# Between Enterprise and Ethics

# Between Enterprise and Ethics

## Business and Management in a Bimoral Society

JOHN HENDRY

OXFORD
UNIVERSITY PRESS

# OXFORD
UNIVERSITY PRESS

Great Clarendon Street, Oxford OX2 6DP

Oxford University Press is a department of the University of Oxford.
It furthers the University's objective of excellence in research, scholarship,
and education by publishing worldwide in

Oxford New York

Auckland Bangkok Buenos Aires Cape Town Chennai
Dar es Salaam Delhi Hong Kong Istanbul Karachi Kolkata
Kuala Lumpur Madrid Melbourne Mexico City Mumbai Nairobi
São Paulo Shanghai Taipei Tokyo Toronto

Oxford is a registered trade mark of Oxford University Press
in the UK and in certain other countries

Published in the United States
by Oxford University Press Inc., New York

First published 2004

British Library Cataloguing in Publication Data

Data available

Library of Congress Cataloging in Publication Data

Data available

ISBN 0-19-926755-3 (hbk.)
ISBN 0-19-926863-0 (pbk.)

1 3 5 7 9 10 8 6 4 2

Typeset by Newgen Imaging Systems (P) Ltd., Chennai, India
Printed in Great Britain
on acid-free paper by
Biddles Ltd., King's Lynn, Norfolk

# PREFACE

In writing this book I had three main aims. First, I wanted to explore what seemed to me to be the biggest and most important challenge facing our society today: the challenge of ensuring that the enormous entreprencurial energies released by today's free market global economy end up by serving society not destroying it. As supporters and critics of business enterprise fought an increasingly vituperative battle for the moral high ground, it seemed that some of our traditional taken-for-granted views of business and morality needed to be re-examined and a framework established for more constructive dialogue, based on contemporary realities rather than outdated ideologies.

Second, I wanted to explore the challenges facing the managers of contemporary business organizations, challenges that seemed to me to be very different from those for which they were still being trained by the business schools, and quite closely related to those facing society at large.

Third, in describing the origins and nature of these challenges, I wanted to emphasize the inseparability of business and management from other aspects of life and the consequent need to root their study in the humanities as well as the social sciences. I wanted to explore my growing conviction that being a manager is not just about using technical skills and knowledge but also about being a person; that the challenges of management, like all human challenges, are shaped by history and events; and that the conflicts of management are at root the conflicts inherent in the human condition.

How far I have succeeded in these aims, time alone will tell. To the extent that I may have succeeded, however, it has been largely by exploiting the efforts of others. Although this book puts forward what is, I think, an original thesis, it is more dependent than most upon other people's insights, ideas, and findings. My main intellectual debts are recorded in the notes and references, but I am also deeply indebted to the numerous friends, colleagues, and students who have taken the time over five years of gestation to hear out and challenge my arguments, comment on my drafts, tactfully point out my errors, and patiently explain things that I would not otherwise have grasped. My strongest personal debts, both intellectual and moral, are to two long-standing friends and colleagues, John Clive and John Roberts. Without them I could not have achieved a fraction of what I have, either as a writer or as a teacher. I should also like to thank particularly my elders and betters, Adrian Cadbury, Charles Handy, Henry Mintzberg, Liz Nelson, and Ken Simmonds, for giving consistent encouragement and unremitting and uncomplaining support whenever they have been called upon; my former Ph.D. students Simon Learmount, Domagoj Racic, Han-Kyun Rho, Paul Sanderson, and David Seidl, for sharing their insights and observations and for always being there when I needed someone to argue with; the participants of the 2002 and 2003 University of Notre Dame London MBA Programmes for acting as guinea pigs and leading me through the finer points of American culture; former students John Carter and Amy Pflueger, for their particularly thorough readings of a rather terrible first draft; David Musson at OUP, for supporting the project throughout and guiding it to fruition; my faculty colleagues at both Girton College and the Judge Institute of Management for being just wonderful colleagues; and Dee, Jamie, and Simon for being just wonderful. The book is dedicated, finally, to the memory of Edith Wise, singer, friend, mentor, and conscience, who died when it was still in an early draft, but who was never far from my mind while I was writing.

John Hendry<br>Foxholes

*March 2003*

# CONTENTS

*List of Figures*                                                                ix
*Abbreviations*                                                                   x

1. Introduction                                                                   1
   Obligation and Self-interest in an Ordered Society                             4
   The Power of Business                                                          9
   The Legitimacy of Self-interest                                              10
   The Weakening of Moral Constraints                                           14
   The Moral Culture of Contemporary Society                                    19
   The Moral Tensions of Management                                             22
   The Challenge of Contemporary Management                                     26
   The Challenge for Contemporary Society                                       32

2. Obligation, Self-interest, and the Development of
   Modern Society                                                               37
   Morality and Social Structure                                                37
   The Growth of Civilization                                                   44
   Entrepreneurial Licence and Moral Duty                                       54
   Moral Obligation in the Business Bureaucracy                                 61
   Conclusion                                                                   67

3. Free Enterprise and the Power of Business                                    69
   The Growth of Business and the Modern Company                                70
   Corporate Freedom and Corporate Power                                        76
   From Local Influence to Global Dominance: Business
   Institutions in the Contemporary World                                       82
   The Failure of Corporate Governance                                          96

4. Economic Culture and the Legitimacy of Self-interest                         98
   The Economic Mindset                                                         99
   Economics and Popular Thinking                                              105
   Economic Ideas in Business: The Flexible Economy
   and its Rules                                                               109
   Economic Thinking in Politics and the Public Sector                         113
   Economics, Self-interest, and Common Sense                                  116

5.  Technology, Liberalism, and the Weakening of Moral
    Constraints                                              120
        The Collapse of Moral Authority                      122
        The Erosion of Cultural Boundaries                   136
        The Suburbanization of Society                       144
        Conclusion                                           147

6.  The Crisis of Morality and the Moral Culture of
    Contemporary Society                                     148
        The Crisis of Morality                               149
        Summary and Review                                   166
        The Bimoral Society                                  168
        Conclusion                                           175

7.  The Moral Tensions of Management                         177
        Management, Morality, and the New
        Corporate Culture                                    177
        The Manager as Boss                                  181
        The Manager as Colleague: The Ethics of Teamwork     191
        The Manager as Employee: Between Work and Home        194
        The Paradox of Freedom                               197

8.  The Challenge of Contemporary Management                 203
        Holding it all Together: The Challenge of
        Leadership                                           204
        Maintaining a Moral Community: The Challenge of
        Management                                           214
        Managing Without Rules: The Challenge of
        Learning                                             224

9.  The Challenge for Contemporary Society                   231
        Globalization and its Problems                       234
        Rights, Humanity, and the Foundations of Moral
        Consensus                                            238
        Regulation and Corporate Governance                  244

10. Conclusion                                               252
Notes                                                        261
Index                                                        291

# LIST OF FIGURES

1  Dimensions of grid and group                                              40
2  Cultural types                                                            41
3  Leaders, artists, and entrepreneurs in a hierarchical or
   role-structured society                                                   50
4  The risks of enterprise in a hierarchical or role-structured society      52
5  Responses to the risks of enterprise in a hierarchical or
   role-structured society                                                   52

# ABBREVIATIONS

| | |
|---|---|
| NGO | Non-governmental Organization |
| OECD | Organization for Economic Cooperation and Development |
| TNC | Transnational Corporation |
| IMF | International Monetary Fund |
| UNCTAD | United Nations Conference on Trade and Development |
| WTO | World Trade Organization |
| PFI | Private Finance Initiative |
| CEO | Chief Executive Officer |
| HRM | Human Resource Management |
| ILO | International Labor Organization |

# 1

# Introduction

In the last few years questions of business ethics, business leadership, and the relationship between business interests and society at large have come to public prominence as rarely before. Events at Enron, WorldCom, Marconi, and other large corporations have thrown into question both the judgement and moral integrity of business leaders and the ability of legal and regulatory systems of corporate governance to protect shareholders, employees, and other stakeholders from the excesses of entrepreneurial zeal. Even in America, for long the spiritual home of free enterprise and individual achievement, the values that drive that enterprise and achievement have been called into question, as businesses have been treated with a degree of suspicion not seen for nearly a hundred years. Meanwhile, the protests of the anti-globalization movement have drawn attention to the immense power of contemporary transnational corporations and the financial institutions behind them. These protests have fuelled a heated public debate between those who see international business and finance as the beneficent source of economic development and prosperity and a small but fast-growing minority who see it only as an agent of social and environmental destruction.

Underlying this debate is a growing realization that, for better or worse, the moral environment in which business is conducted has itself changed; that the old moral certainties can no longer be relied upon; and that behaviours and attitudes that were once associated purely with the world of business—and only with a relatively small part of that world—are becoming commonplace throughout society. So while we may condemn 'fat cat' CEOs for taking massive salaries and stock options while closing pension schemes and making workers redundant, our moral outrage is mixed with envy. Given the chance, most of us would gladly swap places with them and take whatever rewards we could, without any sense of moral guilt. Traditional moral principles still matter, and for some people and in some areas they still matter deeply. But for most people, in most areas of life, they are no longer the only or dominant consideration. Increasingly, it seems, we weigh our perceptions of moral duty and obligation against perceptions of our own legitimate self-interest.

In contemporary society, there seem to be two sets of principles by which people guide their lives. On one hand there are the principles associated with traditional morality. These emphasize our duties and obligations to others: to treat people honestly and with respect, to treat them fairly and without prejudice, to help and care for them when needed, and, ultimately, to put their needs above our own. These principles find expression in the teachings of the major religions and in the laws and customs of nations. They are deeply ingrained in the fabric of society and still dominate behaviour among friends and family, within tightly knit communities, and wherever people feel their fortunes to be closely bound together. There is strong evidence to suggest, however, that they no longer have the force that they once did, and that their field of application has been shrinking.

On the other hand, there are the principles associated with self-interest. Within certain boundaries set by the law—or more accurately by parts of the law, since not all laws on this view are taken as binding[1]—we determine our actions not by their impact on other people, but solely by how well they advance our own interests. These principles find expression in the language of enterprise and free markets, and have always guided behaviour in business dealings, especially those between different communities and organizations. Recently, however—in the last twenty-five years—they have acquired a much wider social legitimacy, as guiding principles for behaviour in general, *within* communities and organizations. To an extent unprecedented in history, the pursuit of self-interest at the expense of others, traditionally condemned as morally reprehensible, has come to be seen as morally acceptable and socially legitimate.

In what follows, I shall refer to these two sets of principles as constituting a 'traditional morality' of obligation and a 'market morality' of self-interest, using the term 'morality' here in a sociological sense, much as Weber and others have used the term 'ethic'. A particular 'morality', in other words, is a particular set of principles of right conduct by which people are observed to live their lives, with no implications as to the absolute truth or correctness of those principles.[2] Where I use the word 'moral', without qualification, or where I refer to morality in the abstract as opposed to a particular, specified morality, I use the words in their everyday sense, as referring to the principles of 'traditional morality'.[3]

Traditional and market moralities are not simply polar opposites. Some expressions of traditional morality have called for complete self-sacrifice and total devotion to the needs of others, but most have been much less demanding. Perfect altruism may be the saintly ideal, but for ordinary people a modicum of self-interest has always been considered normal and morally acceptable. Similarly, the morality of the market is not based simply on self-interest, but also places obligations on market participants. Without some such obligations, indeed, markets could not function. The thrusts of the two sets of prin-ciples are, however, in very different directions, and if applied to the same situation they are apt to lead to different and conflicting prescriptions.

Historically, this conflict has been contained in two ways. The areas of application of the two moralities have been clearly defined and demarcated, and the principles of traditional morality have maintained a dominant position. The morality of the market has been allowed to operate only in certain fields of activity and only under licence, in the service of the greater good. I shall argue in this book, however, that the recent decline of traditional morality and the contemporaneous rise of market morality have upset this balance, producing what I shall call a 'bimoral' society in which we have two conflicting sets of guidelines for living, both of which can be seen as socially legitimate, and the areas of application of which cannot be clearly demarcated.[4]

This raises a number of difficulties at both the individual and societal levels. At the individual level there are already many spheres of life in which the two moralities come into direct conflict. This happens in civic life. It happens in families, when the needs of their members diverge. It is probably most apparent, however, within business organizations. These organizations have rarely been moral exemplars, in the traditional sense. They have often been sites of oppression and discrimination. But in principle, if not always in practice, the bureaucratic business organizations that dominated throughout much of the twentieth century were governed by the rules of traditional morality. The company and its various employees were tied together in a hierarchical structure by webs of reciprocal obligation, with everyone working towards the common good. Today, business organizations are more loosely structured as networks. Managers are encouraged and expected to act as self-interested agents and to make decisions on a purely economic basis, without regard for their impact on colleagues and employees. But they still have to work with those colleagues and employees, and the personal relationships that result would appear to fall squarely within the domain of traditional morality.

This creates two problems. First, managers have to decide how to behave with whom under what circumstances—when to be dutiful, and when to be selfish. Second, they have to cope psychologically with the dissonance that results. So long as the morality of self-interest was confined to impersonal economic relationships, leaving personal relationships to be guided by traditional morality, the two realms could be kept psychologically apart. But when similar relationships become subject to different rules, or when the very same people have to be treated now one way (dutifully, as friends) and now another (instrumentally, as market actors), some psychological conflict becomes inevitable.

One response to this situation, not uncommon in business, is to resolve the conflict by treating everyone instrumentally and abandoning, in effect, the dictates of traditional morality. This works, after a fashion, but it causes problems of its own and it also points to an important problem at the societal level. There can be no doubt that allowing entrepreneurs to act in a self-interested way has brought enormous economic benefits to modern society. All the evidence suggests that successful development depends on free enterprise.[5] Until recently, however, that freedom was tightly circumscribed so that while a market morality was available under licence, so to speak, for the pursuit of enterprise, it posed little threat to the dominant morality of obligation, which acted as the unquestioned foundation of social stability. Now that these constraints have been broken, some interesting and critically important questions arise. Can the two rival moralities coexist in some kind of equilibrium, and if so, how? Or will the morality of self-interest inevitably undermine the morality of obligation, and if so, with what consequences? On the answers to these questions the future of civilization may well depend.

The purpose of this book is to begin to explore the problems and possibilities of our new bimoral society. I shall focus, in particular, on the implications of these problems and possibilities for the relationship between business and society and, more immediately, on the challenges they pose for business managers. The focus on managers is partly a product of my own professional interests. As a teacher, researcher, and consultant, most of my work is with managers. It also reflects the fact that while managers are not the only people who are directly affected by the bimoral society, they do seem to be the first substantial group within our society to encounter its problems systematically, and on a routine basis. It is in the field of management that responses to these problems are being developed, and it may well be from the experiences of managers that other groups will learn.

The book is structured as follows. In Chapter 2, we shall explore the social foundations of the relationship between enterprise and ethics and trace its general development up to the 1980s. In Chapters 3–6 we shall focus on the ways in which this relationship has changed in the last generation. Without exception the changes we shall discuss have deep historical roots, going back at least to the eighteenth-century Enlightenment, but they have all reached fruition and become clearly manifest within the last twenty-five years. In Chapter 3 we shall focus on the growing power and influence of business and financial institutions, in Chapter 4 on the growing dominance of economic thinking and market values and how these are reflected in contemporary business organizations, and in Chapter 5 on the collapse of the institutional structures of traditional moral authority. In Chapter 6 we shall review a range of recent perspectives on a perceived 'crisis of morality' in our society, and set out some of the key features of contemporary moral culture. In Chapter 7 we shall look in more detail at the tensions that face business managers in a bimoral society, and in Chapter 8 we shall address some of the challenges these pose, and how they might be addressed. Finally, in Chapter 9 we shall return to the more general question of the balance between enterprise and ethics in society at large and explore some of the political challenges this poses.

## OBLIGATION AND SELF-INTEREST IN AN ORDERED SOCIETY

In trying to explore the phenomena of changing and competing moralities, we immediately run up against a problem, for on the normal view there is only one morality and it cannot change. For many people, traditional moral principles have an absolute, transcendental quality. For some they are God-given, for others, the product of reason or the essence of humanity, but either way they seem to be rooted in something beyond the mundane experience of social life, and it is this 'beyond' that gives them their imperative force. To say that something is 'bad' 'or wrong' is not to say that it goes against the prevailing social conventions, that it will be disapproved of or sanctioned, but that regardless of law or custom you *should not* do it. What is wrong is wrong, period. From this perspective, the very phrase 'a morality of self-interest' is an oxymoron. The suggestions that there might be more than one kind of morality, that morality might be in some sense socially constructed, that conceptions of right and wrong might vary from culture to culture or from time to time, are dangerous heresies and are resisted as such. Attempting to defend the moral absolute, even the most rational of philosophers become quite irrational and emotional, while the most thoughtful and open-minded believers become quite dogmatic.

There may, of course, be some absolute standards of morality. These may be God-given, though that can never be proven. They may be derivable purely from reason, though no one has yet succeeded in finding such a derivation. The fact is, however, that the moral principles governing people's behaviour have *in practice* varied from period to period and from culture to culture, and have always been closely tied to the particular institutions of different societies.[6] If we look at the prevailing moralities of relatively developed, large-scale societies, these variations are not large. Different societies have different priorities and different sets of moral rules, but underlying these particular expressions the basic principles of 'traditional' morality are everywhere recognizable. If we look at groups within these societies, however, the differences can be quite marked.

The absolutist approach to these differences is to interpret them as aberrant deviations from a moral norm, as reflections of human weakness or a lack of moral development.[7] Perhaps they are, but in a period of great moral uncertainty and changing social perceptions, that is an unhelpful starting point. Quite apart from the great risk of moral ethnocentrism (my morals, whatever they may be, are the right ones, yours are the deficient ones), we need to understand what is happening before we pass judgement on it. To do that, we shall need to suspend our religious or other convictions and treat moralities in the first instance as empirical phenomena, as part and parcel of the structure and fabric of society.

Taking this approach, we shall begin Chapter 2 by reviewing what is known about the moralities of primitive societies, and shall then trace the history of morality and society from early civilization through to the second half of the twentieth century. It is impossible, in a single chapter, to do justice to this history, much of which has anyway yet to be written, but it is important to establish, even if only in very crude terms, where we are coming from. In order to focus the discussion we shall adopt as a descriptive device the cultural typology of anthropologist Mary Douglas. 'Cultural theory', as it is generally known, has its critics, but provided we remain aware of its limitations it is a very useful descriptive tool that helps us to visualize not only the differences between societies but also some of the dynamic processes involved in their evolution and change.

Cultural theory has its origins in Douglas's researches on comparative religion in primitive African tribes and proposes a three-way typology of such tribes based on the psychological effects of social and linguistic classification structures and the relationships between individuals and groups. Each of the three types, which Douglas later labelled as hierarchies, markets, and sects, arises in a particular set of circumstances. Each corresponds to a distinctive pattern of social structuring, which can be seen as the result of a political accommodation among the members of a society faced with a particular set of environmental problems, and each is linked to a distinctive social morality. In particular, the hierarchies are characterized by a morality of obligation and the markets by a morality of self-interest.

When we move from primitive to modern societies, the situation becomes much more complex, and in her researches into contemporary British and American society Douglas found elements of all three cultural types. If we look at the broad historical evolution of civilized societies, however, the way in which the cultural types are combined seems to be remarkably consistent. Wherever we see civilization, we see the development of trade, markets, and an economic subculture based on the morality of self-interest. In all cases, though, this is set within the context of a highly structured, hierarchical society, charac- terized by the morality of obligation. Trade is needed for societies to grow and change, but of the three cultural types only the hierarchy, it seems, has the capa- city to organize on a large scale and to develop the stable institutions and infra- structure on which civilization depends. All the world's major civilizations were established as hierarchical cultures characterized by moralities of obligation.

This basic model of society has survived for several thousand years. It has not been without its problems. In any hierarchical society, there is always a temp- tation for those at the top of the hierarchy to renege on their obligations to those lower down and exploit the hierarchy for their own personal advantage. There has been no shortage in history of tyrants and corrupt leaders. But there has never been any doubt that such corruption has, in the terms of the society as a whole, been immoral. In cultures characterized by the morality of obliga- tion, tyranny could only be sustained by violence and the threat of violence against those it was supposedly serving, and in the long run it has always succumbed to the people's expectation of responsible and moral leadership.

Another endemic problem of hierarchies has been their propensity to ossify as the structuring properties that make them such effective organizers inhibit creativity and change. This problem is familiar to students of organizations, but historical evidence suggests that it applies equally at the level of society. One of the ways in which societies have got round it, historically, has been by licens- ing certain groups to break the normal rules. Artists have been one such group, entrepreneurs another. In the case of entrepreneurs, this licence has operated on several different levels. First, on the day-to-day level, societies have sep- arated out impersonal, 'arm's length' economic relationships from personal ones. As we have already noted, one of the prerequisites for a civilized society was the development of trade and markets, which in the cultural context of the hierarchy replaced or supplemented the central distribution of goods. This inevitably carried with it a legitimation of self-interest, but in the hierarchical context it was a strictly limited legitimation. In market transactions, people were expected, in general, to get the best deals they could, without worrying about the impact this might have on other parties. But they were not expected to exploit other members of their society (though it was all right to exploit foreigners). With this in mind, there were limitations upon the transactions allowed (usury, for example, might be forbidden); and the market principles could always be suspended if they went against the general interest (e.g. in times of famine).

Second, even within their business activities, entrepreneurs have been expected to act with moral restraint and to pursue their self-interest in a socially responsible fashion. This was, for example, a notable feature of the Dutch merchant society of the seventeenth century and of the entrepreneurial boom in eighteenth- and early nineteenth-century Britain. Self-interest in this period was treated as respectable, even virtuous, but only in so far as it was morally restrained and judiciously exercised. As soon as it escaped these bounds it was condemned as self-love, a concept that had no positive connotations.

A third way in which entrepreneurs were licensed was far more specific and explicit. In fifteenth-century Europe, for example, traders and bankers led large companies licensed to operate commercially on behalf of the kings and princes they served. By the early seventeenth century, there were legally chartered trading and colonizing companies and these were followed by chartered or incorporated domestic companies, leading by the mid-nineteenth century to the limited liability company that we know today. All these companies operated under licence within a competitive economic environment according to the morality of self-interest, but what is striking is the extent to which this pursuit of self-interest was isolated from society at large. The early companies were licensed specifically to engage in international competition, on behalf of one nation against another, and not to compete within societies. Their successors were licensed and granted limited liability specifically to engage in commercial activities that were considered to be in the general public interest, such as the construction of canals and railways, the development of water supplies, or the provision of banking or insurance services. In all cases the licences were time limited and conditional upon the public interest being served. To operate a company was quite clearly a privilege, not a right, and was always treated as such in public discussion and debate. Moreover, it was a privilege granted, very sparingly, within the context of a traditional morality of obligation.

In the second half of the nineteenth century, as industrialization gathered pace, the formal constraints on entrepreneurs were gradually removed. In Britain and America (and to a somewhat lesser extent elsewhere) incorporation with limited liability was made freely available and the limited company began to replace unlimited private companies and partnerships as the dominant business form. The number and size of businesses grew rapidly and a new generation of economists and social theorists proclaimed the value of self-interest. By the end of the century the French sociologist of morals and one of the founding fathers of modern sociology, Emile Durkheim, could write of a 'crisis in society' as business and commerce became its dominant functions and the unbridled pursuit of self-interest threatened to undermine the traditional moral foundations of social solidarity. Durkheim's fears were premature, however. For one thing the concept of self-interest remained closely tied to, and bound by, traditional moral virtues. While the growth of business and the growth of the press led almost inevitably to an escalation in the reported cases of financial greed, these were evidently viewed with horror by both society at large and the business community. For another thing, the growth of business had already spawned by Durkheim's time a new type of morally structured business organization. What developed in the early twentieth century was not a market economy of small entrepreneurs but an economy based on large bureaucratic corporations. And while these corporations traded and competed with each other according to the dictates of self-interest, their economic activity was confined to an almost invisible realm of impersonal commercial interactions. What were visible were the corporations themselves and these were, in the main, governed by the traditional moral norms of mutual obligation. Both organizationally and culturally they were hierarchies, modelled on the traditional hierarchical form and moral discipline of the societies in which they operated.

The result of this development was that, right up until the late twentieth century, Western society remained dominated by traditional morality. As ever, this was sometimes honoured more in the breach than in the practice. Hierarchical corporations were no more immune to political exploitation than hierarchical societies, and in the nineteenth century many business corporations were run by despots with scant regard for the welfare of their employees. In the twentieth century, however, standards improved, and while there were always exceptions most corporations came to operate as traditional moral communities. When sociologists came to investigate the prevailing morality in American corporations in the second half of the twentieth century they found a fair measure of political manipulation and calculated self-interest, but the origins of these behaviours lay in a desire to get the job done, to serve the corporation, in situations in which the formal bureaucracy could not cope. It was out of a sense of duty that managers broke the rules, and it was as a consequence of breaking the rules that they found themselves forced to look after their own self-interest, as they sought to secure and defend their organizational positions. When the corporations of the twentieth century functioned properly, they provided an environment in which expected behaviours were wholly consonant with those of society at large, and in which obligation rather than self-interest ruled. This dominance of the hierarchy was also reflected in the markets in which the companies traded (product markets, financial markets, and labour markets), which until the 1980s were very heavily regulated.

## THE POWER OF BUSINESS

While society was able, until recently, to maintain a balance between the traditional ethics of a hierarchical culture and the entrepreneurial self-interest of a licensed market subculture, that balance was always precarious; and for the last 150 years the balance of power has been shifting steadily in favour of an ever larger and more influential business community. For most of this time the increasing power of business was matched by increasing regulation, but in the last twenty-five years this attempt to contain business power has effectively been abandoned and business interests have come to dominate the world in which we live. In Chapter 3 we shall review these developments.

The rise of the business company or corporation as a powerful social institution can be traced back to the industrial revolution. In the late eighteenth and nineteenth centuries, the development of new technologies opened up new possibilities for products and services. Entrepreneurs were keen to exploit these, and societies were keen to benefit from them, but the main benefits came from industrial scale operations and these needed more capital investment than individual entrepreneurs were able or willing to provide. As we have already noted, some companies were granted limited liability incorporation to pursue specific public interest projects. Others raised what money they could on the stock markets. But the distinction between public and private interests proved hard to maintain in practice. The sheer number of business opportunities arising quickly made case-by-case incorporation unrealistic. And the unregulated stock markets proved too precarious for sound business funding. By the middle of the nineteenth century, the constraints on incorporation had been removed. Any company could incorporate, and gain the benefits of limited liability, in exchange for a small measure of regulatory control.

Under the new regime, the number of businesses exploded. With the new technologies of railways, telecommunications, and mass production creating economies of scale and scope, the size of businesses exploded too, and with size came power. This power has continued to grow and is now exerted in all sorts of ways. In America, for example, businesses play a central role in the political process, funding candidates' airtime in exchange for influence and spending heavily on advertising and lobbying to promote their particular interests. Drawing on their immense financial resources, they manipulate public opinion and increasingly control university research. In other countries their influence is exerted more subtly, through personal networks, or more crudely, through outright corruption, but everywhere the outcomes are much the same: businesses call the shots. This is even more the case on the international stage. The largest businesses dictate terms to the developing countries in which they operate, and control the agendas of the international agencies.

More generally, businesses have successfully impressed their own values upon the world at large. Relentless television advertising of consumer products presses home a powerful message: material consumption is what matters. Never mind whether or not you have health, education, or loving relationships: to be deprived is to not have a Coke or a Nike sweatshirt or a McDonald's hamburger. Through expensive public relations, through the media, which they control, and through involvement in educational programmes, businesses also press home the message that business itself, as a social institution, is important and to be trusted—that businesses are responsible and caring, and that any curtailment of their power would damage the prosperity of society.

In the last few decades this message has been accepted by governments, which have moved swiftly since the 1980s to privatize those businesses that were previously state owned and controlled, and to deregulate the conduct of private corporations. At the same time the international growth of transnational corporations, made possible by improved telecommunications and reduced trade barriers, has taken them beyond the reach of individual nation states. The nature, extent, desirability, and effects of the ensuing globalization are all contentious, but whether we conceive of the transnational corporations as the primary agents of economic progress or as agents of social and environmental destruction, there can be little doubting their power and influence. They have not yet usurped the nation state, but their commercial freedom and economic resources give them enormous bargaining power, and a large degree of freedom in determining where, how, and by what rules to operate.

Financial institutions have also benefited from deregulation and globalization and have also grown massively in size and power over the last thirty years. As private institutions whose aim is to make money, without the complications of political constraints, they are freer than governments to protect their own financial interests, and as they have grown they have taken over from governments the dominant role in the global financial system. As currency speculators they dictate exchange rates. As lenders to the developing world they determine the fate of emerging economies, and as shareholding fund managers they exert an increasing influence on the agendas of business, to the cost of traditional stakeholders such as employees and communities.

## THE LEGITIMACY OF SELF-INTEREST

This long-term growth in the power and influence of business, and more recently of financial institutions, has been matched by the growing influence of economic ideas, which is the topic of Chapter 4. The science of economics can be traced to one of the classic works of the eighteenth-century Enlightenment, Adam Smith's *The Wealth of Nations*, but like the institution of business it came to prominence in the late nineteenth and twentieth centuries. And just as business grew in the final quarter of the twentieth century to dominate the other institutions of society, so economic ideas grew in the same period to dominate social and political thinking.

The core idea of economics is that of self-interest. When Adam Smith wrote famously that 'it is not from the benevolence of the butcher, the brewer, or the baker, that we expect our dinner, but from their regard to their own interest', he assumed that this self-interest would be moderated by traditionally moral sentiments. Selfish or exploitative behaviour was, in his judgement, the exception not the rule. As economics developed as a science, however, and concerned itself with the determination of market prices and the distribution of economic goods, these qualifications dropped from sight. In the context of arm's length transactions, self-interested behaviour was both a reasonable assumption and one from which definite predictions could be derived.

Other assumptions, too, were readily deployed in an economic context, even though they were at odds with traditional social values. It was assumed, for instance, that the value of anything could be measured in purely monetary terms, without regard to psychological comfort or traditional moral well-being. This assumption was perfectly reasonable when the goods to be valued were economic goods, and it made calculations of utility possible. The demands of calculation also led to the assumption that economic systems were in equilibrium, so that short-term optimizations could be made without worrying about their longer-term implications.

These assumptions made sense in the narrow context of price determination, but in the twentieth century economists became increasingly concerned with broader social and political issues that had an economic component such as unemployment, taxation, the welfare state, nationalization, privatization, and the distribution of international aid. In these broader contexts, economics became at times almost a parody of a science. Its methods looked like those of the natural sciences, but it lacked their link with hard reality. Natural scientists used hypotheses to generate contrasting predictions, and experiments to test and discriminate between these predictions. Economists also used their hypotheses to generate predictions, but their scope for experiment was severely limited. What mattered to them, in consequence, was not whether the hypotheses worked in the sense of leading to better predictions than alternative hypotheses, since this could never be established, but whether they worked in the sense of leading to any predictions at all. This limitation was no obstacle to the success of economics, however. It looked the part of a contemporary science, and it provided answers to important questions. Indeed the assumption of self-interest, the use of monetary values, and the other staples of economic theorizing proved extremely fertile. In the second half of the twentieth century, economic analysis came to dominate political discussion and debate—often, in America and Britain, to the exclusion of all other considerations. And as their confidence grew economists applied their methodology and market assumptions to an ever wider range of problems. The assumption of self-interest was applied not only to purely economic problems, but also to those arising in personal and political relationships. The monetary measure of value was applied not only to economic goods, but also to social welfare and moral worth. As the mathematical tools at their disposal advanced, economists became able to progress beyond equilibrium situations. But the imperatives of measurement ensured that the claims of the present, which could be measured, continued to dominate over those of the future, which could not—a stark contrast with the traditional, religiously backed moral view in which the dominant claims were those of eternity. Indeed, at the end of the twentieth century commentators could observe that the traditional deities had effectively been replaced by the market as God, so powerful and so ubiquitous had the ideas of the market become.

Unsurprisingly, this late twentieth-century dominance of economic ideas was also reflected in the organization of business. As recently as the 1980s, the business scene was still dominated by large industrial corporations, organized as bureaucratic hierarchies and characterized by ideals of long-term service and mutual obligation. In the 'flexible economy' of the 1990s and 2000s, however, size is measured in terms of market power or added value, not in terms of physical assets or the number of people employed. Manufacturing and other routine tasks have been outsourced to the developing world and speed and agility have displaced coordinating power as the key determinants of success. Employment relationships based on the ideal of a long-term career in which the employees devoted their working lives to the corporation, which in turn was loyal to its employees and looked after their own and their families' welfare, have been replaced by relationships based on the ideal of free market exchange.

To some extent this change was forced on companies by the pressures of competition. As the constraints on international competition were removed and rapidly improving communications technologies allowed entrepreneurs to coordinate resources and copy innovations with unprecedented speed and efficiency, high fixed costs and long-term commitments became an unaffordable luxury. Whatever its long-term benefits, the traditional corporate structure was simply too costly and too slow moving to compete in the short term. The change also had a strong ideological component, however. Traditional employment relationships were the product of a marketplace, but they assumed implicitly that the labour market was not a free one. In particular, they recognized that once people took up employment with a large company the decisions that followed, on where and how to live, on family commitments and so on, restricted their options and created a strong dependence on the company. The loyalty that the company offered in return was in some sense a recognition of this, a recognition that, under traditional morality, the stronger or more powerful party in a relationship has a duty to the weaker. The new flexible economy has no place for such moral considerations, but stresses instead the economic value of the free market, in which trading with one person today does not restrict you from trading with another tomorrow. Short-term employment contracts, made without future commitment, were introduced to maintain the flexibility of the companies, but are idealized as maintaining the freedom of both companies and employees.

Another idea that underlies the practices of the new economy is that of economic agency. First developed in the 1970s, agency theory in economics takes situations that have traditionally been described in terms of moral obligations and recasts them in terms of economic property rights. Property, in economics, covers anything of monetary value over which someone has a claim, including, for the shareholders of a company, the work of its managers. From the traditional moral perspective, it was reasonable to pay managers a fixed salary, of so much a month. Their obligation to the company would ensure that, in return, they worked in the company's interests. From an economic perspective, however, in which all employees are assumed to act as self-interested agents, it makes much more sense to pay by results, using the form of pay to align the employees' interests with those of the company and its shareholders. By the end of the twentieth century performance-related pay, which had previously been restricted to manual workers and salespeople, had become the norm for managers in British and American companies, and was beginning to be introduced in Europe.

Beginning in the 1980s, economic ideas and the practices of the new economy were also applied to the management of public services. Where possible, these services were privatized or opened up to private sector competition. Where these were not possible, competition was introduced through the creation of 'internal markets'. Public services were redefined as businesses and public servants as economic agents, in competition with each other for the custom of the citizens they had once served, now redefined as customers. In areas such as health care and education, customer satisfaction replaced professional judgement as the final arbiter of what should be done.

Taken together, the rising influence of economic ideas, the emerging dominance of business institutions, and the transformation of business in the new economy have had a dramatic effect on our society. In many areas of business and public life, the norms and constraints of traditional morality have become an irrelevance as institutions and practices have been restructured to reflect the assumption of instrumental self-interest. Because traditional morality still has a considerable, if uncertain, hold on us, people are still reluctant to proclaim self-interest as a moral ideal. Whatever their internal realities, most businesses are at pains to present themselves to the outside world as moral in a traditional sense. But even this is changing. In the 1980s, Wall Street financiers, getting rich on junk bond finance deals, proclaimed that 'greed is good', and the world looked on in horror. In the early 1990s people looked back to the 'greed decade' as if it were a one-off event. By the end of the century, however, the idea had become less shocking, and the most admired and most respectable entrepreneurs in America were lining up to make that the point that greed *is* good, because it is greed that drives entrepreneurial capitalism and entrepreneurial capitalism that creates prosperity for society. Meanwhile, political thinking had followed a similar pattern. The 1980s, the decade of Reagan and Thatcher, saw the affluent assert their rights to protect their own self-interest, and not pay taxes towards the welfare or education of the poor. The politics of the 1990s seemed, in comparison, quite liberal, but while the language they used was more conciliatory, and their policies were less extreme, the parties of the centre-left had effectively taken on board the core ideas of market morality. By the end of the decade the politics of self-interest had become almost taken for granted.

## THE WEAKENING OF MORAL CONSTRAINTS

At the very same time as the structural balance between traditional and market moralities was being threatened by the growing power of business and finance and the growing influence of economic and market thinking, the foundations of traditional morality were also being eroded. In Chapter 5, we shall explore the causes and manifestations of this weakening of moral constraints. Like the other processes we have discussed, this process has a long history, but seems to have accelerated sharply in recent decades. We shall focus, in particular, on three aspects: the decline of traditional moral authorities, the breaking down of the traditional boundaries between different cultures, and the suburbanization of society.

Any discussion of the decline of traditional morality is complicated by the problem of what does or does not count as evidence of that morality. The most commonly used indicators are recorded figures on illegitimacy, divorce, and crime, which provide hard statistical evidence and show a clear and consistent pattern. Across the developed world, crime, illegitimacy, and divorce rates, which remained more or less stable through the first half of the twentieth century, all soared exponentially in the second half. This led commentators to talk, often in very bleak terms, of a collapse of moral values. However, the causes of increased crime rates are, to say the least, contentious, and the other figures must also be interpreted with care. They clearly evidence a collapse in the institution of marriage as a lifelong relationship and necessary prelude to procreation, but a change in particular moral values or institutions does not necessarily signal a collapse of traditional morality. Indeed it could be argued that in a strongly moral society, in which people took their obligations very seriously, there would be little or no need for an institution such as marriage.

What the divorce and illegitimacy figures do seem to point to is a collapse of traditional moral *authority*, as a result of which the traditional morality has been left vulnerable and exposed. For it is not just that one particular authority has collapsed and been replaced by another. All of the principal authorities through which the traditional moral code was maintained have been seriously weakened, and nothing has so far taken their place.

The roots of this collapse of authority are very deep, going back at least to the eighteenth-century Enlightenment project of replacing authority by reason. Astoundingly successful in the realm of science, that project was much less so in the moral and political realms, where reason could go only so far. On the one hand the notion of authority, once exposed to the cruel scepticism of reason, was fatally wounded. On the other hand, however much it might criticize authority, reason could not replace it. Intellectually, all attempts at a rational morality ended up relying on some foundation of faith—some moral starting point that could not be proved but had to be assumed. In practical terms, political regimes that were supposedly based upon the dictates of reason and rational moral principles proved no less corrupt, no fairer or more just, than those based upon traditional authority.

In politics, what matters is not so much what is right but what works, more or less, in holding together a bunch of disparate and ultimately irreconcilable interests, and in politics the principles of reason and authority soon got into some kind of pragmatic balance. In morals, however, the principles worked against each other. Traditional morality needed some absolute foundation, some source for its moral imperative, and if this could not be provided by reason alone it had to come from religion. But religion was precisely the area in which the Enlightenment critique was most effective.

This conflict took some time to work itself out, but by the early to mid-twentieth century it was apparent that the authority of the church—the authority of all churches—was in serious decline, especially among the educated classes. The problem was not so much that the existence of God could not be proved, the starting point of the Enlightenment critique. It was, rather, that for the increasing numbers of people with a basic scientific education the myths and dogmas of the Christian churches simply made no sense. In pre-scientific society, the virgin birth and the resurrection could simply be accepted uncritically, on authority. In a scientific society, the authority of the church clashed with the authority of science, and both reason and everyday common sense appeared to favour science. At the same time, as the world changed out of all recognition from that in which the imagery of Christianity had been rooted, the psychological force of that imagery declined. Whereas the Christian religion had been, for most people, an unquestioned starting point, it came to require a very positive act of faith.

The decline in the authority of the church continued throughout the twentieth century. In the early years of the present century the support base of the major churches in England (the Methodists, Anglicans, and Roman Catholics) is roughly comparable to that of the major football clubs. For various reasons, American churches have fared rather better, but even there religious authority is in sharp decline, and increasingly fragmented. Only in the poverty-stricken cities of the newly industrializing world, where messianic hopes provide the only possible escape from total despair, is Christianity still powerful. In the developed world, it seems to be a spent force.

Over the centuries, the churches have been sources of oppression as well as of liberation and support, and while many people lament their decline some see it as long overdue. The fact is, however, that for the past millennium they have been the dominant source of moral authority in our society. What is good or bad has been defined, for the overwhelming majority of people, by what the churches have maintained. Much of that moral framework remains in practice, but for most people in contemporary society the authority which sustained it has collapsed: The churches still have answers to our moral questions but, as a society, we no longer see any reason why their answers should be better than anybody else's.

While the churches have been a particularly important source of moral authority, they have not been the only one. Traditional morality has also been promoted by the state, and through the institutions of family, community, and education. In the last forty or fifty years, however, the moral authority of these institutions has also been in sharp decline.

The state has always been an embodiment of the principles of hierarchical culture, but in the nineteenth and, especially, the twentieth centuries it also came to play a more specifically moral role. Whereas the moral authority of the church derives from religious belief, that of the modern state is based on rational assent, and helped by a broadening of political representation the state was, to some extent, able to take on the mantle of moral authority from the churches when their influence began to decline. By the mid-twentieth century the law, judiciary, and police, even the politicians, were respected as sources of moral authority. The Second World War was fought, as no previous war had been, on ostensibly moral grounds and the domestic politics of the period, from Roosevelt's New Deal to the creation of the welfare state, were also grounded on moral arguments. In the last forty years, however, much of the moral authority of government and its agencies and representatives has been lost. Under the relentless and increasingly intrusive eye of the media, politicians have been exposed for what they always have been: ordinary people with an extraordinary ambition for power and attention but no more claim to moral authority than anyone else. Judges are once again the subjects of ridicule, the law is once again an ass, and the police are disliked and distrusted, even by law-abiding citizens. When morality enters politics, which is not often, it is in pursuit, not in leadership, of public opinion, and as likely as not in the service of a barely concealed attempt at party political point scoring. The idea that you would look to the state for moral guidance has become laughable.

The family, which has always been the most immediate source of moral authority for children in their formative years, has fared no better. The close bond between mother and child remains and might well provide a basis for moral authority, were the notion of male dominance not so deeply embedded in our hierarchical culture. As it is, however, the authority of the mother is fragile, to say the least, and is easily usurped by an incoming—or outgoing—male, whose behaviour is often more notable for its avoidance of obligation than for its representation of traditional morality. Traditional lifelong marriages were not always loving. They could be cruel and damaging affairs. But traditionally married parents could speak with authority about a morality of obligation in a way in which parents who move in and out of relationships, almost inevitably with some bitterness and resentment, cannot.

In modern society, the role of the parents as moral authorities has to some extent been taken over, or at least shared, by teachers. But as the authorities around them have collapsed, making their own tasks massively more difficult, the respect afforded to teachers has also declined. In England and America, where teaching has never been a particularly well-respected profession, teachers are routinely condemned by parents, who cannot exert moral authority themselves, for not doing it for them. In other countries their stock is higher, but they are still fighting against the odds in an area in which they have no training and, as a general rule, more liberal views than the communities they serve. They present an easy target for blame. Many try as individuals to provide some moral guidance, and some succeed, but whatever moral authority they may once have had as a profession has gone.

The contemporary decline in all forms of moral authority has gone hand in hand with another important phenomenon, namely, the erosion of traditional boundaries between countries and cultures. The two are inextricably linked, as in a hierarchical culture both membership and conformity are important. In a culture of mutual obligation, be it an organization or a society, it is necessary to know to whom that obligation is owed. What matters is the common good, and 'common' needs defining. So societies have always had very strict rules on membership, and different rules for members and non-members. It is also important to have a stable and well-defined structure and classification system—what the anthropologist Mary Douglas calls a high grid. A hierarchical society works like a machine in which each part serves its function, and if people fail to fulfil their roles, or act outside those roles, or even think in a different way from other people, the stability of the whole society is put at risk.

Until very recently, the societies in which we live had very strong boundaries, both externally between societies and internally between communities and social strata. Few people travelled outside their home town or village, let alone internationally, and very few had any real experience of alternative cultures. They knew their place, and no other. A deep knowledge of other cultures is still very rare, but in the last few decades the barriers between societies have been rapidly eroded. The political barriers that used to seal off the Soviet Union and Mainland China from the rest of the world, and that complicated travel even between friendly countries, have collapsed. To travel and even to work in other countries is far, far easier than it was just twenty years ago. Travel is easier in a more prosaic way, too, as the development of air transport has made international journeys routine and affordable to millions of people. New communications technologies, such as mobile telephones and the Internet, have also had a big effect. Not long ago, international telephone calls were subject to censorship and the vagaries of primitive and unreliable network infrastructures. Now they are as easy as calling next door. The Internet is even more effective as a breaker of boundaries, as it can carry images as well as words—and unlike the printed press it is virtually uncensorable.

Connected both with the development of transport and communications technologies and with the collapse of political barriers has been the rise of international business and trade. Forty years ago, the overwhelming majority of products were produced in the countries in which they were consumed, and only the largest of companies could conceive of operating internationally. Now both money and goods move freely between countries, and even small businesses operate internationally, as a matter of day-to-day routine. With the money and the products go people and ideas, including a cadre of managers and entrepreneurs for whom words like 'abroad' and 'foreign' no longer have any meaning.

Then there is television. The most obvious effect of television has been the global dissemination of American culture and consumer values, but its documentary and news coverage has also acted in the other direction, giving members of our own society a view, and often an intimate view, of cultures that would otherwise be completely unknown to us. Television exposes the differences between societies, and in so doing points to the social legitimacy of alternative social practices, religious beliefs, and moral codes. It also exposes differences within our own society, challenging traditional moral beliefs about violence, sex, and language. Moreover, it does so in a deeply confusing way, distorting the relationships between social groups and blurring the boundaries between private and public lives, and between fiction and reality.

All of these developments have their very positive aspects. Indeed, few of us would want to go back to a world without free travel, free trade, and state-of-the-art communications. Few people would want to be without their television sets. But all the developments contribute to the undermining of moral authority and the destabilization of existing moral values and belief structures. A further contributory factor to this general weakening of moral constraints is the process of suburbanization.

Suburbanization refers specifically to the movement of the middle classes out of cities, towns, and villages into low-density residential districts on the outskirts of major towns and cities. In our context, however, it can be extended to include the subsequent replacement of the community structures and ways of life that traditionally characterized city centres and villages by struc-tures and ways of life imported back from the suburbs. It is often seen as a peculiarly American phenomenon, but has become widespread throughout the developed world.

Compared with traditional city or village life, suburban life is characterized by a relative absence of intimate relationships and community ties. Suburbs are places where people live, but do not necessarily belong. People live there only as long as it is convenient, and family groupings are rare. Most journeys, to work, school, shops, and services, are made by car, limiting the scope for personal interactions. Often, people do not even know their immediate neigh-bours. In general, the suburbs are peaceful, law-abiding places, and that is often why people move there, but the morality of the suburb is a very low-key affair. In traditional, tightly knit communities, moral transgression is quickly confronted. The community as a whole acts as an institution of moral authority, a kind of extended family. In the suburbs, however, people are much more likely to turn a blind eye to wrongdoing, even when it is carried out against themselves. In practice, the avoidance of conflict takes precedence over the righting of wrongs, and this tolerance is also reflected in people's moral principles. In a recent study of suburban middle-class attitudes, the sociologist Alan Wolfe wrote of 'morality writ small'. The suburbs are relatively conservative places and he found that, by and large, people still believe in traditional moral standards. But they are very reluctant to proclaim those standards, or to impose them on others.

In the last few decades, suburban attitudes and ways of life have spread to the rest of society. The more affluent areas of the cities always shared much in common with the suburbs, with transient populations living their lives in the anonymous city centres, returning home only to sleep and often disappearing at the weekends. But in villages and small towns, too, communities have been weakened. Television has replaced interactive leisure pursuits, and led to the closure of public meeting places. The improved efficiency and reduced costs of telephony, and the advent of the Internet, have made it less and less necessary for people to leave their homes. The concentration of shops in retail parks and malls, the closure of village shops and pubs, and the growing use of cars have all led to increasingly suburban behaviour patterns.

## THE MORAL CULTURE OF CONTEMPORARY SOCIETY

Any weakening of the cultural constraints of a hierarchy provides opportunities for entrepreneurial self-interest. Whenever in history hierarchical authority has been compromised, self-interested entrepreneurs have moved quickly to fill the gap, either exploiting the hierarchical culture for their own ends (as in the opportunistic assumption of political power) or replacing hierarchical with market structures (as do drug barons and racketeers). In the present case, however, the different developments we have described are even more intimately connected, for the very same forces that have led to the weakening of moral constraints have also led to the rapid growth of (legitimate) business, and to the increasing influence of economic ideas. As business has flourished and free markets have brought unprecedented levels of prosperity, support for the alternative morality of market self-interest has grown, and the institutional authorities that have responded, as authorities must respond, by demanding a return to traditional values have lost still more of their credibility.

For many of the advocates of market culture, the associated threat to traditional moral values has not been a great concern. For the most part these advocates have focused simply on the economic benefits to be derived from market structures. They have welcomed the weakening of hierarchical constraints, but have not associated this with any threat to the moral fabric of society. They have assumed that self-interest is constrained by the law, and that the law is an adequate safeguard of traditional moral values. If they have discussed morality more explicitly, it has been to present their ideas as an enhancement of traditional moral virtues, not a challenge to them. They have talked, for example, of an increase in human freedom and equality of opportunity, of the virtue of self-reliance and the moral dangers of dependence, of the moral right to the benefits of ownership.

For many of those who are concerned with traditional morality, however, the developments have naturally been a source of concern, and over the last ten or fifteen years there has been increasing talk of a 'crisis of morality', often described in terms of a 'de-moralization' of society. In Chapter 6 we shall review some of the accounts of this crisis, which, unsurprisingly, vary enormously according to the political ideologies or theoretical commitments of the commentators.

Conservative commentators such as Gertrude Himmelfarb, Michael Novak, and Irving Kristol have lamented the ways in which the moral fabric of society is being destroyed, but have not generally associated this with the rise of market culture. On the contrary, moral conservatives have often aligned themselves with the economic interests of business, responding positively to the free market rhetoric of opportunity and, especially, self-reliance. Our problems are typically attributed not to economic self-interest but to left-wing ideology and the modern welfare state, which destroys self-reliance, encourages dependency, and legitimates illegitimacy, leading to the growth of single parent families and, as a consequence, to the growth of crime, drug dependency, and other forms of moral deviance. The best hope for the future, in their view, lies in the combination of free market economics with a strong reassertion of traditional moral authorities. Francis Fukuyama, in *The Great Disruption*, offers a more sophisticated version of this analysis in which contemporary moral decline is associated with the transition from an industrial society to an information society, a transition that has been significantly aided by the arrival of the contraceptive pill. In this account both the entrepreneurial self-interest that flourishes in periods of technological transition and the welfare excesses introduced to cope with this transition are implicated in moral decline, but as part and parcel of the process rather than as its cause, and the process itself is considered to be a transient one. The disruption may be severe, but it is temporary, and poses no threat to the institutions of liberal democracy. As we adapt to the new technological environment, our traditional moral values and authorities will be restored.

Commentators from the left have taken a very different view. They have seen no danger in the welfare state, no particular virtue in the individualism and self-reliance of market culture, and no future for the traditional moral authorities. Many have stressed the downside of freedom, the dangers of economic greed, and the morally disruptive effects of the flexible economy. But while at the more popular end of the debate commentators have associated the decline of morality with the rise of business power and entrepreneurial greed, scholarly observers have tended to root their analyses in mid-twentieth century perceptions of industrial and post-industrial society. According to the viewpoint taken, the de-moralization of society is associated either with the exercise of technological, and especially bureaucratic, power, as by Richard Stivers and Zygmunt Bauman; or with the dominance of common sense reasoning, based on second-hand perceptions of how people behave (Ralph Fevre); or with the indifference and sense of powerlessness that result from the 'happy conscious-ness' of a media-dominated consumer society (Keith Tester). In the first case, the rise of market culture is represented simply as the replacement of one form of bureaucratic domination by another, of the bureaucratic State by the bureaucracy of the multinational corporation. In the second case, economic thinking with its assumption of self-interest is seen as just a well-developed version of practical common sense, which has proved so successful that it has temporarily squeezed out other forms of thinking based on moral feelings, emotions, and beliefs. In the third interpretation, self-interest is subsumed under the pleasure principle in a world in which morality, like everything else, has become just another commodity.

All these perspectives are valuable and we shall explore them all in some detail. Each has something to teach us, or to remind us, about our present con-dition. They also have their limitations, however. Some commentators seem to seriously underplay the historical significance of the current moral crisis, treat-ing evidently long-term historical developments as if they were temporary, short-term disruptions. Others seriously overplay the crisis, writing as if tradi-tional moral values and behaviours had disappeared altogether, or harking back to some non-existent golden age of moral probity. Many fasten onto a particular 'cause' or causes of the crisis, such as bureaucracy, the welfare state, psychotherapy, contraception, or television, and so miss the broader picture of which all are a part.

One effect of these limitations has been to stifle constructive debate as to how we should deal with the problems with which we are faced. Some writers are content to assume that they will just go away, while others frame them in terms that effectively preclude any solution. Traditional moral authorities such as the Christian Church may not be an entirely spent force, but they are not going to suddenly revive themselves to the extent needed to bring about a traditional re-moralization. The technologies of communication and organization will continue to evolve, but bureaucracy will not disappear and nor will television.

Nor, in the immediate future, will traditional morality. Its institutional structure may be severely damaged, may even be damaged beyond repair, but most people still retain a sense of traditional moral obligation and still accept the social legitimacy of traditional moral values. What has changed is that a morality of self-interest is *also* now socially legitimate. Whether it is manifest in economic enterprise, organizational advancement, reliance on welfare, instru-mental pragmatism, psychological gratification, or indifference to the needs of others, self-interest is generally considered legitimate; and whereas before, the realms of self-interest and obligation were clearly demarcated with one subservient to the other, now they have come together so that we live, in effect, in a bimoral society.

The conflict between traditional moral duty and legitimate self-interest that characterizes this bimoral society is not entirely new. Everyday life has always thrown up countless instances in which people have had to trade off one against the other: giving money to the needy against spending it on oneself, stopping to help against getting on with one's own business, buying from an honest trader or getting the same thing cheaper from someone who might not put the cash through the books. In traditional society, however, these conflicts were resolved by a demarcation of arenas and responsibilities. In people's normal relationships with relative strangers, morality imposed constraints but not duties. To give time or money to charity or good works was morally praiseworthy, but to refrain from giving was not, on the whole, considered immoral. In their relationships with their immediate communities, however, with close friends, family, and, especially, with their parents or children, people were generally expected to be dutiful, to put the interests of the other person above their own. Similar obligations also applied when circumstances threw strangers together, leaving one person uniquely dependent on another for help.

In the bimoral society, such obligations are no longer taken for granted. The growth of self-interest has gone hand in hand with a growing preoccupation with the self and its material and psychological possessions. An outward focus has been replaced by an inward, narcissistic one, and in interpersonal relationships social duty must now vie with psychological gratification. The traditional conception of ourselves as human *beings* has been replaced by a conception of ourselves as human 'havers' and what we have, not only in the way of consumer goods but in terms of less material possessions like time, personality, and emotions, has become an obsession. The result is that we approach situations very differently from the way we used to, and when a conflict between obligation and self-interest arises we do not resolve it just by asking 'what is my relationship to this person or this cause', but also ask 'how does this impact on my self?' It is now considered morally legitimate, throughout much of our society, for people to put their own interests above those of their parents or siblings or even, in some cases, their children. It is certainly considered legitimate to weigh the interests of the other with those of the self, and when it comes to making a judgement there is often no socially 'correct' answer. We are, in the end, our own moral authorities.

## THE MORAL TENSIONS OF MANAGEMENT

In everyday life it is still more or less possible to ignore the values of market culture and take a traditional moral view of our social and personal relationships. For a manager in a business organization, however, the dictates of market culture are not so easily avoided. In traditional business organizations, with their traditional hierarchical cultures, traditional morality and self-interest complemented each other. The competitive advantage of the company was carried in the long-term relationships and experience of its staff. Economic success was based on what people could achieve in a stable and supportive environment in which each worked for the benefit of all, and the loyalty and moral duty of employees were rewarded by financial security. In contemporary business organizations, the need for loyalty and effective working relationships remains, but the timescale is much shorter and there is no longer any assurance that loyalty will be repaid. For today's manager, traditional morality and self-interest are at odds, and in Chapter 7 we shall explore the tensions that result.

These tensions are particularly apparent in relationships between managers and the staff who report to them. However good they may be at allocating resources efficiently, markets cannot direct those resources to a particular end. Business organizations are created for a purpose, and if they are to be effectively focused on that purpose some kind of coordinating structure, some kind of hierarchy, is required. An important function of management, then, is the hiring, supervision and direction, and, where appropriate, termination of staff. In hiring and directing their staff, managers have to ask for their loyalty and commitment to the corporate cause—not, any longer, for a long-term career, but at least for the period that someone remains with the company. They have to require that the company comes first. They also have to build up the personal relationships that will sustain that loyalty. They cannot, however, offer any loyalty in return. The scope for helping staff through personal difficulties, a characteristic obligation of the traditional company, has been drastically reduced. And when the short-term economics say that people should be fired, then people must be fired, regardless of the consequences for them or their dependents. The self-interest of the company shareholders demands it, and the self-interest of the manager, whose pay is performance related and whose own job is on the line, demands it too.

These tensions of the flexible economy go right to the top of the organization. Until twenty or thirty years ago, the Chief Executive Officer (CEO) of a company was generally perceived as a steward. In publicly quoted companies CEOs might dominate the board but they were still employees, better paid than others perhaps, but carrying commensurate responsibilities, in the traditional moral sense, to look after the company for its stakeholders. What this meant varied slightly from country to country, but in Britain and America it meant looking after the long-term interests of shareholders whilst having a proper regard to other stakeholders such as employees and dependent communities. In private, family controlled companies, CEOs might act more as patrons, with benefits and privileges denied to ordinary managers, but again their position carried a moral responsibility, to the family owners of the firm and, on behalf of those families, to the employees and communities to whom they felt responsible. The assumptions underlying these perceptions were the characteristic assumptions of a hierarchical culture: that the role of the leader was to serve the community, and that provided people were treated decently and with respect they would be motivated to perform the roles assigned to them, honestly and to the best of their ability.

In the flexible economy, these expectations and assumptions no longer hold. The growth and sophistication of financial markets and the growing influence of the concept of ownership rights have changed the balance between stakeholder interests, and investors are no longer content to have their interests weighed against others by steward-CEOs. Instead the CEOs are considered to be the shareholders' agents, in the economic sense. Consistent with this, and with the general shift towards a market culture, they are also assumed to act as market entrepreneurs, motivated by self-interest rather than by moral obligation. Reflecting the new assumptions, CEOs have been awarded massive stock options, to align their interests with those of their shareholders. At the same time, they have had to respond to the combination of competitive and investor pressures by taking hard actions, outsourcing work to developing countries, laying off employees, and giving up their firms' traditional responsibilities to their local communities. This has inevitably reinforced the perception of self-interest, isolating them both socially and within their own organizations.

Like any other group of ambitious achievers, CEOs have always had a strong regard for their own self-interest, and there is no doubt that in the past they sometimes abused the trust placed in them, exercising power without accountability. For the truly self-interested, however, there are easier ways to advancement than through management, and most CEOs really do see themselves as stewards, with wide-ranging moral responsibilities. Their problem now is that if they treat one group of stakeholders according to the dictates of traditional morality, this will be interpreted by other groups as an expression of self-interest. If they lay people off, they will be perceived by employees and the public as being motivated by their stock options. But if they accept a moral obligation to their employees, their investors will perceive them as putting personal relationships and comfort factors above their contractual duties as economic agents. The latter complaint carries no moral force, as in a market culture the pursuit of self-interest is perfectly acceptable. It is up to the investors to find a way of making CEOs do what they want. But it nevertheless places the CEOs in an extraordinary and very difficult position. The cultural pressures of traditional society pushed people into moral behaviour even when this went against their perceived self-interest, but at least they were praised for it. The cultural pressures of a market society push people into self-interested behaviour even when it goes against their altruistic instincts, but there is no blame and they get rewarded economically. The cultural pressures of the bimoral society push company CEOs into seemingly self-interested behaviour, and reward them for it, but in a bimoral society they then get blamed, not praised, for their success.

While the flexible economy impacts strongly on the management of relationships within the vertical hierarchy, its most pronounced impact on middle and junior managers is on their lateral or non-hierarchical relationships, which are increasingly set within the context of teamwork. In many organizations, bureaucratic offices and rigid matrix structures have effectively been replaced by flexible networks of self-organizing teams. For the company, effective teamwork provides a flexible, responsive, and efficient way of organizing that is perfectly suited to the contemporary competitive environment. But its success depends on a strange dynamic. In any situation, effective teamwork requires and generates loyalty and commitment, old-fashioned moral values. But the teams of the new economy are based on the logic and morality of self-interest. On one hand, team members are partners, working together to achieve an out-come for the company. On the other, they are competitors, competing to work on the next, more challenging, prestigious, or remunerative project. Entry to a team is a competitive process, managed not hierarchically but through network contacts and an internal labour market. Survival in the team is also competitive. Those considered unsuitable or unproductive will not be man-aged and developed, either within the team or from outside, but simply ejected, their reputations damaged and options reduced. The hierarchical supervision of traditional organizations is replaced by the peer-control of team members whose pay and prospects are closely tied to performance.

One way of succeeding in this environment, at least for a while, is to cultivate a veneer of cooperativeness but rigorously pursue your self-interest. Many contemporary managers network avidly to get onto the best and most visibly successful teams and, when things do not work out, move on before they are moved on, and leave others to carry the can. For other managers, such a ruthless self-interest is not an option. Team relationships are personal relation-ships, and personal relationships carry traditional moral obligations. But it is no longer an option simply to behave dutifully and trust that the rewards will come, because the chances are that they will not. So somehow people have to combine duty and self-interest and work out when, and with whom, each is appropriate.

In practice, in this highly competitive environment, the cooperative qualities fundamental to teamwork are created largely by the common need of the team to perform and by the shared excitement of the task. A team challenge creates its own dynamic and teams perform best when they capture their members' lives. But this itself creates conflict, for while some people may be in a position to give their all to the team, others have quite legitimate commitments outside the work place, most obviously to their families. For many women, this situa-tion is sadly ironic. For years they fought prejudice in traditional hierarchical companies, reluctant to invest in women as they did in men for fear that the women would disappear to bring up families and their investments would be wasted. Contemporary businesses, with their shorter time horizons, have no such problems and will in principle employ and promote women on the same basis as men. But in practice, juggling the obligations to a family with the obligations to a team and the need to network and be visible can be extraordin-arily difficult, if not impossible.

A key feature of the flexible economy is that the responsibility for dealing with these conflicts of responsibilities is thrust squarely onto the individual. In a bimoral society the pressures of traditional morality still operate, but they are effectively pushed down from the institutional to the personal level. Traditional societies were built on moral constraint, but because that constraint was institutionalized it was not problematic. People simply operated within it. In a market society, constraint is replaced by freedom, and at first sight that seems very attractive. Everybody wants to be free, and freedom of a kind—the freedom from torture or oppression, for instance—is one of the distinguishing marks of a well-developed traditional society. But the freedom of the market society is in fact very different. The rhetoric, naturally enough, emphasizes the positive side: the economic benefits of free trade and free markets, the benefits to consumers of free choice, the freedom for people to make their own life decisions, instead of having them made for them. But in a market society, freedom cuts both ways. Because there is no institutional hierarchical responsibility, in the traditional moral sense, people are on their own. They are free to prosper, but free to starve, free to exploit but free to be exploited. They are even free to oppress and free to be oppressed. Words like exploitation, oppression, and coercion, drawn from the moral vocabulary of the hierarchy, are neutral or even, in the case of exploitation, positive in the market context. If people starve or suffer, are exploited or oppressed, that is not the responsibility of society: it is their own responsibility, their own fault. In any competition there are losers as well as winners, and the freedom to take charge of your own career, to take one of the clarion calls of the new economy, is also the freedom to find yourself without a job.

Many people today are clearly finding that freedom in the market sense can be genuinely liberating and invigorating. For those able and willing to take them, the flexible economy creates opportunities of a kind that were previously not available. People are taking charge of their own careers, building lives to suit themselves, and finding new energies in the process. For many others, however, the uncertainties of the market are disabling, a source of insecurity, despair, and despondency. In a bimoral society, legitimate expectations of security sit side by side with an experience of pervasive insecurity. The framework of a traditional social structure, able to limit the effects of oppression and exploitation, remains but seems increasingly under threat. People expect to be looked after, but they are expected, or feel expected, to look after themselves.

## THE CHALLENGE OF CONTEMPORARY MANAGEMENT

The tensions of management in a bimoral society present today's managers with a range of challenges, some of which are not only very different from those that faced their predecessors of a generation ago but also very different from those for which they are still trained in many of the world's leading business schools. Business schools have now latched on, a little belatedly, to the importance of entrepreneurship and career self-management, and managers are learning fast how to fend for themselves in the flexible economy. But in the enthusiasm for the discourse of enterprise and markets very little attention has been paid to the core of the new management challenge, which is to combine enterprise with humanity, in such a way that the driving force of entrepreneurial self-interest is not merely released but constructively employed in the interests and service of the company (and ultimately of society) as a whole. This does not mean suppressing self-interest. One of the great benefits of the new flexible economy has been that people's entrepreneurial instincts have been released and turned to productive economic use rather than to political infighting within an unproductive hierarchical organization. It does, however, mean balancing that self-interest with the traditional moral concern necessary for the effective and productive management of organizational structures and the interpersonal relationships on which these are built. In the context of the flexible economy, this cannot be done through traditional hierarchical systems of rules and constraint. We have to find new ways of giving life to the morality of obligation.

The specific challenges this brings to management are manifold, but we shall focus on three. The first is a challenge primarily for senior managers and is a challenge of leadership. It stems from the need to coordinate and direct divergent self-interests so as to serve the interests of the corporation and its stakeholders. In the old economy this was done through hierarchical control, but the new economy calls for more subtle means of achieving a shared purpose. The second challenge affects all managers, but particularly those in the middle and senior levels of management or in human resource management. It is the challenge of managing the business organization as a moral community in the absence of any long-term commitments by the company. The third challenge affects all managers equally and is a challenge of learning. Old-fashioned hierarchical organizations were characterized by well-defined rules, routines, and procedures, which both governed the management relationships within the organization and acted as a store for organizational know-how. Flexible organizations can neither sustain nor afford such systems of rules, and managers must find other ways of learning and of managing the learning process.

The transition from hierarchical to network organizations has not only been beneficial in terms of efficiency and responsiveness, it has also released enormous entrepreneurial energies. Unless these energies are harnessed to the purpose of the organization, however, they can easily become destructive, as employees put greater effort into competing against each other than into competing for the business. Some people have seen the solution to this problem in self-organizing networks, but while such networks can adapt effectively to their immediate environments, resolve differences between their members' interests, and organize around a given purpose, they are not, in themselves, purposeful. If they are to serve the needs of the business they need to be directed in some way. In the early stages of the transition to flexible organizations, this has not been a problem. On the contrary, companies have on the whole been able to impose a market discipline on their employees without sacrificing the traditional hierarchical demand for loyalty. The combination of market freedom and hierarchical dedication is a recipe for supernormal profits, and business has been booming. But this situation is unsustainable. It takes time for people to lose their hierarchical loyalties, but as the market culture continues to undermine traditional hierarchical authority, in organizations as in society, this loyalty will be eroded and other kinds of direction will be needed.

Providing this direction, including a vision for the organization and a strategy to achieve it, aligning people behind the direction, and motivating and inspiring them to hold to it and not be diverted by their personal interests, are the challenges of business leadership. The processes of leadership—directing, aligning, motivating, and inspiring—are essentially the same in flexible organizations as they were in a more traditional bureaucratic organizations, but the change of context brings significant new challenges. In the bureaucratic context, the key leadership challenge was change. In a stable bureaucratic culture, a well-defined 'grid' of roles and relationships, rules and conventions, ensures that direction and alignment are not problematic, while a strong moral compact provides the necessary motivation. Only when change is required and a new direction and new alignment are needed does leadership become an issue. In a flexible organization, in contrast, which has neither the constraining structure of bureaucracy nor its moral compact, leadership is a permanent requirement, needed as much to maintain stability as to generate change.

The change of context also impacts on the style or type of leadership that can be employed. In a hierarchical context, authoritarian leadership styles could often be very effective. People looked to a leader, that is, to someone filling the leadership role, to lead. Oddly enough the same was true, for rather different reasons, in the less formal organizations, such as criminal gangs, to be found in market cultures. Here, the problem was to control members' self-interest, but in the absence of any moral constraints the most effective way to do it was through a strictly hierarchical and oppressively authoritarian use of power. In flexible organizations, however, there is neither the cultural basis for legitimate authoritarian leadership nor that for coercive autocracy. An authoritarian style of leadership is not an option, and today's business leaders must—and do—adopt more participative leadership styles.

The question is: how participative? Most contemporary CEOs, at least of large companies, appear to treat their leadership responsibilities in a very individualistic way. They encourage participation, but without relinquishing any control, treating the vision and strategy as almost their personal property and devoting most of their time and effort to their effective communication. Instead of simply telling people what to do they sell them a product, but they do not really give them any say over what that product is. In many ways this is understandable. From a cultural perspective, both hierarchies and markets favour strong, individual leadership. In the competitive environment of flexible organizations a CEO's closest colleagues, with whom he might otherwise share his knowledge and leadership tasks, are also often his strongest rivals. CEOs also know that they will be held personally to account, both internally by their boards and externally by investors and the media, for any failure or supposed failure, whoever's fault it may be. These factors all contribute to the role of CEO being quite a lonely one, and this separates the CEOs still further from other people, encouraging them to see themselves as different and reinforcing a hubristic image of individual leadership.

It is very doubtful, however, if this is the most appropriate way of leading today's business organizations. To some extent it is certainly necessary for the leader to maintain control. The more purely empowering forms of leadership, which may work in other settings, are not generally appropriate in business, partly because the objectives of the business transcend those of the group that can be empowered (empowering the employees will not always serve the interests of the shareholders or other legitimate stakeholders), and partly because in a complex and rapidly changing competitive environment the distributed processes of an empowered organization sometimes have to be short-circuited by someone with a strategic overview of the whole. But if the benefits of the flexible organization are to be secured, and the entrepreneurial drive of its members harnessed, control cannot be too rigid: some degree of empowerment and genuine autonomy is also necessary.

What this suggests in leadership terms is an approach that balances an element of top-down leadership with some elements of what has been described as servant leadership or transforming leadership, in which the leader's personal interests are suspended, the emphasis is on providing guidance rather than instructions, and this guidance is based on a deep awareness and empathetic understanding of the tensions people are facing. This is a demanding challenge, and not just because the ability to listen is very rare. To get to be CEO of a large company in a highly competitive job market requires not only great ability and dedication to one's work but also qualities that are very different from those required for servant leadership—great personal ambition, a drive to succeed, to win, to do better than the next person. To turn round having got the job and suspend one's personal ambition is extraordinarily difficult and requires great maturity. However, it is only by listening to people and empathizing with them that the leader of a flexible organization can lead effectively, building on and directing people's personal interests in such a way as to serve the interests of the organization as a whole.

A related and in some ways still greater challenge may be to break out of the mould of individual leadership altogether, and move towards a model of team-based leadership. Team structures may not fit naturally in either hierarchical or market cultures, but by mediating between individual and common interests they do provide an effective compromise solution to the challenges of management in a bimoral society. Like the function or office in a bureaucracy, they can also survive changes of individual membership, so ensuring a continuity of organizational functionality in a world of high mobility. They have become the basic building blocks of flexible organizations. At top management level, however, even the most flexibly organized of companies have so far retained a bureaucratic hierarchical structure, with well-defined functional roles and a single leader. There are strong cultural and political reasons for this, but there are also considerable costs associated with it, and it seems very likely that managers will at some stage have to explore new and more cooperative modes of leadership.

A fundamental aspect of servant or transforming leadership is taking account of the other, and this leads to the second challenge facing managers today. Nothing is more important for the creation and maintenance of a moral community than the actions of the leadership. But moral leadership may not be enough. Especially in large multinational and operationally decentralized organizations, the leader or leaders can be quite remote. In listed companies they may also be ousted, and often are ousted, at very short notice, when a company's performance fails to live up to the expectations of the investment community. As recent events at Enron have shown, organizations also need, just like societies, to protect themselves against the excesses of self-interest, against leaders whose drive and charisma obscures a financial greed or lust for power that knows no moral constraints. While only the leaders of a business organization can formulate the vision and purpose that will make that organization cohere strategically, the responsibility for managing a moral community must run right through the organization, and in the absence of a strong hierarchical culture this poses a challenge for each and every manager.

'Moral management' is not a familiar phrase. In traditional hierarchical organizations, the rules of the hierarchy effectively looked after the moral side of the organization and ethical issues only came into play when those rules were broken. Management itself was often described as amoral and instrumental and there was a long tradition of mechanizing managerial work so as to remove as far as possible the elements of judgement. This tendency has become particularly pronounced in recent decades, in the transition from hierarchy to network organizations. In a penetrating analysis of late twentieth-century managerialism, the critical theorist Stanley Deetz has observed that contemporary business organizations tend to deny any legitimacy to questions of values, which are either translated into value-neutral economic terms, thrown back onto the individual manager to deal with at a personal level, or suppressed completely. In the context of the hierarchy, this can, perhaps, be seen as one of the effects of terminal malfunctioning. When hierarchies break down, it is quite normal for legitimate morality to be replaced by instrumental power, for the organization to become an agent of tyranny. Its carryover into network organizations, with their emphasis on market morality, is also quite natural. If network organizations are to thrive, however, they must act as traditionally moral as well as economic communities, and they must be managed as such. People need to be free to act as enterprising economic agents, but they also need the benefits of community: an environment of mutual trust, awareness, and support, in which multiple responsibilities and accountabilities are recognized and in which they can learn and grow.

In the absence of any long-term organizational commitments, this can only come from interpersonal relationships in which 'management' becomes the exact opposite of the instrumentalist characterization: an explicitly value-oriented activity. Once the purpose and priorities of a company are determined, allocating economic resources between rival projects needs little in the way of management. Market structures can do that pretty well. But determining purpose and priorities is essentially a matter of values. For senior managers, the challenge is to balance the divergent interests of the various stakeholders of the company—shareholders, employees, communities, suppliers, and so on. For middle and junior managers it is to balance the interests of individual employees, including themselves, in the context of those of the company as a whole. Judgements of this kind cannot be reduced to economic formulae because, from a traditionally moral perspective, they depend upon specific relationships. A company's responsibilities to an arm's length supplier who operates in a free market and has many other customers for its goods or services are not the same as those to a supplier that has been encouraged in some way to dedicate itself to the company. The responsibilities to employees who were taken on in recent years, explicitly without commitment, are different from those to employees who joined in an earlier era and devoted their lives to serving the corporation. The development needs of one employee, at a particular point in life, may be very different from those of others in the same company position but at different stages of their life trajectories. The commitment that can be expected from a working mother or grieving son or daughter is necessarily different in *kind* (not necessarily in extent) from that which can be expected from someone without family responsibilities. The time and energy that a manager can reasonably devote to the company, and to the needs of its employees, will inevitably vary from time to time according to the demands of home and family—and vice versa.

These differences were recognized in traditional organizations, where they were built into the rulebook. How people were treated depended on their particular positions in a complex social structure, with carefully worked out procedures to cope with the different circumstances that might arise. There were even rules to say when the rules could be overruled by management discretion. Contemporary organizations have much more limited rules, and those they have are not always effective, so managers have to make their own judgements, to manage without rules. And the only way of managing without rules, other than by adopting a pure market culture and basing everything on economic value, is to manage through relationships. The starting point is moral concern, an attitude of awareness to people's particular needs and circumstances, and to the specific aspects of different relationships that might generate specific moral obligations. Prominent among these, in a business organization, must be the economic demands of the company and its shareholders. But however prominent, these are not everything. Other needs must be recognized too. In the end, of course, not all the needs can be met, but that is the nature of life. The moral imperative is not to get the right answer, because there is not one, but to try and ask the right questions, to answer them as best we can in the circumstances, and to continually keep learning and helping others to learn.

In today's knowledge-based economy, learning is a key source of competitive advantage, and a central function of management in flexible organizations is to manage the learning process. The knowledge that most matters, however, is not the codified explicit knowledge that can be carried in databases but the tacit or implicit know-how that can only be learnt from experience and communicated through shared interpersonal understandings. In bureaucracies this know-how was part of the stable corporate culture, a source of advantage but also of resistance to change. In flexible organizations it has to be actively managed, with managers taking responsibility both for its development and dissemination in and between teams and for its exposure and questioning, when it ceases to be productive or interferes with new learning.

This is a tough challenge, but it is entirely consistent with the other challenges facing managers today, and requires much the same skills: listening, empathy, and personal engagement, trusting and showing trust. Only by engaging in this way can the manager become part of the learning process and so a conduit for the tacit knowledge that is generated. Only in this way can she create an environment of open, critical, and constructive reflection.

## THE CHALLENGE FOR CONTEMPORARY SOCIETY

Managing in a bimoral society will always be challenging, though it should be very rewarding too. What makes it especially challenging in the short term is that society at large has not yet found a way of expressing its bimoral character. There is widespread, if tacit, recognition that the traditional morality of obligation and the market morality of self-interest are both indispensable for continued prosperity and survival, and we are prepared to accept both as socially legitimate. But we have not yet found a satisfactory means of balancing them, either conceptually or institutionally. The political doctrine of the 'Third Way', as employed by New Labour, asserts that both are important and attempts to steer a path between them, between a market-based libertarian capitalism on one hand and a social democratic welfarism on the other. But since it has found no way of grounding its traditional moral side other than in the old institutions of church, state, and family authority, it has not, in practice, been able to place any significant restraint on commercial self-interest. Theoretically more sophisticated versions of the Third Way, such as that proposed by Anthony Giddens, do not fall into this trap of traditionalism. They recognize that morality will in future have to take a non-traditional form closely akin to the kind of moral concern that is now called for from managers. But they do not show us how to get from here to there.

This failure to find a way of expressing the traditional morality of obligation that transcends the limitations of traditional hierarchical authorities complicates the manager's task, because it leaves her without any societal resources on which to draw in her own attempts to balance entrepreneurial self-interest with the common good. Its most obvious manifestations, however, are at the societal level. It is reflected, for example, in the current failure of attempts at corporate governance and the regulation of financial markets, especially at the international level; in the deep rift of misunderstanding between big business and governments on one hand and environmentalists and anti-globalization campaigners on the other; and in a chronic failure to understand and reconcile the moral foundations of different cultures and societies.

These are big issues and we shall certainly not resolve them here. But in Chapter 9 we shall look briefly at two questions that are central to our theme. First, on what commonly acceptable principles might a morality of obligation appropriate to the twenty-first century be based? Second, in the light of our answers to this, how might we most effectively approach the regulation and governance of international business and finance, so as to ensure that they serve the public interest?

Before exploring the first of these questions, we shall need to address an issue that is central to contemporary political debate, namely that of globalization. There has been a lot of argument over the last few years about the extent to which globalization is or is not occurring, and about the future or otherwise of the nation state, but beneath the froth of the debate a few things seem evident. On one hand, the nation state is not going to disappear, at least for some considerable time. Politically, culturally, and economically, we are a long, long way from living in a global society, and the cultural interconnectedness characteristic of globalization is still serving more to emphasize a plurality of values than to homogenize those values. On the other hand there are important ways in which we *are* moving toward a global, or globally interconnected, society. International trade may still be dwarfed by intra-national trade, but global currency markets, international loans, and the conditions attached to them are producing a kind of global economic integration. Cultural differences may still be massive but as cultures come more and more into contact the pressures to resolve these differences are growing. Environmentally, the activities of one country routinely affect the environments of others, and the most serious sources of environmental risk are global in their impact. The natural resources of the earth may be far from exhausted, but a country can no longer increase their availability by conquering or expanding into new territories: the limitations of the globe impact increasingly upon us. These and other changes are tying the fates of nations inextricably together. They are also producing financial and environmental risks that impact upon nations but cannot be controlled by them.

In this environment, it is not enough to seek a moral consensus at the national level. There is also a growing need for the international governance and regulation of business and finance and for a global moral consensus on which to base these. Such a consensus will have to be based, moreover, on the recognition of cultural pluralism and the search for a modus vivendi, rather than upon any particular cultural tradition. It will have to be post-traditional.

The most obvious basis for a global moral consensus is the idea of individual human rights. This idea already commands widespread cross-cultural assent, being embodied in the Universal Declaration of Human Rights and in cross-national European legislation. Whereas systems of moral constraints, which are at the core of traditional moralities, appear to look backwards to a past that is no longer relevant and to constrain people unnecessarily, rights appear to look forward and to offer liberation. Whereas systems of moral constraints vary noticeably from culture to culture, rights appear to be in some way universal. In fact, the origins of an ethics of rights are peculiarly Anglo-American, but there seems to be almost universal agreement, based on an argued rational consensus, that being human entitles one to some inviolable rights, and that these rights should be protected in law. There is also a remarkable amount of agreement on what people's rights should be.

Individual rights may well provide the most promising basis for an institutionalized global morality of obligation, but if a workable system of rights is to be developed a number of issues will need to be addressed. First, there is the problem of the politics of recognition: of how to balance individual rights against the collective rights claimed by particular social groups in a pluralistic society. Second, there is the problem of property rights. This is one area where the Anglo-American roots of the law and ethics of rights are reflected in culturally specific features that are not universally shared. It is also an area in which the discourse of rights can readily be adapted to serve the cause of self-interest. Third, there is the issue of corporate rights. The idea that a business corporation should be treated as a legal 'person', as it currently is, appears at first sight to have some moral value, to impose on the corporation a responsibility akin to that of a moral individual. In practice, however, corporate personhood has, like property rights, been used more to shield people from traditional moral responsibilities and to defend their self-interest than it has to constrain that self-interest.

There are also two more fundamental problems with the ethics of rights. One is that, with a few exceptions, most of the rights people claim are not absolute. Different rights can conflict with each other, and perceptions of rights vary over time and across cultures. The other is that many important human rights are effectively meaningless without the existence of corresponding obligations. A right to life imposes a duty on everybody not to kill, but a right to subsistence or education, or to any of the so-called welfare rights, does not impose any universal moral obligation. To be effective, such rights have to be accompanied by an institutional framework (such as, for example, that of public services and taxation) for allocating obligations. This poses a serious political problem, for while everybody wants rights there is generally much less enthusiasm about obligations. Universal subsistence, education, and health provision may be universally agreed to be desirable, but someone has to pay for them, and to protect even the basic welfare rights of the world's population would impose a massive—and at present unacceptable—burden on the wealthier members of society.

What this means is that while a system of individual rights can perhaps provide a good explicit basis for moral consensus, it cannot do all the moral work that will be required. We shall also need some principles for determining the rights to be included and for interpreting them in practice. These will need, moreover, to be powerful enough emotionally to engage our moral concern, while being free of both the outdated trappings and the cultural specificities of the traditional religions. I shall suggest tentatively that these might be found in the essentially humanitarian notions of loving-kindness and human-heartedness that can be found in very similar form in all the main world religions, as well as in the secular ethics of Confucianism. Indeed Confucianism, which is religiously neutral and which originated as an attempt to escape the conventionalism of hierarchical culture, may well provide a model on which we can build.

What can all this tell us about our more immediate concern with the regulation and governance of business? It is one of the ironies of our present situation that in an age in which rules and regulations are becoming less effective they are also becoming much more prolific, especially with regard to business. This proliferation of regulation is partly the natural response of any hierarchy to a loss of control, but it also serves as a reminder that the state is the one institution of society that has no alternative but to be hierarchical. Its primary function is indeed to determine and enforce laws and regulations. Much contemporary regulation is essentially trivial—the form-filling compliance triviality of bureaucracy—but that should not be allowed to obscure the fact that there are many areas of business where regulation is needed: to set environmental, health and safety, and food and drug standards, for example, to control the risks inherent in financial markets, or to provide a framework for corporate governance. In these areas and others, the preferred choice of market participants would be self-regulation, but this would not work. For one thing, it would be vulnerable to abuse by the most successful—and, hence, most powerful—of the market participants. For another, the mutual interests of the participants differ significantly from the interests of society as a whole.

Some form of external regulation is, therefore, required, and in many areas this will need to go significantly beyond what is already in place if it is to effectively modify the effects of commercial self-interest. It will also need to operate on a global level. This will have to be achieved, however, in an environment in which the authority of governments is increasingly questioned and in which there is still no global government or regulatory body with any credibility at all. This in turn suggests that the effective regulation of business will be possible only if it can be founded on a process of global dialogue, built upon some commonly acceptable framework of principles.

Following our earlier discussion, one basis for global regulation might be a framework of human rights. As in the more general situation, however, this would need infusing in some way with an attitude of moral concern and awareness, and even if such a concern were developed at the social level we would still need some means of ensuring that it was carried into the business context. This takes us back to the issue of trust and trustworthiness. Most current approaches to corporate governance and financial regulation, heavily influenced by economic thinking, are based on the agency principle of mistrust. While corporate managers, for example, insist that they can be trusted, the tendency in corporate governance is to assume that they are self-interested and untrustworthy and to try and devise mechanisms to contain their self-interest. These mechanisms effectively separate them still further from the (implicitly moral) community that is trying to regulate them, and so accentuate the problem. An alternative approach, more in tune with the character of the bimoral society, would be to assume that like anybody else they are capable of either trustworthy or non-trustworthy behaviour, and to seek to build up their trustworthiness.

If we follow this approach, we find that corporate governance becomes above all a question of interpersonal engagement, of finding ways to link the managers who run corporations directly to the communities affected by them, in such a way as to engage these managers in moral dialogue and stimulate their moral imagination. This suggests a new and explicitly moral role (as opposed to the current primarily economic role) for the company's board. No system will be perfect. There will always be charismatic entrepreneurs who can gull people into thinking they are moral when they are not. By and large, however, they do this by choosing as their associates people who are gullible and by avoiding engagement with those who are not. A governance system in which boards were in some sense representative of the public interest, and not just of particular stakeholder groups, might go some way towards addressing this problem.

The same general reasoning also applies to the regulation of financial markets. Some regulators, appointed in the United Kingdom by parliament, already engage directly with the firms they regulate and already see themselves in some sense as protectors of the public interest, but they do not yet see themselves as its promoters. Nor does their conception of the public interest yet extend beyond the national interest. Broadening their terms of reference in both respects might well increase their effectiveness.

Why, finally, should firms consent to governance and regulation of this kind? Why should they engage in a traditionally moral dialogue, and not just insist upon pursuing their self-interest? Because, despite their considerable power, they still depend upon society for some kind of licence to operate, and while they may resist the old hierarchical idea of a moral compact they are still open to the idea of a social contract. Indeed the very idea of a social contract, in which people accept certain social or moral obligations as the 'contractual price' of certain individual benefits—in this case benefits such as limited financial liability, corporate personhood, and an immunity from liability for the unforeseen consequences of one's economic actions—combines rather neatly elements of both hierarchical and market cultures and may well prove a rather useful device for navigating our way through the bimoral society. Provided, that is, that we recognize that it can never provide a basis for absolute truth, and that like everything else in politics its terms will need to be constantly debated and renegotiated.

# 2

# Obligation, Self-interest, and the Development of Modern Society

## MORALITY AND SOCIAL STRUCTURE

Whichever way we look at it, morality is important. On one hand, it is the bedrock upon which societies are based. Philosophers have argued for centuries as to whether people are 'naturally' altruistic or egoistic, and whether a 'state of nature' would be one of harmony or terror. These same arguments continue to rage today within the context of evolutionary theory and economic game theory. Both game theorists and evolutionary theorists start out from the assumption of individual egoism and show how over time, or over a sequence of repeated interactions, this self-interest can lead to cooperative and apparently altruistic behaviours. But how is this to be interpreted? Evolutionary theorists have argued that any genuine genetic altruism would place those possessing it at a disadvantage, that we are all fundamentally egoistic, and that what looks like altruism is merely a strategy for survival under certain social conditions. Their critics retort with evidence suggesting that human altruism is so deeply rooted that any explanation of its egoistic origins is at best irrelevant: If apparently altruistic actions are undertaken from consciously altruistic motives, and are not consciously and calculatedly selfish, then the altruism they reflect is as 'real' as we could ever ask for.[1] Game theory-inspired attempts to test for egoism and altruism under experimental conditions appear to suggest that self-interest is at least moderated by some sense of fairness, but their interpretation is at best controversial and they do little to resolve the basic argument.[2]

The arguments over human nature will no doubt run and run. Meanwhile, however, neither side disputes either that cooperative behaviour and the (real or apparent) altruism on which it depends are an essential part of the foundations of society, or that these cannot always be relied upon. Wherever we find people living together we find, in practice, both altruism and egoism. We also find moral rules of conduct and behaviour, without which a stable social existence would be simply impossible.[3]

On the other hand, at the individual level, morality is also central to the formation of character and identity. We define ourselves in relation to others, and in both the childhood development of self-consciousness and the adult development of character, the development of the self becomes inseparable from that of a moral attitude.[4] In a very real sense, how we behave in relation to other people determines not only how they see us but also how we see ourselves. Even the contemporary tendency to identify the self with some deeply private psychological interior, accessed not through normal social intercourse but through the private world of analysis, carries clear moral overtones.[5]

Morality is evidently important, but it is also notoriously difficult to analyse and observe. Early anthropologists inevitably imposed their own late modern European conceptions of morality upon their subject matter and their more recent successors, consciously restricting their analyses to empirically observable data, have tended to focus on explicit laws or rituals and treat moral attitudes or behaviours only implicitly, if at all.[6] For the self-consciously relativistic anthropologist, attempting to treat every society strictly in its own terms, the very definition of the term 'morality' is indeed problematic.[7]

Back in the 1960s, Mary Douglas, a social anthropologist specializing in the comparative religion of primitive African tribes, attempted to overcome these problems by developing a form of cultural typology. The comparative study of religion, like that of morality, is hampered by the fact that its key terms are meaningful only in the context of the particular social practices in which they are found. As she later explained, 'where religion is concerned, there is no theory comparing dogmas that does not take its own position for dogma'.[8] As Wittgenstein famously pointed out, this seems to be true of all language,[9] but in the case of religion or morality the problem is compounded by the absence of any directly observable physical basis for comparison. Douglas, who saw religious symbols as the products of social structure, wanted a way of describing objectively the differences in social structure and religious symbolism between different primitive societies. As a keen observer of debates within the Roman Catholic Church, in the wake of Vatican II, she was also looking for a way of applying the methods of anthropology, developed for the study of primitive societies, to the contemporary problems of late industrial society.

On the basis of her African research, Douglas identified three types of social organization, each of which could be related to the particular circumstances with which a society was faced in its formative or transformative years—the availability of food sources, the types of husbandry that resulted, and the comings and goings of colonial powers. One type was essentially undifferentiated, one was differentiated cooperatively, and one was differentiated competitively. She later called the three types sects, hierarchies, and markets.

In *sects*, the defining influences were the need to stick together in order to survive and the corresponding fear of defection. The social structure evolved around the importance of maintaining a strong boundary, and the moral order that resulted was a strictly egalitarian one. To be good was to conform, to be 'the same' as everyone else. To transgress was to sin, and almost inevitably resulted in expulsion from the community.

In *hierarchies*, the defining circumstance was the need for coordination and for people to perform specific roles if others, dependent upon them, were to survive. In these circumstances the society needed to develop a role structure, with different groups (e.g. men and women, or kin groups) developing different skills and the fruits of their labours being shared round in a mutually accept-able way. The social structure was built around hierarchical bonding and mutual dependence and the morality was one of obligation. To be good was to perform one's role competently and to behave responsibly and in the service of the common good. To be bad was to be selfish, to not pull one's weight, or otherwise to put oneself ahead of the community.

In *markets*, the defining influences were the need to trade and exchange in order to survive, and the corresponding fear was of subversion of the market. The social structure evolved around institutions of contract, private property, and the protection of individual freedom to negotiate, and the morality was one of pragmatic egoism. What worked was good, so to be good was to be suc-cessful. To be bad was to interfere with the success of others, by inhibiting their freedom or subverting the institutions on which the market depended.[10]

Douglas's terminology needs treating with care. She later regretted the use of the term 'sect' with its pejorative overtones, and suggested the alternative 'egalitarian enclave'.[11] The term 'hierarchy' is also potentially misleading, as although some vertical element of structuring is required to ensure coordina tion, it is the division of labour that is central. 'Role-structured society', 'ordered society', or, for an organization, 'bureaucracy' would be more accurate terms. In a management context it is also important that we do not confuse Douglas's cat-egories with those of the economist Oliver Williamson, whose own well-known categories of market and hierarchy both refer to forms of transacting within what would, on Douglas's definition, be a market society.[12] These qualifications apart, however, Douglas's cultural typology provides us with a very useful language with which to describe and analyse the moral structure of society. Moreover, by going a little deeper into the origins of her theory we can also use it to understand how different moralities can coexist in a complex, pluralistic society and, through that, how the moral structures of our own society have evolved over time.

The basis of Douglas's typology is an analysis of the social context of an individual in terms of two categories of classification and control, which she called *grid* and *group*. Her use of these categories varied, but in the version of her theory that we shall use here, they refer to the socio-cognitive context in which an individual person finds herself. As indicated in Fig. 1, *grid* describes the scope and coherence of a dominant system of classification structuring the individual's world view. The more someone is constrained to think and act within a single, tightly structured, socially shared system of language, institu-tions, and social norms, the higher she is located on the grid dimension. As the constraints of the system weaken, whether through a lack of coherence or through the availability of alternative systems, so her location on the grid dimension moves down towards zero. Zero itself represents confusion, the lack of any system, while below zero grid represents the dominance of increasingly

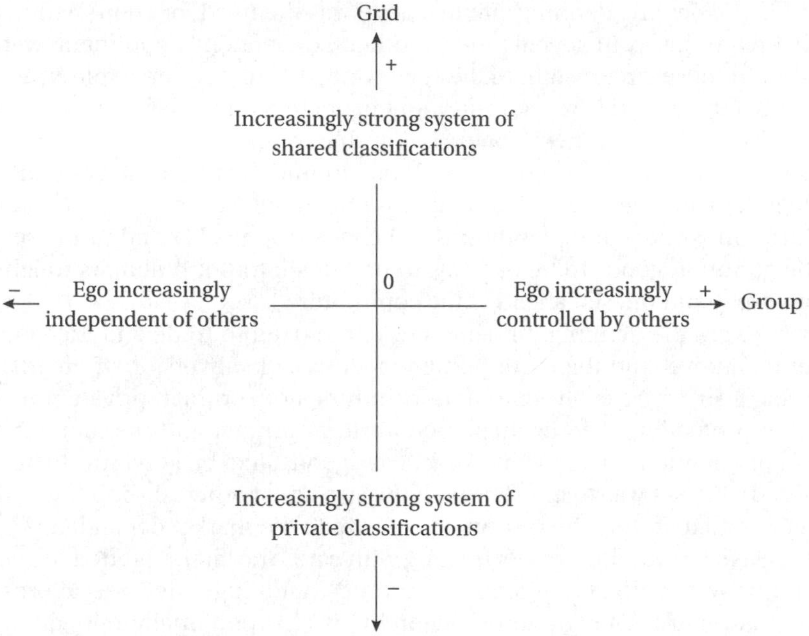

Grid

+

Increasingly strong system of
shared classifications

0

−    Ego increasingly
independent of others

Ego increasingly   +   Group
controlled by others

Increasingly strong system of
private classifications

−

**Fig. 1. Dimensions of grid and group**
*Source*: Based on Douglas 1973/1996, p. 60.

strong and coherent private systems of classification: the realm of creative thought and, at the extreme, of madness. *Group* describes the control exerted on the individual ego by the rest of the community. At the right hand side of the diagram (high group), the ego is totally dominated. At zero it is completely free of pressure, either because of social isolation or because different pressures effectively cancel each other out. To the left of zero, rather than being subject to group pressures, the individual is exerting pressure on others.[13]

Although this model has some conceptual problems (strictly speaking neither the grid nor the group dimension is single-valued), as an aid to description it is both rich and dynamic.[14] Thus, any individual can be pictured as a point moving across the space of the chart through life, beginning with a childhood move up the grid dimension, as the classification systems of society are absorbed and internalized, and from right to left along the group dimension, as total dependence is replaced by a measure of autonomy. Societies or other collectivities (communities, organizations) will normally embrace individuals of many kinds and in various stages of development, and can be pictured as scatter diagrams, each made up of many individual points forming a particular pattern on the chart. These patterns will themselves evolve over time. They may also take distinctive forms, and it is in the form of three 'typical' scatter diagrams that Douglas described her three cultural types. She did not actually provide pictures

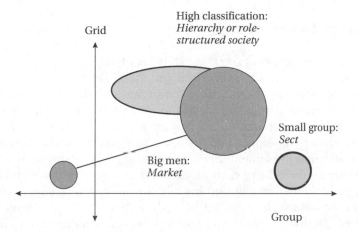

Fig. 2. Cultural types

to go with her descriptions, but on the basis of her descriptions we can visualize the types as shown in Fig. 2.

In typical sects, or 'small group' societies, the classification system is relatively weak: there are minimal institutions and little internal differentiation. Thinking and acting are tightly constrained, but by strong group pressure rather than by language or other classification systems. Everybody inhabits more or less the same socio-cognitive space and the boundaries of the society are very strong.

In hierarchies, or 'high classification' societies, the constraints imposed by the system of classification are strong and relatively uniform. These societies are characterized by strong institutions, clearly defined and often complex rules of behaviour, and well developed language systems. On the group dimension, the community dominates over the individual. In a smoothly functioning hierarchy, some people experience more group pressure than others, but no one is autonomous: Even the leader is a servant of the community. The boundary is strong, as the definition of group membership is important for the determination of duties owed, but it is not as strong as in the sect.

Finally, Douglas's market societies consist of two distinct groups of people. On one hand there is a relatively small group of market entrepreneurs, who exploit the classification systems for their own utility. (Douglas describes this in the primitive context as a 'Big Men' society and this term also seems apt for more contemporary market settings.) On the other hand, there is also a larger group of labourers and camp followers, a subservient majority who for one reason or another (opportunity, ability, effort or luck) have failed to become entrepreneurs themselves and whose lives and fortunes are dominated by the leadership figures.[15]

## Cultural and moral change

One of the advantages of expressing Douglas's typology in graphical terms is that it helps us to visualize how social and moral structures can change over time. Because of its deeply embedded nature, any culture, whether social, institutional, or organizational, is resistant to change. Social structures of power, legitimation, and domination constrain the social practices of individuals, which themselves reproduce and reinforce those same social structures.[16] In a high classification or hierarchical culture, the language, institutions, and social rules dominate thought to such an extent that changing those classification structures becomes literally unthinkable. In the strong group environment of a sect, departures from group norms are met by the expulsion of those concerned, so that the norms themselves remain immune from change. In markets, the power lies with those who benefit most from the status quo. Changes do occur, however, and using the visual device of the grid–group space we can begin to see how.[17]

First of all, there are changes within moral types, changes that do not affect the basic morality of society but do affect the specific rules through which that morality is expressed, especially in a role-structured society. Such changes occur when changing circumstances and environments lead to changes in the details of classification systems, either gradually at an unconscious level, across the whole of society, or by creating opportunities for individual action. We noted earlier that the space below the line of zero grid represents the realm of creative thought, and in hierarchical societies it is the space of artists, poets, and other people whose personal visions in response to nature or humanity are powerful enough to overcome the constraining effects of orthodox language and classification systems. When these visions are strong enough, and powerfully enough expressed, they can become a source of social change. The artist, in effect, moves from right to left in the lower half of the chart and her ideas begin to exert influence and become absorbed into society's ways of thinking. Immigrants or returned travellers introducing new languages and new customs can be similarly influential, and political or commercial entrepreneurs can exploit emerging opportunities to challenge or subvert existing social structures.

The exploitation of opportunities created by environmental changes can also lead to changes between social types. In a stable hierarchical society, resources are normally under the control of the centre, but if the social structures become weakened through exposure to environmental changes, it may become possible for market-oriented entrepreneurs to escape from their control and play the system, capturing the resources needed to create their own market sub-society. Historical examples might include the later Roman Empire or the Roman Church of the Renaissance period. The process begins when those holding powerful positions within the hierarchical culture begin to operate in their own interests outside its rules, to the left hand side of the grid–group space, or when they license others to do so on their behalf. The emerging community of Big Men begin by using the classification systems of their host culture to control those they exploit, but if their numbers and influence are allowed to grow sufficiently the networks employed in their service expand and the classifications of the market culture gradually usurp those of the hierarchy. This change can take place without the majority of the community moving very far through the grid–group space: All that happens is that one form of grid and group control gets substituted by another.

A weakening of classification systems may also allow space for groups of oppressed or dissatisfied individuals to band together and seal themselves off from the dominant hierarchical culture in egalitarian sects. Such are the origins of religious sects such as the early, pre-hierarchical Christian church in the context of the Roman Empire, or the Plymouth Brethren in post-Reformation England. Another example, discussed by Douglas, is the British Trades Union movement. Whereas the equivalent movements in Sweden and Germany evolved within the cohesive and structured hierarchies of Swedish and German industry, the British movement, which grew up within a weaker and more fragmented industrial structure, exploited the freedom this gave it to develop its own counterculture. The consequence, according to Douglas, was its emergence as an isolated sect with its own structure and culture independent of, and so lacking influence on, the hierarchical institutions of British society.[18]

Moreover, if history offers examples of sects emerging from hierarchical cultures, contemporary observation suggests that they may also form within the oppressed communities of a market system. For their members these communities are in many ways like oppressive hierarchical societies but without the certainty and consistency that hierarchical culture affords. Though the systems of classification may be weaker than in the hierarchical case, the group pressures can be just as powerful. Both, however, are fragmented by competition and the uncertainty produced by this fragmentation provides a perfect breeding ground for sects. In the visual terminology of the grid–group space these communities literally drop out of their host societies.

In a large and complex society, sects are constantly being generated, but in most cases their lifetimes are relatively short. The sect is a natural type of social structure for small, threatened communities, but as the numbers in a sect grow or its members move physically apart it inevitably becomes more difficult both to maintain its boundaries and to operate by egalitarian consensus. If the need for the strong boundary of a sect continues, any growth simply leads to schism. If, however, the sect is successful in securing its members' needs, it either negotiates, from its strengthened position, a return to the main culture, or develops its own hierarchical coordinating structures. Either way the members move up and to the left in the grid–group space, exchanging the defences of group control for the benefits of higher grid. In his way, small egalitarian sects either outlive their purpose or grow into larger hierarchical bureaucracies.

Finally, in the face of a severe crisis affecting the whole of a community, a market society might also turn or return to a hierarchical form. All three cultural types have their weaknesses, and the weakness of a market culture is that its individualism renders it insensitive to communal risks. When war or famine become opportunities for profiteering rather than risks to be averted, the very existence of a society is threatened. Societies can respond effectively to the ensuing crisis only by suspending the market and reverting to a strict hierarchical structure with centrally coordinated defences and the central distribution of scarce resources. Power here is likely to remain with the Big Men, but instead of competing they pool resources in the interests of the whole community, moving voluntarily from left to right in the grid–group space.

## Cultural and moral pluralism

The grid–group diagram is rather less well suited to the visualization of cultural and moral pluralism, which really calls for more than two dimensions, but here too it can be helpful. In a pluralistic society, which is to say in any large complex society, we are faced with a multiplicity of classification systems and social groupings. Sometimes these may be more or less discrete, but then it makes more sense to talk of multiple societies than of a single pluralistic society. More typically, both classification systems and groupings will overlap. A person may, for example, live within a predominantly hierarchical society, work as an entrepreneur within a competitive marketplace, and worship as a member of an egalitarian Protestant sect. And for this to be possible without engendering intolerable cognitive dissonance, there must be some common ground between the groupings: a common language, perhaps, or a shared set of basic ground rules.

One way of depicting a pluralistic society would be by drawing different grid–group diagrams for each social grouping. What is interesting about such societies, however, is not so much the fact of pluralism as its consequences, in terms of the interactions between the different groupings. In what ways do their classification structures overlap, and in what ways do they differ? In what ways might participation in one group compromise the structural integrity of another? How do people cope, socially and psychologically, with the conflicting demands of the different cultures in which they participate? If we begin by depicting one social grouping in terms of the classification structures appropriate to it, we can start to address these questions by asking how far and in what specific respects individuals or subgroups fall outside the normal boundaries of the type: towards or below the line of zero grid; outside the bounds of group control; able, in certain respects, to exercise control of their own, or subject to control from different groups or classification systems. As we trace the growth of civilization and the moral development of modern society, this imagery will be useful.

## THE GROWTH OF CIVILIZATION

Having explored some of the possibilities of Douglas's cultural theory we now need to put it to use in understanding the evolution of moral structures in society. Although Douglas was trying to get away from Emile Durkheim's much older classification of societies into mechanical and organic types, there are strong surface similarities between these types and her sects and hierarchies. It is very tempting to latch onto these similarities and to present the history of civilization, as many people have done, as a straightforward progression from organic sects, which for Durkheim were characteristic of primitive societies, through mechanical hierarchies, characteristic of traditional modern societies, to markets. As we shall see, this has an element of truth, but the reality is much more complex. In the first place, Douglas found all three of her cultural types in relatively primitive societies. In the second place, we can still find all three of them present in contemporary society. Not only does our society contain institutions of all three types, but the values associated with these institutions are also mixed. For example, we have markets that are hierarchically regulated and hierarchies in which self-interest is allowed to flourish. Egalitarian ideals can be found in both markets and hierarchies and not just in small sects. Conceptions of morality remain closely tied to the hierarchical ideals of obligation but have long been intermixed with elements of individual freedom and self-interest, on one hand, and equality, on the other. What has changed over time, and is indeed continuing to change, is not the type itself, or even the combination of types, but the ways in which the different types have been combined within increasingly complex and pluralistic societies.

A limited moral pluralism can be found even in primitive tribes, with different rules applying to domestic and political interactions, to kin and non-kin relationships, or to different types of kin relationship.[19] This pluralism becomes clearly apparent, however, as soon as we move from primitive tribes to civilized societies, all of which display strong elements of both hierarchical and market structures and moralities.

The basic cultural type of the civilized society would seem, in all cases, to be that of the ordered hierarchy. All of the world's civilizations appear to have emerged as hierarchical cultures, and they have all retained this basic form, right up to the present day. They are characterized by central governments using bureaucratic structures to raise taxes and coordinate public services such as defence, policing, and, in more developed societies, transport infrastructures, health care, education, and welfare; by laws, customs, and rules of behaviour based on the morality of obligation; and by hierarchical ideologies in which political leadership is equated to service, whether of God or of the people.

This dominance of the hierarchical form reflects the fact that, up to now at least, only hierarchies have been able to organize on a large scale and create and maintain the stable institutions and infrastructure on which civilization depends. Whether this might change with the introduction of ever more powerful and sophisticated information technologies is a topic for later in the book, but without such technologies the market and sect cannot operate effectively on the scale needed even for a small town, let alone a city or nation state. Sects, as we have already noted, are severely size limited. When primitive tribes organized as sects grow beyond a few hundred people, they typically split into two or more new tribes.[20] When sects do grow successfully, they quickly develop hierarchical features. Market societies are not limited in the same way, but based on an ethic of competition they are in constant danger of fragmenting. They are also vulnerable to external risks, as under threat of attack or in times of shortage entrepreneurs look to their own interests rather than to those of their communities.

A hierarchical basis is, therefore, necessary for the growth of civilization. But it is not sufficient. For one thing, all civilized societies are economic as well as social entities. Historians have often noted that the dawn of civilization is associated not just with structures of coordination and control (structures that made possible the Egyptian pyramids, the Greek city state, and the Roman army), but also with the development of trade and markets.[21] However regulated or constrained it may be, some element of market culture seems to be a necessary component of an evolved society. Once it grows beyond a certain stage of complexity, hierarchical government itself also relies on market institutions. Governments incur costs and must, therefore, raise revenues, and when the costs are temporarily greater than the revenues available governments must borrow. In particular, the waging of war, which of all social activities is arguably the most dependent on hierarchy, requires both large and irregular expenditures and has been intimately associated at least since the Middle Ages with the operation of financial markets as kings, princes, and more recently nation states have borrowed from international merchant bankers to pay the short-term costs or their armies.[22]

Hierarchies also have their own problems. In particular, they are vulnerable to exploitation by self-interested individuals, and in constant danger of stagnation or ossification.

The more obvious of these problems, from a historical perspective, is the danger of exploitation. Built around the principle of service to others, hierarchical societies are always vulnerable to self-interest. A hierarchically ordered structure invests those at the top of the hierarchy, or occupying roles in which they are responsible for key resources (those in charge of the armed forces, for example, of state finances, or of foreign relations) with enormous potential power, and depends on them exercising that power responsibly and in the public interest. But the temptation to use that power to one's own advantage is inevitably great and throughout history ambitious leaders and would-be leaders have constantly escaped the 'group' bonds that hold hierarchical societies together, moving to the left of the grid–group diagram and using the tight controlling structures of these societies to serve their own personal ends. Moreover, the ways in which societies choose their leaders almost inevitably exacerbate these tendencies. The philosopher king of Plato's *Republic* is a rare phenomenon in practice. Hereditary leaders are as likely to be self-interested as altruistic, and the inevitable arguments over succession favour those hungrier for power, not those best able to wield it responsibly. Elected leaders, likewise, are chosen from amongst those seeking election, and the characteristics of candidates for public office seem to have changed remarkably little from

Pliny's Rome to contemporary America.[23] Candidates are bought; votes are bought. The ideology may be one of service, but the reality is often one of naked political ambition.

To some extent this problem is self-correcting. Because hierarchies are typically very stable, a period of exploitative leadership is unlikely to be fatal. The society holds together. Things go on working, more or less. But as the effects of exploitation become apparent, the behaviour of the leader becomes unacceptable, attention becomes focused on the restoration of order and one way or another, by succession (forced or otherwise), revolution, or election, normal service is resumed. The very stability that enables hierarchies to survive periods of exploitative leadership is, however, the source of another problem, that of ossification or resistance to change. This problem is familiar to students of management and business organization, for whom the word 'bureaucracy' carries much the same connotations as 'dinosaur' (the two were commonly linked in the popular management literature of the 1980s—a form superbly suited to a stable and wholly predictable environment, but quite unable to adapt to change.[24] The problem is less immediately obvious at the societal level, because we tend to look at our societies from inside rather than outside, but it is no less serious. The culture of the Chinese Empire of the Ming and Qing dynasties (1368–1912), and of the Republics that succeeded it in the mid-twentieth century, was arguably the most purely hierarchical of modern times. Almost every aspect of social life was coordinated and controlled by state bureaucracy. 'There are', observed the sinologist Etienne Balazs, 'clothing regulations, a regulation of public and private construction (dimensions of houses); the colours one wears, the music one hears, the festivals—all are regulated. There are rules for birth and rules for death; the providential state watches minutely over every step of its subjects, from cradle to grave. It is a regime of paperwork and bother, endless paperwork and endless bother.'[25] Balazs characterized the Chinese culture as totalitarian, and other totalitarian states, such as that of the Soviet Union in the mid- to late twentieth century, are indeed good examples of hierarchical cultures. But the word as used in the West in this period carries misleading connotations. Like communist party officials, Chinese mandarins ruled with a firm hand, but as far as we can determine they ruled as servants of the society as a whole—with diligence, loyalty, and duty and, in principle and for the most part in practice, with humility. They were honoured to serve the Emperor and his people.[26]

By European standards, this pure Chinese hierarchy was extraordinarily stable and long lasting, but it was also extraordinarily unproductive. Having been scientifically and technologically the most advanced country in the world in the thirteenth century, China simply stopped developing, and stayed stopped for centuries. On a much shorter time scale (shorter because improved communications made it impossible to insulate the society, as Chinese society had been insulated, from outside developments and influences), the modern Soviet Union showed a similar capacity for stagnation.

The two problems faced by hierarchical cultures are, of course, connected. If the problem of exploitation can be characterized as arising from the exposure of an altruistically constructed society to egoism, the problem of ossification can be characterized as arising from the failure of such a society to capture the benefits of egoism. Indeed, it seems evident that as civilized societies have developed, their progress has been closely correlated with the existence of free, unregulated markets. Thus, against the examples of Imperial China and the modern Soviet Union we may set those of the Roman Empire of the first century CE, of the Netherlands in the fifteenth and again (after a period of Spanish domination) in the seventeenth centuries, of eighteenth- and early nineteenth-century England, or of late nineteenth- and twentieth-century America. In each case we see a hierarchical culture, but one that is unusually open, for its period, to free market competition and the pursuit of personal gain, and one that is also unusually successful.

In the early Roman Empire, customs duties were reduced, monopolies abolished, and travel restrictions removed. There was a developed banking system, manufacturers and merchants were actively encouraged, and business enterprise faced fewer hierarchical restrictions than it ever had done before, or would again for nearly two millennia. The result, by all accounts, was an exceptional level of prosperity, not only for the entrepreneurs themselves but also for society as a whole.[27]

In the fifteenth century, the Dutch established themselves as the merchants and traders of Europe and built a society of merchant republics, based upon business and enterprise. Internally, this was tightly regulated and relatively non-competitive: the product of a classically hierarchical culture. The scope for free enterprise and profit came in this case from relatively unregulated (and lightly taxed) international trade, which the Dutch exploited to the full. In the seventeenth century, the heyday of the Dutch East India Company, business was in theory heavily regulated, but in the open seas of the East Indies there was always scope for self-interested enterprise, which the Dutch were again ready to exploit. A small country with few natural resources, the Netherlands was by the late seventeenth century the most prosperous nation in the world.[28]

For the England of the second half of the eighteenth century, the period leading into the Industrial Revolution, international trade was also important, but it was the free internal market that struck contemporary observers. England had long been free of the tolls and tariffs that still bedevilled travellers on the continent, and by mid-century it had a comprehensive (and unique) system of public turnpikes, or metalled roads. It had low taxes and a very limited state bureaucracy. The medieval guild system that still regulated the price and quality of goods in many European countries had been effectively disbanded. There was a developed banking system with easily negotiable bills and easily obtainable credit. As nowhere else at that time, business entrepreneurs were free to exploit what opportunities they could, and they did. 'There was never from the earliest ages', wrote Dr Johnson, 'a time in which trade so much engaged the attention of mankind, or commercial gain was sought with such general emulation'.[29] It is from this period that the foreigners' picture of England as a nation of shopkeepers dates (and the shops, uniquely for the period, had windows, and the newspapers had advertisements), but it was also a land teeming with wholesalers and middlemen, all bent on securing a quick profit. Everything, it seemed, was for sale, and the country was uniquely prosperous. As continental visitors were quick to comment, even the poor drank tea and ate white bread. Not always so, perhaps, but they were evidently much better off than in other countries.[30]

The fourth example, of twentieth century America, needs little elaboration. In recent history, the hierarchical constraints have been weaker in America, the markets freer, and self-interest more acceptable than anywhere else, and while other countries have from time to time matched or even surpassed American economic performance, none can show such a continuous long-term growth in prosperity.

These examples raise a number of difficult questions, to which we shall return. The Roman Empire collapsed, and took prosperity with it.[31] In some respects the living standards of the first few centuries CE were not to be matched again until the eighteenth or even the nineteenth century. In Holland and England, the hierarchy reasserted control, limiting the freedom of entre-preneurs, and in economic terms both countries lost their leadership positions and fell behind their neighbours.[32] But whether these were cases of wasted opportunity or of social self-preservation, avoiding the Roman precedent of fragmentation and decay, it is hard to tell. The American example also poses questions, for American culture is the product of unique and very unusual cir-cumstances, and may not be an appropriate model for others. We shall return to this question later in the book. Whatever the particular significance of the different examples, however, the overall message is very clear. The standard model of a civilized society is a pluralistic one made up of a fundamentally hierarchical culture, but with significant market elements; and in successful societies marked by growing economic and cultural prosperity those market elements tend to be very strong.[33]

The question this raises is: how are the hierarchical and market elements related in such societies, and how do they coexist? Here the visual presentation of the grid–group diagram is helpful. As we have already discussed, one of the most important problems of any hierarchical or ordered society is the risk of ossification. And one of the most important ways in which societies have got round this problem, historically, has been by permitting a certain amount of aberrant behaviour—activity that in grid–group terms is at the bottom of the diagram, below the line of zero grid (Fig. 3). More specifically, three groups of people have been licensed or permitted to live in some respects outside the dominant classification system. These three (overlapping) groups are artists, travellers to or visitors from other cultures, and business entrepreneurs.[34]

Artists are both the historians and the innovators of culture. As historians they keep alive a culture's energy sources, the myths and stories associated with its birth or rebirth that in a hierarchy would otherwise get lost beneath the red tape of bureaucracy. As innovators they challenge and extend the hierarchy's classification systems, introducing new language, new images, new ideas.

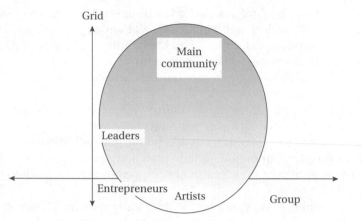

**Fig. 3. Leaders, artists, and entrepreneurs in a hierarchical or role-structured society**

Pushing beyond the limits of convention they tend to live outside the social mainstream, breaking its surface rules (of dress, of habit, of personal relationships) as well as its deeper structures. Much of the time their innovations are stillborn, unpublished, unexhibited, or simply ignored by all but a few fellow spirits. Much of the time they are aborted, unfinished, and unexpressed. Sometimes, however, they capture something that society can use to meet a pressing challenge or exploit a new opportunity, and an idea or image filters through into accepted language. Occasionally, an artist succeeds so well as to become influential in his or her own right, moving to a space on the left of the grid–group diagram and visibly shaping the lives and experiences of society at large.

Travellers are a society's link with a changing environment. Influenced by different cultures, they behave oddly and at times disrespectfully, but they bring in new knowledge, new ways of doing things, and proven solutions to what for the host culture may be new and difficult problems.

Entrepreneurs, motivated by self-interest, quite openly breach the most fundamental principles of hierarchy, those of obligation and service in the common good. But they also find solutions to society's problems, locate and capture valuable resources, and bring to a society the energy and dynamism that only self-interest can generate.

The purest hierarchical cultures, like Imperial (and later communist) China and the Soviet Union, have had no room for any of these groups. Borders were closed to travel, private enterprise banned, and only 'official' artists, whose work reproduced and reinforced the established classification systems, were allowed.[35] Anything else was considered a threat to the integrity of society. Most hierarchical cultures have been more pragmatic, however, and artists, travellers, and entrepreneurs have been tolerated, sometimes even encouraged, even though they have routinely broken the normal rules of society. At least, they have been tolerated up to a point, for while the potential benefits of art, business, and cultural exchange have been recognized, so have the potential risks.

As individuals, artists have not generally been considered a threat. They tend to live in a world of their own, they are recognized as being rather odd people, and their strange mores can be tolerated just as can those of, for example, the mentally subnormal and other 'characters'. When their work is seen to be of value they can be brought in to society proper; when it is not, they can simply be ignored. The artistic product, however, can have a life independent of its author, and most societies have sought to control art through some kind of censorship, putting limits on the degree to which the existing conventions can be challenged. When we look back, historically, at some of the more prominent examples of censorship—at the banning of Galileo's *Dialogo*, say, or of Lawrence's *Lady Chatterly's Lover*—it is easy to be critical. But if an ordered society is to be maintained and not descend into anarchy or expose itself to exploitation, it must set some limits on what is acceptable. Individual acts of censorship may, in retrospect, look misguided, but in a hierarchical culture censorship itself is perfectly sensible—and we still do it.[36]

In the case of travellers, it is the people themselves who pose the risk, for while artists tend to shy away from mainstream society travellers tend to be inveterate mixers and talkers. Until relatively recently in history, foreign travel was something that only a very few could engage in, and because hierarchical societies distribute resources between their members, they have always needed border controls anyway. Contemporary European concerns with illegal immigration from the Balkans and Asia-Pacific—based on the fear that the immigrants will consume resources that would otherwise be available for the native community—are simply the most recent manifestation a long-standing problem. Membership of a society has always carried some privileges, even if only the right to work common land or, more tenuously still, the right to be treated as a member of the community, and these have always been jealously guarded. Even once travellers or immigrants have been allowed into the country, societies have often sought to put limits on their influence, restricting them to certain districts, monitoring their movements, or otherwise making clear that their practices and mores are not to be emulated.[37]

The risks associated with entrepreneurs are of two kinds, as illustrated in Fig. 4. The first risk is that the self-interest that drives their business enterprise may contaminate other areas of life, undermining the morality of obligation on which a hierarchical society depends. This was the risk identified by Emile Durkheim a century ago when he agonized over a large and increasingly dominant business sector acting 'outside the sphere of [traditional hierarchical] morals and . . . almost entirely removed from the moderating effect of obligations', and the potentially destructive effects of this sector on the moral structure of society as a whole.[38] The second risk is that individual entrepreneurs might gain sufficient economic and, thereby, political power to exploit the structures of the hierarchy for their own ends, turning the dutiful community of an ordered society into the oppressed community of a Big Men market system.

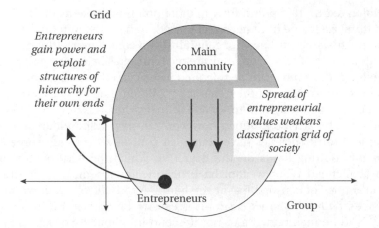

**Fig. 4. The risks of enterprise in a hierarchical or role-structured society**

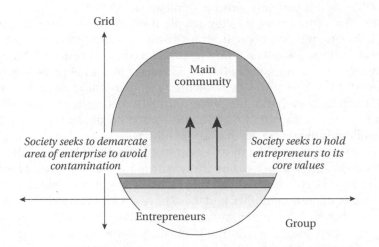

**Fig. 5. Responses to the risks of enterprise in a hierarchical or role-structural society**

Historically, societies have sought to control these risks in two different ways (Fig. 5). On one hand they have tried to restrict the scope or effects of entrepreneurial self-interest by holding entrepreneurs as far as possible within the hierarchical culture of society—in terms of the grid–group diagram by pulling them up above the grid line. This has been achieved both by formally regulating entrepreneurial activity, traditionally, for example, through trade guilds or state monopolies, and more recently through the more sophisticated regulation of markets and competition; and by informally binding the interests and mores of the entrepreneurs to those of society (or at least to those of its ruling classes), for example, by affording them social privileges and status in return for declarations of allegiance to the society. The international bankers of renaissance

Europe were often co-opted as advisers or administrators into the hierarchies of the states they bankrolled. On the other hand societies have tried to clearly demarcate the boundaries of enterprise and self-interest—in terms of the grid–group diagram to build social barriers between the main body of society and the community of entrepreneurs.

One aspect of this demarcation has been based on a distinction between community members and outsiders, or foreigners. As we have just noted hierarchical societies have good practical reasons for controlling their boundaries and keeping out those who are not entitled to their privileges. They also have good reasons for holding in, psychologically, those on whose duty and obligation they depend. So while the boundary of a hierarchical society is not normally as rigid as that of a sect, it can still be extremely strong. Desertion from the army (a very strict hierarchy) is a criminal offence. Members of the Roman Catholic Church are required to routinely recommit to membership through creed and confession. Exit from the Soviet Union, through the 'Iron Curtain' dividing it from Western Europe, was even more tightly controlled than entry to it. And even in less rigid hierarchies, there is always a very clear distinction between insiders and outsiders. Thus, even today, an American living and working in Britain, paying British taxes, subject to British law, and living within the institutional structure of British society is still classed as an 'alien', able to work only with the state's explicit permission, required to report periodically to the authorities, and with far fewer rights than a British citizen, even though that citizen may never have lived in the country at all.

In the control of enterprise, this distinction between insiders and outsiders serves two purposes. First, it makes it possible for certain activities, which are in some way beneficial to a society but go against its rules and ideology, to be conducted by outsiders. In ancient Athens, for example, trade was considered an improper occupation and was largely restricted to foreigners who possessed no civic privileges.[39] In medieval Christendom usury was morally unacceptable, but without it economic development would have been impossible. The solution was, in effect, to license it to the Jews, who were very clearly identified, by religion, appearance, and residence, as outsiders. In this way the practice was effectively separated from the community whose classification systems it might otherwise have threatened.[40] Second, the distinction opens the way to international business, as it allows a society to have one set of rules for relationships with insiders (the rules, typically, of duty and obligation) and another set (those of self-interested exploitation) for relationships with outsiders. In crude terms, ripping off foreigners has always been OK. This is the basis on which European imperialism and the slave trade were built.[41]

The other important aspect of the demarcation of enterprise and self-interest has been the demarcation of action rather than of people—a combination, in effect, of the two responses to the risks of enterprise. By defining quite clearly and setting limits upon the circumstances and activities in which the pursuit of self-interest is acceptable, societies have sought to keep business people within the bosom of society while at the same time preventing their self-interest from contaminating the main body of social life. The simplest and most common demarcation of this kind has been that between personal and 'arm's length' relationships. Even in medieval societies, where domestic prices were quite tightly regulated, barter and negotiation were evidently a fact of life. Buying food in the market, or trading cloth for a pig, people have always sought a good deal and such self-interested behaviour has always been acceptable—but only within limits. Exploiting another person's ill fortune, for example, or driving a hard bargain with one's own neighbours or relatives, do not appear generally to have been considered acceptable.

We also find in hierarchical societies another, more explicit form of demarcation of self-interest and enterprise: the licensing or chartering of people and companies to engage in business in specific areas and under specific conditions. As business activity has grown through the centuries, this licensing and associated regulation of business has played a critical part in the evolving relationship between the hierarchical morality of obligation and the market morality of self-interest.

## ENTREPRENEURIAL LICENCE AND MORAL DUTY

The growth of business enterprise as an integral part of society occurred first in what we now think of as Europe but was historically identified as Christendom. The reasons for this have been much debated by historians, but would seem to be bound up with the different kinds of hierarchical societies that developed in different parts of the world. The Chinese empire, as we have already noted, was a powerful hierarchy but too tightly controlled for enterprise to flourish. For several centuries international trade was prohibited, and domestic business was very tightly regulated. In India, in contrast, the socio-religious and political structures of the hierarchy seem to have developed separately and a rigid and restrictive caste system combined with political fragmentation and instability, the one limiting the scope for enterprise, the other frustrating the development of an infrastructure capable of supporting the development of industrial and economic life. In Islam too, though in a very different way, conceptual rigidity combined with political instability and while trade flourished the development of urban centres was constantly frustrated. Only in Europe was the relative political stability necessary for the growth of business combined with enough political pluralism to prevent the resultant market subcultures from being totally stifled by the hierarchy.[42]

Within Europe, business activity grew up gradually during the Middle Ages. Towns and cities grew up as centres of trade and craft manufacture, and the economy became monetarized (it had been so in the Greek and Roman periods, but not in the intervening centuries). By the fifteenth century, business was thriving in hundreds of centres across Europe, but for the most part it remained very tightly controlled. Entrepreneurial self-interest was certainly present.

As the historian David Landes has pointed out, 'Business, like love, laughs at locksmiths.'[43] Both international traders and those specialist craftsmen who operated in international markets shunned any regimes that sought to constrain them too tightly. But overall, the locksmiths, who in this case sought to lock people in to the moral values of the hierarchy, were pretty much in control. Domestically, business was regulated by craft guilds, which themselves were regulated by the city authorities, which in turn governed on the basis of privileges granted by the crown. The basic principle of the game was that the moral imperatives of the hierarchy took precedence over the individual desire for gain. Typically, within the city (and beyond if the authorities were powerful enough) there was no free market competition. Prices, quality, and trading hours were fixed. A craftsman could do well by producing goods of superior quality, but he could not charge extra for them, nor could he make money by trading inferior goods for a lower price. There was no scope for middlemen.[44]

International trade was, inevitably, less tightly regulated. Foreigners were often barred from selling in the local market, but entrepreneurs with sufficient resources could profit from wholesale trade and by the end of the fifteenth century this seems to have been big business with active sea trades in sugar, salt, gold, alum, and indeed slaves, as well as in the traditional cloths and spices. These trades were undoubtedly conducted according to market principles, but dependent on royal patronage for resources and safe conduct they were still tightly bound to the hierarchical structure of society. A merchant could pursue his self-interest only under licence to a royal protector and, while in negotiating deals he might have a fairly free hand, the bulk of the profits ended up, one way or another, in the coffers of the state. In all other respects the merchant remained subject to the rules of the hierarchy. The real market competition was between societies, not within them.

Making this competition possible, one small group of people do seem to have stood in some way outside the constraints of the hierarchy. International merchant bankers such as the Medici, most of them operating from small city states, provided funds for both trade and war. They expected debts to be honoured and were beholden to no one, not even to kings. The world of high finance was, however, and was to some extent to remain, a very secretive one, with its workings well hidden from view. Neither the bankers nor their clients had anything to gain from spreading the market culture of finance any further than was strictly necessary, and it posed no threat to the moral structure of society.[45]

This situation seems to have continued essentially unchanged through the sixteenth and well into the seventeenth centuries. The merchants gradually acquired some wealth to trade on their own account, and growing prosperity and the farming out of local monopolies increased the numbers of noblemen with reserves of capital to invest in trading ventures. By the late sixteenth century a business 'company' or trading venture could raise capital from a range of sources and a single country could support a number of different companies.

In the early seventeenth century the introduction of international bills of exchange between merchant bankers facilitated the funding process. However, the larger companies especially remained in the service of the hierarchy. The English and Dutch East India Companies, founded in 1599 and 1602, respectively, to exploit the trading possibilities of the Indian Ocean, are often thought of as precedents of the modern business corporation, but both were very clearly the products of hierarchical cultures. The English East India Company secured a charter that gave it not only a monopoly of English trade beyond the Cape, but also delegated authority from the Crown to defend that trade by force and to make and administer law in any colonies that might be established. The Dutch East India Company, a state-sponsored merger of a number of private companies, also secured monopoly rights and also found itself engaged as deeply in battle and politics as in trade. The two companies did not even compete directly with each other, except upon the high seas. As far as business went, they effectively divided the spoils, the Dutch securing the trade in and around the Spice Islands (which became part of the Dutch East Indies) and the British that with India. Once the colonies were established, the companies do seem to have provided scope for the pursuit of enterprise and self-interest. Adventurers seeking to make their fortunes would join the companies and once out of reach of the homeland would plunder and pillage or trade on their own, private account. In so far as the companies interacted with their home societies, however, it was more as colonial administrators than as market entrepreneurs.[46]

What the Dutch East India Company did do was to open the way to speculative investment through the innovation of transferable (so tradable) shares, and in the later seventeenth century this innovation was vigorously developed in England. With parliament ascendant in the wake of the English Revolution, the traditional system of crown monopolies that had governed international trade came under attack and the first institutions of a capitalist society were put in place. By the late 1680s there was an active London stock market, and by 1695 there were at least 150 companies listed, with liquid markets in about ten of these, dominated by the Old and New East India Companies, the Hudson Bay Company, and the Bank of England, created in 1694 to finance government debt but financed itself by private shareholders.[47] Established monopolies were challenged both in law, through the parliamentary process, and in fact, as new companies set out to trade regardless. A pivotal case was that of the Royal African Company, a joint-stock company that had in 1672 (following the insolvency of its predecessor) been granted the monopoly in the slave trade from Africa to the sugar producing colonies of the West Indies. The company eventually lost its legal monopoly in 1714 after twenty-five years of political argument, but it had already lost the power to enforce the monopoly much earlier. By 1700 rival companies had already taken about 80 per cent of the market.[48]

It is notable, however, that the arguments used in the debates over the Royal African Company were those of the hierarchy, not the market. There can be little doubt that the main protagonists were motivated by self-interest, but the arguments they used were based on the premise that self-interest is bad. Defenders of the monopoly argued for the interests of the country as a whole in a regulated trade rather than one dominated by competing private interests. Their opponents argued that a monopoly served the self-interest of the few who possessed it, to the cost of everybody else. It is also notable that the London stock market had much more to do with the funding of state debts than with that of private enterprise, and that it was initially short lived. The share issue for which it is best remembered, that of the South Sea Company in 1710, was devised to fund short-term government debt, converting high-interest annuities issued to meet the costs of the Wars of the Spanish Succession into shares in a trading monopoly, and following the boom and bust of the bubble market in these shares it was effectively closed down by the Bubble Act of 1720, which prevented the creation of companies with freely transferable shares.[49]

Somewhat ironically, the suspension of a market in transferable shares seems to have encouraged rather than to have inhibited the growth of free enterprise. For the most notable feature of the South Sea Bubble was not the bubble itself (which was hardly unique) but the very effective way in which it was managed by the government. Investors were partially compensated for their losses, as shares were converted into fixed interest annuities and the standing of government debt was maintained. Contemporary French attempts to employ trading ventures in the service of government debt finance, which were based on hierarchical rather than market structures, were in contrast an unmitigated disaster, as the bubble and bust of the *Compagnie des Indes* in 1719 brought down not only that company but with it the *Banque Royale*, the French equivalent of the Bank of England, and the entire system of government debt funding.[50] The financial environment of Britain was by comparison a model of stability. By the 1750s Britain had developed instruments of debt funding similar to contemporary government bonds, and the country was positively abuzz with private enterprise.

At first sight, indeed, the British society of the later eighteenth century looks remarkably like a market culture. It was certainly an extraordinary period. The conditions for business, even before the technological advances of the Industrial Revolution, were exceptionally favourable. Britain was by then a nation rich on trade, and undepleted by war, with low taxes and unobtrusive government, free from the tolls, tariffs, and heavy bureaucracy that still characterized the rest of Europe. A country joined up by metalled roads (which reduced journeys from weeks to days), with regular coaches; and, later in the century, by canals, on which a horse-drawn barge could carry goods at a minute fraction of the overland cost. A country of free markets, unfettered by the old guild system that still prevailed on the continent, and with no restrictions on the putting out of work to country labourers working on a contract basis. A country with a stable currency and widespread capital reserves, and with an effective banking system, including a network of private local banks, able to deploy these. A countryside of private enclosures, with an inheritance system that allowed the land to be maintained intact as economically viable private properties, and (above all, some historians would argue) a country in which private property rights were effectively protected by law.[51]

In this environment, enterprise flourished: everybody seemed to be in business, making something or selling something. Manufacturing boomed and for the first time in modern Europe there was a domestic mass market in non-staple fashion and luxury goods. For the first time, too, business appears to have escaped the bonds of the hierarchy. The improved transport infrastructure opened the way to wholesalers and middlemen, buying cheap and selling dear and trading at a distance, free from the constraints and obligations of face-to-face relationships. The freedom of travel and the availability of work also led to an unprecedented level of internal migration, as people moved from community to community in search of opportunities, again opening the way for calculating, arm's length relationships to replace those of duty and obligation. Advertising puffery was another new phenomenon, as producers sought to reach the widespread markets to which they could now deliver. Moreover it was not just produce that was traded. At this time you could buy a public office, or a naval commission. The market penetrated deep into the hierarchical structure, and everything had its price.

Meanwhile, church attendance dwindled (and in a country of free religion even those who did worship were divided amongst different churches, so that communities no longer worshipped together as a whole). Sexual mores loosened. The pursuit of pleasure became respectable as never before and so, it has been suggested, did the pursuit of self-interest. 'There was nothing new', writes the historian Roy Porter, 'about seeing people as grasping and go-getting. What was new was treating egoism, and even greed, not as sinful and anti-social but as natural and even admirable'.[52]

But did people really see egoism as admirable? The classic reference here is to Adam Smith's *The Wealth of Nations*, published in 1776, and in particular to a famous quotation: 'It is not from the benevolence of the butcher, the brewer, or the baker, that we expect our dinner, but from their regard to their own interest. We address ourselves, not to their humanity, but to their self-love.'[53] Taken out of context, however, this quotation is wholly misleading. In the first place, Smith in this section was not making a general argument about the value of self-interest but a relative one. He was arguing that there were situ-ations where it was appropriate (as in the conduct of business) and situations where it was not. In the second place, the whole thrust of the book was to argue *against* unbridled self-interest and in support of a foundation of traditional, hierarchical morals as a basis for economic growth. The very word 'self-interest', in Smith's language carried connotations of moral restraint. Unrestrained by the traditional virtues, self-love (the word he used for pure self-interest) subverted individual freedom, hindered the division of labour, and led to economic stagnation. Elsewhere, he took issue strongly against Bernard Mandeville, who in a famously controversial book first published in 1705, *The Fable of the Bees, or, Private Vices, Public Benefits*, had argued that economic life was based upon vanity, greed, and self-love, and that these were accordingly the basis of successful civilization. Mandeville, he complained, 'seems to take away altogether the distinction between vice and virtue'.[54] Self-interest could be productive, but only if pursued in conjunction with virtuous motives, with duty and obligation, goodwill, prudence, and self-restraint.[55]

This theoretical position appears to have been reflected in both popular perceptions and practice. The period undoubtedly had its libertines and its sharks, but the evidence we have suggests that greed, which was more commonly associated with public office than with commerce, was condemned rather than admired and that business was carried out, for the most part, with a moral seriousness. Businessmen vied for the moral respect of their peers and customers. A good reputation, not only for financial prudence and probity but also for moral decency, was important. When merchants and manufacturers grew prosperous, their thoughts turned to philanthropy, not as a source of self-importance but as a simple duty.

Not only in the works of Adam Smith, but in the other political, moral, and economic writings of mid- and late eighteenth-century Britain, we find a lot of attention being given to individual freedom and private property rights, but the context remains throughout traditionally moral. Where duty and obligation are not preached they are assumed to be inherent in human nature, and where they are not assumed they are preached as being essential to salvation. Self-love or selfishness is routinely distinguished from a morally constrained self-interest. In general, the period witnessed a much closer relationship than hitherto between business and society, and a new and much more sophisticated understanding of the interweaving of self-interest and obligation. It also witnessed a strong confirmation of the sanctity of private property, an institution that was, as we shall see, to provide an important bridge between the values of the hierarchy and those of the market. But the hierarchy remained firmly in control.

The hierarchical structure of British society was, of course, different from and in some ways more developed than those of its continental neighbours. Governed by parliament rather than by the monarch, it offered more scope for individual expression and public debate. Politically and religiously it was the result of a negotiated compromise and toleration rather than of hegemonic imposition, and this characteristic seems to have been reflected in its attitude to enterprise and market values. Whereas rival European powers sought to hold their market elements tightly within the hierarchy, regulating them tightly and ruling them as far as possible from the centre (the first of the two responses to the risks of enterprise that we discussed above), the focus in Britain appears to have been rather more on the demarcation between market and non-market areas of activity. Whereas on the continent private enterprise was still seen as being in itself a threat to the social order, and was largely suppressed, in the more tolerant climate of Britain it was seen only as a potential threat, quite acceptable so long as it stayed within firm limits.

When those limits were broached, the hierarchy reasserted itself, and before the century was out a deep reaction against the occasional excesses of a generation drunk on freedom was already under way. Sexual mores began to tighten and the churches resumed their position of authority—an authority that was no longer imposed but now freely welcomed. Inspired, perhaps by the example of George III, the family became the model and focus for moral relationships, with a stress on such virtues as duty, loyalty, and forbearance. From being a taken for granted aspect of life, traditional morality became an obsession. Moral sensibility, a sensitivity to the needs and problems of others, became the recognized mark of a good character.

This new obsession with the traditional morality of obligation proved to be much more long-lasting than the flirtation with market values that preceded it. Throughout the nineteenth century traditional virtues, often linked with the family as a moral ideal, reigned supreme. The factory owners of the new industrial age exploited and abused their workers in much the same way as previous generations had exploited and abused their slaves, but they do not appear to have been driven by greed. There was a widespread ethic of self-improvement through hard work, and the iniquities of the factory system seem to have been more a product of thoughtlessness than of self-serving. For those who could afford it, philanthropy remained a social duty, not an optional extra or public relations exercise. Inevitably, the dislocations of industrialization and the growth of the cities, with their anonymity and fluid populations, released or tore people from their social ties and created opportunities for the self-serving. Honoré de Balzac wrote famously of mid-century Paris that, with the ties of obligation broken,

Virtue is slandered here; innocence is sold here. . . .[E]verything is sublimated, is analysed, bought and sold. It is a bazaar where everything has its price, and the calculations are made in broad daylight without shame. Humanity has only two forms, the deceiver and the deceived.[56]

Around the same time, in the *Communist Manifesto*, Marx and Engels blasted the naked self-interest of the bourgeoisie.[57] In the 1870s the novelist Anthony Trollope, returning to London after a period away, was shocked by the extent of corruption and self-seeking manipulation, especially in the world of finance.[58] But neither the aristocratic Balzac nor the founders of communism were the most reliable of witnesses, and Trollope's readers were as shocked as he was by what were seen as exceptional scandals, not as normal behaviour.[59]

There were important moves in this period toward the legitimation of self-interest. In particular, in the second half of the century, Herbert Spencer and the English economists presented self-interest not only as the foundation of economic prosperity, but also as the triumph of reason over superstition, and an expression of human emancipation and development. In Spencer's evolutionary model of society (originally Lamarckian but later the basis for social Darwinism) human development depended on natural selection and the 'survival of the fittest' (his phrase, not as is commonly thought Darwin's). Self-interest served to further this aim and altruism and traditional structures of moral authority, in particular the established church, to hold it back.[60]

Underlying this grand thesis, however, was the same balanced view of self-interest that we saw in the eighteenth century. Everyone who worked for a living was, in Spencer's language, 'selfish', and egoism and altruism properly understood were mutually dependent, each being necessary for the successful pursuit of the other.[61] For his contemporaries, for whom altruism was both a moral duty and a way of helping other people to help themselves, this was familiar ground. His ideas certainly caused a stir but they do not seem to have challenged the established consensus that the way forward was through a combination of hard-earned self-advancement and traditional moral virtue.[62] Durkheim's concern a few years later with the 'crisis' of society resulting from the rise of business and the resulting erosion of traditional morals may have been unwittingly prophetic, but in terms of his own time he was fighting a chimera.[63]

## MORAL OBLIGATION IN THE BUSINESS BUREAUCRACY

The one thing that did change quite radically from around the middle of the nineteenth century, especially in Britain and America, was the structure of business. Up until the 1840s there were essentially two types of business company, the basic forms of which had remained unchanged since the seventeenth century. The great majority of businesses were relatively small-scale affairs, whose capital needs could be met from local resources. Some were set up as joint-stock companies, but most were partnerships or sole traders. Private banks provided lines of credit to cover investment or working capital needs, but did not normally take an ownership stake. Alongside these private businesses there was also a much smaller number of relatively large chartered (in America, incorporated) joint-stock companies. These were the successors to the East India Companies and took essentially the same form. The capital was still raised privately, but the state limited their risks by granting them monopolies and the protection of limited liability (unlike in a private joint-stock company or partnership, the legal liability of the shareholders was limited to the amount invested).

The chartered companies and corporations were the classic hierarchical solution to the need for economic development. With limited liability and the right to retain whatever monopoly profits they could generate, the shareholders were granted privileged exemption from the normal hierarchical rules and licensed to pursue their economic self-interest, but only in the interests of society. Charters were limited to ventures deemed to be in the public interest— initially foreign trading companies, later utilities, canals and railways, and 'essential' manufactures—and were granted for a limited period only. The pursuit of profit was quite clearly a licensed privilege, and the company principals were, in effect, the agents of the state.

As the industrial revolution gathered pace in the 1830s and 1840s, and new technologies called for ever-larger financial investments (the railways were particularly capital intensive), this system began to split at the seams. In Britain, private joint-stock companies had to draw on larger and larger numbers of shareholders, creating growing problems of accountability, and parliament could not keep up with the demand for charters. A series of measures designed to address the two problems converged on a single solution, and by the middle of the 1850s limited liability status could be gained by a simple act of company registration, in exchange for a requirement (on all companies with more than a limited number of shareholders) to submit annual audited accounts.[64] In America an increase in incorporation led to a blurring of the line between public and private interests and to concerns that the privileges of incorporation were being abused, concerns that were heightened by the evident and growing prosperity of those holding corporate stock. Some states responded by tightening up on the controls, but some took another route. Instead of trying to limit the rewards to the stockholders, they opened them up to the complainers, by removing the restrictions on incorporation. By the 1880s the benefits of limited liability incorporation were freely available and had come to be seen, as they were by then in Britain, as rights rather than as privileges.[65]

Symbolically, the extension of limited liability to any company filing audited accounts, irrespective of public interest considerations, marks an important stage in the social legitimation of business. Self-interest was no longer bound quite as closely to self-restraint. It became acceptable, in effect, to take risks with other people's (banks' and creditors') money. The move was only possible, however, because that was not considered a danger. Of course, the politicians who endorsed it were themselves investors and, with the opportunities for profit growing, self-interest cannot have been absent from their deliberations. But the moral virtues of the hierarchy were probably more firmly entrenched in this period than in any other. Meanwhile in continental Europe, for a number of reasons, the development of business structure took a rather different path. As in earlier periods, European societies sought to keep control of enterprise strictly within the hierarchy rather than licensing and seeking to benefit from a more market-oriented subculture. Government-sponsored investment banks (in Germany and central Europe) and direct state finance (in the Mediterranean countries) played a much larger part in the funding of industrialization and the stock markets a much smaller one. In Japan, too, industrial development in this period was largely government-sponsored. In both regions the bonds between big business and the moral priorities of a hierarchical society stayed much tighter, and have remained so to this day.

The second great change in the structure of business to have its beginnings in the mid-nineteenth century was to greatly reinforce these bonds across the developed world. It was the birth of the bureaucratic business organization. As advancing manufacturing, transport, and communications technologies brought economies of scale in production and distribution, so the size of businesses grew. The small-scale putting out that had characterized the early part of the century was replaced by the large-scale factory, the individual wholesaler by the large-scale distributor. Small retailers were supplemented first by department stores and then by retail chains. In each case forms of hierarchical structure replaced what had been free market relationships. The department store and retail chain brought back fixed, non-negotiable prices. The factory labourer, though supposedly hired in a free labour market, was bound by duty more than by contract. In the putting out system, people had been paid for what they produced and had been free to choose when and how they got the work done. In the factory system they worked fixed hours in a fixed place. They did so out of necessity—the labour market was weighted seriously against them—but the practice was socially legitimated in terms of a moral obligation to the company, as a kind of mini-society.

Over the next hundred years or more, continuing technological advances favoured the development of ever larger and more complex business organizations, with ever more complex rulebooks and role structures.[66] These businesses were economic entities competing with each other in a market setting (albeit, as we shall see, one constrained by hierarchical values), but that aspect of their existence was barely visible. To the man or woman in the street, the twentieth-century company was either a source of desirable products, sold at fixed prices and in a manner and environment that veiled the interests of the company and created an experience that was as far removed as possible from that of a market transaction; or it was a place of employment, with all the trappings of a traditional hierarchical community. The companies were hierarchically structured, with people occupying well-defined roles, subject to well-defined rules, and bound together by common systems of classification (company language and symbolism, dress codes, grading systems, etc.), all working towards a common end. And they embodied a hierarchical morality. The employees, even at the most senior levels, were expected to serve the interests of the company. The company, in turn, looked after the interests of its employees, providing secure employment (interrupted only briefly in the great depression of the 1930s) and support in times of ill health or family troubles. In many cases, the company almost replaced the traditional town or village as the basis of community, providing extensive recreational facilities and taking on responsibility for community affairs. The first question people asked of a stranger was not 'where are you from' but 'who are you with?'

These hierarchical organizations inevitably faced much the same problems as hierarchies everywhere. Their tight classification structures made it difficult to respond to changing environments, and especially to the changing demands of competitive markets. Loosening the classification structures, however, opened them up to political exploitation. In one of the classic studies of management and organization the sociologist Melville Dalton observed how American manufacturing firms in the late 1940s and 1950s responded to these problems.[67] The companies he studied were all structured as bureaucracies, but Dalton found that their rigid designs simply could not cope with the complex and changing demands of customers, with unpredictable production or maintenance problems, with problems with suppliers, or with the human frailties of employees. A human need to personalize situations and respond to emotion as well as logic meant that the interactions between offices almost inevitably departed from the logic of the organizational design. And the people who occupied the different bureaucratic roles did not always fit the real requirements of those roles: nor could they, given the limitations of bureaucratic procedures for hiring and promotion.

Faced with these circumstances, the only way in which responsible managers (responsible, that is, in the hierarchical sense) could make their organizations work effectively was by going beyond their formally assigned roles and breaking the formal rules. Once these rules were broken, moral conflicts became inevitable. Sometimes the rules clashed both with requirements of effectiveness and with personal moral claims on the manager: the claims, for example, of subordinates who did not fit their formal roles but were good at managing informally, or who were just decent, hardworking, and able people. At other times, the requirements of effectiveness clashed with personal moral responsibilities, as the only way to get things done effectively was by being dishonest, or by sacrificing or exploiting others in the organization. Once managers began to depart from the formal rules, moreover, the problem of role fit created a vicious circle, as managerial jobs increasingly demanded informal management skills that formed no part of the official job description. All this opened the way for political action and the pursuit of individual self-interest. In a politicized environment in which the most effective managers were precisely those most able to work around the rules, while maintaining an upward semblance of working within them, conspiracy and deception flourished. As well as seeking what was best for the organization, managers had no option but to look after their own interests, and those of their associates. Some inevitably took this further, exploiting the situation to advance their own interests against those of the organization.

The picture Dalton presented was not, on the whole, one of self-serving behaviour, whether by intention or default. A few of the managers he observed could be described in this way, but they were the exception rather than the rule. The picture was rather one of people seeking to act dutifully, to do their best for the business and behave decently to their colleagues, but being forced by the failings of the bureaucratic system to achieve those moral ends by immoral means, by deception, subterfuge, and the exploitation of those who were not their close colleagues.

A generation later, in the 1980s, another sociologist, Robert Jackall, conducted a similar investigation and painted a similar but subtly different picture.[68] The difference, to which we shall come back later, was that whereas Dalton's companies were prospering Jackall's were struggling, in mature declining industries. Survival was the name of the game, and preoccupied with this the managers were beginning to lose any meaningful sense of the corporate purpose, or of how this might relate either to their own interests or to the common good. The political manoeuvering had become an end in itself and the pursuit of self-interest had become much more prominent. This was, however, a self-interest born out of adversity and the need for survival, not one based on greed, and its origins lay as before in the practical limitations of bureaucracy to cope with change, not in the intrusion of market values. Jackall's book is famous today for a single quotation, attributed to a manager at one of the companies he observed and frequently cited to support the idea that business is immoral: 'What is right in the corporation is not what is right in a man's home or in his church. What is right in the corporation is what the guy above wants from you. That's what morality is in the corporation.'[69]

But what is the morality of church or home if it is not doing what you are told? The problem in this case was that the guy at the top was breaking the rules to cover his own backside. The manager interviewed by Jackall, an outsider with his own professional loyalties, had been sacked when he uncovered this and was understandably shocked, but the other managers were more philosophical. This happens in hierarchies, when things are going badly. It always has. But it passes. Unless you have the power to change it you respond, as Jackall observed, by sticking together, by forming communities within communities, in which the values of the culture can be preserved and protected.

We should also note that both Dalton and Jackall carried out their research in America, with its unique tradition of entrepreneurial individualism, where the tensions within business bureaucracies seem to have been rather more marked than they were elsewhere. The American business bureaucracy was on the whole very effective, but for many of the Americans attracted to a career in business the bureaucratic structure seemed unduly constraining. It was much more readily accepted in European culture, where people seem to have been happy to work within rather than around it.

The bureaucratic business corporations of the twentieth century, so long as they functioned properly and as intended, provided an environment in which the moral rules and expected behaviours were entirely consistent with those of the hierarchical cultures of the societies in which they were situated. Obligation, duty, a concern for one's fellow men or women; these were what mattered. The market aspects of the business were kept well out of sight and barely intruded on most people's lives. Moreover, these aspects were themselves very strongly conditioned by the values of the hierarchy. Competition, for most of the century, was not exactly a cut-throat affair.

For a start, competition was largely domestic. International business was restricted mainly to imperial, or former imperial territories, and where the larger companies did move into genuinely foreign markets it was largely through licensing agreements with local firms. This was partly due to the problems of coordination involved in multinational and, especially, multicultural operations and marketing. It was partly due to import quotas, tariffs, and restrictions placed by national governments on the foreign ownership of assets. To the extent that international competition was present, it was characterized as in previous periods more by the competition between nations than by that between companies. Where the companies were not actually state-owned (as many of the large European companies were), they tended to receive strong government support, either directly through subsidies or indirectly through favourable civil and defence contracts and the protection of tariffs. Especially in extractive industries such as oil exploration and production, and in technology-based manufacturing industries, where each country supported its 'national champions', the pursuit of international business remained closely tied, as it had been since the days of the East India companies, to the pursuit of the national interest.

Domestically, economies of scale combined with government policies to give high levels of industry concentration. An industry would be dominated by a small handful of companies, and with no threat of external competition it was in their interests to cooperate. Cartels, commonplace in the early part of the century, were gradually outlawed, but there was nothing to be gained from price competition. So companies competed on product and service, and in an era of generally growing prosperity there was plenty of business to go round. In more fragmented industries, where economies of scale were not so important, business was divided up locally and competition was restrained. Entrepreneurs knew each other well, through trade associations, chambers of commerce, and general social intercourse, and recognized that they were bound by mutual interests.

Meanwhile the other markets in which companies engaged, in particular those for labour and finance, were also very heavily regulated. Companies were restricted in their negotiations with employees not only by a general morality of obligation, but also by legally recognized trades unions and works councils. Currency exchange was tightly regulated, and so was bank lending. In America, commercial and investment banking were strictly segregated by the Glass–Steagall Act, introduced in 1933 and not repealed until the very end of the century. Share dealing everywhere was in the hands of a professional monopoly.[70]

Edward Luttwak has described this situation as 'controlled capitalism', with the emphasis on the 'controlled', and this captures it well.[71] The controls used varied from country to country and from government to government, but consisted largely of regulatory constraints, mixed with a greater or lesser degree of direct government influence and involvement. In cultural terms the demarcation of market from non-market activities that had characterized the growth of British and American business was still important, but the impact of business on the rest of society was so great that this was no longer sufficient to insulate society sufficiently from the effects of market self-interest. Even in America, where the controls were at their weakest, the unions provided a check on corporate power, small-scale agriculture was subsidized, tariff barriers provided protection from international competition, anti-trust measures were vigorously pursued, and many industries were very heavily regulated, especially where issues of public safety were concerned. Across Europe, government regulations protected weak or vulnerable groups from adverse market forces.

The interests of employees, in particular, were protected by strict redundancy laws, generous holiday and benefit entitlements, trades union closed shops, and, in some countries, compulsory employee representation on company boards. Small-scale, uneconomic agriculture was heavily subsidized, shop-opening hours were limited; and firms in strategic industries were heavily supported by the state. High taxes supported a comprehensive welfare state, including free health and education systems, and most public service industries. Together with other firms and industries considered crucial to the national interest (oil companies, defence contractors, and in France at least a range of other manufacturers) were nationalized. Britain, though it relied less than other countries on state intervention, followed this general European pattern. In the other major world economy, Japan, where the main aims of government were full employment and industrial leadership, a similar set of circumstances prevailed. Across the world, business activity was growing fast, but it remained closely monitored and controlled by hierarchically structured societies pursuing traditional hierarchical values.

## CONCLUSION

The social history of morals is a precarious activity. For the most part, our knowledge is restricted to the views of a very small segment of society and even there what people do not say, because they take it for granted, is often more important than what they do say. From the seventeenth century onwards—the period for which documentary evidence is reasonably prolific—public debates about morality and business have consistently focused on issues of mercantile monopoly and the role of the state rather than on issues of business practice. This was the context of Adam Smith's *Wealth of Nations*, and of many of the writings of Herbert Spencer. Literary treatments, such as those of Balzac, Zola, or Trollope, have focused more on the iniquities of fraudulent dealing than on the rights or wrongs of legally pursued self-interest. With these qualifications, however, we can assert with reasonable confidence that, at least until the 1980s, the pursuit of entrepreneurial self-interest was sanctioned by society only within quite tight moral bounds. This does not mean that entrepreneurs always stayed within these bounds. Many very evidently did not. But for self-interest to be socially legitimate it had to be confined to its proper area, accompanied by traditional moral virtues of duty, obligation, and restraint, and exercised through traditionally moral institutions and organizations—most notably, in recent times, the bureaucratic business organization in which the traditional moral rules of a hierarchical society prevailed, and the self-interest of market dealing was almost completely hidden from view.

Using the resources of cultural theory, it is evident why this should have been the case. Civilized societies are, without exception, cultural hierarchies, the cohesion of which depends critically on a 'high grid' social structure. If they are to develop and grow, culturally and economically, such societies need the creative input of people who can challenge this structure—people like artists, travellers, and entrepreneurs who inhabit a space below the line of zero grid on the grid–group diagram. They also need financial entrepreneurs, to fund their wars and other activities. But all these people, and the challenges they bring, are also an inherent threat to social stability. Entrepreneurs, in particular, not only operate within a market morality that is sharply at odds with the morality of the hierarchical society but are also well placed to exploit the structure of such a society in their own self-interest. Enterprise captures resources, resources bring influence, and a successful entrepreneur, unrestrained by the constraints of moral obligation, could easily move into a very similar position, vis-à-vis the body of society, to that of a would-be despot who has successfully captured the resources placed in his leadership care. As the role of business in society grows, and the values of the market become more widespread, there is also a risk that these values will undermine the tight value structure of the hierarchy, compromising its ability to coordinate activities and resources in the common good, encouraging the pursuit of politically motivated self-interest, and generally threatening its stability. Whether real or imagined—and this is an issue to which we shall return—such threats are naturally defended against.

# 3

# Free Enterprise and the Power of Business

We saw in Chapter 2 that up until a generation or so ago, despite the steady growth of business and enterprise, the moral structure of society remained remarkably consistent. A market subculture characterized by entrepreneurial self-interest has always been necessary for cultural and economic development as well as for the funding of government debt, but it was always set in the context of a dominant hierarchical or ordered culture, characterized by a traditional morality of obligation and duty. Enterprise was pursued under licence, subject in varying ways and in varying degrees to the constraints of traditional morality.

Although this balance between entrepreneurial self-interest and the traditional morality of obligation was successfully maintained over many centuries, however, it was always a bit precarious. For most of those who engaged in business, whether as managers or on their own account, it worked well. By and large, people engaged in business to make a living, not to make a killing. They worked hard and got by, and in so doing they not merely accepted but positively embraced the social norms of moral restraint and dutiful obligation. As business proprietors they were glad of the protection that these norms provided from unscrupulous and predatory competitors. As managers they appreciated the social benefits and psychological comforts of working in bureaucratically structured organizational communities. Such an attitude has never been typical, however, of the truly enterprising. Entrepreneurial success, as opposed to mere survival, demands a more individualistic, more risk-taking, and less restrained approach, unhindered by the social conventions of duty and obligation, and determined entrepreneurs have always sought to escape the bonds of society, even while sharing in its benefits. This is true, moreover, not only of the pirates, drug barons, extortionists, racketeers, fraudsters, and other criminals who have always exploited the cracks and weaknesses in the hierarchical structure for their own selfish ends, but also of the entrepreneurial heroes, the builders of legitimate businesses, on whom societies have depended for their economic growth and prosperity.

Business entrepreneurs have been able to escape the constraints of society in a number of different ways. Some have positioned themselves between different societies. International trade has long provided a competitive arena in which entrepreneurs could operate free from the local restrictions of their home countries—and free, as strangers, from many of the restrictions of the other countries in which they have traded. Others have built up their own market communities within, but effectively untouched by, their home societies. The world of finance impacts enormously upon society, but because money is intangible and its movement invisible it does so only indirectly and obscurely. Though nominally subject to sovereign states, financial markets have historically set their own rules and regulations, basing these on the ethics of the market rather than on those of the hierarchy, but shielding them effectively from public view.

Some entrepreneurs have used their economic power to influence social values, arguing that either business in general or their own businesses, in particular, are socially beneficial and that the shackles of regulation and moral constraint will rebound against the public interest. This course has been adopted historically by both financial and industrial entrepreneurs, but has been particularly characteristic of the latter, whose physical activities and labour needs have tied them more closely to society and kept them more open to the public gaze.

Societies, of course, have resisted all these moves, and as business has become progressively more powerful so it has become more closely regulated, at least until very recently. But for at least 150 years now, the balance of power has been shifting slowly but inevitably in favour of business as the forces unleashed in the Enlightenment and Industrial Revolution have spawned an inexorable growth in the size, number, and power of business enterprises, and in the social legitimacy of the economic values by which they are driven. In the last twenty-five years, the traditional hierarchical resistance to the market ethic finally seems to have collapsed. Free market economic ideas have come to dominate public policy and regulation has receded. From being constrained by the traditional institutions of society, business has itself become the dominant social institution. Entrepreneurial self-interest, traditionally treated with suspicion, has become socially legitimate. In this chapter we shall explore the rise of business power and influence and the role of business in contemporary society. In Chapter 4 we shall look at the rise of economic values and thinking and the growing social legitimacy of market self-interest.


## THE GROWTH OF BUSINESS AND
## THE MODERN COMPANY

Until well into the nineteenth century, business was mainly a private concern, carried out by individual proprietors or business partnerships. The chartered or incorporated joint-stock company with limited liability, which is the antecedent of contemporary business corporations, had been around since the sixteenth century. But such companies (as they were called in England) or corporations (to use the American term) were few in number and tightly regulated and controlled, being created only to undertake specified public interest projects (canals, water supplies, banking, insurance) and for periods limited to those projects.

In England, the power to grant charters moved from the monarch to parliament and, as the industrial revolution of the nineteenth century gained pace, the limited liability needed to encourage large-scale capital investment was increasingly granted by special acts of parliament (to the railway companies) or letters patent. But these privileges were still an exception, granted for a limited period and justified on a case-by-case basis by the supposed contribution of the company concerned to the public interest. With unchartered joint-stock companies effectively outlawed by the Bubble Act of 1720, repealed only in 1825, the great majority of business activity in the eighteenth and early nineteenth centuries was carried out through private partnerships, with unlimited liability. Capital was supplied by the partners and supplemented as necessary by bank loans and overdrafts. Moreover, the country banks that provided most of these loans were themselves private partnerships, limited by law to just six partners. Both in industry and in industrial finance, business was intimately tied to the social positions and reputations of the people engaged in it.[1]

Although the precise institutional structures varied considerably from country to country, this close linkage between the business company and the state (in the case of chartered companies) or its individual proprietors (in the case of sole traders or partnerships) was common throughout Europe.[2] The situation in America was similar. There, the power of incorporation lay with the individual states and was sparingly exercised on the basis of the local public interest, incorporation being for a specified period and requiring a special act of the state legislature. With a strong puritan ethic and an emphasis on local communities, America held fast to the ideal link between incorporation and public service and while in the early nineteenth century some states incorporated manufacturing as well as transport and utility companies, it was always in response to a perceived requirement for a statewide franchise, justified by some public need. Unlike their British counterparts, the local American banks were chartered as joint-stock companies, but prohibited from operating across state borders they remained tied to their local communities.[3]

Of course, not everything to do with business was so closely linked to society. Financial markets such as Wall Street and the London Stock Exchange operated as unregulated market enclaves, where the norms and practices could be far removed from those of private business or society at large. The early Wall Street traders, for example, were notorious for being social outsiders. Moreover, while these markets were dominated by trades in government and municipal bonds, they also traded bonds issued by the chartered companies and, to a lesser extent, shares in those companies. With the dramatic growth of canals and, especially, railways in the first half of the nineteenth century, this trading grew in importance, especially on Wall Street. Purely speculative traders were joined by investment bankers, proprietors of private unregulated banks who not only invested their own capital but also managed investments for their clients (primarily overseas investors) and helped to place new issues. However, it was still possible in this period to draw a clear line between the world of speculative finance, in which the market ethos ruled, and the world of business and commercial banking, in which enterprise remained closely linked to social convention and moral restraint.[4]

Up until the middle of the nineteenth century, then, we may think of the business corporation as embodying a form of social contract in which society granted certain privileges, in particular the privilege of limited liability, in exchange for some desired public service. For the majority of businesses that did not have a public service basis, there were no such privileges. Businesses were identified with their proprietors and sole traders and partners did business as individuals, with the normal rights, responsibilities, and obligations of individuals.[5] In the second half of the century, however, this social contract was radically changed. Between the 1850s and the 1880s, beginning in England but spreading quickly through the developed world, the privileges of the limited liability joint-stock company were effectively made available to all companies, subject only to fairly modest minimal share values, capital values, and registration and reporting procedures. In England, from 1856, even these basic controls were absent. The only requirement for the registration of a limited company was the filing of a memorandum of association signed by seven shareholders who had taken up (but need not have paid for) one share each.

The immediate reasons for this dramatic change remain unclear. In England, which moved from having Europe's tightest controls on companies to its loosest in just a couple of years in the mid-1850s, there was discussion of such things as the need to raise capital for the rapidly growing number of new ventures, of the need to provide appropriate domestic outlets for savings, and of the need to provide safe (limited liability) investments for the working classes. There was discussion too of the virtues of free markets and of the iniquities of imposing unlimited liability on those who were in effect sleeping partners (or, after the repeal of the Bubble Act, simple shareholders). But analysis of the debates suggests rather more opposition to limited liability than support for it, and while a large proportion of English capital was certainly being invested overseas, on Wall Street, at a time of considerable domestic industrial growth, there is little evidence of UK companies actually being short of funds for investment.[6] What seems almost certain is that many in parliament at that time will have been thoroughly confused by the matters under discussion, and unclear about the implications of the various measures proposed. All sorts of bills were proposed, with a wide variety of objectives, and in a parliament in which seats were either inherited or bought the success of the bills that became enacted may well have been due as much to personal and political bargaining as to any genuine support for their contents. What is quite clear is that once the change had taken place it could not easily be reversed.

In America, the pace of change varied from state to state, and the debate followed a slightly different tack. A key issue there, during and after the Civil War of the early 1860s, was that in a relatively individualistic culture, in which the control of corporations was increasingly in the hands of Wall Street bankers and 'robber barons', the line between public and private quickly became blurred. Definitions of what was or was not in the public interest were easily influenced by bribes or personal relationships. The terms of incorporation, which normally included some element of monopoly over the public service provided, could also be influenced. The Union Pacific railroad scandal, in which a group of private investors used an incorporated company to cheat the US government to the tune of about $50 million (an immense sum for that period), was one of the most notorious examples, but the railroads generally were no great advertisement for the public service ideal.[7] The directors and stockholders were often in cosy relationships with the state legislatures and in many cases got rich even when their corporations failed, as all the risks of the venture were loaded onto innocent and uninformed bondholders. In other cases the shares were cornered by speculators who managed the companies for their own short-term interests.[8] The association of the corporation with public service gave way to an association with unfair privilege, and as the owners of business corporations prospered so opposition to this privilege grew. There were two responses to this reaction. First, states sought to limit privileges, both by introducing free competition legislation and by strengthening their control over the corporations. Second, however, they sought to remove the perception of privilege by extending it to all, introducing legislation to allow businesses to incorporate as a matter of course, and without the time constraints that had traditionally been imposed. Thus, in America, the extension of incorporation and limited liability to all businesses appears to have come about not primarily because that was thought to be a good thing, but because restricted incorporation became discredited.[9]

In continental Europe, change came about more slowly and with greater safeguards. Strongly influenced by the English example, the unchartered limited liability joint-stock company became established in France in the late 1860s and in Prussia in the 1870s. In both cases, the restrictions on incorporation were lighter than in England and markets in shares were also more tightly regulated, but the general principle of granting companies limited liability as a matter of course, without any specific governmental approval, was conceded.[10]

To some extent these different patterns of company deregulation in different countries reflected different political circumstances, but they can also perhaps be seen, tentatively at least, as reflecting different hierarchical structures and cultures. In Britain, the moral fabric of society was uniquely strong in this period. In a relatively stable democracy with stable social and moral structures untroubled by the threat of revolution, business enterprise posed relatively few risks. Given the country's record of industrial success, it could indeed be seen as an opportunity rather than as a threat, and society could afford to relax its controls. In continental Europe, in contrast, most societies were faced with continuing social and political turmoil. Their cultures remained strongly hierarchical, but the hierarchical structures themselves were contested and relatively weak. Business and politics remained closely bound. As they sought to catch up with the industrial advances of Britain, European countries naturally turned to English legislation as an exemplar, but they remained cautious about market enterprise and business remained very closely tied to the institutions of family, community, and state. America was different again. Its unique history as the creation of enterprising communities fleeing from the religious constraints and perceived moral iniquities of European hierarchies had given it a much more pluralistic culture than anywhere in Europe. Both the individual self-interest of the market and the egalitarian ideals of the sect formed much stronger elements of the mix, while the forces of hierarchy were correspondingly weaker.[11] Although it was already the largest and most populous of Western countries, it was marked by a pervasive distrust both of size itself and of the centralized power that is characteristic of hierarchy. Business enterprise was seen as less of a threat than was entrenched privilege.

In the decades following business deregulation, the cultural attributes of American society combined with more material factors to make America the home of business enterprise. By the late nineteenth century, the legal form of the modern corporation was clearly established in all of the world's main economies, but while in most countries firms were quite slow to take advantage of the possibilities this offered, in America things developed rapidly. A key factor here was size. In a large country, with a population already around 70 million, a well-developed railroad network, the arrival of telegraph communications, and new mass production manufacturing technologies gave rise to tremendous economies of scale. Aggressive entrepreneurs responded by seeking to take over their competitors while other firms joined together in self-defence, and a wave of mergers around the turn of the century led to the creation of massive corporations.[12] Although America operated as a single large market, however, it was divided for legislative purposes into a host of much smaller states, and here the cultural resistance to size and to the centralization of power came into effect. American commercial banks were prevented by law not only from holding shares themselves but also from operating beyond state boundaries. They could, accordingly, play little part in the growth of businesses so the manufacturing entrepreneurs turned, as had the railroad entrepreneurs before them, to the investment bankers of Wall Street, who arranged equity financing for the mergers.[13] The result was that the large American corporation quickly became characterized by widely dispersed ownership, geographically dispersed operations, and a separation of ownership (shareholders) from control (managers). As corporate governance scholar Mark J. Roe has pointed out, 'even John Rockefeller, the richest man in America, ended up owning only a fraction of Standard Oil'.[14]

The structure of English business, in contrast, changed much more slowly. The first uses of the new corporate form were for speculative bubble companies, and with capital needs being significantly lower than in America (in a much smaller country the scope for scale economies was smaller) and investment bankers being much more interested in government bonds than in the promotion of industry, the partnership form of business continued to dominate well into the twentieth century. Gradually, however, equity financing took over and by mid-century limited liability joint-stock companies dominated the British economy too. Large family shareholdings, which maintained a link between ownership and control, continued to be important into the 1970s, but by the end of the century shareholdings in quoted British companies were even more widely dispersed than in their American counterparts.[15]

Meanwhile in France and Germany, where securities markets remained under tighter state control and where a well-developed commercial banking sector was able to meet the financing needs of industry, shareholdings remained much more concentrated and ownership much more closely linked with control. In both these countries, too, a close bond between business and society remained, and to a large extent remains to this day.[16] In France, prior to the reforms of the 1860s, the larger companies had typically been structured as a kind of limited partnership in which the principals carried full liability but the liabilities of sleeping partners were limited to their investments. Growth had been financed mainly through family networks and from retained earnings. After the reforms, companies gradually moved over to the joint-stock company model, but ownership remained tightly concentrated. In the twentieth century, French big business was characterized by interlocking networks of private funding and close state involvement, its leaders often drawn from same educational elite (and, in consequence, the same social networks) as the civil service. Small business remained rooted in the social and political networks of local communities. In Germany, too, though the modern corporate form was gradually adopted, share issues were a much less important form of funding than bank loans or internal reserves. In the twentieth century industrial development was guided, with active government involvement, by a small number of powerful universal banks, and co-determination legislation required companies to include employee representatives on their boards. At both local and national levels, business was harnessed to the interests of society.

Both in terms of ownership and control and in terms of the more general relations between business and society, market, and hierarchy, the French and Germany systems were much more typical of twentieth century business worldwide than were those of Britain and America. The other major industrial power of the twentieth century, Japan, also developed an insider-controlled business system closely bound to both government and the social hierarchy, and elsewhere too control by a majority shareholder remained the norm. In the late twentieth century the dispersed shareholdings of British and American companies were still unique, and so too was the relative emancipation of British and, especially, American business enterprise from the hierarchical constraints of government and society. By the turn of the twenty-first century, however, this situation was beginning to change rapidly, as France, Germany, and other countries dismantled the constraints they had traditionally placed on the market. By this time, moreover, it was neither the French nor the

German nor indeed the British companies that dominated the economic arena, even in their home countries, but American corporations, and these corporations were not only remarkably free of social or legal constraints, but also immensely powerful and influential institutions.

## CORPORATE FREEDOM AND CORPORATE POWER

In some ways the separation of ownership and control protected American businesses from the extremes of market culture. In the early twentieth century J. P. Morgan and other prominent investment bankers played an active part in the direction of the corporations in which they held investments, even when those investments were relatively small. Their primary role, however, appears to have been to protect their (mainly foreign) investors from the risk of appropriation by unscrupulous corporate raiders.[17] As the sheer scale of the merged corporations gradually put them beyond the reach of these raiders, and as public concerns about the concentration of power in the hands of the financiers (who were accused of operating a 'money trust') grew, the investment bankers withdrew from direct involvement, leaving the corporations in the control of professional managers. And it was under management control that the corporations developed their modern functional and multidivisional organizational forms, bureaucratic and hierarchical in both structure and moral values.[18] In Britain, meanwhile, social and class differences kept the worlds of industry and finance well apart, even hostile to each other, but as British companies gradually grew in size they copied the American model.[19]

In other ways, however, the separation of ownership and control loosened corporate ties to society and gave business corporations and the people who ran them enormous, unprecedented power. One of the characteristics of the early corporations had been that as creations of the state they had had legal identities separate from those of their shareholders or directors, and this legal personhood was carried over to the new business corporations. In 1886 the Supreme Court of the United States ruled that the business corporation qualified as a 'person' for the purpose of the Fourteenth Amendment, giving it the rights of liberty, property, and free speech previously granted only to individuals, and with this confirmation the language of privilege that had dominated earlier discussions of incorporation gave way to that of rights. In particular, whereas limited liability had been seen as a privilege granted for a limited purpose and time, it came quickly to be seen as an inalienable right, available to any business enterprise in perpetuity. Whereas before corporations had been able to do only what was expressly licensed by their charters, they were now able to do anything that was not expressly outlawed.[20] Coupled with the nationwide growth of industrial enterprises, this change also had significant consequences for the relationship between business and politics. Whereas previously the state legislatures had generally sought to limit and control business corporations, some of them now saw financial and political advantages in encouraging businesses to incorporate within their own states rather than others, by affording particular freedom or protection. Most notoriously, they limited the liability of corporations to their workers and communities. Insurance records suggest that around the turn of the century industrial accidents (mainly, but not entirely, in mining and extraction) were killing about 100 workers a day—about 600,000 over a twenty-year period—with many, many more serious injuries. Just as in many developing countries today, working conditions were appalling, wages minimal, and child labour commonplace—in 1910 about two million American children between, the ages of ten and fifteen were in employment.[21] The courts ruled that the workers were legally responsible for their own injuries and that any challenge to employment practices was a violation of corporate rights. The common good, the traditional yardstick in matters of incorporation, became identified with industrial production. Any business activity, however conducted, created wealth and was therefore in the public interest.[22]

An important factor in these developments was that companies were no longer incorporated in the states in which they carried out their business. In part, this was because it was the states without substantial natural resources and employment opportunities that had most to gain from encouraging incorporation: the 'race to the bottom' of states competing for incorporation by promoting company-friendly legislation was led by Delaware and New Jersey. More fundamentally, though, it was a direct consequence of the growth of the business corporation and the associated separation of ownership and control. When people express concern nowadays about the separation of ownership and control, they usually have in mind Adolph Berle's concern, first expressed in the early 1930s, that this separation leaves management unaccountable to shareholders.[23] As one of Berle's contemporary critics, E. Merrick Dodd, pointed out, however, there is another side to the problem. In the traditional family-run company, there was a strong bond between the owners (who were also the managers) and their communities. The company relied on the community for a social infrastructure, for workers, and for goodwill. The community relied on the company for jobs and security. This bond was reflected in the company's activities. It was, perforce, morally responsible, and restrained in its interaction with workers and community—a community in which the proprietors lived and of which they were a part. In many cases it was also an active contributor to the community welfare, developing roads, housing, and recreational facilities. By today's standards the attitude may have been overbearingly paternalistic and authoritarian, but it was marked by a genuine sense of responsibility and moral obligation, a genuine moral bond. Once companies began to operate nationwide and to be run by managers who were responsible for economic performance and had no remit to give away the owners' money in charity, this bond was broken.[24]

In the course of the twentieth century, businesses in all developed countries came under increasing regulation as governments responded to cases of fraud and blatant exploitation. Employment and health and safety laws were introduced to protect workers, customers, and communities. Monopolies and mergers legislation was developed to promote competition and outlaw cartels and monopolies. Accounting regulations and financial disclosure requirements were progressively tightened, especially for quoted companies. However, the laws introduced to control corporate activities were not always effective, and they did little in practice to curtail the power of business, which grew as the businesses grew. Large companies in particular continued to influence the political and legal agenda. In Britain no less than in America, continuing geographical diversification and the continuing dispersion of shareholdings acted to progressively loosen the bonds between companies and communities.

The freedom of businesses to resist the controls that society sought to impose on them was in part a direct consequence of their legal status. Lord Thurlow, Lord Chancellor of England, observed in the nineteenth century that while those directing a corporation might have moral duties and obligations the corporation itself could not be a moral being.[25] 'Did you ever expect a corporation to have a conscience', he observed, 'when it has no soul to be damned and no body to be kicked'.[26] As a legal person, a company is legally responsible for its actions, but because it is not a moral person it cannot be 'morally' punished, for example by imprisonment. As the law evolved, however, the directors of a company could not be punished at all. The formula that came to be adopted was that while they might *in extremis* be held responsible for gross negligence, they could not be held to account by the law for their business judgement. If, then, a company breached the environmental, health and safety, or employment legislation that was introduced during the twentieth century, the only remedy available to the courts was to fine the company. But with the directors unscathed this turned an essentially moral misdemeanour into a purely economic cost, for which companies could easily account and even plan.

Large corporations break the law regularly and with complete impunity—a freedom that in developed countries is denied even to the wealthiest of individuals.[27] They are occasionally fined, but the fines are small and are seen as a cost of doing business. Even for serious and knowing breaches of environmental or health and safety laws—breaches that cause serious injury and death—no individual gets taken to court, and no one gets sent to jail. The only sanction is public opinion, but even when a corporation gets into serious trouble, as Exxon did, for example, with the Exxon Valdez oil spillage, it can generally buy itself out with a public relations campaign.

The story of public relations is probably one of the best examples of the growth of corporate power through the twentieth century. The giant business corporations that emerged in America at the beginning of the century may have had legal power and the ability to influence (or bribe) state legislatures, but they did not have great social legitimacy. For one thing, the cavalier way in which many of them treated their employees did not endear them to the population at large. For another, Americans retained their traditional distrust of concentrated power.[28] In the language of the time, business corporations were described as 'soulless'—remorseless inhuman machines whose actions impacted on everyone but whose decision makers were remote from the communities in which they operated, out of human contact and with no sense of public duty. This charge hit home, especially as the rapid unionization of the workforce was strengthening its bargaining position, and the corporations responded in two ways. First, they improved their employment practices, introducing welfare programmes for their workers and seeking to build a sense of organizational belonging and loyalty. In this they followed the earlier example of family companies such as Cadbury in England, where strong moral values (in the Cadbury case, Quaker values) had been put to effective business use. Instead of simply hiring and firing, the corporations provided lunchroom amenities, educational and recreational programmes, and housing assistance, presenting themselves to their employees as caring and responsible families, models of the traditional (hierarchical) moral order. Second, they worked on their public image by advertising their welfare programmes and, more generally, by using advertising to promote not so much their products as their desired corporate images. If a corporation could be associated with an individual founder, it could almost be guaranteed that the face of that founder would appear on its advertisements, regardless of how little control or influence he now exercised, or in what direction. The important thing was to show a human face. Corporations could not hide their size, indeed they did not want to. Pictures of large gleaming modern factories assured customers that they were buying from the best and most reliable firms. But if the corporation was engaged in mass production, the advertising would also emphasize its artisan roots, showing the first small shop from which Burroughs sold its adding machines, or the 'little house' that housed the early Heinz company and was shipped five miles to sit next to its massive new factory—'a constant reminder', the advertising noted, 'of the ideals established there, the principles on which the Heinz business has been built'.[29]

In the course of the ensuing century, companies have spent many billions of dollars presenting themselves to the public in an attractive light. Indeed, by the end of the twentieth century, public relations was a £2 billion a year industry worldwide. The companies have proclaimed themselves as devoted public servants in times of peace and the nation's saviours in times of war, as caring employers and pillars of the community. They have emphasized their creativity and inventiveness, their conservatism and respect for tradition. They have reminded people constantly of their honesty and integrity, their trustworthiness, and sense of responsibility. They have done so, moreover, in an ever more skilled and calculated way, and while public relations can be used to promote the truth it can also be used to obscure it. The word 'reputation' used to be closely linked to behaviour: one secured a reputation by acting in an appropriate way. But modern business reputations are manufactured as well as earned. Photographs or films of women and children, soft focus and pastels, often have little or nothing to do with the ostensible product, everything to do with the corporate image being promoted. Green fields signify an extractive or highly polluting industry.[30] If a company promotes a story about the good it is doing, it is a fair bet that it is trying to counter or distract attention from something less praiseworthy. In early 2001, two stories appeared in the British newspapers about the multinational tobacco corporation, BAT. One reported that it was sponsoring athletic events for teenagers in West Africa—and distributing free cigarettes to the children who took part. The other reported that it was funding a professorship and centre of business ethics and social responsibility at a leading British university.[31]

While public relations covers a wide range of activities, including sponsorship and press relations, much of it is carried out through advertising, and this also enhances the power of business in other ways. By the 1990s, global expenditure on advertising, packaging, and product promotion, at over $600 billion a year, was over half that on education.[32] To a certain extent, advertisements for competing products cancel out each other's effects. But successful brands shape people's lives in the most powerful of ways, by shaping their identities. Consumer culture has been traced back by historians to the eighteenth, even the seventeenth century, but there can be little doubt that people's identities have been moulded more and more by corporate advertising over time. There is also a powerful cumulative effect: the creation of a 'must-have' consumer culture in which people are driven to work more and more to buy more and more, not to satisfy any physical need or to achieve any satisfaction or contentment, but to try and satisfy an ultimately insatiable psychological need created by, and serving the interests of, the business corporations.[33]

As a final illustration of the growth of corporate power, we might consider the relationship between business and politics. Business entrepreneurs have always sought political influence, both to advance their particular ventures and to protect themselves from public criticism. Indeed, the very fact that they have departed from the common norms of society, in placing self-interest above obligation, has made it imperative that they seek political as well as entrepreneurial power. Traditionally, this power was gained through the time-honoured means of bribery. Since many of those engaged in politics have always been after power themselves, the parties understood each other well. Even today, in most countries of the world, the relationships between business entrepreneurs and politicians are very direct. In well-developed democracies, straightforward bribery is no longer accepted, but money still talks, and large businesses have developed effective means of exerting political power.

As in public relations and advertising, American corporations have led the way. A particular feature of American politics is the liberal conception of free speech, to which corporations as legal persons are entitled, as implying no constraints. What this comes down to is that to be elected to a political office in America you not only need more popular policies than your opponent, you also need more advertising (nowadays, airtime), which costs serious money of a kind that individuals or political groups do not themselves have.[34] The business corporations have the money and they give it freely, in exchange for political influence and protection—to the tune of $1.5 billion dollars in 1997–8, which was not a presidential election year, and over $1 billion for the 2000 Presidential elections.[35] Much of this money comes from businesses for which government policy decisions are critical, and by and large their money seems well spent. When the European Union and the American government were in negotiation about banana import quotas in the late 1990s, the head of one of the American companies affected, Carl Lindner of Chiquita, was reported giving $1.4 million to the Democrats and $4.2 million to the Republicans.[36] During the 1990s, the tobacco industry contributed about $3 million a year to the funds of both parties.[37] Before it collapsed, the Enron corporation is reported to have been funding three quarters of all US Senate and House of Representatives members on a regular basis, and the money appears to have been well spent. Enron benefited from tax breaks and from crucial regulatory decisions, and it played a central role in the formation of US energy policy.[38] Monsanto, the leading producer of genetically modified seeds, also seems to have successfully acquired significant influence over policy formation in its area.[39]

Most large American businesses pay into campaign funds, but that is not all they do. They also spend money on political advertising themselves, on political lobbying, and on university research and educational programmes proclaiming the virtues of their products and activities and the moral superiority of the economic system from which they benefit. Since the early 1970s, when they came under attack from environmentalists and consumer activists, they have funded the so-called 'public-interest' law firms such as the Pacific Legal Foundation, which was set up to defend businesses against clean air and water legislation, nature protection, and workers' rights, and which attacked environmentalists for their 'selfish, self-centred motivation . . . ; their indifference to the injuries they inflict on the masses of mankind . . . ; and most of all, their power to inflict monumental harm on society'. They have also created and funded a host of political lobbying associations masquerading as citizen's groups: the National Wetlands Coalition, sponsored not by the defenders of the wetlands but by oil and gas companies and property developers wishing to operate there; Consumer Alert, created to campaign *against* product safety legislation; or Freedom Forum, the creation of one of America's largest media corporations. Everyone in America has the right to free speech, but not everyone can be heard: for a long time now the business corporations have dominated public discourse. And of course, the newspapers, television stations, and other media outlets are also controlled by a few, very powerful business corporations.[40]

Even when taken individually, their spending power and control over investment and employment give large American corporations enormous power in relation to the communities in which they operate and the political representatives of those communities. When, as in the cases just cited, the power of the corporations is pooled to protect the interests of an industry, or of business itself, it can achieve awesome dimensions. The classic example at the industry level is that of the tobacco industry. In the post-war period the big six American cigarette companies, under strong public pressures for controlling the industry on health grounds, withheld from the public findings from their own scientific research that demonstrated the ill effects of smoking; they also used their advertising power to proclaim what they knew to be false, that smoking did *not* have any such harmful effects. Given the importance of the industry to the economy, government was rendered powerless. In later years the American government used its own very considerable diplomatic power to prevent or repeal legislation in developing countries that, while clearly in the public interests of those countries, ran counter to the commercial interests of the US cigarette manufacturers.[41]

Elsewhere in the world, corporate influence has been exerted in different ways, and in many cases to somewhat lesser effect. But even at its weakest the influence has still been very powerful, and always increasing. In Italy and, until recently, Japan, corporate influence has been built on political links between business and the ruling political party, manifest in widespread corruption. In France it has been built on close ties between industry and government, reinforced by the 'old boy' networks of the two elite Grandes Ecoles. The ENA, which is the graduate training school for the civil service, and the Polytechnique, which is that for the armed forces, turn out only a few hundred graduates a year but have long provided the majority of large company chief executives and directors. In Britain, the political power of business has traditionally been quite modest—indeed reluctance on the part of politicians and civil servants to listen to the concerns of business has often been blamed for the country's relative economic underperformance in the twentieth century.[42] In recent decades, however, American practices have gradually been imported. Corporate political funding is still very modest, but business influence on regulatory processes, such as those affecting the food and drugs industries, and on local politics, in particular with relation to planning, now appears to be very significant.[43] The power of business over society at large, exerted through advertising, sponsorship, and the media, has grown substantially.


# FROM LOCAL INFLUENCE TO GLOBAL DOMINANCE: BUSINESS INSTITUTIONS IN THE CONTEMPORARY WORLD

The growth in the relative power and influence of business has been a long-term process. Ultimately it has been based on the technological advances of the Industrial Revolution, which themselves rested on the intellectual achievements of the Scientific Revolution and Enlightenment. It is possible, however, to discern a significant enhancement of corporate power in the closing decades of the twentieth century, partly as a result of the extensive deregulation of businesses at the national level and partly as a result of the dismantling of trade barriers and the political and economic globalization that has accompanied this.

## The deregulation and privatization of business

Across the developed world the 1980s and 1990s were characterized by the extensive deregulation of private business, the privatization of previously state-owned public services such as telecommunications, transport, and utilities, and the use of private sponsorship to support those services that remained in the public sector. The most visible, most commented upon, and politically most contentious of these developments was the movement toward privatization. This movement, which started in Britain under the government of Margaret Thatcher, was based partly on the growing influence of free market ideas, which we shall discuss in the next chapter, and partly on the recognition that with ageing populations, leading to rising health and welfare costs, governments would find it increasingly difficult to square what people expected from public services with what they were prepared to pay in taxes. Privatization, which was justified on the grounds that private corporations operating within the disciplines of the market would be more efficient than state-owned monopolies, provided governments with immediate cash windfalls. It also created a new cadre of very large and powerful companies, many of which, such as water utilities or national post and telecommunications companies, still enjoyed elements of natural monopoly.[44] Where services were split up, for example, into regionally based utilities, they were soon re-incorporated into large international groupings.

In Britain in the late 1990s the focus shifted from privatization by stock market flotation to public–private partnerships and the private finance initiative (PFI). Whereas before they would have invested public funds in the building of new hospitals, say, those services that remained in public ownership (e.g. health, schools, prisons and police forces, and some transport systems) were required to contract with private sector suppliers to build the facilities as private ventures and rent them back to the public services concerned. The theory was again that the private sector would do the job more efficiently, but by this stage theory, driven by market ideology, seems to have gone somewhat awry. For what was being privatized now was not the construction of the hospital, which would have been done by private contractors anyway, but its funding—and governments still have access to funds at much cheaper rates than consortia of private companies, especially as the latter have to give their shareholders a significant return on investment. The effect was to further empower business while tying the public services into long-term, inflexible, and relatively high cost contracts.[45]

In contrast to the PFI, corporate sponsorship of services such as education did enable expenditure on these services to be improved without committing any further public funds. Even without any educational involvement, however, businesses already exerted a strong influence on youth culture, for the simple reason that young people watched a lot of television, enjoyed consuming, and were susceptible to advertising. By the end of the century many companies also enjoyed the freedom to sponsor products in schools and to design and supply television programmes and curriculum modules propounding their own corporate values and ideals. This is furthest developed in America, where 40 per cent of schools subscribe to a broadcasting service that places advertising routinely in the classroom and where a 1999 Consumers' Union report found 80 per cent of teaching packs distributed to schools by business corporations to be biased or inaccurate in ways that supported the corporations' interests. But it is also a growing trend in Britain and elsewhere.[46] At university level, where they had previously bought influence through generous benefactions, businesses now 'buy' whole science departments, in some cases claiming property rights over and limiting publication of the research outputs and taking explicit responsibility for the management and control of the departments as well as for their funding.

Engaging as it did with the traditional politics of capitalism versus the state, privatization inevitably stole the limelight, but more significant in its effects was the gradual deregulation of businesses that were already in the private sector. We noted at the end of Chapter 2 that up until the 1980s business in the developed economies was still quite strongly regulated, a situation described by Edward Luttwak as 'controlled capitalism'. By the early twenty-first century, however, this had given way to what he calls 'turbo-capitalism', in which businesses are much more loosely regulated. The sheer number of relevant laws and regulations has not decreased; indeed it has continued to grow. But the burdens imposed by these regulations have been substantially reduced. In America, long-standing restrictions on the operations of banks and other financial institutions have been removed. Federal and state controls on the pricing of fuel, transportation, and other services have been removed or relaxed. Anti-trust proceedings have shifted their focus from the protection of the consumer from monopoly power to the commercial competitiveness of American industry. And while environmental, food and drug, and health and safety regulations have proliferated, they have increasingly acted in rather than against the interests of big business, relying on the professional judgements of industry insiders and enhancing standards as and when advancing technologies make this economically viable for American companies (and not, typically, for their overseas competitors). In Britain, radical legislation has been introduced to free businesses from the constraints imposed by trades unions, facilitating redundancies and increasing flexibility in pay and working conditions. Price controls have been removed and competition laws relaxed. Both government constraints on privatized firms and government support and protection for 'strategic' industries have gradually been withdrawn, and banking controls have been relaxed.[47]

Elsewhere in the world, similar changes have taken place. In Japan, rocked by corruption scandals, government gradually disentangled itself from the control and direction of industry. Australia and New Zealand, which had traditionally been very highly regulated economies, had by the mid-1990s become very lightly regulated. In the late 1990s even France, traditionally by far the most sta-tist of the leading economies, went through an intense period of rapid deregu-lation. Throughout South America and South-east Asia, privatization of the banking sector effectively freed business from government control. None of these changes has been particularly dramatic, but together with reductions in international tariffs and the removal of currency exchange regulations they have transformed the nature of big business in the developed world. Whereas the businesses of the 1960s and 1970s operated within tightly defined frameworks of constraints, contemporary businesses are, in commercial terms, unfettered. In most industries, compliance with government regulations and commercial and employment legislation has become a matter of operating routine or main-tenance. It is no longer a constraint on strategic direction.

## Globalization and the transnational corporation

If privatization and deregulation represent one aspect of the 'retreat of the state' in the late twentieth century, globalization represents another. It is widely accepted that globalization has resulted in a significant shift of power from the nation state to the multinational or transnational corporation. Whatever the technicalities of their incorporation, the large transnational corporations (TNCs) have effectively moved beyond the control of individual governments. They remain subject, in principle at least, to the laws of nations, but they operate routinely across borders, conducting operations wherever it is most efficient to do so—which often means wherever the legal and regulatory con-straints imposed by society are weakest. In many respects their powers, when compared with those of nation states, are severely restricted. Most obviously, not even the largest and most powerful of the TNCs can raise taxes or enact and enforce legislation. But in purely economic terms, their wealth and resources dwarf those of many of the countries in which they operate. The turnovers of the six largest TNCs exceed the GDPs of all but the twenty-one largest nation states and by these measures too the fiftieth largest company is larger than the fiftieth largest country. The debt ratings of the large TNCs are higher than those of many smaller countries, and they also own a large proportion of the world's physical, financial, and intellectual assets. Through the international patent system, for example, Monsanto effectively owns the rights to all future modifica-tions of the soya bean, a staple of world food supplies, while other companies now 'own' human genes.[48]

The effects of this power, and the extent and effects of globalization gener-ally, are hotly debated. The 'official' view, shared by the International Monetary Fund (IMF), the World Bank, and the governments of the world's largest devel-oped economies, is that globalization has been an unalloyed success, and that the power of the TNCs has, for the most part, been exercised responsibly. The counter view, advanced by what has come to be called the anti-globalization movement, is that globalization has been a disaster, and that the power of the TNCs has been used to exploit the developing world and expropriate its resources.

The first of these views focuses on the exceptional economic achievements of the late twentieth century and interprets these, in self-congratulatory mode, as the simple consequences of a triumph of reason: of the economic reason of free markets and the political reason of democratic capitalism. This is the message proclaimed both by those who have benefited (or expect to benefit) from economic growth, and by those who would seek credit for it: by businesses and entrepreneurs, by international economic agencies, and by national governments. It is also, by and large, and for a variety of reasons, the dominant perspective of the press and public media. It is most clearly stated in the pages of publications such as *The Economist* and *Business Week*, or in the reports of international agencies such as the IMF, the World Trade Organization (WTO), and the World Bank, or even, in recent years, the United Nations Commission on Trade and Development (UNCTAD). But it is also advanced, implicitly or explicitly, throughout the financial and economic press, in most college courses on macroeconomics, in the corporate publicity of multinational corporations, and in the political rhetoric of governments worldwide.

The storyline of the triumph of reason is compelling. The freeing of markets and the removal of social and institutional constraints on the exercise of economic self-interest have undoubtedly brought with them fantastic economic growth. Whatever 'protectionist' tariffs and trade barriers may have offered in the way of genuine protection to local lifestyles and emergent domestic industries, there can be no doubt that they also harboured gross inefficiencies as well as widespread corruption. The collapse of trade barriers in the last thirty years has brought in a large-scale international transfer of technological skills and equipment and allowed the most efficient companies to compete and win business in most countries of the world. At the same time, the collapse of communism and the wholesale removal of state restrictions on ownership of the means of production have made it possible for literally millions of entrepreneurs worldwide to contribute their skills and energies to the process of wealth creation.

As a result of this process, economic output has soared and even in the less developed countries, where populations have also soared, people are massively better off, in economic terms, than they were a generation ago. The figures speak for themselves. In the last fifty years, world output has multiplied by a factor of between five and six and much of this growth can be attributed to the growth of the developing world. In the twenty-five years from 1970 to 1995, during which time the world's population almost doubled, the per capita GNP of Britain and the United States, measured at constant prices, grew by about 50 per cent. That of India, the World's second largest country, grew by about 80 per cent. That of Indonesia, the fourth largest, more than tripled. That of China, the world's most populous country, multiplied fivefold. During the same twenty-five year period, developing country infant mortality roughly halved, crop yields nearly doubled, and life expectancy increased by about ten years.[49]

By any standards these are extraordinary achievements, but they have not been achieved without costs and it is on these costs that the counter view focuses. This counter view tells a story of massive environmental and ecological damage, the destruction and exploitation of indigenous communities, and increasing economic inequalities leading to poverty and social disintegration. It is a story of ecological disaster and the triumph of greed and it is every bit as compelling, in its own way, as the story of the triumph of reason. Development guru David C. Korten sums up the problem as[50]

a crisis of governance born of a convergence of ideological, political, and technological forces behind a process of economic globalization that is shifting power away from governments responsible for the public good and toward a handful of corporations and financial institutions driven by a single imperative—the quest for short-term financial gain . . . These forces have transformed once beneficial corporations and financial institutions into instruments of a market tyranny that is extending its reach across the planet like a cancer, colonising ever more of the planet's living spaces, destroying livelihoods, displacing people, rendering democratic institutions impotent, and feeding on life in an insatiable quest for money.

The storyline of the triumph of greed, as told by Korten or in more measured tones by the Nobel Prize winner and former World Bank and Clinton administration economist Joe Stiglitz, accepts the facts of economic growth, and accepts that, in monetary terms, this growth is creating wealth for developing as well as developed countries.[51] But it questions how that wealth is measured, how it is being created, and where it is going. The wealth is measured, it suggests, by economic production statistics, which means that even a few people earning meagre wages while others beg count for more than a large number living more comfortably off their own smallholdings, the produce from which is not included in the economic statistics. It is being created from a wholesale destruction of environmental resources, from the exploitation of child labour, and by forcing people in developing countries to live and work in conditions we would not ourselves consider acceptable. It is going overwhelmingly to the shareholders of multinational corporations and, when it stays within a developing country, to small entrepreneurial elites, drugs barons, and corrupt government officials. Moreover, while China and some of the South-east Asian economies may have grown rapidly over the past twenty-five years, the per capita GNP of Latin America has changed little and that of Africa has actually declined, in many countries quite dramatically. The number of people living in poverty has, on most measures, increased, with 1.2 billion people now living on less than one dollar a day and 2.8 billion (nearly half the world's population) on less than two dollars a day.

The point about measurement is probably the least familiar part of this argument, but is quite important. Over the last twenty-five years, economic growth in developing countries has been closely linked to the activities of the World Bank, which provides loans to countries for the purpose of development, and the IMF, which provides emergency loans in times of crisis. These loans are typically accompanied by conditions, which guide—or, more accurately, dictate—the debtor nations' economic policies, the general aims being to generate the foreign exchange needed to enable these nations to pay their international debts and to integrate them into the world economy. In the 1980s, following a change of leadership at the IMF and its adoption of policies based on a free market ideology, these conditions were packaged and promoted as 'structural adjustment' programmes, which typically involved reduced trade tariffs, privatization programmes, export subsidies, and subsidies and other incentives for direct foreign investment. These policies undoubtedly led to economic growth, as portrayed in official government statistics, and were at the time proclaimed a success. But the people who were deeply involved with development issues 'on the ground', through working with charities and aid agencies, saw a very different picture. For example, while the incentives offered to foreign companies drove up both production and employment, both in city factories and on large commercial farms, they tended to drive down wages. Income statistics, which measured total wages but took no account of the self-employed—the subsistence farmers and smallholders who had traditionally made up the great majority of the population in most developing countries—showed a growth, but real per capita incomes declined. The same criticism can be made of more recent claims that the economic growth of developing countries has benefited the poor as well as the rich.[52]

If economic statistics on development are misleading in the narrow sense that they do not measure what they claim to measure, they are even more misleading in the broader sense that they measure only what can be measured in terms of money. Critics of the structural adjustment programmes of the 1980s and of their more sophisticated successors in the 1990s and 2000s have pointed, for example, to the infringement of national sovereignty by IMF hegemony, to the bypassing of due political process and overriding of local community interests, and to the social and psychological pressures of ever-increasing debt burdens, none of which can ever be costed. The IMF does not suggest to countries what their economic policies should be, or debate the possibilities with them. It tells them what to do, on the basis of what many would argue is simplistic and outdated economic theory and in ignorance of the specific circumstances of the society concerned. Lending, in recent years, to countries that have already developed some kind of industrial base but not a regulatory infrastructure or welfare state, it has enforced policies resulting in large-scale unemployment, corruption, and rapid capital outflows, which have often led to social and political unrest.[53]

The main concern of critics has been with the direct social and environmental impacts of economic development. Across Central and South America, Central Africa, Russia, and South-east Asia, the world's main hardwood forests are being destroyed at rates that would be completely unsustainable, even if they were all replanted. They are not replanted, and in the last twenty years between 15 and 30 per cent of the forests in these regions have been lost. Not only that, the soil is too poor to sustain the cattle farming or export crops that replace them and within a few years vast areas of land that once supported indigenous communities lie barren.

The early stages of industrial development, with their focus on extractive industries and the production of iron, steel, and concrete, have always caused high levels of pollution. But in developing countries today this is supplemented by the effects of other high pollution industries, such as copper and aluminium smelting, heavy chemicals production, and toxic waste processing, which are not needed for the local economy but have been 'exported' from the developed world. Less pollution for the rich, but more for the poor. Moreover, all these industries displace rural communities and traditional subsistence, but without giving rise to significant employment themselves.

Where rural communities do survive, many of them are now turned over to the capital-intensive production of luxury food products for the consumers of the developed world, leaving basic foodstuffs to be imported and hundreds of millions of agricultural smallholders without any means of subsistence. In many countries, small farmers have been encouraged to make the shift from producing food for their own needs to producing export crops. When world prices are high, the export crops generate cash that could, in principle, take economies out of subsistence and into growth. Unfortunately, world prices have tended to fall, in some cases dramatically, leaving the farmers in debt and without the food to meet their own needs, and prompting developed countries to introduce import quotas and subsidies to protect their own agricultural industries. The export crops are also heavily dependent on seed, fertilizers, and pesticides supplied by the large multinational corporations, the prices of which have not fallen; and with little control over pesticide use many parts of the world are now plagued by contaminated water supplies. Very often, the pesticides supplied have been those banned as unsafe by the developed countries. Pharmaceuticals exports show a similar pattern.

What employment there is in the developing countries is increasingly in the growing cities, and much of it is in appalling conditions. In Guangdong in southern China, the official figures for 1994 showed over twenty industrial deaths a day. In the Philippines and elsewhere, the assembly of microscopic electronic chips destroys workers' eyesight in the space of a few years. In the sweatshops of Latin America and southern Asia, and the carpet factories of India and Pakistan, women and children work in conditions bordering on slavery. Many of the children really are in slavery, sold off by parents who literally cannot feed them. And those who find themselves working in an airless room for fifteen hours and no pay are the lucky ones. By some estimates there now a million child prostitutes in South-east Asia, the vast majority of whom are likely to develop AIDS.[54] Even in a relatively developed country such as Mexico, in the *maquiladoras* across the border from the United States, hundreds of thousands of workers receive from their American employers just 10 per cent of American pay rates, and work in conditions that fall far short of even the official Mexican health and safety requirements, never mind those of the developed world.

These examples could be multiplied ten- or a hundredfold, and provide evidence that, at the very least, the story of global prosperity and the triumph of reason is not as straightforward as it seems. There are losers as well as winners.

Early stage industrial development is still accompanied today by the same tragic by-products as a century ago, but with the pace of development forced some of these by-products are even more severe. And at the global level, it is now evident that economic development goes hand in hand with con-sequences that could easily turn triumph into disaster. The destruction of the rainforests, for example, is not just impacting on indigenous communities, but on carbon dioxide levels in the atmosphere. The industrialization of developing countries is not just polluting those countries but also contributing to world pollution levels. Even without this contribution, the prosperity and affluence of the developed world is fuelled by levels of emissions, from power stations, cars, and planes, far greater than nature can absorb. As a result of all these develop-ments, global warming, seen ten years ago as a figment of the environmentalists' imaginations, is now an accepted fact. No one yet knows, of course, just quite how severe its consequences will be, but since the affluent countries of the world are unwilling to contemplate anything beyond a marginal reduction in power consumption, and the governments of developing countries quite reasonably see no reason why they should stop developing, there seems little prospect of averting them. And if China should continue growing in prosperity until it reaches the per capita power consumption and emission levels of Japan or the United States, the effects could well be disastrous.

Moreover, while global warning may be the biggest environmental threat to our society, it is not the only one. The depletion of oil and gas stocks may put some kind of limit on global warming, but not before it has caused massive political problems as there is not enough to go round. As scientific education advances, the technologies of biological, chemical, and nuclear warfare are becoming more widely disseminated, and the potential destructive power of terrorists and tyrants is growing. As a result of technological developments and economic globalization, our capacity to generate food is currently outstripping world population growth, but the oceans are being depleted, as are vast areas of previously fertile land. Genetically engineered crops offer improved yields but like other new technologies they carry unknown risks. These risks tend to get dismissed, but history would suggest that is unwise. Not one saw a risk in asbestos, or tobacco. Incredible though it seems, no one saw a risk in feeding beef cattle (naturally vegetarian) with protein supplements made from beef meat, and as the technologies get more and more advanced, so the risks grow greater.

From the point of view of the environmentalists and other critics of market culture, a central feature of all these developments is financial greed, an unquenchable desire on the part of business enterprises for more and more wealth regardless of the consequences. It was greed that prompted people to feed beef with beef, or to proclaim cigarettes safe and keep marketing aggres-sively when the tobacco companies' own research had already showed they caused lung cancer, and it is greed that now drives the producers of GM foods and mobile telephones. (It is rumoured that the telephone manufacturers already have evidence that their telephones, which demonstrably heat up the brain, are causing increases in brain cancer.) It is greed that causes people to vacuum the oceans, killing off the young fish to catch the fully grown, or to cut down forests without replanting. It is greed that prompts entrepreneurs to set up factories in developing countries with below-subsistence wages and minimal regard for health and safety, and greed that prompts multinationals to encourage this by negotiating rock-bottom prices from their suppliers. Above all, it is the greed of the financial institutions for short-term profits that pushes companies to behave in this way.

It is evident that the two contrasting stories of globalization, one focusing on the triumph of enlightened reason and the other on the triumph of greed, both contain important truths. It is also evident that neither tells the whole truth and that the different effects on which they selectively focus are to some extent incommensurable. Only time and the judgement of history will tell whether the benefits in terms of economic development are worth the social and environmental costs. Both views, however, recognize that the power of the TNCs is a critical factor in the outcomes observed. For the intergovernmental organizations and the governments of the leading economies that dominate them, empowered TNCs are the crucial agents of change, bringing foreign direct investment to the developing countries, importing their employment, environmental, and health and safety standards, improving both economic and resource efficiency and using their bargaining power to help bring these countries up to Western standards of business propriety and governmental accountability. For the anti-globalization critics, the power of the TNCs enables them to exploit the developing countries, which are increasingly dependent on them for the investment and technological skills needed to generate the exports to repay IMF and World Bank debts. Far from improving standards, it is argued, they use their power to exploit the low standards prevailing in the developing world, securing land appropriation or protection from local special interest groups, exporting their most polluting activities, or exploiting cheap labour or minimal environmental and health and safety standards.

The difficulty of deciding between these views in practice is apparent when we look at some of the cases that have been highlighted by critics. In the late 1990s, wage rates for clothing manufacture in the Far Eastern subcontractors of apparel firms such as Nike and GAP were of the order of 15–25 pence an hour. By modern, developed world standards the working conditions were appalling. By local standards, however, the pay rates and working conditions were both rel-atively good. There was no shortage of would-be employees, and no apparent desire on the part of those who were employed to leave.[55] Indeed, the people who seemed from the critics' perspective to be suffering most from the TNC policies often saw themselves as their greatest beneficiaries.

Another example illustrates nicely the twin facets of the power of the Western corporation in developing countries. In the 1990s Tesco, the UK supermarket chain, sourced its mange tout peas from Zimbabwe. As it does in the United Kingdom, and as its competitors also do, it started by encouraging farmers to invest in their businesses and devote their production to the company, then began to turn the screw, squeezing them on both price and quality—the latter determined in this case by the smallness of the pea pod. The higher the quality specification, the more of the harvest was wasted and the less the pickers got paid. There was nothing exceptional in this, and although the television documentary in which it was portrayed evidently set out to explore the iniquities of international business (an agenda that may only be possible in Britain, with its unique public service television channels), the situation was no different from that faced by many British farmers. What was different, however, was the positioning of the company. In Britain it is a company. To the Zimbabwean workers it was presented as a god—a 'higher being', as one of them said, struggling to describe it. When the Tesco buyers visited they were entertained by the children from the village school, supported by the company, singing songs in its praise: 'Tesco is our king!', they sang.[56] What Tesco does in a small way, through its supply chains, the big consumer corporations do through their advertising. For American consumers, Coke and Pepsi, Nike and McDonalds may produce desirable products, but they are still business corporations. For the young people in developing countries, they are truly god-like: a glimpse of heaven, of an American dream. That is power.

The process of globalization has also enhanced the power of business less directly, but just as effectively, through the operations of international agencies such as the World Bank, the IMF, and the WTO. As we have already noted, in the 1980s and 1990s the Washington-based consultants of the IMF effectively wrote not only the trade policies but also many of the internal social and economic policies of debtor countries—which is to say of most of the developing world— and these policies consistently favoured American corporations. Again, when the World Bank has lent money to a less developed country it has generally been for projects involving large procurement contracts with the European and American corporations. US Treasury Department officials were quoted in the 1990s as saying that for every dollar of US contributions to the World Bank, two dollars come back to US corporations in procurement contracts.[57] Though both these organizations are concerned primarily with the developing world, both are firmly controlled by the governments of the large developed economies and in particular by that of America. Through the medium of their governments, large Western corporations have exerted a powerful influence on the bank's policy and, thus, on the social structure of the communities in which they operate.

The corporate interest is even more effectively represented on the international stage through the WTO, created in 1995 to eliminate barriers to free trade. A key requirement of the WTO agreement is that any national legislation restricting a company from competing in its markets can be challenged. This sounds reasonable enough, but what it has meant in practice is that countries trying to impose health, safety, or environmental standards stricter than the WTO's own 'international' standards, or trying to use trade quotas to advance humanitarian ends, have been prevented from doing so. Thus, whereas one might expect an international agency to set minimum standards of, say, environmental risk, and so to control the actions of corporations, the WTO will effectively set maximum standards and so protect the corporate interest against any communities wishing to limit it. The aim is harmonization, but as in other areas, such as food standards, the committees setting the standards are dominated by corporate interests, so that there is always pressure to harmonize downwards.[58] Meanwhile UNCTAD, which until recently was the one agency that provided a balancing force within the United Nations, taking the part of developing country communities against the large corporations, has shifted its position, joining the other UN agencies in singing the praises of international business, foreign direct investment, and free trade.[59]

## The global financial system

Business corporations were not the only institutions to gain power in the 1980s and 1990s. In the same period there was also a dramatic growth in the size and power of institutional investors such as mutual funds, insurance companies, investment companies, pension funds, and, especially, the institutions that managed and invested these. Financial institutions generally grew massively in both size and influence and for many critics of global capitalism it is they rather than the industrial corporations that are primarily to blame for its ill effects. Thus David Korten, one of the most eloquent and informed of these critics, suggests that[60]

even the world's most powerful corporations have become captives of the forces of a globalized financial system that has delinked the creation of money from the creation of real wealth and rewards extractive over productive investment. The big winners are the corporate raiders who strip sound companies of their assets for short-term gain and the speculators who capitalise on market volatility to extract a private tax from those who are engaged in productive wealth and investment.

We saw earlier that in the nineteenth and early twentieth centuries the world of finance tended to set itself apart from society and out of the public eye. In America this tendency was exacerbated by the insurance scandals of the turn of the century, concerns about the 'money trust' in the 1910s, and the fallout from the Wall Street crash of 1929. The first of these bouts of bad publicity resulted in restrictive legislation on insurance companies, preventing them from holding corporate shares or bonds and consigning them to a relatively passive role in the financial markets. Between the second and third, the commercial banks, whose loans financed the consumer revolution of the 1920s, became increasingly powerful. But in the wake of the crash they, too, were subjected to a raft of regulations, including the Glass–Steagall Act of 1933 that prevented banks from operating in both commercial and investment banking. The financial institutions of other countries were not so curtailed, but nor did they wield exceptional power. The large universal German banks played a strong role in the direction of German industry, but within a well-defined social compact that placed industry itself at the service of society and limited rather than encouraged the entrepreneurial self-interest of business. The French banks were also financially powerful, but were closely allied to government and effectively under state control. In England, where in contrast to America it was finance that was considered socially acceptable and industry not, the City of London pursued a conservative path, devoting itself to the trade in government securities and being left free to set its own rules and regulations. In the genteel world of the City, it was a morally restrained and communal rather than an individual self-interest that ruled.[61]

In the early 1980s all this began to change dramatically, as a combination of new information technologies and free market ideologies led to the removal of restrictions on capital movement and the opening of financial markets to global competition. In America many of the post-crash regulations were swept aside, and although the Glass–Steagall Act was not repealed until the end of the century its provisions were effectively bypassed. The restrictions on insurance companies were also removed. In London the traditional cosy world of investment banking was turned upside down by the arrival of American, German, and Japanese competition. The world's financial centres competed aggressively for business, relaxing their regulations in order to attract it. Using junk bond financing, financial corporate raiders and asset strippers enjoyed a 'market for corporate control' reminiscent of that of eighty years earlier but on a much larger scale. A rapid international consolidation of the banking and financial services sector concentrated power in the hands of a relatively small number of companies.[62]

The financial sector exercised its new powers in various ways—through speculation in the currency markets, through international lending, and through the ownership of corporate stock and speculation in the derivatives markets. In today's deregulated global financial system, both national governments and private financial institutions are important players. But operating globally and unconstrained by either domestic political considerations or any global political or regulatory framework, it is the private institutions that effectively wield the power. It is their speculations that provide the markets with liquidity and set short-term prices, and their decisions that determine the flows of investment capital.

This power of the financial institutions first became visible to the British public in 1992 when currency speculators, lead by George Soros's Quantum Funds, forced the devaluation of the pound against the wishes of the British government. To the great surprise of both politicians and public, the Bank of England, acting on behalf of the government, proved completely powerless to halt the slide in sterling, and succeeded only in losing large amounts of taxpayers' money to the private institutions with which it was trading. The power of these institutions was then confirmed through a series of financial crises affecting developing countries: Mexico in 1994–5, the economies of South-east Asia in 1997, and Russia in 1998. The causes of these crises remain a matter of fierce debate, but one important factor seems to have been the premature exposure of developing economies, in line with IMF requirements, to capital market liberalization and the speculative currency flows that this made possible. Western financial institutions not only dominated this currency speculation, but also acted as key international lenders, setting interest rates and calling in loans. The institutions suffered losses, but they had the power and relative freedom to control those losses and, as Soros has noted, the means by which they did this—hedging currencies, imposing stop-losses on transactions, calling in debt—all served to accentuate rather than ameliorate the crises.[63] These effects were reinforced by the actions of the IMF, which typically required countries to hold exchange rates for long enough for the institutions (and indeed the rich and powerful in the countries concerned) to get their money out.[64]

We shall return later in the book to Soros's observations on the inherent instability of a largely unregulated global financial system, in which the risk management techniques of the most powerful players increase the risks of the system as a whole. For now, it will suffice to mention one further example of the power of the financial institutions, the stock market collapse of 2000–2002, which followed a speculative bubble in technology and Internet stocks in the late 1990s. There was nothing particularly unusual about the stock market movements. Though company shares have a notional 'fundamental' value, based on the company's expected future earnings, day-to-day stock prices are always based on estimates of short-term future changes in those prices and at times of speculative fever the fundamentals get eclipsed. Expectations of higher prices drive up prices, which drive up expectations, which drive up prices, and so on. For a considerable period in the recent bubble the Internet retailer Amazon boasted a share price that, it seemed, could only have been justified on fundamentals if the company had grown to be larger than the entire American economy; but so long as the price kept on rising it remained a 'good buy'.[65] Eventually, the bubble bursts and the reverse process sets in. What was striking about the recent bubble, though it was scarcely remarked upon, was the extent to which the financial institutions, in particular the investment banks, were for a long time relatively unharmed by the collapse. The City of London experienced a sharp drop in graduate recruiting and a few small-scale redundancies, but nothing like the cutbacks that had accompanied previous stock market falls. The reason for this is simple. Crudely put, what was invested in the stock market was other people's money, much of it invested by the institutions as fund managers on behalf of pension funds. As the market fell, so did the management fees, but trading remained active and profitable. The institutions' own money, and that of their richest individual investors, was moved into hedge funds, which made excellent profits—much of them from short-selling the market and thus contributing to its further fall. Meanwhile the pension funds themselves, constrained by their regulations and accountable to their trustees, refrained from such 'risky' investments, while for small individual investors they were simply not available.[66]

## THE FAILURE OF CORPORATE GOVERNANCE

There is a certain irony in the situation we have just described, for at the same time as the institutions were driving share prices down they were also increasingly exercising their power as shareholders. Uniquely among the advanced economies, Britain and America had in the post-war period developed fully funded pension schemes, in which contributions were invested to pay for future pensions rather than used to pay current ones. By the 1980s the largest of these schemes had amassed enormous investments, which were beginning to dominate the equity markets. In America, in the mid-1960s, about 85 per cent of share value on the New York Stock Exchange was held by private investors, just 15 per cent by institutions. By the early 1990s the institutions owned the majority of shares, and by the mid-1990s they were completely dominant. In Britain, the change happened even faster. Because there was a relative profusion of pension funds and other institutional investors, and because they spread their investments relatively widely, corporate shareholdings remained relatively dispersed. However, the largest pension funds could hold a few per cent of a large corporation's shares, far more than any individual and quite enough to ensure that their voice could be heard. The smaller funds put their assets in the hands of professional fund managers, the largest of whom by the end of the century controlled hundreds of billions of dollars of funds, and they too began to flex their financial muscles, insisting that corporate managers focus on the maximization of shareholder value (new measures of which were quickly developed) rather than on their traditional goal of corporate growth. Increasingly, moreover, they did so internationally, outside the British and American markets.[67]

The growth in the power of the institutional investors has generally been discussed in terms of the problem of the separation of ownership and control, as formulated in the 1930s by Berle and Means, and that is certainly how it appeared to the participants in the power play. In America in particular corporate managers responded to the growing power of financial entrepreneurs in the 1980s by using their own considerable power to persuade state legislatures to support anti-takeover measures such as poison pills. In the 1990s institutional investors put pressure in turn upon the corporations to rescind such measures; 'corporate governance' became a public policy issue and beginning in Britain but moving rapidly across the world codes of conduct were developed to protect shareholders from unscrupulous or merely incompetent managers and incorporated into stock market listing requirements.

As recent events at Enron, Worldcom, Marconi, and other large, failed corporations have shown all too vividly, the effects of the corporate governance movement have been limited. Senior managers may, in general, be more accountable (if massively richer) than they were, but good corporate governance practice did not protect Marconi shareholders and employees from disastrously incompetent top management decisions, or Enron employees, shareholders, and pensioners from the cataclysmic effects of the company's fraudulent accounting practices. The focus on the power struggle between finance and business also obscures the fact that in relation to society at large, the power of both groups has been growing rapidly. Despite a lot of talk of 'stakeholders' and 'corporate responsibility', the most significant effect of the battle for corporate control has been the disempowerment of traditional stakeholders such as employees and communities.

We have already noted how small shareholders and the beneficiaries of pension funds have lost out to the large financial institutions. The most visible losers in the corporate governance struggle, however, have been employees. In a few countries, such as Germany, employees have rights of representation that have, until now, protected their role as stakeholders in the corporation. In most countries, however, the dismantling of trades unions and the easing of employment legislation have reduced them to relative powerless onlookers. In the final decades of the twentieth century, under relentless pressure from the shareholding (though not necessarily share-owning) institutions to produce ever-improving economic performance, business corporations in Britain, America, and elsewhere dramatically reduced their headcounts. Manufacturers outsourced their operations or shifted them into low-wage developing countries. Service companies replaced their full-time workers with part-timers, often firing and then re-hiring the same people, but without either the social benefits or the participation rights or union recognition that they had previously enjoyed. They did so, moreover, with impunity, for whatever their differences the combined power of business and finance was enormous. From a traditional emphasis on the control of entrepreneurial self-interest, legislation shifted to its support and encouragement. What was good for business and finance was now seen, almost without qualification, as being good for society.

# Economic Culture and the Legitimacy of Self-interest

Inseparable from the growth of financial and business power in the late twentieth century was a growth in the power and prominence of economic and market ideas. Like other changes with which we shall be concerned, this growth can be traced back to the eighteenth-century Enlightenment, and in particular to the pioneering work of Adam Smith. However, it was only a hundred years after Smith's *Wealth of Nations*, in the second half of the nineteenth century, that economics began to emerge as a separate intellectual discipline, and only in the early twentieth century that it began to take shape as a formal academic discipline with a well-defined conceptual framework. By the middle of the century, economists were beginning to wield serious political influence, but only on a distinct subset of government policy. By the last quarter of the century, the scope of economics as a discipline and the scope of its influence in the political arena were both widening rapidly. In Britain and America in the 1980s and 1990s, almost every aspect of public policy came to be interpreted primarily from an economic perspective. Politics became, in effect, a branch of applied economics. Meanwhile, some of the core concepts and ideas of economics, divorced from the rigorous constraints and conditions under which they were originally developed and applied by economists, had come to enjoy a still wider currency, being employed with sometimes religious fervour.[1]

We shall discuss the nature and extent of this recent dominance of economic thinking shortly. First, though, it will be helpful to enumerate some of the core ideas that make up the economic way of thinking about the world. In doing so we should note that the ways in which these ideas are employed in economic analysis are often a source of contention between economists themselves. There are substantial differences between the underlying assumptions and ideologies of Chicago School economists such as Milton Friedman or Gary Becker or business economists like Oliver Williamson, on one hand, and their institutional or Schumpeterian critics on the other, and to a certain extent the characterization that follows is more typical of the former than of the latter group,[2] but only to a certain extent. Apart from the fact that it is the former group who have been by far the most influential, both within their profession and on wider public perceptions, the elements of the economic mindset described here are, to some extent, common to almost all economic thinking, of whatever school or persuasion.[3]

## THE ECONOMIC MINDSET

### Economic self-interest

A key assumption of most contemporary economic theorizing is the assumption that people act solely to further their own self-interest or, to put it another way, to maximize their own utility. The publicity afforded Adam Smith's brief comment on self-interest, which we discussed in Chapter 2, has led to the impression that this was, from the very beginning, the basis of economics. In fact, as we saw, Smith's conception of self-interest was bound up with notions of moral restraint. In the second half of the nineteenth century Herbert Spencer and the Manchester School of economists sang the praises of self-interest as an emancipating rational principle (and in so doing, incidentally, found a warm welcome on Wall Street), but classical economics assumed only that in simple economic markets, all other things being equal and in the absence of any moral considerations, people would sell for the best price and buy whatever combination of goods maximized their total satisfaction. Its exponents did not suggest that the same considerations would apply outside economic markets, in social and civic relationships, and they did not argue that people would, in practice, absent moral considerations from their calculations—or that they should.

From the point of view of social scientists trying to build predictive models, however, the assumption of economic self-interest proved to be an enormous asset. Taken together with the assumption of rational competence, it meant that if economists could specify people's economic interests they could in theory predict their actions. As the science of economics developed during the twentieth century, the qualifications attached to the self-interest assumption were gradually forgotten, and when in the 1970s economists began to break free from some of the other assumptions that had been forced on them by the need for simplicity—the assumption that information about rival products was free and universally available, for example, or the assumption that market transactions were costless—they found the assumption of self-interest, narrowly defined, to be exceptionally fertile. By the early 1990s the dominant theories of economics were based firmly on the assumption that people in general are not just self-interested, but opportunistically self-serving, that they will do whatever they can get away with (shirking, guile, deceit) to maximize their own interests, regardless of the impact on others.[4] Critics dubbed this model of man *homo economicus* (and not, by implication, *sapiens*) and argued that it was inconsistent with the facts of social and organizational life, but as well as being scientifically fertile it is extraordinarily difficult, if not impossible, to disprove.[5] As we shall discuss below, it also appeals to at least some part of our common sense perceptions. We may not see ourselves or our friends and loved ones as self-interested, but our experiences make it quite easy to believe that 'other people', people we don't know well, *are* self-interested. Economists argue that even if their assumptions are not strictly accurate they are a good enough approximation to cover most situations reasonably well, and that argument has proved to be very persuasive.

## Money as the measure of good

A second common assumption of economics is that we measure our welfare or utility in essentially material terms, without taking account of any moral well-being or psychological satisfaction, such as the satisfaction (and for a religious person the hope of salvation) that might be derived from altruism. More generally, economics assumes that everything that is valuable or good can be measured in monetary terms.

Within the narrowly economic realm of prices, wages, rents, and profits this assumption is perfectly reasonable. From this perspective economics is concerned with what, to quote J. K. Galbraith, 'determines the prices that are paid for goods and for services rendered. And how the proceeds from this economic activity are distributed. And what determines the share going to wages, interest, profits, and, although less distinctly, the rent of land and other fixed and immutable objects used in production'.[6] For these things, money is a natural measure. But economics has always had wider aspirations too. Alfred Marshall, who was one of the most influential economists of the first half of the twentieth century, defined it as 'a study of mankind in the ordinary business of life', and while few economists now would take quite such a broad view, few would restrict themselves to the determination of prices, wages, and so forth. For most of the last century economists have been centrally concerned with national and, increasingly, global policies covering not only such purely 'economic' issues as the management of inflation or exchange rates but a whole range of related social issues: unemployment, taxation, the welfare state, the nationalization and privatization of core services, and the nature and distribution of international aid.

When addressing issues such as these, it is of crucial importance not only what something costs, but also how that cost and the associated benefits are distributed through society: not only how people benefit or suffer materially but also, and critically, how they feel about it psychologically. The economist, however, has no means of addressing this last question. Money is the only measure available, and everything is, therefore, measured in money. Similarly, in the case of legal and contractual relationships such as those of business and management—but also of marriage and community—to which economists have turned their attention in the last thirty years. By assuming that people's welfare can be measured in material terms, and that they will act so as to maximize this welfare, economists have been able to model these relationships in logical and mathematical terms and so bring them within the domain of their discipline. The assumption was adopted for the sake of simplicity, but once adopted it almost inevitably became part of economic dogma. As in the case of self-interest, to challenge the assumption is in effect to challenge the legitimacy of economic analysis.

In the days of the 'Cold War' between the capitalist West and communist East, in the 1950s and 1960s, a lot was made of the materialism of Marxist ideology and its rejection of all religious or spiritual aspirations. This materialism was condemned as a moral outrage, and from the point of view of those who condemned it the charge was justifiable. What few people seemed to notice was that the materialism of Marxist economics was more than matched by that of the home-grown capitalist kind. People did not notice this because they did not want to. At the time, the traditional cultures of the West were still paying lip service to the authority of religion. In the aftermath of the Second World War the non-economic values of freedom, deeply rooted in both European and American cultures, were also to the forefront of people's minds. The idea that American or British economic policies might be based upon the same materialism as those of the Soviet Union was simply unthinkable, even to the economists themselves.[7]

It was only in the 1980s, by when freedom was taken for granted and the war against communism was won, that the economists of the West could admit to their materialist assumptions, and even then they kept their distance from Marxism by expressing them in terms of the monetary value of goods and services rather than in terms of the material goods themselves. Express them they did, though, and it was no accident that that period saw the rise of explicitly monetarist economic policies, based on economic ideas that had first been developed sixty years earlier, but had lain dormant since the Second World War. Accept that all value is measured in monetary terms and it makes sense to place the supply of money at the centre of economic regulation. Of course, the monetarist view did not go unchallenged, any more than did the egoistic morality with which it was often associated. But with it the idea that everything of value can be measured by money, that money is in the end what matters, came out into the open and ceased to be socially taboo.

## Property and possession, agency and control

When people are assumed to be narrowly self-interested and their interest is measured in monetary and material terms, the concepts of property and possession inevitably become important. The analysis of property rights and their legal and moral basis dates back to the early Enlightenment and was an important part of the intellectual context within which the American Constitution was framed.[8] Whereas the leaders of the French Revolution promoted the values of liberty, equality, and fraternity and embodied the latter in a powerful state, their American counterparts settled for liberty and equality with the role of the state minimized and that of individual property rights maximized. It has been said that the greatest freedom of the American people is the right to possess property, and that the second greatest freedom is the right to defend that possession, by force if need be, from anyone seeking to take it away. From this follow the American obsessions with litigation and the law, which provide the institutional framework for the defence of property rights; and with gun ownership, which provides the physical means of achieving the same end.[9] In the late twentieth century, through the influence of American economists, the importance attributed by Americans to property came to be reflected in economic thinking worldwide.

In the last twenty-five years the economics of property rights and the contracts by which they are enforced has become one of the most vibrant areas of economic theory and, in the context of business and management, one of the most influential. But what is property? To most people, the word property refers to something tangible and clearly owned, like a house, a car, or a piece of furniture. But to the economist it refers to anything over which an individual has rights, to which some (inevitably monetary) value can be attached. It includes things that nobody owns, such as fresh water or the air we breathe. It also includes things like a worker's time, and especially that part of it which is not at the worker's discretion. With slavery abolished it is no longer possible in our society for one person to legally own another, but whenever people enter into contracts they generate what economists call property rights.

Suppose, for example, that somebody agrees to do some consulting for a company: three things happen. First, a deal is struck. Second, an obligation is entered into: the person agrees to deliver. Third, a property right is created: the company has a right to having the person's time used in accordance with the agreement. Of these, the modern economist is interested primarily in the third. With respect to the first, he will assume that there is a market for the services sought and offered, and that the price agreed is a product of this market. With respect to the second, he will assume that the consultant is selfish and self-seeking and will try and get away with as little as he can. What interests him, though, is the problem that this generates for the third part of the agreement. The company, having bought, let us say, £30,000 of the consultant's time, has property rights of that value that it wishes to enforce, and the question that arises is: how might it do this?[10]

This problem is known as an agency problem, and from the viewpoint of economics  much of our social and organizational life can be expressed in terms of such problems. How do I control my property rights over a gardener or plumber? How does the university for which I teach control its property rights over me? If I share the teaching on a programme, how do I ensure that my colleague carries her full weight? If I take out insurance on a valuable object, how does the insurance company ensure that I am as careful with it as I would be otherwise? If I pay for music lessons for my children, how do I ensure that the teacher teaches, and that the children put in the practice time to make the lessons worth (my) while?

Agency theory takes situations that have traditionally been described in terms of moral obligations and recasts them in terms of economic property rights, specifically the right to a fair return on monetary expenditure. It stresses the importance of property and possession and it reinforces the view that people are selfish and deceitful and that money is what matters. If I pay for your time, if I am the one spending the money, it is my welfare and mine alone that matters: yours does not count.

## The magic of markets

We have so far identified three characteristic features of the economic mindset: the assumption that human beings are motivated by self-interest; the assumption that everything of value can be measured in monetary terms; and an emphasis on property and possession, leading to a view of life as an agency problem. A fourth feature, which has become increasingly influential, is a belief in the magical power of markets.

Like the assumption of self-interest this can be traced back to Adam Smith, only this time legitimately so. Writing at the beginning of the Industrial Revolution, when the abuse of mercantilist power was evident but large scale industrial organization had not yet emerged, Smith suggested that free trade and free markets, by coordinating the inputs of specialist craftsmen, would increase the efficiency of the manufacturing process. It was also through the 'invisible hand' of the market that society's needs were matched with the interests of suppliers: butchers, brewers, and bakers, to take his famous example, did not supply us with meat, beer, and bread out of pure kindness of heart but because there was a market for these products.

The theory of markets, and especially of the price mechanism, remained the main focus of economic theory right up until the middle of the twentieth century and still forms the core of what is taught to economics students today. For simplicity, it makes some fairly massive assumptions: that the market is characterized by complete (and free) information; that market transactions are cost-free; and that the goods traded can be described completely in terms of price and quantity, with no variations in quality. The market, in other words, is like those for commodities or foreign exchange, where a barrel of Brent crude is a barrel of Brent crude and a euro is a euro, regardless of whom you buy it from. It is not like the markets for software, legal advice, motorcars, or industrial machinery, where competing products vary in quality and specification—but because the realities of those markets are difficult to model it is used to describe them anyway.

As in the case of human motivation, economists use these assumptions primarily because they allow them to develop theory and make predictions, rather than because they are well-founded in reality. But here again, this has implications. If the world were really as assumed by neoclassical economics, markets really would be magical, because there would be no need for firms or business organizations. All transactions, of every kind, could be carried out in the market place, at no cost and to optimal effect.

In the two centuries following the publication of *The Wealth of Nations*, large firms came to dominate the economies of the developed world, but economists persisted with a core model in which there was no room for such firms. Only in the 1930s did economists such as Ronald Coase and Joseph Schumpeter begin to develop economic theories of the firm and of entrepreneurship, and only in the 1970s did this work begin to have any real influence.[11] Throughout the period in which the bureaucratic business organization was most dominant as the source of economic growth, and in which free market mechanisms were most severely curtailed, economics was effectively restricted to the economics of markets. Then, when economists did eventually come to analyse what should be conducted through business organizations and what through the market, the assumption of self-interest ensured that the idealized market remained the optimal state of the affairs, the organization a second best substitute for when ideal markets could not be achieved. It would, after all, be irrational to risk building an organization around people you assumed to be irredeemably self-seeking: far better to deal with them at arm's length, through the mechanism of the market.[12]

## The priority of the present

A final characteristic of economic thinking that should be mentioned in this context is its focus on the present or, at least, on the very short term. This is not a universal characteristic, for there are economists who concern themselves with the evolution of markets and economic systems. It is also in large measure accidental. Like the emphasis on rational behaviour, monetary value, and perfect markets, it comes about largely because of the technical difficulties of modelling anything more complex; but unlike those emphases it has not acquired any ideological status. Neoclassical economics concerned itself with steady-state equilibrium because that was what it could model, and modern transaction cost economics seeks to maximize short-term efficiency because that, too, is all it can model.

Whatever its origins, however, this focus on the present has important implications, for it reinforces the bias against hierarchical organization and in favour of the market. If all businesses were concerned about was turning a short-term profit, it is unlikely that they would have developed the large and complex organizations that they have. What such organizations do, and what role-structured cultures in general do par excellence, is coordinate activities over time, maintaining stability while building for the future. Markets, on the other hand, are most efficient for the short-term distribution of goods and services to those who want them now.

The short-termism of economic thinking also accentuates some of its other characteristics. The agency problems of opportunistic self-seeking, for example, are more severe when the principal and agent have only the short term to worry about. Take a longer-term view and the agent has to consider her long-term reputation as well as her more immediate interests, while the principal has to consider the benefits of trust and an established working relationship. It is also easier to place a monetary value on short-term than on long-term effects, and on instant transactions than on enduring relationships. Given a trade-off between easily measurable present benefits and uncertain future costs, economic thinking will always give much greater weight to the present than did the role-structured thinking of our traditional culture, which fought wars and made investments for its children's children and gave weight, in the extreme, to the infinitely long-term effects of heaven and hell.

## ECONOMICS AND POPULAR THINKING

Until relatively recently, the influence of economics and the economic ideas we have been discussing on public policy and popular thinking was fairly modest. Public policy debate was conducted in essentially moral terms. Following a tradition that can be traced back to Aristotle, politics was seen as applied ethics, and political arguments were about what was morally right or wrong; or, more instrumentally, about how best to achieve the common good. Economics only came to the fore as something more than an academic pursuit in the wake of the great depression of the 1930s, and even then it was slow to respond—mainly because in the economic theory of that time such things as depressions could not occur. As we have noted, economic theory needs simplifying assumptions, and one of the assumptions on which it had been based up until then was that of full-employment equilibrium. The depression was, however, quite clearly an economic problem, and because of its length, severity and sheer unexpectedness, after the century-long growth of the industrial revolution, it dominated public debate as nothing else had, apart from war. In due course, and in particular through the work of John Maynard Keynes, economics responded, and quickly claimed a place toward the top of the political agenda.

After the Second World War, the political influence of economists and economic ideas grew steadily. In mid-1960s Britain, there were about forty-five professional economists in government service, more than half of whom were in the Ministry of Agriculture. Ten years later there were over 350. By the 1980s professional economists completely dominated both policy formation and public policy debate in both Britain and the United States. In Britain today, we have active policy debates about social security provisions and the health service, education and the arts, but the arguments are framed almost entirely by economists. Fifty years ago, even thirty years ago, debates of this kind were conducted by philosophers and historians, doctors and teachers, writers and artists. But now such authorities are at best on the fringes of the debate.[13] Moreover, though some countries have been slower to come round to the new way of thinking than others, this observation can also be applied to most of the developed and developing world. Whether the economic analysis is carried out within a country's own policy-making process, or imposed from outside by the IMF, it is the principal, and uniquely authoritative, input to the overwhelming majority of political decision making.

In some ways this influence is even deeper than at first appears, for the very terms 'developed', 'developing', and 'underdeveloped' are essentially economic constructs. The concept of underdevelopment, in its contemporary usage, can be traced to President Truman's inaugural address of 1949, when he outlined a global programme for economic growth and development. Over the ensuing decades, classifications of the world's nations in terms of their cultures and geography gave way to a dominant classification based on economic statistics. The great majority of the world's people gradually lost hold of their previous cultural identities and were recreated as the underdeveloped, failed versions of the economically wealthy.[14] Even the concept of sustainable development, with its implied emphasis on environmental protection, retains this economic influence. Within the discourses of sustainable development the overriding emphasis is not in fact on sustaining natural resources, cultures, or communities, but on managing those resources to sustain economic growth.[15] (Much of the time, indeed, it is on managing the resources of the developing countries to sustain the economic growth of the developed.) Environmentalists may campaign against economic culture, but their very choice of labels already implies significant concessions. Classified as 'environment', nature is already made subservient to man, a resource to be exploited rather than conserved.[16]

The influence of economic ideas can also be seen much more directly, in the dominance of public discourse by a set of connected propositions drawn straight from the repertoire of economic ideas discussed above: (1) Free markets are economically most efficient; (2) Whatever is economically most efficient is best; (3) [Therefore] free markets are inherently good; (4) Free markets depend on self-interest; (5) [Therefore] self-interest is not only normal but also positively good.

The last of these propositions remains controversial. In the early 1960s, in a work somewhat ahead of its time, Milton Friedman, who was to become the economic guru of the Thatcher and Reagan governments of the 1980s, argued that any departure from self-interest in the economic sphere could only lead to market inefficiencies.[17] This provided the legitimacy for the financial entrepreneurs of the 1980s, such as Ivan Boesky, Michael Milliken, and Dennis Levine, to declare, as Boesky did when addressing a graduating class of MBAs in 1986, that 'Greed is healthy. You can be greedy and still feel good about yourself.'[18] The greed of these entrepreneurs eventually took them beyond the realm of what was legal, and though heroes of Wall Street they came to be seen by the public as the quite unacceptable face of capitalism. Society at large was not yet ready to see greed as a virtue. By the late 1990s, however, the idea that greed is good was winning mainstream support. Jonathan Hoenig's 1999 book, *Greed is Good*,[19] earned him the title of 'Voice of finance for Generation X' from *Forbes* magazine, and in a CBS documentary the following year the great and good of American industry (business entrepreneurs, not financiers) lined up to explain how greed was indeed good. In a free market greed drove entrepreneurship which created wealth, the benefits of which would trickle down to society at large.[20]

While the legitimacy of the more extreme forms of self-interest has grown only gradually, the efficiency benefits of free markets and the identification of what is most desirable with what is most efficient (or, more generally, of what is best with what has the greatest economic value) were quickly and almost universally accepted. In Britain and across the world, governments of all political persuasions set about breaking up the tightly regulated economic systems that had characterized the 1950s and 1960s, privatizing state-owned industries and services, deregulating those that were already in the private sector, and systematically replacing (and encouraging firms to replace) long-term relationships with short-term contracts. In health and education policy, traditional service goals increasingly took second place to efficiency goals. In general, as Edward Luttwak has observed, the traditional practice by which economic policies were used to achieve social ends was replaced with one in which social policies became subservient to economic ends.[21] In Alan Wolfe's phraseology, a capitalist economy, operating within a moral society was replaced by a capitalist society.[22]

In America, and to a lesser extent in Britain, economic ideas were also deployed to argue the case for lower taxes and lower government spending on welfare and education. Alongside the traditional moral argument against welfare, that it harmed its recipients by making them dependent on others, it could now be argued by those of comfortable means that redistributive taxes introduced market inefficiencies and so reduced the wealth of society as whole.[23] In populist American thinking, the free market ideal even became identified with that of democracy itself as proponents of regulation or control, from judges to environmentalists, were branded as privileged elitists and would-be dictators, out of touch with the common people and hell-bent on curtailing their democratic rights.[24] Most people would not go so far, but at the turn of the twenty-first century belief in free markets as a source and embodiment of what is good is both firm and widespread. In some sense, as Harvey Cox has observed, the market has taken over from God.[25]

If the market is the new God (and while the analogy is too extreme it makes a serious point) then money is the new Holy Spirit. In earlier times the ventures of Boesky and Levine would have been described as 'lucrative', meaning that they were morally tainted by the purely pecuniary greed that motivated them ('lucre' has traditionally been 'filthy'). Today, the word has lost its pejorative connotations and making money has become a laudable aim, regardless of what motivates it or what the money is to be used for. Asked about their life objectives in the 1960s, around 40 per cent of UCLA freshmen classed 'being very well off financially' as essential or very important. This proportion rose steadily over the next twenty years, reaching 75 per cent by the late 1980s and staying there through the 1990s. Similarly, in American national polls the proportion of people listing 'lots of money' as one of the elements of a good life rose from 38 per cent in 1975 to 63 per cent in 1996.[26]

This attitude reflects the economic idea of money as a measure of good. It also reflects the practical fact that in a world in which ethical and aesthetic values are increasingly contested and uncertain, money is often the only value measure on which there is consensus. We shall look more closely at moral values in Chapter 5, but the general point can be simply made in the context of aesthetics and modern art. Each year, in Britain, the award of the Turner Prize reopens the debate on what is art. Can a pile of bricks, an unmade bed, or a light switch going on and off be compared with the sculptures of Michelangelo or the paintings of Cézanne? Is there such a thing as objective beauty? Does a work of art have any intrinsic value? Contemporary postmodern philosophers argue that all supposedly 'objective' values are simply cultural products, and that in today's multicultural society one person's judgements are as valid as another's: in short, anything goes. But as one of these philosophers, Jean-François Lyotard, has observed,[27]

Eclecticism is the degree zero of contemporary general culture: one listens to reggae, watches a western, eats McDonald's food for lunch and local cuisine for dinner, wears Paris perfume in Tokyo and 'retro' clothes in Hong Kong; knowledge is a matter for TV games. It is easy to find a public for eclectic works. By becoming kitsch, art panders to the confusion which reigns in the 'taste' of the patrons. Artists, gallery owners, critics, and the public wallow together in 'anything goes,' and the epoch is one of slackening. But this realism of the 'anything goes' is in fact that of money; in the absence of aesthetic criteria, it remains possible and useful to assess the value of works of art according to the profits they yield.

If people from different cultures disagree about the aesthetic value of a work of art, they will, nevertheless, be able to agree about its monetary value, because in a free market that is quite objective: it is whatever the highest bidder will pay. In much the same way, moral values too can be reduced to an objective monetary value. In a free market society, the price people are prepared to pay for a product or the terms under which they are prepared to contract, as suppliers of labour or services, with an entrepreneur, should reflect their moral evaluation. In contemporary society, moral values are increasingly reflected in monetary measures, in the form of taxes or fines, and the differing values of different societies are reflected in their different fiscal structures. In politics everything, morality included, has its price.

If politics now follows economics in treating money as the measure of all value, at the individual level money is even more dominant. Economists may measure everything in monetary terms, but they recognize that the value of money is ultimately an exchange value, and not an intrinsic value. Intrinsic value, from an economic viewpoint, comes not from a big bank balance but from the satisfaction of preferences through the consumption of goods and services. There can be little doubt, however, that many people today are motivated simply by money, without any particular idea as to how they will spend it. This is partly a consequence of affluence. People who are hungry or homeless have an obvious reason for earning money, but once spending becomes discretionary the thought process gets split into two: how to earn money, and how to spend it. It is also a consequence of uncertainty. As traditional cultural values and expectations have been questioned, many people have been left not knowing what they want from life. Money, for these people, is an intermediate goal, but one that many of them never get beyond. The same uncertainties, which we shall explore further in Chapter 5, have also left people increasingly reluctant to judge the motives or actions of others, with the result that the stigma traditionally attached to making money for money's sake has largely disappeared.

Finally, many people are now economic actors in a way that as traditional employees they were not. They are either self-employed or working on fixed term contracts, within an economic environment that is dominated by business and financial companies for which money, in the form of profits, is quite clearly the primary objective. To compete and survive in this environment they have little choice but to engage with the monetary values of these companies.

## ECONOMIC IDEAS IN BUSINESS: THE FLEXIBLE ECONOMY AND ITS RULES

Listed companies, as opposed to partnerships or family firms, have always been dominated by the profit motive, but their character has also changed in the last quarter century as the economic mindset that has so influenced our political and public discourse has informed a profound transformation of the way in which businesses are organized and managed. Well into the 1980s the characteristic form of business organization was the large multidivisional hierarchy or bureaucracy. As we noted earlier, the business bureaucracy had evolved in response to the opportunities created by technological developments in transportation, communications, and mass production in the nineteenth century. As it developed it acquired the moral characteristics of the hierarchical culture of the societies in which it was located and, with these, the self-reinforcing characteristics of a cultural system.[28] The multidivisional form of hierarchy had then evolved between the two world wars, in response to the business opportunities created by changing population and income levels and further waves of technological innovation.[29] Just as technological innovation created and sustained the business hierarchy, however, it also threatened its existence. In the 1970s advances in information technology began to erode the economies of scale experienced by the large firms and open up the competitive environment to entrepreneurial newcomers. With increasingly rapid and voluminous communications, competitive cycles shortened dramatically and the proprietary knowledge bases of the established firms, built up over many years of substantial investment, were duplicated rapidly by leaner, more agile, and more innovative rivals.

As we noted when discussing hierarchical societies in Chapter 2, all forms of hierarchical organization, based as they are on very detailed and specific classification systems, are inherently resistant to change. Their natural tendency is to respond to threats by reasserting control and strengthening the authority structure,[30] and the first response of businesses to the new competitive threats was to try and build the linkages needed for rapid and successful innovation into the hierarchical structure through the adoption of increasingly complex and sophisticated matrix organizations. As Tom Peters and Richard Waterman pointed out in their best-selling book *In Search of Excellence*, however, the formal matrix structure was precisely the wrong way to encourage innovation.[31] Far from strengthening and elaborating the grid classification, what was needed was a loosening of grid, to create the space in which innovation could flourish.

The picture Peters and Waterman painted of the innovative organization, with its skunk works and intrapreneurs, its ambiguity and informality, its relaxation of social controls on appearance and behaviour, and its toleration of failure, was revolutionary. It contained everything that, on anthropologist Mary Douglas's account, a hierarchical collectivity most fears.[32] That it was arguably the most influential book on business ever published seems to have rested on two factors. One was the evocation of market rhetoric, at a time when the ideology of free markets was just beginning to take hold and the profitability of the firm, which had traditionally been taken for granted, was emerging as a real concern. The other was the offer of something to replace the control that would be lost by a weakening of detailed grid classifications, in the form of a corporate culture that was at once innovating and constraining. On one hand, they suggested, a strong corporate culture could support and encourage innovation and risk-taking. On the other hand, it could compensate for the loss of bureaucratic control (i.e. in the language of cultural theory, of detailed grid classification) by reinforcing the organization's underlying shared values (strengthening the core aspects of the grid and using these as a basis for group control). With group allegiance secured and a strengthened grid foundation, individual freedom need no longer be perceived as a threat.

The idea of a corporate culture combining innovation and control proved to be a seductive but elusive chimera. Many large bureaucratic companies tried to follow the Peters and Waterman recipe, but most failed to bring about the changes they needed.[33] By the late 1980s and early 1990s, with competitive pressures still mounting and increasingly powerful shareholders making increasing demands on profitability, more drastic measures were needed. Firms turned to the remedies offered by pure market thinking: cut costs, improve efficiency, replace long-term relationships with short-term contracts, and use self-interest, rather than group interest, as the primary motivation.

The young firms that had stirred up the competitive market place were already organized around market principles. Instead of seeking economies of scale and scope by doing everything in-house, they minimized overheads and maximized flexibility by operating networks of subcontractors, keeping in-house only a few core activities. Instead of employing people for the long term, with planned careers, extensive training, and rewards for loyalty, they employed them on fixed-term contracts, for specific projects, with rewards linked to economic performance. When new positions were created or old ones vacated they were filled by competition rather than by planned succession. Instead of organizing around fixed roles and fine-grained hierarchies, they organized around flexible project teams. To try and compete, the older firms adopted the same principles. Costly manufacturing plants were closed down, often with large-scale redundancies, and the manufacturing outsourced from low labour-cost suppliers in developing countries. Other activities no longer seen as core to the business, from accounting to personnel and from canteens to information systems, were also outsourced. Even in service organizations, massive redundancies became commonplace. In many cases staff who had been employed on a secure contract with generous benefits were made redundant, only to be re-hired on short-term, sometimes part-time contracts, and with much more limited benefits. Many managers were also made redundant, as management structures were de-layered, vacancies opened to competition, and vertical reporting relationships supplemented by networks and teams.

These changes were both substantial and profound. Contemporary businesses are not only organized in different ways from their predecessors, they also use a whole different language, emphasizing certain qualities and de-emphasizing others, so that the very notion of what it is to be a manager is changed. Thus, the sociologist Paul du Gay writes of a wholesale transition from a bureaucratic culture to 'an "enterprise culture" ... in which certain enterprising qualities—such as self-reliance, personal responsibility, boldness and a willingness to take risks in the pursuit of goals—are regarded as human virtues and promoted as such'.[34] Even if people do not overtly subscribe to the values of this culture, he suggests, the structuring of contemporary organizations and the discursive contexts in which these structures are set lead inevitably to them acting out the values in their work.

In some respects, du Gay's characterization is almost certainly too extreme. Bureaucracy and enterprise are not polar opposites, and the changes that have taken place do not represent a complete rejection of bureaucracy. Although they make extensive use of market mechanisms to reward their staff and put together projects and ventures, contemporary business organizations remain basically hierarchical, with a strong residue of bureaucratic procedures, a clear chain of command, and well-structured, if much more flexible, roles and responsibilities. As organizations they still look much more like hierarchies than like markets.[35] But in important respects they have broken radically from traditional hierarchical values. The cultural values of hierarchy are not consistent, for example, with the rejection of members of the collectivity, even those at the bottom of the pile, and they are certainly not consistent with the rejection of those in the responsible, middle ranks of the hierarchy, who are the guardians of its classification structures.

The use of performance-related pay also signifies a significant departure from traditional values. In the bureaucratic organizations of the mid-twentieth century, performance-related pay was used only for sales staff and, in some cases, factory workers, and it signified that in some sense these groups were not fully a part of the hierarchy. Salesmen, typically, were on probation, learning the product and the market and demonstrating their abilities and commitment before moving on, if successful, to salaried jobs. For a variety of reasons, factory workers were not always to be trusted. They were members of the collectivity, but not full citizens in the way that salaried members of staff were. For salaried employees the assumption was that if they were not giving their all, it was for a good reason, deserving of sympathy rather than punishment. A steady salary was recognition of a commitment to the organization. Today, the widespread use of performance-related pay suggests that no one is to be fully trusted. The company may be structured as a hierarchy, but it is no longer a moral community, in which loyalty and commitment can be assumed.

In a similar way, the secure employment of the traditional bureaucracy also represented a moral compact. When people agreed to work in the management of a corporation, it was not merely a market exchange of money for effort but a commitment on the part of the manager to the organization—a commitment that would affect his whole life. The manager committed to doing whatever jobs were asked of him, to living wherever he was posted, and to building his marriage and the upbringing of his children around these commitments. For the corporation, the power it had over the manager's life gave it responsibilities—to provide secure employment, and help in times of sickness and need. With short-term contracts there is no such moral bond: No moral commitment and no recognition of the traditional moral obligations of power.

The new business organizations also come close to breaking one of the fundamental principles of hierarchical legitimation, namely that those at the top of the hierarchy must be seen to be the servants of the community as a whole.[36] This equation of leadership with service has on the whole survived within the hierarchical structures of society at large. It is what we still expect of our political leaders, for example. It is also a prominent feature of the corporate hierarchies of Germany, Scandinavia, and Japan, and was long implicit in those of America and Britain. So long as profitability was not seriously at risk and redundancy was not an issue, the top managers of large corporations were seen by their employees as servants of the corporation. Even where they were also the owners, the model of ownership was the paternalistic one of the caring and responsible parent. With financial difficulties and the emergence of a market for corporate control within the 1980s political ideology of popular market capitalism, all this changed dramatically. Top management now professed public allegiance to their shareholders rather than to their corporate communities, and were increasingly remunerated according to the rules of the market rather than those of a hierarchical culture. As this trend continued through the downsizing of the 1990s, the credibility of top management as the servant-stewards of hierarchical collectivities was strained to breaking point and the integrity of the corporate hierarchy as a cultural system was seriously challenged.

## ECONOMIC THINKING IN POLITICS AND THE PUBLIC SECTOR

### The flexible economy and the public sector

When we talk about the flexible economy we think mainly of private sector businesses, but the application of economic ideas and market values has not been confined to the private sector. Indeed much of the late twentieth-century enthusiasm for replacing organizational with market-based structures and incentives seems to have been stimulated by the introduction of such changes in the public sector.

Although a relatively recent creation, the public sector bore until the 1980s all the hallmarks of our traditional role-structured culture. Public sector organizations were bureaucratically structured and removed from the marketplace. They were not motivated by profit, but by public service. The public they served were not conceived of as customers, or even clients, but as citizens and subjects to whom they were tied by all the rights and obligations of shared community membership. In the 1980s, and especially in the Britain of Margaret Thatcher and the America of Ronald Reagan, all this changed. Influential economists condemned bureaucracies as inefficient and sang the praises of competition and open markets. Governments sympathetic to business, open to economic ideas, and keen to encourage individual initiative and entrepreneurship by cutting taxation, moved rapidly to bring market discipline and its promised efficiency savings to public sector operations. Where possible the services were privatized. Where that was not feasible they were exposed to economic forces, either through the deregulation of competition or through the introduction of internal markets.

In the last twenty years, what started in America and then Britain has spread rapidly to the rest of the world. What started as a policy of the political right has been taken up by governments of all political hues. In Britain the providers of water, electricity, and gas, of rail and bus services, of telecommunications and even of some prisons have all been privatized. The post office has been exposed to competition. The health service has been split up into small-scale units, competing through an internal market. The administration of social security benefits and other services has been farmed out to agencies. All this has undoubtedly increased efficiency, as it was intended to. The old bureaucracies carried a lot of slack, and the ethos of public service favoured expenditure over cost control. But the application of flexible economy rules to the public sector has also undermined key aspects of our traditional hierarchical culture. As Henry Mintzberg has observed, parodying the economist Milton Friedman, 'When the enterprises are free the people are not.'[37] In a role-structured culture, the needs of the society come first and public servants give, as members of that society, what they expect to receive. All citizens share the same rights and obligations. They are in it together, for better or worse. In a market culture, on the other hand, you get what you pay for, and while you may benefit as a customer from the efficiencies of the privatized firms and market-oriented agencies, you can no longer rely on their obligation. Nor can they give it, for however much they may still be motivated by ideals of public service they are accountable for performance and required to behave as economic entrepreneurs.[38]

## Citizenship and consumption in public life

These changes in the conception of the public sector are reflected in political life more generally. Representative politics is one arena of life in which moral obligation and self-interest have always sat, rather uneasily, side by side. The theory of democratic politics is that the candidates for election openly declare the values by which they will be guided and the electorate choose from these, but it has never been that simple. The political party is built on values, which are almost always derived from the values of traditional morality: freedom, equality, solidarity, justice, fairness, and the virtues of moral restraint. However, the particular choice and expression of values varies from party to party and is closely bound up with interests—the interests of a particular social class, a particular generation, a particular ethnic group, and so on. Moreover, the very process of representative politics places the parties in the position of competitors in a political marketplace, advancing their own interests and pitching their campaigns so as to appeal to the interests of their potential customers, sectors of the electorate. As the sociologist Pierre Bourdieu expresses it,[39]

[T]he political field is the site in which, through the competition between the agents involved in it, political products, issues, programmes, analyses, commentaries, concepts and events are created—products between which ordinary citizens, reduced to the status of 'consumers', have to choose, . . .

This aspect of the political process would seem to be intrinsic to representative democracy, and essentially no different now from how it has been for a long time. Aided by the tools and techniques of opinion polls, media presentation, and focus groups, the marketing process is both more sophisticated and more visible than it used to be, but the relationship between values and interests remains much the same. However, the discourse of politics—what Bourdieu describes as the political products on offer—does appear to have changed. Over the last twenty years, political rhetoric has increasingly cast the citizen in the role of consumer, replacing the notion of citizenship rights, with their traditional moral basis, by that of consumer rights, the basis of which is implicitly contractual and rooted in the legitimate self-interest of the citizen as contracting consumer. The change is not total. In foreign policy and law and order contexts, for example, the imagery of citizenship is still routinely evoked. But in the more discretionary, and so more controversial, areas of domestic policy, the imagery of consumption now dominates.

Good examples of this can be found in the political discourses of education and health care. In education a discourse based on the needs of the child, the obligations of a civilized society, and (secondarily) the costs and benefits to society at large has given way to one based on the wishes of the parent and the cost to the taxpayer. The earlier discourse focused on the citizen: the child being educated, the member of the body politic. The current discourse focuses on the consumer: the parent choosing the child's school, as the consumer, in a market sense, of the education provided, and the parent and taxpayer as consumers of political products. Similarly in health care, the focus of discourse has shifted from the responsibility of society for the patient as citizen to the interests of patient as consumer. And again, the 'consumer', though ostensibly a consumer of medical services, must also be seen alongside the taxpayer as a consumer of political products—in short, as a voter.

This political transformation of citizen into consumer has several dimensions, all of which can be related to the growth of market culture. It can, for example, be seen as a reflection of the introduction of market ideas into the public sector, a development that was itself partly a political response to the growing prevalence of economic ideas and partly a pragmatic response to the problem of rising costs and declining service in burgeoning public sector bureaucracies. It can also be seen as a direct reflection of the growing legitimacy of self-interest. While in some areas appeals to voters' self-interest still have to be hidden behind some kind of traditional moral language (policy on immigration and asylum seekers, where the prescriptions of traditional morality seem to run directly against voters' perceived self-interest, would be one such example), in other, less emotive areas those appeals can now be made more directly. It might also be related to a growing political apathy. If, as Noreena Hertz has suggested, people no longer feel like citizens, if they no longer feel engaged in a political process that impacts less heavily on their lives than the actions of multinational businesses, it makes little sense for the politicians to treat them as such.[40]

However we may explain the consumerization of political discourse, one thing is clear. It is not something for which people have explicitly asked or expressed a preference. As Bourdieu notes, political products are the creation of political professionals. In the oligopolistic marketplace of politics, ordinary people generally have little choice but to select from what they are given by the established parties, and if the parties concur in a certain problematic, in this case one based on the citizen as consumer, people have in practice to go along with it.[41] We are cast as consumers whether we like it or not.

This inevitably has implications for the way we live our lives. Citizenship implies a rich web of rights and privileges, duties and obligations. In particular, it implies membership of a community of fellow citizens, an obligation to con-tribute to that community and a guarantee of the privileges and protections that membership affords. Consumption, in contrast, is by nature a solitary state characterized by caveat emptor and contractually limited rights, on one hand, and by the freedom to walk away on the other. Each in itself is balanced, but in the politics of contemporary society this balance gets lost as politicians inevitably stress whichever aspect seems more attractive in any particular circumstances, downplaying the obligations of citizenship and glossing over the limitations of consumer culture. The overall effect is to create an illusion of a world in which people's naive self-interest can be satisfied without imposing any risks on themselves (the risk, for example, of choosing an inappropriate education or medical treatment—the customer is always right) or any costs on anybody else. It is an illusion of a competitive market culture in which there are no losers.

## ECONOMICS, SELF-INTEREST, AND COMMON SENSE

In this chapter we have defined the mindset characteristic of contemporary business and politics as 'economic' and linked it explicitly to a market culture. It is in the science of economics and the operation of economic markets that the ideas we have been discussing find their purest expression, and it is primarily through the advocacy of economists that they have entered into public and political discourse. It would be a mistake, however, to associate the ideas too closely with one particular science or one particular professional grouping. In the first place, as we have already noted, not all economists are of one mind. Numerous economists have in fact attempted to limit the application of and even, albeit less successfully, to break out altogether from what has been described here as the economic mindset. In the second place, the kind of thinking described here is by no means limited to economics, or even to those social sciences (most notably political science) that have been strongly influenced by the economic paradigm.

Indeed the sociologist Ralph Fevre has suggested that the rise of economic thinking is only a particular, technical manifestation of a much more general growth of what he calls 'common sense' reasoning.[42] This terminology seems at first to be confusing, as for many people the one thing economics, with its nar-row and artificial assumptions, does not correspond to is common sense. Common sense, it may be argued, suggests that people are not pure egoists, that money is not everything, and that the long term does matter. But as we have already noted in the context of self-interest, these assumptions do corres-pond to some sort of common sense about how 'other' people behave. *We* may be morally responsible, but *other* people, according to office gossip or the tabloid press, are all too often selfish.

In Fevre's definition, common sense is a form of sense-making that 'requires that we rely solely on reason, that we act towards others only on the basis of what we know and never on the basis of what we take on trust or that which requires an act of faith'.[43] Here, 'what we know' refers primarily to what we know '*about people*, about their thoughts and behavior',[44] and it refers both to what we *all* know (or know in *common*), and to what we know through the experience of our *senses*—what we see (directly or through television), what we hear (directly or through gossip), and what we read in the papers.

Common sense knowledge, then, is what people 'know' from the evidence of their combined senses. In small communities it is the product of gossip: that innkeepers water their ale; that market scales are biased; that the local councillors takes bribes; that respectable spinsters have illicit affairs. Whether any of these things are true or not, they are common knowledge. They also have *enough* truth in them, typically, to be worth knowing. In contemporary society, common sense knowledge is more a product of the media, of journalism, of supposedly true-to-life soap operas, and of surveys and opinion polls of one kind or another. Again, these may not be entirely reliable sources of information, but they convey a working view of the world that people can share and on the basis of which they can order their lives, without having to think too hard about it, and without having to resort to their feelings or emotions. Indeed common sense reasoning has no place for feelings or emotional non-sense, and no place for belief, whether religious or humanistic.

As Fevre stresses, common sense rationality is absolutely essential to daily life, and always has been. It is the necessary basis of everything from shopping to politics, and of administration of all kinds—of all those areas of life in which emotions and trust are dangerous or inappropriate. In contemporary society, however, it has also come to dominate areas, such as interpersonal relationships, in which emotions should perhaps more properly reign. We have become so used to applying common sense to everything around us that we have lost access to the world of inner feelings, of emotion, belief, and morality. The Croatian philosopher and social theorist Stjepan Meštrović, who focuses on the tyranny of reason and its relation to barbarism, captures something of this when he writes provocatively of a 'post-emotional society'.[45] But Fevre himself is more matter-of-fact. Discussing everyday human relationships, he writes of lives filled with common sense and so emptied out of morality.

The history of common sense reasoning is complex, but its rise is evidently bound up with the rise of science, even though they are not the same. The Scientific Renaissance and Revolution rested not only on the rediscovery of mathematical reason, but also on the insistence upon the evidence of the senses—and in particular on the common sharing of such evidence—as against that of scriptural authority. The witnessing of experiments or observations was crucial.[46] As science, and especially the popular knowledge of science, have advanced, so common sense has advanced with it and has in the process changed its allegiances. In the Middle Ages, for example, common sense incorporated a common awareness of the existence of miracles and of the truth of Christian dogma. With the development of scientific awareness, miracles came gradually to be attributed to natural causes and human gullibility, and Christianity came gradually to be a matter of personal belief rather than of common sense. In the twentieth century the sciences of psychology and sociology, with their emphasis on abnormal or deviant behaviours, also conditioned common sense, as what was scientifically deviant, being what was popularly reported, became the basis of a common sense view of normality. Technology is also implicated, as the advancing technologies of communication and mass media have made it possible to discover an ever-wider common sense on ever more aspects of life.

This last process is epitomised by the opinion poll, and Fevre illustrates his argument with an analysis of the American response to President Bill Clinton's sexual engagement with White House intern Monica Lewinsky. When the story broke in January 1998, only 28 per cent of Americans thought that it was true (and, consequently, that the President had lied under oath), but 67 per cent said that if it were true, Clinton should resign, and 55 per cent that if it were true and he did not resign he should be impeached. Over the ensuing months two things happened. The proportion of people who thought Clinton was lying grew steadily (reaching 68 per cent in August), and at the same time the proportion who thought he should resign or be impeached fell steadily (to 40 and 33 per cent, respectively). This story can be interpreted in several ways. It can be seen, for example, as illustrating a contemporary reluctance (which we shall explore in Chapter 5) to make moral judgements on others. When Americans' thought Clinton was innocent they were happy to make a (purely theoretical) moral judgement, but the more evident it became that he was guilty the more reluctant they were to impose their moral values. It can also be seen, as it is by Fevre, as a process of common-sense-making, for as the polls fed back regular reports on what the consensus view was, they also reported the extent to which peoples' responses were tied to their political affiliations. As the story unfolded, it became apparent that while Republicans were somewhat more likely than Democrats to think Clinton should resign or be impeached, they were much more likely than Democrats to believe he was guilty in the first place. And as people witnessed each other making political rather than strictly moral responses, so they seem to have shifted their own views from the moral to the 'common-sensical'. By the November elections, the American public was taking an entirely pragmatic common sense view of the whole situation, with opinions split clearly along party lines.[47]

Within this conception, economic reasoning appears as a particular, rather sophisticated form of common sense that has grown with the spread of capitalism and with the growing dominance of the activities—earning, spending, consuming, trading—for which it is most appropriate. In particular, the assumption and acceptance of self-interest arises not from any thoughtful reflection or introspection but from common sense observations, captured in traditional proverbs, of how other people behave in everyday life, and it has no moral significance or connotations. If people are self-interested, then for the contemporary public as much as for contemporary economists that is neither good nor bad. It is just a 'fact' of life.

Like common sense rationality in general, economic rationality is perfectly appropriate in a whole range of situations, and has indeed been exceptionally productive in bringing material benefits to society. As with common sense rationality in general, however, it has come to be applied to areas where it does not necessarily belong. Two areas Fevre picks out, in particular, are education and child care. In the former case, he suggests, the fundamental moral purpose of education has been subsumed under an economic rationale of enhanced productivity and economic competitiveness. In the latter, decisions to do with a child's upbringing and with the emotional relationship between child and parent are actually made on the economic basis of the parent's earnings and the relative return on investment from parenting or working and paying some-one else to parent.[48]

As these examples illustrate, the main concern of Fevre's analysis is with the impact of common sense on traditional morality. He argues, indeed, that the rise of common sense reasoning, and the legitimacy of self-interest within this, has brought about a wholesale 'demoralization of Western culture'. We shall return to this argument in Chapter 6, where we shall review the widespread perception of a 'crisis' of morality in contemporary society. First, though, we shall need to take a closer look at what has happened to moral attitudes, and especially to perceptions of moral authority, over the last few decades.

# Technology, Liberalism, and the Weakening of Moral Constraints

In Chapters 3 and 4 we have explored how the traditional balance between ethics and enterprise, between a dominant hierarchical or ordered culture characterized by a traditional morality of obligation and duty and a licensed market subculture characterized by entrepreneurial self-interest, has been challenged by the growth of enterprise and its values. In the last decades of the twentieth century, business and financial enterprises grew to be massively more powerful, economically, politically, and culturally, than at any previous time in history. During the same period, economic ideas and the values of market culture also became enormously influential, dominating public and political discourse and transforming the way in which businesses are run and organized. Self-interest, in particular, acquired a social legitimation and acceptance it had never previously enjoyed. In this chapter we shall look at the other side of the equation, at what has happened to traditional morality and the values of hierarchical culture during the same period. We shall conclude that while traditional moral values still seem to be intact, the social structures that have supported them have been seriously weakened.

The traditional morality of obligation and the hierarchical type of culture with which it is associated have been dominant for so long and in such a wide variety of contexts that it is tempting to take them for granted. Most people do. We saw in Chapter 2, however, several indications of their potential vulnerability. From the viewpoint of cultural theory, hierarchical cultures are vulnerable to the effects of strong market subcultures on at least two counts. First, any profusion of values that run counter to those of the hierarchical orthodoxy (values that place people in critical respects below the line of zero grid in the grid–group diagram) must weaken the classification structure of the hierarchy, exposing it either to the risk of anarchy and fragmentation or to that of tyranny and despotism, as powerful leaders escape the constraints of society. Second, in a weakened hierarchy, there is also the possibility that self-interested entrepreneurs will use their economic power to exploit the structure of the hierarchy for their own ends and turn it into a 'Big Men' market culture.

From a historical viewpoint, the dominance of traditional morality appears to have been threatened on a number of occasions. One was in the Roman Empire, when the economic freedom and progress of the first and second centuries were followed by a fragmentation and collapse of civilized society from which Europe did not recover for centuries, if not millennia. We know little about what really happened in this period—far too little to make any assertions about a causal link between the rise of market culture and its effects—but the instance serves as a sober reminder that we cannot take the continued flourishing of a society, however prosperous, for granted. The second occasion was in Britain in the second half of the eighteenth century, when unprecedented enterprise and a thriving free market were associated both with increased prosperity and with an evident slackening of traditional moral constraint, at least in respect of religious observance and sexual mores. As we have already noted, market self-interest in this period remained under much tighter constraints than at first appears, and to the extent that moral constraints were loosened they were quickly tightened again. However, the late eighteenth century cannot be dismissed simply as a moral 'blip' without any significant consequences. The strength of the reaction to it, in the form of the nineteenth-century obsession with the moral virtues of constraint, is testimony to the risks it posed. Moreover, while this reaction may have been effective on a practical level, the intellectual insights of the eighteenth century, the insights of the Enlightenment, remained. These insights were to powerfully shape both the thinking and, in due course, the practice of the next 200 years. One consequence of this was that by the time the market culture next threatened to break free from its hierarchical constraints, in the closing decades of the twentieth century, the intellectual grounds for these constraints had been very seriously weakened.

Meanwhile, alongside this intellectual development, the material consequences of the Enlightenment had been working in very much the same direction. As we saw in Chapter 2, the technological innovations of the Industrial Revolution encouraged hierarchical forms of organization. Mass production technologies, rail transport, and telegraph communications made possible economies of scale and scope and so gave birth to the business bureaucracy. As described in Chapter 4, however, the successors to these technologies had an opposite effect, prompting businesses to move away from bureaucratic structures. More fundamentally, they also served to break down the physical and communication boundaries that, until recently, bound communities together and kept different societies and different specific value systems apart. These pressures on the structure and fabric of society were not felt until well into the second half of the twentieth century, but by the last quarter of the century they had become very powerful indeed. By the 1980s and 1990s the traditional moral constraints of society were being seriously undermined on both the intellectual and the practical fronts.

## THE COLLAPSE OF MORAL AUTHORITY

Many commentators have pointed to a collapse of moral standards in the late twentieth century. Most famously, Francis Fukuyama has written of a 'Great Disruption' in social values, commenting that[1]

Although conservatives . . . are often attacked for harping on the theme of moral decline, they are essentially correct: the breakdown of social order is not a matter of nostalgia, poor memory, or ignorance about the hypocrisies of earlier ages. The decline is readily measurable in statistics on crime, fatherless children, reduced educational outcomes and opportunities, broken trust, and the like.

Between 1840 and 1900, recorded crime rates in Britain fell by more than half, finishing the century at about 2.5 cases per thousand people per year. By 1940 they were roughly back to where they had been a century earlier at around six cases per thousand. By the early 1990s they had soared to well over 100 cases per thousand of population, an increase of about 4,000 per cent over the century.[2] The figures dropped back a little in the later 1990s, but by historical standards the fall was insignificant and it may even have masked a continuing rise in real crime. Finding from experience that nothing was done about them anyway, people gave up reporting minor crimes and the police, having responded to public concerns by directing resources towards a preventative presence on the streets, were left with a severe and chronic shortage of administrative staff to record those that were reported. A survey in 2003 found that over 40 per cent of crimes went unreported, and 18 per cent of those that were reported received no police response.[3] The rise in violent crime over the same period was even steeper, and the figures for the United States and continental Europe are very similar to those for Britain. By the late 1990s, the number of inmates in American jails had risen to nearly two million, with another three and a half million on probation or parole.[4] Moreover, this order of magnitude change may in itself be an underestimate of the real state of affairs, as many previously indictable offences, such as vagrancy and public drunkenness, were effectively decriminalized during this period.[5]

In Britain, the United States, and many other developed Western societies, with remarkable consistency, divorce rates doubled between the late 1960s and early 1980s. By the end of the century about half of all marriages were ending in divorce. There were also fewer marriages. Throughout the nineteenth century and up until the 1960s, British illegitimacy rates had remained relatively stable at between 5 and 7 per cent. Between the mid 1960s and the early 1990s, they quadrupled. In America the increase began earlier but from a lower base. By the end of the century about a third of all births in Britain, France, and the United States, and half of those in Denmark and Sweden, were to unmarried mothers. In other countries the growth of illegitimacy was more delayed, but the basic pattern was consistent across the developed West.[6]

These figures must be treated with care. Quite apart from the problems attendant on all such statistics, their connection with the oft-proclaimed collapse of moral values is not necessarily as straightforward as it may appear. The causes of increased crime have been hotly debated. Because most crime has always been committed by young men with more time than money, changing demographics and unemployment rates are important factors with no immediate link to morality. In America, crime figures are also closely correlated with income inequality.[7] Changing patterns of life and work are also important. In mixed use, low-rise neighbourhoods, 'eyes on the street' act as a powerful deterrent, while high-rise residential areas are easily colonized by criminal elements.[8] Social disruption of all kinds is consistently associated with high crime levels. Thus the high crime rates in Russia and the former Soviet Union following the collapse of communism are clearly linked to a collapse of a particular hierarchical structure, but do not necessarily reflect a collapse in the moral values of hierarchy in general. In nineteenth-century Britain crime rates began to rise in the 1810s, with the early disruptions of industrialization, and peaked in the 1840s, a full two generations after the moral excesses of the eighteenth century had begun to give way to what we now term 'Victorian' moral values. The subsequent fall in crime through the rest of the century can surely be associated with a strengthening of those values, with an increasing rigidity of moral constraint during Victoria's reign, but it can also be associated with a stabilization of living patterns following the upheavals of the industrial revolution.

Figures on divorce and illegitimacy also need to be treated with care. From the particular perspective of the Roman Catholic Church, both divorce and sex outside marriage are morally wrong, but this is a reflection of a specific set of moral values rather than of traditional morality per se. Shocking as they once seemed, few impartial observers would now claim that the high illegitimacy rates of the Scandinavian countries are a reflection of moral weakness. Many people would argue, indeed, that if the morality of obligation is sufficiently well embedded in society, there is little need for the artificial constraint of marriage. From this perspective the Scandinavian countries may be characterized by a relatively high level of traditional morality, not by a collapse of moral values.

Other evidence on moral values has been collected by researchers looking at indicators of community and social capital. In surveys carried out in 1981 and 1990 people were asked whether a range of traditionally immoral behaviours were ever justified. These included, for example, avoiding paying the fare on public transport, cheating the taxman, buying stolen goods, and keeping money one had found rather than handing it in to the police. In each of these cases a large majority of Britons over the age of thirty responded that they were never justified (68, 60, 80, and 59 per cent, respectively), while only a minority of those aged thirty or under responded the same (48, 40, 49, and 30 per cent).[9] Much of this difference may well be accounted for by a life-cycle effect, with the young being more cavalier than the old, but responses to other questions suggested that there may also be a generational effect, with the new generation holding (permanently) to different values from those of previous generations. As Robert Putnam has shown, this is almost certainly the case for related changes in people's perceptions as to the morality of others. When asked in 1952 whether people then lived as good lives, in terms of honesty and morality, as they used to, 50 per cent of Americans replied 'yes'; but by 1998, only 27 per cent did. When asked whether most people could be trusted, 55 per cent of Americans said 'yes' in 1960, declining to about 30 per cent in 1999. The comparable figures for school leavers changed more sharply still, averaging under 25 per cent for the 1990s.[10] Summarizing the conclusions from this literature, we can say that in Britain, America, and indeed elsewhere, the generations who grew up in the last quarter of the twentieth century do seem, in some ways, to be both less moral and less trusting of others' morality than their elders. However, the evidence on people's perceptions of others' morality is much more compelling than that on their own moral values.[11]

Overall, the evidence available from surveys, interviews, and social statistics does not seem to support any strong claims as to a collapse of moral *values*. It does, however, suggest a collapse of traditional moral *authority*, and the institutions associated with it, and this collapse has inevitably left moral values vulnerable. It has quite often happened in history that one particular authority or institution has ceased to be relevant to the changing circumstances of a society and has collapsed or fallen into disuse, only to be replaced by another. So the divine authority of kings has been replaced, at various times in different societies, by the authority of a secular state. The authorities and institutions of imperial powers have been replaced by those of their conquering successors, or by those indigenous to the country concerned. In the late twentieth century, however, *all* of the principal authorities through which traditional moral constraints have been imposed appear to have been seriously weakened, at the same time and across most of the developed world. From this perspective Fukuyama's term, the Great Disruption, is almost an understatement.

## The Enlightenment heritage

The intellectual roots of the Great Disruption can be traced back to the eighteenth-century Enlightenment project of replacing superstition and authority (primarily the authority of the Roman Catholic Church) by science, reason, and freedom.[12] In some ways this project was hopelessly ambitious. In the first place, dispensing with authority proved to be much more difficult than it seemed. In a hierarchical culture, most attempts to break away from authority altogether resulted, in practice, in the replacement of one version of authority by another. Scientists bowed to the authority of Newton. Philosophers exchanged the authority of Aquinas for that of Cicero.[13] The French Revolution replaced the authority of the monarchy with the no less severe or, in cultural terms, hierarchical authority of the Republic. Much later, in the twentieth century, this experience was repeated to even more devastating effect in the Russian Revolution.

In the second place, reason had its limitations. Employing it sceptically, to explore the flaws or hidden assumptions in someone else's argument, was one thing. Using it constructively was quite another. Emmanuel Kant's critical philosophies of science and ethics, published in the 1780s, stand as extraordinary monuments to Enlightenment rationality.[14] They revolutionized philosophical thinking and Kant's moral writing, in particular, still exerted a powerful influence on philosophers (including such major figures as Rawls, Habermas, and Derrida) over 200 years later. As an attempt to derive the principles of morality from reason alone, without reference to religious or other forms of authority, it was and is magnificent. But it was already apparent to the first generation of Kant's students that it ultimately fails, and it quite quickly became apparent that this failure was inevitable. The principles of morality could not be derived without some assumptions based on faith or authority.[15] Meanwhile, in the world of practical politics, it also became apparent that reason could be put to a multitude of purposes and that, contrary to the hopes of the Enlightenment, regimes based on the dictates of reason were not necessarily any fairer, any more just, or any less corrupt than those based on traditional authority. The French republic did not exactly live up to expectations.[16]

In retrospect, the political debate initiated in the Enlightenment was not really about replacing authority with reason, but about combining the two, so as to replace an arbitrary hereditary authority with a rationally defensible one, which in practice meant one that recognized individual freedom and equality. The French Revolution was grounded on the principles of freedom and equality and the hope that if these were granted people would be able to govern themselves in a rational manner, imposing on themselves and accepting as legitimate the authority that was necessary for any form of political government. This proved optimistic at the time, but the ideal persisted and political debate since has been largely concerned with the question of how far individual freedom should or should not be sacrificed to communal authority in the interests of the common good. In contemporary Britain and especially America this takes the form of a debate between liberals, who emphasize the value of freedom, and communitarians, who emphasize the value of community ties and authoritative social norms. To the extent that this is a debate about politics, however (and not about the ontological relationship between individuals and society), the difference is one of emphasis rather than of principle. Both sides are agreed on the need for both freedom and authority, in appropriate measure.[17]

If politics required a reconciliation of reason and authority, however, in ethics they worked against each other. For while politics are essentially about compromise, about balancing the disparate, often conflicting needs of different members of a community, morals are about absolutes, about imperatives. Enlightenment thinkers sought to replace traditional moral authorities, and in particular the authority of the church, by the authority of reason. That project failed, in the sense that reason alone proved unequal to the task. But it succeeded in the sense that the authority of religion was fatally undermined.

## Religion and the church

Throughout Europe and North America, the Christian church has been the dominant moral authority of the past millennium. Indeed, outside the confines of academic philosophy it is probably only in the last hundred years that it has even been possible to think of moral judgements other than in a Christian or Judaeo-Christian context. Throughout the Middle Ages and the early modern period, the church was regarded as the sole ultimate authority on such matters. Such education as existed was under church control and it was the teaching of the church that formed the basis of parental instruction. Even rulers could go against this teaching only by invoking a higher religious authority and pro-claiming the divine right of kings. When King Henry VIII of England failed to get the Pope's permission for divorce he countered this not by questioning the moral authority of the church, but by setting up an alternative church, almost identical in its teaching to the Roman one and differing only in that it reported to him and not to the Pope.

By the sixteenth century, when Henry ruled, the Roman Catholic Church as an organization was scarcely a model of moral rectitude. Corruption was endemic and the excesses of its leaders were only too apparent. Support for the protestant churches of Luther, Calvin, and Zwingli was growing and was to keep on growing, and it would not be long before Henry's own Church of England was itself challenged by the puritan movement that was to provide the moral basis of early American society. The Reformation, however, was about a battle for authority *within* Christianity, and it was important precisely because the authority *of* Christianity continued to be paramount. It was only in the eighteenth century that the authority of the church was seriously questioned.

This questioning took two forms. At the intellectual level, Enlightenment thinkers challenged both the general concept of religious authority and, espe-cially, the specific assumptions of the Christian faith.[18] On a practical level, people stopped going to church. The statistics are patchy, but for England in the second half of the eighteenth century it would seem that only about 10 per cent of the population were Church of England communicants on anything like a regular basis. The dissenting protestant churches were undoubtedly more popular, especially in the expanding cities, but it seems likely that over half of the population were not regular church-goers. In the late eighteenth and early nineteenth century religion made something of a come-back, with the membership of the dissenting churches quadrupling over a thirty-year period. By mid-century the organizers of the 1851 census could report a weekly turnout rate in Christian places of worship of 58 per cent of the population of England and Wales, and it would seem that by this time the Christian faith could again be taken for granted. Even if people did not attend church, they were most likely believers, and for the overwhelming majority of the population the dominant moral authority was that of church, priest, or bible.[19]

This situation seems to have persisted throughout the nineteenth century, but over the last hundred years the authority of the church has again waned. In the middle of the twentieth century, the church was still an important part of the social fabric, but for those educated to think for themselves it was ceasing to be a dominant authority. By the last quarter of the century it was becoming an irrelevance. Educated and brought up with a Christian view of morality most people probably still held that view, and many of the older generation still held to the religious beliefs underlying it. But the church as an institution (and not just this church or that church, but any church) seemed increasingly irrelevant to daily life. By the end of the century, though a third of all Britons claimed that religion (unspecified) was important to them, the practice of that religion had become a minority interest, with regular church-goers reduced to around 5 per cent of the overall population, and a much, much smaller proportion of the younger generations.[20] Manchester United could claim more supporters in England than all the Christian churches put together.

This pattern was reflected elsewhere in Europe. Though the proportion of church-goers varied significantly from country to country, all the main European churches experienced a sharp decline in attendance, and in most cases a sharp increase in the age of their congregations, in the last third of the twentieth century. Across Europe as a whole, average reported weekly church attendance halved in this period from about 40 per cent to about 20 per cent of the population, and at the end of the century this decline seemed to be accelerating.[21] The proportion of people reporting that religion was important to them fell to just 21 per cent in Germany and 11 per cent in France.[22] The decline in America was much more gradual, with reported church attendance holding up at around 37 per cent in the late 1990s, but even here the time devoted to church and to related activities fell sharply.[23]

As befits its antiquated image, the church still plays a ceremonial role in the celebration of births, marriages, and deaths, but even this is declining rapidly. In France, for example, 92 per cent of children born in 1958 were christened, but only 64 per cent of those born in 1987 and, we may be sure, a much lower percentage still in the early twenty-first century.[24] Whether or not they tell us anything about moral values, the increased illegitimacy rates to which Fukuyama draws attention surely speak volumes about the reduced need for the legitimacy granted by the church ceremonies of marriage and baptism, and the reduced authority of the churches. In public, the bishops and archbishops still speak as if from positions of moral authority, but the sad truth is that nobody listens to them any more. Even within the churches, authority is compromised as people find the traditional moralities out of touch with contemporary reality. The Roman Catholic Church has a powerful hierarchy and strict line on moral dogma, but in many countries the instructions of the Pope on such matters as birth control are quite simply ignored, even by those few of reproductive age who remain within the church. There is a kindly respect for those in positions of supposed spiritual authority, as no one would want to hurt their feelings, but it is the respect we afford people for what they once were rather than for what they now are.

For those to whom the church is a vocation, this is all very difficult to accept. Given their religious beliefs they hope, they have to hope, for a recovery, a turnaround, a return of the people toward their Christian God. But it is very hard to find a reason why that should happen, and very easy to find reasons why it should not. One can try to draw parallels with the eighteenth century and hope for a new 'Victorian' revival, but a lot has changed over the intervening centuries. For over one and a half millennia from the dawn of the Christian era, the Western mind remained relatively stable, the symbols and stories of Christianity caused no significant difficulties, and the Christian message retained its relevance. But the explosion of scientific knowledge in the last few hundred years, and the social, technological, and educational changes that have accompanied it, have dramatically changed the way we think. Commenting in 1932 on a drift away from the protestant churches of Europe after the First World War, the psychologist C. G. Jung observed that 'modern man has an ineradicable aversion from traditional opinions and inherited truths'.[25] This is as succinct a summary of modernism as you could find, and Voltaire had said much the same thing nearly 200 years earlier. But in Voltaire's time it applied only to a small intelligentsia and even there was more wishful thinking than reality. By Jung's time it was spreading throughout the educated classes. In Britain and other developed countries today, the educated classes account for the vast majority of the population.

Of course, science and Christianity are perfectly compatible, and in that sense there is no obstacle to belief.[26] But that belief is no longer a matter of course. It requires a deep commitment and arises only, if at all, where the peculiar combination of psychological need and personal experience makes such a commitment appropriate. For both children and the parents of children, such circumstances are rare. Life in the modern world is too full and too busy to allow much dwelling on its meaning. For those who do have time the television is both an easy and an addictive alternative to thought. The serious illnesses and premature deaths that might prompt a deeper reflection are now mercifully few and far between. For most people the story of Christ is a rather macabre tale, the church seems obsessed with tragedy and death, and the fundamental tenets of Christian belief appear, from both a scientific and a common sense perspective, to be downright nonsense. In an increasingly pluralistic and liberal society, in which much of religious education is comparative, Christianity also appears as just one of a range of religions, each of which appears to contradict all the others while claiming that it alone is right, and all of which lose credibility as a result.

At some stage in their lives, many people encounter a psychological need for some kind of religion, for some kind of meaning or purpose to life. They discover, in other words, that for them religion *does* matter. But in today's world this tends to come fairly late in life, with the death of parents or of friends, and with the vacuum created by retirement or the departure of children from the family home. For the generations that were brought up steeped in Christianity it made some sense to return to it: The symbols and myths were familiar from childhood, and however archaic they could still make some connection with half-forgotten meanings. Once the thread of tradition has been broken, however, there is no going back. For most people Christianity is no more meaningful and no more able to meet their needs than any other set of beliefs.

The processes of change are ongoing, and if we look at Britain today, it would still be going too far to say that the moral authority of the Christian church has collapsed completely. Such moral debate as still exists in our society is still influenced by senior church figures, and the views of the church are still held in some sort of respect. But this seems increasingly to be a vestigial effect. The fact that someone speaks as a bishop or archbishop, say, is becoming incidental, and the authority of the church as an institution is waning fast. Moreover the same is true, in various measures, throughout the developed world. In France and Scandinavia, as in Britain, the churches have long been in decline and have long ceased to wield any significant moral authority. Elsewhere in Europe, the decline is more recent but no less marked. In Catholic Europe, the authority of the church dominated society well into the last century. The priests wielded unquestioned authority in their communities and religiously imposed norms dominated both education and family life. Today, however, the church is only one influence among many and the influence of the priesthood on the young is marginal. In Germany, where the protestant churches are strongest, the story is similar. Turn outside Europe to Japan and we find a different religious tradition, incorporating a mix of Shinto and Buddhism, and a different set of institutions, but the same basic story of the collapse of religious authority.

America is different, of course, but not that different. We have already noted that church attendance in America has remained relatively high and other indicators also suggest a continuing role for religious authority. The name of God is routinely invoked in public and political discourse in a way that would have been familiar to nineteenth-century Europeans but seems alien to their twenty-first-century successors. Religious arguments for creationism and against evolutionary biology still seem to carry weight, nearly a century after they were dismissed in Europe. In general, the geographical isolation of America and the world dominance of the American media seem to have resulted in modern Americans being far less exposed to external cultural influences than the people of other developed nations, and this is reflected in a relative stability of ideas and institutions. Against this stability, however, and against the continuing reference to a Christian God, must be set the profound individualism of American culture. Individual conscience has always weighed more heavily on American minds than church authority, and as urbanization, suburbanization, and an ever-growing variety of church denominations have broken the bonds between church and local community, the little authority the churches did possess has been lost. In contemporary America the churches offer competing products for consumption in the religious market place. Each element of guidance, moral or otherwise, carries the name of God, but it is up to the individual which one she chooses.

A rather different market for religion can be seen in parts of the developing world. Amongst the poorer communities of South America and parts of

South-east Asia, the Christian churches are vibrant and growing and the authority of the church would seem to be in the ascendant. But there is always a market for religion among the poor or oppressed, who have no other hopes for the future, and the current activity owes more to a breakdown of traditional authority structures and the consequent freeing of the religious marketplace than to any increase in the actual or perceived need for church authority. Religious activity is high, but the competition between religions is intense and in an open market it is driven more by what the different churches can offer in terms of salvation or support than by what they might require in terms of moral standards or behaviour. Even when we look at the world's Islamic communities, in which the authority of the church appears to have grown markedly in the last few decades, what we see in the violence and repression associated with the new fundamentalism is not so much a rise in the moral authority of the church as a desperate response to the threatened destruction of tradition, and to the collapse of more peaceably ordered authority. Where the authority of the Islamic church has grown, as for example in Nigeria, where much of the country is now ruled by Islamic law, it has been to fill a void left by failing state authorities that can no longer deliver the basic infrastructure of a peacefully ordered society. Where this has been accompanied by violent assertions of authority, it has been in response to the absence of any peaceful avenues for dialogue. Fundamentalism has been described as a traditional defence of tradition, and the growth of Islamic fundamentalism is a reflection not of the strength of the Islamic churches but of their threatened extinction at the hands of Western materialism and American hegemony.[27]

As some of the consequences of the recent emergence of fundamentalism make clear, the decline of religious authority has its positive side. Over the centuries the Christian church has probably abused its authority as much as it has used it properly. It has at times been a powerful liberating force, and still is so in some developing countries. But it has also been a powerful force of oppression, maintaining its control by the instillation of fear and the perpetuation of ignorance. It would not be unfair to suggest that it had ceased to earn its authority long before it actually lost it. But liberty always has its costs. In this case, the freedom from religious authority is also the freedom from direction, the freedom to doubt, the freedom to suffer in that doubt, and the freedom to lose one's way. The simple fact is that for most people in our society the moral authority of the church has collapsed. If they want to know what is right, they must look elsewhere.

## The state

To some extent, the moral authority of the Christian church was replaced in the twentieth century by that of the state. In a hierarchical society, the state had long been a source of authority, which it had exercised partly through force and partly through the rule of law. On moral issues it had traditionally ceded to the 'higher' authority of the church, basing the law upon Christian teachings and leaving its enforcement largely to church institutions. As the authority of the established churches declined, however, the maintenance of law and order became increasingly a state activity. And as the moral authority of religion in general declined, so that of the state increased.

By the middle of the twentieth century the moral authority of the state and its institutions, in Britain and elsewhere, were impressive. In the Britain of the 1950s, the police officer was seen not only as part of the apparatus for capturing criminals but also as a moral authority, a source of friendly guidance and fair constraint to be treated with the utmost respect. The same respect was afforded to the judiciary and to the legal profession in general. Even politicians, whose legitimacy had been enhanced by universal suffrage and whose status had grown as a result of the Second World War (there is nothing like a successful war for building up a leader's image), were respected as sources of moral authority. The Second World War itself was fought, on both sides and as no previous war had been, on ostensibly moral grounds. Territorial disputes, the traditional grounds for war, were secondary. The cold war that followed was probably concerned more with the balance of world power than anything, but it was again presented in moral terms. Communism (or, from the opposite perspective, capitalism) was morally repugnant. Domestic politics too were shaped by moral concerns. The post-war creation of the British National Health Service and the education reforms of the same period were justified, as the pre-war American New Deal and Fair Deal had been, on the basis that they were 'right', 'fair', 'good'.

Impressive though it was at the time, however, the moral authority of the state and its constituent institutions appears to have been rather short lived. In the Britain of the 1950s and early 1960s, most people respected the judgements of the politicians and judiciary. They respected the law as a proxy for moral correctness, and they respected the integrity of the police in trying to uphold that law. By the late 1990s, however, all that had changed. Despite having in Tony Blair a prime minister who carried as an individual more moral authority than any of his predecessors since Churchill, the general perception at the turn of the century was that politicians are in it for power and glory and to further their own ambitions, rather than out of any sense of public service. The relentless attention of the press on political sleaze and corruption, both real and imagined, has exposed remarkably little, and there can be little doubt that politicians are far less corrupt now than they were in any period prior to the First World War, but the perception is fair, nevertheless. What has happened is that we now know much more about our politicians, through press and television, than we did before, and we can recognize them for what they are: ordinary people, with an excess of ambition and a craving for attention, who are no more and no less qualified to speak with moral authority than the rest of us are. These changes are reflected in the statistics. In Britain and throughout the developed world, levels of voting and political participation, respect for politicians and confidence in their honesty and integrity, and trust in political institutions have all fallen sharply in the last thirty years.[28]

Meanwhile the judges, after a few decades of unaccustomed respect, have also resumed their traditional role as figures of fun, quite out of touch with reality, and the stock of the police has also taken a tumble. In just forty years we have moved from a position in which police officers were universally liked and respected, and could act as moral authorities within their local communities, to one in which they are isolated from many of the communities in which they serve, widely (if incorrectly) assumed to be both incompetent and open to corruption, and avoided at all costs even by perfectly upright and law-abiding citizens. It is not hard to see how this has come about. Most people encounter the police when they get stopped for a driving offence, get caught in possession of some relatively harmless and very widely consumed drug, or experience a burglary or theft, which the police never solve. They naturally see the police as punishing them for things they do not think are wrong and failing to punish anyone for things they do think are wrong. Add to that a measure of heavy-handedness and a few well-publicized instances of police corruption, and the idea that a contemporary youth would take moral guidance from a police officer becomes little short of preposterous.

As in the case of the church, the collapse of state authority is not without its benefits, for in many societies that authority has been and continues to be oppressive. Experience suggests, indeed, that the greater the moral authority of the state—the greater the influence of the state on people's moral judgements— the more suspect are the morals concerned. The moral authority of Hitler's Third Reich was immense, and succeeded in corrupting a whole nation. The moral authority of the communist states of Eastern Europe was also extremely powerful, but even though its collapse has left a vacuum in which criminal activity has spiralled out of all control, it is scarcely lamented.

The collapse of state authority in the Soviet Union cannot really be compared to that in Britain or Western Europe. The institutional structure of Soviet society, characterized as it was by a command economy and a suppression of religious activity, was far cruder and less sophisticated than those of Western Europe, so that when the state authority collapsed, suddenly and completely, there was simply nothing left to hold things together. Everything had to be constructed afresh. The changes in the West have been gradual and evolutionary in comparison. The fact remains, however, that any erosion of institutional authority leaves a vacuum to be filled. In most of Western Europe, the state gained its recent authority when the church began to lose its. Now both are in decline and the question they leave behind is becoming ever more urgent. Who will tell us what to do? Where do we go to find out what is right?

## The family

People learn their morals as children, and although these may derive from the authority of church or state they are normally transmitted through more immediate authorities, in particular through parents, grandparents, and other family members, and through teachers. The authority of the family is particularly important, and the institution of the family is central to most human societies, including our own. Very young children are almost completely dependent on their parents, and it is from our parents that we learn as young children what is and what is not acceptable behaviour. Much of this is about manners and etiquette rather than morality. It is good to say 'Thank you' when we are given something; it is not good to throw our dinner round the room. But we also learn from our parents that it is good to be nice to people and bad to hurt them, and whether through explicit instruction or implicit example we model our behaviour on theirs.

As we grow older, the role of the parent becomes more ambiguous. We rebel as well as conform, and on many matters—such as music or clothes—our parents cease to be convincing role models. Sometimes we also rebel in more serious ways, too. As a general rule, however, the history of our society has been characterized by a very strong family institution and strong parental authority. It has always been considered the duty of the child not only to follow the parents' instructions but also to respect their wisdom and judgement on matters of right and wrong.

As we saw in Chapter 4, the notion of the family as a moral unit played an important part in the reassertion of moral authority at the end of the eighteenth century and was again strong during the Victorian period. It has recently been revived with vigour by more conservative politicians, eager both to champion family values and to shift the burden of responsibility for youth crime, unemployment, and other costly failures of our society away from the state. As the statistics presented at the beginning of this chapter indicate, however, families are not what they were. Until relatively recently it was the norm for couples to marry, have children, and stay together 'till death do us part', in the words of the marriage service. Quite apart from any religious or moral convictions this lifelong bonding has some very clear practical advantages and it will no doubt survive, with or without the formal element of marriage, but it can no longer be described as the norm. Relationships now are for the duration of mutual satisfaction and for many people that duration is not very long. The affluent still preserve the form: they marry, have children, separate, and remarry. Each stage takes time, each stage costs money, and the number of changes is relatively small. But whereas once it would have been unthinkable for the separation to occur until after the children had grown up, now it might happen at any time. For the less affluent such formality is, quite simply, too expensive, so they move in and out of relationships more quickly. A mother might have quite a number of partners between the conception and maturity of her child—or she might have none at all.

The implications of these changes for parental authority are substantial. Perhaps the most striking effect, though that least commented upon, is that many children now look to their mothers for authority rather than, as has traditionally been the case, to their fathers. In the traditional family it was the father who gave guidance and wielded authority while the mother succoured and supported. In the absence of a father, or the presence of a half-father or of multiple fathers, the authority devolves to the mother.

On the face of it, this seems quite encouraging. Although our culture has perpetuated the myth of male responsibility—man as protector and provider— few men can experience the responsibility felt and taken by a mother for her child. We need only look at the crime figures, or at the behaviour in any social gathering, to see that women on the whole provide better role models for moral behaviour than do men. Research into male and female conceptions of moral- ity also suggests that women's approaches, with their emphasis on relationship, fit much more naturally into our traditional culture and its role-structured institutions than do the more individualist approaches of men.[29]

It is not, however, that simple. In the first place, the notion of male domi- nance is so deeply embedded in our history that the woman's authority is at best a fragile one, which is all too easily displaced when a partner comes along. The woman gives up her authority role, the man takes it on, and the child needs no encouragement to fall in with the new order. After nearly three millennia of male dominance the father figure has come to occupy a crucial place in the human psyche, and one that cannot be taken by the mother, who has her own psychological role to play. There is a sense in which a child needs a father fig- ure, and the absence of a real father can lead to difficult problems of psycho- logical development. However, the presence of two or more alternative fathers, or of a succession of neo-fathers, can cause even more damage and confusion.

The second problem is that the very behaviour of the parents in moving between relationships very easily erodes their moral authority. Few separations are entirely amicable. There is almost always some bitterness, some rancour. People are let down; responsibilities are not discharged. In these circumstances, it is very difficult for parents to provide real guidance, because however hard they try there is inevitably some dissonance between what they say and what they do.

The third problem is that an increasing number of parents are themselves brought up in divided or discordant families. They may want to do better for their children, but they have no experience of effective parental authority on which to draw.

## Education

Aside from family, the main authority figure for children in the twentieth century was the teacher. Both the content of the school curriculum and the institutional power of the education system vary tremendously from country to country. In some countries, such as Japan and Germany, ethics have been formally taught as part of the core school curriculum. In Britain and America they have not. Moreover, the institutional power and authority of the education system have always been traditionally much weaker in Britain and America than in France, Germany, or Japan, where syllabuses and teaching methods have been kept under tight state control, and teachers have been afforded, ex officio, considerable social respect. In these countries the authority of education derives directly from that of the state. In Britain and America, with their much more liberal educational traditions, it depends much more on the teacher as an individual, and the respect that that individual can command. The teaching profession in these countries has always been badly paid and has always attracted a mixture of those deeply committed to teaching and those unfit for anything else, so that respect could never be taken for granted.

Even for the deeply committed, really good teaching, of the kind that gives people guidance and contributes to their growth, is extraordinarily difficult, and correspondingly rare. The teacher has a responsibility for conveying the conventional wisdom, but also for challenging that wisdom; for instructing her pupils or students in the accepted truths, but also for developing their critical faculties so that they can progress beyond those truths; for guiding people in a direction, but also for enabling them to choose their own direction. Even in the protected atmosphere of an expensive private school or an elite university this is difficult. In an ordinary state school with large classes and minimal resources, communicating anything is a challenge, and as school budgets have been cut in the name of economic efficiency and the collapse of other moral authorities has removed the support that teachers could traditionally expect from church, state, and family, this challenge has become harder and harder to meet.

As the institutions around them have collapsed, schools and teachers have taken much of the blame. Unable to exert moral authority themselves, and unwilling to subscribe to the decaying authority of church, state, or community, many parents now expect teachers to do it for them, and get angry when they cannot. The politicians side with the parents, who wield the votes, and the church attributes its own downfall to the lack of a 'proper' religious education in schools. Branded as incompetent or misguided or both, the teachers find it progressively more difficult to maintain any kind of authority and a vicious circle develops.

The teacher's role as moral authority has been made even more difficult by the growth of pluralistic and multicultural societies. In America, where the assertion of individual rights and freedoms has undermined traditional patterns of moral discipline, teachers are no longer expected to act as moral authorities. A sociological study carried out in the early 1980s compared schools with shopping malls in which the pupils' freedom of choice took absolute priority. Moral sanctions, if they were imposed at all, were weak, and moral judgements were avoided. As one teacher put it, both succinctly and accurately, 'our job is not to teach morality'.[30]

In Britain teachers still have some moral discretion, but with multicultural and multilingual classes, with no background of shared and stable values, exercising that discretion is difficult. It has not been helped by changes in the curriculum away from the supposedly peripheral subjects of the humanities (and especially from history) towards the more immediately relevant and economically productive. These changes have been entirely well motivated, but they have had the unintended effect of taking away from education any foundation for moral discussion and debate. Moreover, these changes, though they have waxed and waned over the years, are now sufficiently advanced that many teachers are themselves relatively uneducated. Faced with what is going on around them they still do their best to provide some kind of moral guidance and authority, but in school as in family it is the blind leading the blind.

It is worth repeating that a collapse of authority, even on the scale and across the range of institutions described here, is not necessarily a bad thing. As we noted in Chapter 2, if societies are to grow and develop such changes are sometimes necessary. Institutional structures are created for stability, not change, and are innately conservative. When societies change the institutions lose their relevance and have eventually to be replaced. Some of the institutions and authorities we have been discussing here have been in decline for a long time now, and it may be that they are already living on borrowed time. But until and unless they are replaced by something more appropriate to contemporary needs, their collapse leaves a vacuum in the authority structure of society that cannot but weaken the constraints of traditional morality.

## THE EROSION OF CULTURAL BOUNDARIES

The weakening of institutions and the collapse of moral authority described in the last section have been inseparably linked with another major recent change in our society: the disappearance of the traditional boundaries between cultures and communities. We saw in Chapter 2 how strong boundaries are an integral part of the hierarchical culture, keeping out those who are not entitled to its benefits, keeping in those on whose support and commitment it depends, and maintaining a pragmatically useful distinction between insiders and outsiders. The underlying political logic of the hierarchical or role-structured society is that all should work together, and adopt their various roles and responsibilities, in the interest of the common good. This logic is powerful when membership of the community is well defined, and especially when it is both physically and psychologically fixed, when the members have neither the option to leave nor any concept of what they might leave for. But when the barriers of membership break down, the logic also comes into question.

Until very recently, the societies in which we live were remarkably closed, not only in terms of their national and cultural boundaries, but even in terms of their internal structures. A man who lived in a particular town or village and belonged to a particular church and a particular segment or stratum of society had little idea what belonging to a different town, church, or social stratum might be like, and no prospect of finding out. At the national level, the number of people who had even read about different cultures and countries was small. The number who had travelled internationally was minute. And the number who had any real experience of alternative cultures was minuscule. Even those who lived for an extended period in a foreign country were more likely than not to be protected from its culture, living and working in a community of 'ex-pats', the only locals they ever talked to being manual employees or domestic staff who spoke only when spoken to.

A true understanding of a foreign culture is still extraordinarily rare, but over the last few decades the barriers have come tumbling down. This is true both within countries and between them. In Britain, for example, the traditional class divisions have been breaking down, mobility has increased, and despite some continuing racial tensions most people now live in a multicultural society. This is especially true of children. In the cities and large towns, most schools are racially mixed, and even at 'middle class' private schools, which remain predominantly white and notionally Christian, children now learn something about Islam, Buddhism, and Hinduism as well as about Christianity. Internationally, dramatic improvements in travel, communications, and business have opened up the world to view.

## Politics and freedom

The most obvious examples of the breakdown of national boundaries are as much the result of a collapse of institutional authority as they are its cause. Twenty years ago, for a Westerner to travel freely to the Soviet Union was virtually impossible. Europe was divided by an 'Iron Curtain' into the democratic West and the communist East. Even postal or telephone communications between the two sides were difficult and subject to strict censorship. Travel from West to East was extremely rare, and the few who did travel were restricted to approved itineraries and accompanied by state officials throughout their stay. Travel from East to West was even more rare, and most of those who attempted it were shot.

The breakdown of the Soviet Union was partly a result of improved communications. Despite all the precautions taken by the state, people did find out about the West, and some at least were attracted by its freedom and prosperity. But it was also a result of institutional collapse. Through a combination of corruption, incompetence, and inflexibility, the coordinating hierarchies of the command economy simply failed to deliver what they were designed for, and lost their credibility. Once the psychological contract that maintained the hierarchy collapsed, the boundaries could not hold.

Other political barriers, in other parts of the world, have come down for other reasons. China's gradual move toward a more open society has been intentional, not forced. So has the dismantling of barriers between countries in the European Community. In all cases, though, the results are much the same. It is now possible for people to travel in and out of both mainland China and the former Soviet Union and its satellite states. And while the numbers doing so are still relatively small they are growing very rapidly. For a citizen of one of the countries in the European Community it is possible not only to travel freely throughout the Community but to do so without customs controls, without loss of welfare benefits, and without any restrictions on employment. Moreover these changes are being reflected, on a smaller scale, across the world.

Fifteen years ago, a British citizen needed a visa to visit the United States. Now that requirement is waived: you just fill in a form on the aeroplane.

## Technologies of transport and communication

These freedoms would have made little difference if they had not been accompanied by a rapid development of the technologies that make it possible to exploit them. Air transport, which until recently was a rare and exciting luxury, is becoming a routine part of everyday life, and millions of people now travel from one country to another in pursuit of work or leisure. Once in a foreign country, it is also much easier to get around, as more and more countries develop sophisticated transport infrastructures.

Improvements in telecommunications have also had a radical effect. Forty years ago an international telephone call was an adventure that needed to be planned well in advance and was still of doubtful outcome. Now you can direct dial to any part of the world with every expectation of being connected. Even where the local infrastructure is lacking, satellite technology can often find a way round it. Email has also had a dramatic effect. Because the two parties to a communication do not need to be online at the same time, email communications can be made as a matter of routine even in countries where telephone connections are fragmentary and unreliable. The Internet café has become a ubiquitous feature of the developing world.

Even with Internet cafés, the proportion of the world's population with access to email is still very small, but it is growing very fast. Within the academic community, the Internet has long been the main form of communication, both at the local level and internationally, and is rapidly rendering older technologies obsolete. The business community was slower to react, mainly because of security concerns, but it too now operates mainly online. Moreover, the Internet is not just a medium for email, e-commerce, and e-business, though the last of these has taken many of the headlines. It is above all a medium for transmitting uncensored and in practice virtually uncensorable information, including images as well as words, around the world. Through the Internet a person in one culture can get intimate access to another, finding out not only what the hierarchical authorities would like her to know, through official government or agency websites, but also the views of critics, protest groups, and dissident minorities. The Internet may not be quite everything it is hyped up to be, but it is certainly an effective breaker of boundaries.[31]

## Economics and free trade

Another factor in the breaking down of boundaries, connected both with political freedom and with transport and communications, has been the rise of free trade and international investment. This happened first in the developed countries of the world. Forty years ago, most British products were made in Britain and sold in Britain. Some were exported to (and raw materials imported from) the former British colonies. Thirty years ago there was already much more international trade, but international operations were still largely restricted to a few large corporations, mainly in extraction and chemicals. Even these were limited in their global coverage. By the 1980s, international investment and operations were rapidly becoming the norm. Japanese car and television manufacturers were setting up plants in Europe and America; American and European manufacturers in all sectors were establishing operations overseas. Privatized or deregulated industries such as utilities, telecommunications, and defence saw a spate of cross-border mergers and acquisitions. In the last ten to fifteen years, similar developments have also spread to the less developed countries.

Encouraged by international institutions such as the World Bank and the International Monetary Fund (IMF), and motivated by the desire for investment capital and financial loans, the less developed countries of the world have followed the more developed in moving increasingly away from systems of trade protection and national ownership toward systems of free trade and inward investment by multinational corporations. This movement has not been without its problems. As mentioned earlier, the economic policies needed to secure international grants and loans and to provide an attractive environment for business investment have often imposed considerable suffering on large sectors of the population. And in many emerging economies the relaxation of state control has been accompanied by massive levels of corruption and exploitation, as the opportunities for entrepreneurship in a transitional, fragmented hierarchy have been taken up energetically by racketeers, gang bosses, government officials, and others with power and few scruples. At the time of writing, Russian industry and commerce would appear to be overwhelmingly controlled by criminal elements, and even the more law-abiding entrepreneurs seem more intent on moving assets out of the country than on investing in it. The massive economic growth of southern China has also been accompanied by endemic corruption. For China and for many other newly developing countries, however, the consequences have also included a massive flow in inward investment. Over the past decade the total foreign direct investment of multinational corporations (which occurs, for example, when a company from one country takes over a company or sets up manufacturing facilities or sets up a joint venture in another country) has risen from about $200 billion to over $1700 billion a year, and of this an increasing proportion has been going into the less developed countries. About $10 billion a year in the mid-1980s, foreign direct investment to less developed countries had reached nearly $240 billion a year by 2000.[32]

Unlike other forms of funds flows such as grants, loans, and equity investments, foreign direct investment represents a real crossing of boundaries as both managers, materials, and end products move from one country to another. And $1700 billion a year represents an awful lot of movement. Communist China, for instance, used to be a closed culture, with rigidly preserved boundaries, but since the mid-1990s it has received a massive inflow of over $40 billion a year of foreign direct investment. And with the investment have gone people and information and ideas, all eroding the cultural barriers between China and the West.

## The globalization of business

All of the changes described above have been both encouraged and exploited by the world of business, and it is within business that the cultural boundaries have eroded most quickly. Most fields of social and professional activity are still dominated by national institutions, even if they now transcend them. In Britain, for example, questions of law are dominated by British statute, by the British legal system, and by professional lawyers trained and licensed to operate in that system. Here as elsewhere the barriers between countries are breaking down. Many British statutes now derive from the European Community, as Britain and the other member states try to bring their legal requirements into line. In some areas there is a right of appeal beyond the British to the European courts. But the British legal system remains the primary context for the resolution of legal matters in Britain, and where international coordination is needed it is handled through international institutions created specifically for that purpose. The same is true of professional activities, such as medicine or accountancy. Again, people are trained and practise within a national system, leaving to supranational institutions the problems of reconciling differences and bringing about convergence. In the social realm, most sports and hobbies are also organized nationally and coordinated through supranational institutions.

Business is different, though. First, as the philosopher of business Richard de George has pointed out, there are no supranational institutions for the governance of business or the international coordination of its practices.[33] There is nothing to compare with the institutional frameworks of international law or international sport. Second, the international aspects of business practice are not special cases, apart from the day-to-day activities in which people are primarily engaged. They *are* the day-to-day activities in which people are primarily engaged. To holiday in a different country from one's own, to play football against a foreign team, to resolve a difference in international medical ethics or procedure: all these are in some sense special events that stand out from the routine of everyday life. But for a business to purchase an item in one country, assemble it in another, and sell it in a third; or to use software engineers in one country to maintain systems in another; or to pass management instructions from one country to another: all these are now routine. For a new cadre of senior managers trained in the world's top business schools, the very idea of national boundaries is almost an anachronism. Part of an international peer group, most have lived, worked, and studied in a variety of different countries and cultures and, unlike businessmen of a previous generation, they have really lived in those countries, and experienced something of their cultures.

## The impact of television

The final and perhaps the most dramatic force in the destruction of national and cultural boundaries has been television. By the mid-1990s the average teenager in a household with a television, based on a worldwide forty-one-country survey, was watching six hours of television a day, and even in a country like China the majority of households had a television. The average American household had 2.4 and the proportion of Americans reporting that they turned on the television regardless of programming, as opposed to turning it on only to watch a specific programme, had risen to over 60 per cent.[34] This growing domination of leisure time by television has had four main effects.

First, television has been the vehicle for a global dissemination of American culture. Go to almost any country in the world, turn on the television, and you can see American soap operas, American comedy series, American cartoons, American films, and American-style commercials. The commercials are, of course, backed up by American products. Coca-Cola is more readily available than drinking water and the *Economist* magazine calculates the relative strengths of currencies worldwide in terms of their Big Mac purchasing power. But it is television and billboard advertising that lead the way. The young and affluent across the world live in a curious blend of indigenous and American cultures. So, in a different way, do the old and the poor. They may not drink the Coke or eat the hamburgers, but they do see the television programmes, for even in the shanty towns of Caracas or New Delhi people have television, if nothing else. Across the world, moreover, attempts by developing country governments to impose a state monopoly on television programming have fallen apart in the face of satellite technologies and the power wielded by the giant international media corporations.[35]

Second, through its news and documentaries, television provides people, in both developed and developing countries, with a window on the rest of the world. Before television, our knowledge of foreign cultures and societies was restricted to what we might read about, in travel books or gazettes. It was very limited, very distant, and available only to the educated minority. Now television takes us all into the nooks and crannies of cultures all over the world. We see major events, such as wars or riots, famines or floods, as they are happening. When tribes or countries go to war the main news broadcasters have reporters and camera teams in both of the rival camps. Television news has taken us into the centre of Khabul and Groszny in the midst of civil wars, and into the refugee camps of Somalia and Rwanda. Television documentaries have taken us into the homes of Inuit Eskimos and New Guinea tribes; into Japanese weddings and Polynesian feasts; into Buddhist temples and nomad camps. The experience is vicarious, and the 'reality' that we see can be deeply misleading— socially and historically decontextualized, and distorted by the particular aims and interpretations, or misinterpretations, of the producer. But it is vivid and immediate, and we really do learn something (accurate or otherwise) about the different religions, customs, and lifestyles to be found around the globe.

Third, through both films and documentaries, fact and fiction, television introduces us to values that are sometimes very different from those authorized by our social institutions. Our children have been taught that they should not swear, and should not be violent. But when people swear on the television, no one tells them off. Violence too is endemic on television, where it is statistically far more prevalent than in the real world and perpetrated by glamorous hero-figures as much as by villains.[36] But it passes without comment. Sex, in the authorized version of our society, goes with love, but that's blatantly not the case on television. In these cases the boundaries that are being broken down are those within our society, the barriers between social classes and between communities, the barriers between what we profess and what we do, and the barriers between the moral world of social practice and the amoral world of fantasy. But values also differ between societies and these differences too are exposed by television. So we not only find out about the life and customs of Afghan Muslims or Japanese Buddhists: we also discover that some of their values are different from ours, that our authorities are not the only ones by which people can live, and that the rules by which we were brought up are not as universal as we thought.

Fourth, as Richard Stivers has pointed out, in introducing us to these worlds television creates a kind of social chaos. Television documentaries pick out the features of a social group or culture on the basis of what will be meaningful or entertaining to their audiences, rather than to reflect reality. The pictures we get are grossly distorted, but because they are *pictures* they are absorbed without question. We may not always believe what we hear but we do tend to believe what we see. By playing to our visual sense, television also tends to eliminate both spatial and temporal context. The visual is always present, but watching television we move incoherently from one present to another, all of them equal in their claim on our attention, but with no narrative connection. In television fiction, characters from different social groups or contexts are reconstructed so as to make them more accessible to the average viewer and then put together in combinations, proportions, and situations that would never occur in real life. In television talk shows and soap operas the boundaries between public and private life, and between fiction and reality, are blurred. The so-called 'reality television' ('Big Brother', 'Castaway', 'Wife Swap') takes this to the extreme, inviting us to watch real (but carefully selected) people taking part in real (but totally artificial) activities, in the real (but utterly distorting) context of the cameras. The precious distinction between reality and fantasy becomes ever harder to sustain.[37]

## The consequences of interaction

Just as the erosion of moral authority has its benefits, so does the erosion of cultural boundaries. When the barrier between two liquids is removed, the liquids intersperse. As the boundaries between cultures are dissolved, the cultures interact. What was strange becomes familiar and ideas that, to begin with, seem completely incommensurable are gradually absorbed into each other until dialogue and discussion become possible. Put two people together, neither of whom speaks the language of the other, and for a while it will seem that no communication can be made. But it will not take long before they find a way around their differences, and what is true for language is true for other aspects of culture too.

This interaction produces all sorts of positive and encouraging effects. The more you know people, for example, the better you understand their customs and religions, and the more intimate your connection with their lives, the harder it is to go to war with them. War is only possible when people are prepared to kill for their society, and that is only possible when the boundaries of membership are strong. In parts of Africa, tribe can still fight tribe. In Bosnia or Northern Ireland, creed can still fight creed. But these are now exceptional cases. We no longer see nation fighting nation, because through most of the world the boundaries of nationality are no longer that strong.[38]

It is also harder, as one learns more about societies, to use ignorance or poor knowledge of their customs as an excuse for bad behaviour. In business especially, an enormous amount of unscrupulous behaviour has been justified in the past by the erroneous use of the principle of 'When in Rome, do as the Romans do.' Throughout the less developed world environments have been destroyed, people have been abused, and communities split asunder on the basis that 'that's how they do things over there'. Corrupt regimes have been sustained by businesses mistaking the presence of corruption for its social acceptability. Incalculable damage has been done by the aggressive marketing of food products (such as infant formula milk powder) in ignorance or disdain of the social context in which they will be used. Thousands upon thousands of businessmen have betrayed their partners for the pleasures of the foreign brothel, convincing themselves—or convincing themselves that they had convinced themselves—that it was somehow expected of them. As the boundaries between societies break down, however, caricatures will gradually be replaced by more realistic images, based on the knowledge and understanding of real, ordinary people, of the lives they live and the values they hold. The scope for the exploitation of misunderstanding will surely diminish.

Meanwhile, we live in societies that are increasingly pluralistic, and increasingly confusing. With the traditional authorities no longer providing us with the values that we seek, we look around us and see a dazzling variety of alternatives. A schoolgirl growing up in Britain today may well share a classroom with Christians and Muslims, Hindus and Sikhs. She is unlikely to fully understand the cultures and beliefs associated with those religions. Such understanding takes a very long time, and a much deeper involvement than school encounters or television can provide. Most children, anyway, have very little understanding of their own cultures or religions. But the differences in values and social customs are apparent and so a question is raised which cannot be answered: which, if any, is right?

A young man growing up in southern China sees the traditional Confucian ideas of respect and obligation side by side with the self-assertion and egoism of aggressive entrepreneurship. Are relationships and agreements sacrosanct, or are they not? A Turkish or Algerian woman struggles with the conflict between traditional Islamic customs and values and those of the West, each of which are violently asserted in her country. How should she behave? In any European or North American city a teenage boy learns from his TV screen that violence is cool and that the heroes get sex with whomever they want. OK, so maybe the violence needs some cause, but how much? As he scans through the channels or watches the people in the city around him it becomes clear that the boundaries of acceptable behaviour vary enormously from community to community.

As we survey the range of different cultures, different religions, and different values to be found in our societies or on our television screens, three things become painfully apparent. The first is that while we might know about all these cultures we cannot possibly understand them, because we cannot experience them. Seeing how a community lives on television, or talking to one of its members, gives us only the most superficial of insights. The second is that without such an understanding and experience we are simply in no position to make judgements between the values we see. The third, and probably the most disturbing, is that while we cannot fully grasp these new alternatives to which we are constantly being exposed, we are rapidly losing whatever grasp we had on the traditional moral values and belief structures of our own societies.

## THE SUBURBANIZATION OF SOCIETY

At first take, the idea of suburbanization being a major factor in the weakening of moral constraints seems all back to front. Are not the suburbs, as compared with, say, the inner cities, the epitome of moral correctness? In a way they are. The suburbs are generally peaceful and law-abiding districts, in which crime rates are low and people can walk the streets without feeling threatened. That is often why people move there. But compared with small towns and rural areas suburban life is also characterized by relatively weak community and family ties and by low levels of social interaction: In simple terms, people *don't* walk the streets. They stay at home or drive. Moral values may be high, but moral constraints are low. For the suburbs themselves, this is not a serious problem, but in the past few decades many of the same technologies we have already discussed in the context of eroding cultural boundaries have also been instrumental in transferring the social patterns of the suburb back into the town, city, and countryside, where the weakened moral constraints are potentially much more damaging.

Although the suburbs are a worldwide phenomenon, they are probably seen in their purest form in North America, and it is in America that their moral aspects have been most deeply studied. What has been found is what

M. P. Baumgartner has called 'moral minimalism' and Alan Wolfe, 'morality writ small'.[39] Baumgartner concluded her ethnographic study of a middle-class American suburb in the 1980s by stressing the inhabitants' aversion to moral engagement: [40]

Moral minimalism dominates the suburbs. On a day-to-day basis, life is filled with efforts to deny, minimise, contain, and avoid conflict. People shun confrontations and show great distaste for the pursuit of grievances or the censure of wrongdoing. In fact, only when they can be assured that someone else will bear the full burden of moral authority, allowing them to remain completely anonymous and uninvolved, do suburbanites approve the exercise of social control . . .

[Residents of suburbs] are happy to have police act as their champions in preventing and resolving troubles that unknown persons might cause, but beyond this they have very little use for law. When problems occur, most people do not seriously consider recourse to legal officials, and, in fact, they generally act as if law did not exist at all. In this sense, suburbia is a kind of limited anarchy.

This 'limited anarchy' is evident even in family relationships. Suburbs are relatively transient places, in which the mobile nuclear family is the norm. Extended families and family clusters, as found in traditional villages and cities, are rare. Instead, relatives are dispersed around the country and most family relationships are voluntary rather than enforced. Even within the nuclear family, Baumgartner found a high degree of physical and emotional separation. Family members had their own space and possessions, and lived their own lives, passing each other by in the course of the day, but rarely spending much time together. Parental authority was weak.

Friendship and neighbourhood ties were even weaker. People got along fine, but they did so largely by avoiding each other and by putting up (preferably at a distance) with behaviours they disliked, even when they considered these highly immoral. Again the transitory nature of residence and the physical separation between households was a factor. Because people took the car any place they were going—to work, to school, to the large anonymous shopping mall—they simply did not encounter each other on the street. Often, they did not even talk with their immediate neighbours. And if they did not like something that was going on they could simply stay in their own house or yard until it went away.[41]

A decade after Baumgartner's research, in the mid–late 1990s, Alan Wolfe conducted an interview survey of the moral views of middle-class American suburbia and found a consistent picture. The moral values people reported were very traditional: 'I just believe', said one typical respondent, 'that we were put here by God to love and care for each other and to make a difference in this world'.[42] But their morality was very quiet, very low key. In a pluralistic society, tolerance was the greatest virtue and 'making a difference' did not mean imposing any moral constraints on others, or even talking publicly about one's views. The weak ties with family and community reported by Baumgartner were also strongly evident. Only the church-based networks seemed strong, and they were somehow separate from day-to-day life.[43]

The suburbs are essentially a product of technology. Early, relatively high-density suburbs, such as those that characterize many British cities, were made possible by the railways that ferried people into work. More modern, low-density suburbs are a product of the motorcar, on which they are almost totally dependent. Changing technologies, including the motorcar, have also been a key factor in the transfer of suburban lifestyles and social patterns to towns, cities, and the countryside.

Country villages were once self-contained communities, but today they are almost wholly residential. Village residents drive to work or to the supermarket or retail park exactly as suburban residents do. They also drive where they used to walk: to the village shop if there is one, or the recycling bins. Town centres that once housed a mixture of residential and working activities are now mainly commercial, and even those people who do live in town are quite likely to work out of it. In city centres mixed neighbourhoods have given way to well defined commercial, shopping, or residential areas, and for the more affluent residents of the city centre, most of whom are young and single, 'home' is likely to be somewhere else. They live in the city because it is convenient for work, but they live there only to sleep, leaving early, returning late, and disappearing by train or car for weekends and holidays.

The other major technological factor in the suburbanization of society, as in so many other developments, has been television. The average person in Britain, as in other developed countries, now spends four hours a day watching television. Take away eight hours for sleep, eight hours for work or school, and another two for travel, shopping, and domestic chores, and that is two thirds of the time left. Television is entertaining and absorbing, and much easier than talking or going out. It sucks people in, expands to fill the time available, and provides ersatz-communities of soap operas and dramas, quiz shows, and sport. Whether in suburbs, villages, towns, or cities the result is that people no longer communicate as much with each other as they used to. They go out less and in smaller groups, and when at home they interact less. What is commonly referred to in Britain and America as the 'family room' is in reality a locus for communal television watching. The institution of the family meal has been eroded to the point at which to sit down together at table is an exceptional event rather than the norm.

If television reduces the desire to go out, other forms of technology reduce the need. Fridges and freezers mean that shopping is no longer a daily activity. Improved telecommunications and the Internet have meant that the postal service as a means of interpersonal communications is almost redundant. Mail (mainly bills, statements, and promotional leaflets) is received (without leaving home), but no longer sent (which did require leaving home). Banking can be done without visiting the bank.

Between them, television, the motorcar, and other technologies have left us with communities in which people no longer communicate, no longer know each other, and no longer care. Such communities cannot provide moral exemplars, for none are visible. They cannot provide support when families break down, because no one knows what is going on. Above all, they cannot provide any moral constraint. If a young boy vandalizes someone's property, there is a good chance that no one will see him or hear him, because they are all watching television. If anybody does see him, there is a good chance they will not recognize him. If they do recognize him, there is a good chance that they will not know his parents.

Fortunately for the boy's community, but not for society at large, there is also a good chance that he will go somewhere else to do his damage—into town, or across town, to where he can be quite sure that nobody knows him. And if things go wrong, if people catch on to what he's doing, or if, a few years later, he gets fed up with his girlfriend and does not want to pay for her baby, he will just move on, as easy as that. No need to tell anyone, no need to sort anything out, and no one to ask, as they would once have asked, 'What is that boy doing? Perhaps someone could have a word with him.'

## CONCLUSION

The late twentieth century was very obviously a period of great technological and political change. We have seen in this chapter that it was also a period of tremendous moral change. It is not so much that people now are any 'less moral' in a traditional sense than they were twenty years ago, though attitudes to families, colleagues, and communities have certainly altered. It is more that, in the space of a single generation, the institutions and authorities on which the traditional morality of obligation has depended for support and enforcement have very largely disintegrated.

In part, this has been a consequence of the more obvious changes. Political and economic globalization, the motor car, air travel, television, and the Internet have all contributed to breaking down the social structures within cultures and the barriers between them, exposing domestic institutions and authorities to critical scrutiny. In part, it has been the culmination of a much longer historical process of rational critique, an inevitable if much delayed consequence of the Enlightenment project. Whatever the causes, however, the effect has been to substantially weaken the constraints imposed by traditional morality.

# 6

# The Crisis of Morality and the Moral Culture of Contemporary Society

The collapse of traditional moral authorities, the weakening of cultural boundaries, and the suburbanization of society described in Chapter 5, and the rise of economic ideas, the growing power of business and finance, and the adoption of market values described in Chapters 3 and 4, were intimately connected. In historical terms they can all be seen as manifestations of the gradual working out of the Enlightenment project, as products of a particular kind of 'scientific' rationality that first found expression in the seventeenth and eighteenth centuries, and of the scientific and technological developments with which that has been associated. The way in which all the developments we have described gathered pace in the closing decades of the twentieth century reflects their close links to technology, and in particular to communications technology. Fostered in earlier times by the technologies of metalled roads and canals, railways, and the telegraph, their recent acceleration is in large measure due to the accelerated communications of air transport, television, telecommunications, and computer-based systems.

In terms of the cultural theory outlined in Chapter 2, the developments can be seen as two sides of the same coin. On one side we can see the gradual weakening and fragmentation of the traditional hierarchical culture of a role-structured society. As the ties of hierarchy have been loosened, the shared values and classification systems maintained by those ties have become neglected or thrown into question, and the moral authorities to which people traditionally turned have been undermined. On the other side of the coin we can see the growing exploitation of this fragmentation of the hierarchy by entrepreneurs, and the gradual intrusion of ideas and institutions associated with the market culture—ideas and institutions that can be applied readily across cultures and belief structures.[1] Just as, in the absence of any consensus on aesthetic values, a work of art can always be valued by its market price, so too when the traditional religious and social underpinnings of morality get called into question, people can fall back on a shared perception of self-interest.

Given these developments, the critically important question arises as to whether the balance between enterprise and ethics still holds, in any meaningful way. Does it still make sense to talk of a society structured by the traditional morality of obligation in which entrepreneurial self-interest has an important but essentially limited role? Or have the roles been reversed, so that we now live in a predominantly market culture characterized by the morality of self-interest, in which the morality of obligation is limited to specific situations or circumstances? Or are both sets of values in some sense equally legitimate?

One manifestation of the changes we described in Chapter 5 has been a widespread concern with a perceived 'crisis of morality'. Ralph Fevre's analysis of the rise of common sense reasoning, which we used in Chapter 4 to contextualize our own account of the rise of economic thinking and the legitimacy of self-interest, was set out in a book titled *The Demoralization of Western Culture*, and other recent titles reflect the same theme: Fukuyama's *Great Disruption*; Himmelfarb's *De-Moralization of Society*, Stivers's *Age of Cynicism: American Morality in Decline*. In this chapter we shall begin by reviewing some of the more prominent accounts, both popular and academic, of our society's moral decline, its causes, and its remedies. We shall conclude that while these accounts shed valuable light on various aspects of our present situation, they tend either to overstate the extent to which moral attitudes have actually changed or to misinterpret the nature, and underestimate the extent, of the structural changes affecting our society. In most cases, they are also distorted, or at least constrained, by political and ideological considerations. People who write about moral issues tend to have particular moral axes to grind. In the second half of the chapter we shall, therefore, put forward an alternative, and we hope more balanced, view of contemporary society as a 'bimoral' society, in which the traditional morality of obligation and the market morality of self-interest are *both* socially legitimate and in which, in the absence of any strong moral authority, it is left up to the individual to decide which set of values to adopt in which situation.

## THE CRISIS OF MORALITY

Contemporary accounts of the crisis of morality can be classified, very crudely, by their view of human nature, optimistic or pessimistic, and by their political leanings, to left or to right.

The philosopher Richard Rorty has remarked that a key difference between American pragmatism and the continental European philosophies to which it is most closely related rests in different perceptions of human nature.[2] The Americans, who have never been subjected to fascist or communist regimes, are optimists. They tend to believe that people, in general, are inherently benevolent, and that if left to their own devices they will use their freedom not only to advance their self-interest but also to protect the common interest. With this belief, they see little need for hierarchies and are favourably disposed toward free markets, in both economic goods and ideas. So pragmatists, who equate what is good with what is most beneficial to society, argue that society be left free to experiment with different versions of the good, and to choose that which is most effective. Similarly in economic life, Americans tend to favour free markets with a minimum of regulatory controls. Continental Europeans, on the other hand, who have a long history of political oppression, are more pessimistic about human nature. They tend to believe that if left unchecked, people will exploit positions of power, and this makes them deeply suspicious both of free markets and of rigid vertical hierarchies.

On the political dimension, views from the right tend to emphasize the positive value of economic self-interest, not only as a source of economic wealth but also for its associations with individual freedom and the moral virtue of self-reliance. Although they see the world as suffering, and suffering seriously, from a collapse of moral standards, they broadly subscribe to the view we labelled in Chapter 3 'the triumph of reason'. The market, from this perspective, is not so much a threat to traditional morality as its potential saviour, rescuing it from the misconceptions of socialism and the welfare state. Views from the left embrace the rival view we earlier labelled 'the triumph of greed', but are not restricted to it. They see traditional morality under threat, but from bureaucratic rationality and the comfortable indifference of consumer society as well as from economic self-interest.

From the perspective of the triumph of reason, morality, or at least the morality of advanced democratic capitalist societies, is not always considered an issue. There is a concern—a very deep and fearful concern, in the wake of the World Trade Center disaster of 11 September 2001—with the perceived immoralities of certain developing country societies. There is a concern, too, with the moral standards of the underclass in Western society. In both cases, immoral behaviour is seen as a threat to the safety and security of society. But in both cases that threat is widely seen to come from outside society. For whatever lip service the affluent middle classes may pay to the needs of the poor and underprivileged, they treat them in practice much as they might people in another country altogether. That is to say, they treat them with hostility and suspicion, and avoid them as far as possible. For the prosperous beneficiaries of economic growth, the 'society' of their emotional lives is a society from which criminal or potentially criminal elements are effectively excluded, and while this society is certainly characterized by self-interest there is little sense of any threat *from within it* to traditional morality.[3]

For some commentators, however, the perception of a collapse of traditional morality is simply too strong and its implications too serious to be so easily dismissed. It is not enough simply to associate immorality with an excluded underclass. Some account must also be given of why that underclass exists and why the habits associated with it are so steeply on the increase. We shall consider, here, two such accounts. The first, expounded by Francis Fukuyama, treats the contemporary decline of traditional morality as part of a process of cyclical adjustment, an inevitable but temporary by-product of technological and economic progress. The second, expounded by conservative thinkers such as Gertrude Himmelfarb, Michael Novak, and Irving Kristol, treats it as a much more fundamental problem, but associates it with the politics of social democracy and the welfare state and looks to the market culture itself for a cure.

## A cyclical adjustment

Francis Fukuyama is in no doubt about the existence or severity of contemporary moral decline. In *The Great Disruption*, he documents the data on crime, divorce, and illegitimacy and presents a sombre picture of the breakdown of social order across the developed world.[4] He is no doubt either that the individualism of market culture, spilling over from the world of enterprise into society at large, has played a large and significant part in this decline. In many ways, indeed, his analysis is very close to that offered here, accepting the need both for entrepreneurial self-interest and for traditional morality and hierarchical social structures, and recognizing that the balance has swung uncomfortably far towards the former. For Fukuyama, however, the contemporary decline of traditional morality is not part of a long term process going back to the Enlightenment but a much more recent phenomenon arising out of the shift from an industrial to a post-industrial or information society in the last third of the twentieth century, and out of contemporaneous developments in medical technology. What happened, he argues, was that the shift of emphasis in the developed economies from physical to mental work (and from manufacturing to services) led to the inclusion of women in the workforce, undermining the traditional institution of the family. At the same time, increased longevity and the technologies of contraception reduced the role of reproduction in life. And in a period of rapid economic change and great business opportunities for those prepared to grab them, the exuberant individualism of market entrepreneurship spilled over into society and weakened both the traditional authorities and the traditional social ties that held families, communities, and nations together.

This story fits quite well with the recent statistical evidence, for the rise of information technologies, the availability of contraception, and the decline of the family can all be dated quite accurately to the 1960s. Inconveniently for Fukuyama, the steep rise in crime rates, which he would like to see as a consequence of the breakdown of the family and, therefore, lagging behind the other indicators, occurred at the same time, but given the complexity of the relationships involved that is a minor anomaly. In general terms the story is a convincing one, and when set in a historical context it is also reassuring.

The key point, historically, is that the great disruption of the late twentieth century was not unique. For something very similar happened in the last great technological and economic revolution, the Industrial Revolution of the late eighteenth and early nineteenth centuries. Then, too, technological changes led to a massive disruption in patterns of work and family life, with the change from village-based outsourcing to city factories. Then, too, the change impacted particularly upon women, breaking up family structures. Then, too, the changes opened the way for entrepreneurial individualism, which spilled over into society. And then, too, the end result was a steep rise in the crime rate and the breakdown of social order. But that breakdown was not permanent. By the Victorian era, as we saw in Chapter 2, the institution of the family had recovered, crime rates had fallen, and the values of traditional morality were once again ascendant.

This suggests to Fukuyama that while changes in technology are cumulative, changes in morality are cyclical, and that what we have been witnessing over the last forty years is essentially no more than a transitional phenomenon, a temporary if painful side effect of what Joseph Schumpeter called the 'creative destruction' of technological and economic change. Arguing on the basis of evolutionary biology that human beings are naturally, biologically, cooperative moral beings, and also that it is in our long-term self-interest to maintain a foundation of traditional moral norms upon which markets can operate effectively, he asserts confidently that moral values will be restored. The social structures of the information society will inevitably be different from those that characterized the industrial society, just as the structures of the industrial society differed from those of the agrarian society that preceded it. In particular, he suggests, there will be a somewhat greater reliance on self-organizing networks and less on formal hierarchies, at least in local settings. But the hierarchies will still be there. And as the Information Revolution works itself through and people work out how best to organize themselves in its wake, traditional morals will reassert themselves, just as they did 150 years ago—a process that he sees as already well under way:[5]

The process by which societies regenerate social capital is complex and often difficult. In many cases, it is a multigeneration process that leaves many victims in its wake, as older cooperative norms are destroyed without anything to take their place. The Great Disruption will not correct itself automatically. People have to recognize that their communal lives have deteriorated, that they are engaging in self-destructive behaviors, and that they have to work actively to renorm their society through discussion, argument, cultural argument, and even culture wars. There is evidence that this has happened to some extent already, and earlier periods in human history give us a certain confidence that renorming or remoralization is possible.

Fukuyama is at pains to dissociate himself from the more extreme advocates of the free market. He recognizes that for all its achievements the market culture (aided, it would seem, by the contraceptive pill) has also produced significant collateral damage and he takes that damage seriously. His account of the Great Disruption is carefully researched and historically aware. But somehow it does not quite ring true.

In the first place, Fukuyama seriously downplays the differences between the early nineteenth and late twentieth centuries. His suggestion that both should be seen as periods of social dislocation associated with revolutionary phases of technological and economic growth is powerful and, as far as it goes, convincing. Both the industrial and the information revolutions can indeed be characterized as periods of entrepreneurial exuberance and social disruption due to changing work patterns, leading to a loosening of moral standards and a rise in criminal activity. There is, undoubtedly, a cyclical element to social order, and this is manifest especially in the crime figures on which Fukuyama builds his case. But even those figures are twenty times higher in the late twentieth century than they ever were at their nineteenth-century peak; and the collapse of moral authority, the erosion of cultural boundaries, the growing power of business, and the rise of economic culture, while they have accelerated sharply in recent decades, are all longer-term developments. At the time of the Victorian remoralization of society the effects of the Enlightenment had hardly begun to work themselves out. Developments in science and technology had produced an industrial revolution, but the mindset of ordinary people remained thoroughly traditional. The Victorians did not have a modern scientific education, for example. They did not have television. And they still had religious belief.

In the course of the Industrial Revolution, church attendance fell off and there was a shift from the established to the dissenting churches, but Christian belief was not seriously threatened and religion played an important part in the remoralization process. Fukuyama suggests that it might do so again, not necessarily out of belief but out of a desire for community:[6]

[P]eople will return to religious tradition not necessarily because they accept the truth of revelation, but precisely because the absence of community and the transience of social ties in the secular world make them hungry for ritual and cultural tradition . . . They will repeat ancient prayers and reenact age-old rituals not because they believe that they were handed down by God, but rather because they want their children to have the proper values and want to enjoy the comfort of ritual and the sense of shared experience it brings.

In the American context this may seem faintly plausible, though even there the evidence is that church-going is based more on continuing belief and a continuing mistrust of science than on any desire for ritual, but in Europe the idea of a mass return to Christianity seems hopelessly far-fetched.

Fukuyama discusses religion in the context of his assertion, based mainly on a slight decline in crime rates in the early–mid 1990s, that the process of remoralization is already under way, and his insistence on this, while insignificant in itself, illustrates the limitations of his perspective. If his argument that the present disruption is essentially just like the previous one were stronger, he would have no need to show that we have turned the corner. As we have just seen, however, that argument is suspect. Some aspects, like the rise in crime, might be the same, but others are different. To bolster his argument he therefore needs to show that, in effect, the similarities outweigh the differences, and for this purpose strong evidence of a contemporary remoralization would clearly be very helpful. The problem is that his evidence is not very strong. As we noted in Chapter 2, crime statistics are notoriously difficult to interpret, but the fall in the early 1990s probably owes more to demographic changes (a fall in the number of young males of criminal age) and the boom phase of an economic cycle than to any fundamental remoralization of the underclass. Moreover it has not been sustained. Nor, more significantly, has the apparent retreat from the market excesses of the 1980s that seemed to characterize both business practice and political perspectives for a brief period in the mid-1990s, when Fukuyama was writing. From the perspective of the early twenty-first century it is the continuation of the trends of the late twentieth century that is most apparent, not their reversal. Of course, this perspective may itself be misleading and in ten years time the situation may well look different again, but if we are going through a process of cyclical readjustment, it still has some way to run.

Fukuyama makes some very important points, but he ends up by reinforcing the comfortable contentment of those who believe in the triumph of reason, and so fails to address the problems with which we are faced. Perhaps everything *will* be OK in the end, but if a traditional remoralization of society is to occur it will not happen overnight and it is unlikely to mirror the recovery of the nineteenth century. Moreover, it is unlikely to happen by itself. Accepting with Fukuyama that people have some kind of inbuilt moral instinct (an issue to which we shall return) and that it is indeed in people's long-term self-interest to re-establish and maintain social norms of cooperative behaviour (an argument that few would challenge), it does not necessarily follow that those norms *will* be re-established, let alone that they will be re-established in time to contain the potentially destructive forces of self-interest.

On this issue, Fukuyama is distinctly unconvincing. He emphasizes the importance of self-organizing networks as the appropriate coordinating structure for the information age, and suggests that such networks can act spontaneously to generate social norms. But having set up what looks like a possible solution he then destroys it with an impeccably clear-headed analysis of the limitations of networks and the continuing need, in a large-scale society, for a basically hierarchical culture. The future, it seems, lies with some kind of rational, politically negotiated hierarchy that formalizes spontaneously generated moral norms and helps people to order their lives, but without recourse to irrational authority or the infringement of liberties. It lies, in other words, with the modern liberal democracy. This conclusion should come as no surprise from the author of *The End of History*, in which the liberal democracy was presented as the end point of political evolution. But the confident assertion that existing political structures will in the end cope with the pressures to which they are being subjected tells us nothing about how to cope with them now.

## Moral markets and the virtue of self-reliance

For all his complacency, Fukuyama does at least recognize that an excess of market self-interest can have a destabilizing effect on morality and social order. In contrast with this, many free market economists and their political supporters would be quite horrified at the idea that their advocacy of economic self-interest and unregulated competition presents any challenge whatsoever to traditional morality. Milton Friedman, for example, one of the most influential of the Chicago school of economists and economic guru of the Thatcher and Reagan regimes, defended the right of company shareholders to pursue profit maximization at the expense of corporate social responsibility. He argued, indeed, that corporate social responsibility initiatives could do nothing but harm, interfering with market processes and so reducing overall efficiency. From his perspective, however, the duty of managers to run a company in the economic interests of its shareholders was a traditional moral as well as a legal one, and the pursuit of profit was also subject to 'the basic rules of society, both those embodied in law and those embodied in ethical custom'.[7] The ethical customs he had in mind seem to have been such things as the honouring of contracts and restraint from fraud and deception rather than any kind of altruism, but there is no doubt that he saw his position as being a moral one, in the traditional sense.

For Friedman, as for another of the influential figures of the 1980s and 1990s, the Austrian economist Friedrich von Hayek, economic markets need a foundation of traditional moral rules if they are to function effectively. What they suffer from is an inappropriate excess of moral sentiment. There are two lines of argument here, which tend to get confused. One starts from the premise of self-interest, treats traditional moral rules as a product of that self-interest, and the market as the primary medium through which it is expressed. From this perspective the traditional association of morality with duties and obligations is maintained, but the association with altruism is erroneous. As Norman Barry puts it in a recent article in which he takes up Friedman's attack on notions of social responsibility and business ethics,[8]

Good ethical conduct does not require a change in the moral personality, it simply requires the capacity in business agents to follow those conventions which are to their long run advantage. It requires that they be prepared to forgo opportunities to make immediate gains in the interests of sustaining those rules and conventions that make for long-run success.

In a family situation, he suggests, more demanding moral rules may well be appropriate, but that too will be a function of the self-interest of the parties involved. There is no conflict here between traditional morality and self-interest because one is the product of the other. If an act is in your long term self-interest, it is moral. If it is not, it is not.

The other line of argument treats individual freedom and property rights, both of which can be grounded in traditional morality, as supreme goods, and obligations that curtail these as being morally harmful. From this perspective, constraints such as respect for property, honesty in dealing, and the observance of contract act in the long run to maintain individual freedom, while more exacting moral demands limit it. Thus Barry, in the same article, distinguishes between a minimal set of moral rules that direct self-interested behaviour into socially productive channels, and 'a more expansive view of ethics [that] actually undermines [this] acceptable morality' by infringing on individual freedom.[9]

An apposite example of these lines of reasoning is found in free market critiques of the welfare state. The economic argument here is fairly straightforward. Welfare, it is said (by Hayek and Friedman among others), distorts the price mechanism that in a market economy directs self-interest to its most productive ends. In particular, welfare payments discourage people from working and the taxes needed to pay for them discourage employers from employing. But it is the moral arguments that are most interesting.

The first argument, from the perspective of morality as an aid to self-interest, focuses on the importance of self-reliance and the dangers of dependency. When the state allows people to become dependent upon it (however noble the intentions behind this), it allows their personal sense of responsibility to atrophy. Having once experienced the security of welfare, they become less eager to seize the opportunity of work and self-advancement when it presents itself, and more inclined to fall back into dependency when things get difficult. They take what is offered whether they need it or not. Dependency, in other words, breeds dependency in a vicious circle, encouraging passivity and irresponsibility, destroying people's innate capabilities, and so acting against their own self-interest as well as against the collective interests of society.[10] Welfare, beyond the care of the elderly and genuinely infirm, is therefore immoral. Of course, the recipients of welfare no longer recognize that it is against their long-term interests, but that is because their minds have already been corrupted.

This line of argument, with its emphasis on self-reliance as the basis of moral character, can be traced back to de Tocqueville and Burke who criticized the English system of poor relief in the 1830s in almost exactly the same terms as are used by critics of the welfare state today.[11] A few years later, in his famous essay on self-reliance, Ralph Waldo Emerson captured what has remained the characteristic American view of the moral person as thinking for himself, working for himself, and putting his own interests first.[12] For conservative thinkers today, the neglected virtue of self-reliance is a natural moral counterpart to the market culture, with its reliance on economic self-interest.

The second argument presents welfare as championing material equality (perceived as an aim of dubious moral value) and a perverted notion of the equality of opportunity at the expense of freedom and the true equality of opportunity associated with that. From this perspective state intervention not only distorts the priorities of both welfare recipients and taxpayers, but also takes away their freedom. In the process, it undermines the civil society that is the basis of a free society. This argument is a direct descendent of capitalist critiques of communism and has more to do with the general level of state intervention than with welfare specifically. The high taxes that result from modern welfare systems evidently limit the freedom of the taxpayers, as do public sector monopolies, minimum wages, and other products of social democratic government, but the claim that welfare payments limit the freedom of the recipients is more tenuous. It depends, in effect, on the earlier argument that dependency erodes autonomy. What it does, however, is to give that earlier argument a traditional moral force and enable the proponents of a free market culture to take the moral high ground and claim for the market a traditional moral authority. From this point of view, the free market is not merely set in the context of traditional morals, but is their central support. As in the first argument, the decline of traditional morality, instead of being associated with the rise of market culture and the morality of self-interest, becomes a direct consequence of the rise of the welfare state.

It should be said that economists like Hayek and Friedman do not generally take this step. But others do. The historian Gertrude Himmelfarb's book, *The De-moralization of Western Society*, is in fact an account of a very moralized society, that of Victorian England, but in an epilogue that rather curiously gives the book its title, Himmelfarb compares this society with those of contemporary Britain and America.[13] Her starting point is much the same as Fukuyama's, the 'two powerful indexes of social pathology, illegitimacy and crime'.[14] But whereas Fukuyama sees in the statistics a cyclical process, Himmelfarb sees the fluctuations of the nineteenth century as trivial in proportion compared with the steep rises of the late twentieth century. She identifies the latter not with technological and economic change, but with a demoralization of the public sphere. 'In Victorian England,' she writes, 'moral principles and judgements were as much a part of social discourse as of private discourse, and as much a part of public policy as of personal life'.[15] In contemporary life, in contrast, 'Most of us are uncomfortable with the idea of making moral judgements even in our private lives, let alone with the "intrusion", as we say, of moral judgements into public affairs.'[16] There is a deep reluctance to make moral judgements on others, to argue questions of public interest on moral grounds, or to enter into any kind of moral discourse.

We have already encountered this moral reticence in our discussions of the suburbanization of society and of the shift from social to psychological conceptions of identity. It is a central and well-documented feature of contemporary society. The question is, though: where has it come from? The answer, according to Himmelfarb, is from left-wing intellectuals seeking for their own ends to break the bonds of social conformity, and from their twentieth-century creation, the welfare state, which has de-legitimated traditional moral values and put in their place the values of the underclass. In the nineteenth century, poor relief or philanthropy had to be justified in terms of their moral as well as material benefit to the poor, which meant, among other things, discouraging dependency and restricting relief to those who 'deserved' it. In the welfare state of the twentieth century there are no moral preconditions to state funding. As a result of an unholy pact between the affluent left and the indigent underclass, moral judgements have been outlawed. What the Victorians classified as moral vices (e.g. illegitimacy or alcohol and drug dependency) have been legitimated by the state and reclassified as disabilities.

Stronger still are the arguments of Michael Novak, a writer on capitalism and civil society whose ideas have gained both widespread popular support and significant political influence, both in America and in Britain. For Novak, the welfare state in its late twentieth-century form corrupts the individuals it supports and because its benefits go overwhelmingly to divorced, separated, and (especially) unmarried women it is directly responsible for today's high levels of illegitimacy and, thus, for the rise in violent crime. Interpreting a correlation between prosperity and marital stability as showing that 'the simple fact of being married gave Americans a 93 per cent chance of not being poor' [sic], and noting that the children of single parents are much more likely to turn to crime than those of traditional families, Novak claims that it is not poverty but the state support of unmarried mothers that is to blame for the contemporary collapse of traditional moral standards.[17] Similarly Irving Kristol, another high profile social commentator, attributes to the welfare state the destruction of the family and, with that, 'a poisonous flowering of those very social pathologies—crime, illegitimacy, drugs, divorce, sexual promiscuity—that it was assumed the welfare state would curb if not eliminate.'[18]

What we have in this perspective is fervent support for the market culture coupled with a passionate defence of traditional moral standards and, in many cases, of traditional moral authorities. There is a deep contradiction here, because the market culture is inherently suspicious of authority and in most circumstances its proponents argue strongly against it. The problem they face here, though, is that in a world corrupted, in their terms, by welfare state thinking,[19] people no longer know where their true self-interest lies. Specifically, they think that taking welfare payments like unemployment benefits is in their self-interest when, because of the consequences of dependency, it really is not. There is, therefore, a pressing need for the powerful reassertion of the traditional moral virtues, in particular that of self-reliance, and this need can be met only by the reassertion of traditional, hierarchical, moral authorities. So Himmelfarb, for example, notes that it is not enough to get rid of welfare and rely on free markets, valuable as they are. So long as the state remains morally corrupt, immorality will remain legitimate. Government itself must, therefore, be remoralized and resume its proper role as the moral authority of a secular state.

Other writers look to religion rather than government to play this role. Thus Novak, who writes as much on Roman Catholic theology as on economics, quotes the conservative Pope John Paul II in support of his condemnation of the welfare state, and many other, more moderate, commentators also look to traditional religion to provide the moral basis for a market culture. For Robert Sirico, for example, the market is 'the most powerful institution imaginable for making prosperity and productivity possible, for calculating and coordinating resources in society . . . ' But:[20]

The market does not work automatically; markets have no moral compass built in; the culture of the market also needs a moral precondition in the recognition of certain fundamental values. He who values the market must also value the sanctity of the human person, the broadest possible definition of wealth, the greatest possible opportunities for economic creativity and a place for every person in the productive capacity of society. To be sure, this means placing strong emphasis on the indispensable institutions of private property, the freedom of contract, rivalrous competition and entrepreneurial enterprise; it also means understanding that these are not ends in themselves but instruments to be used to the higher glory of the Creator . . .

Whereas the irreligious proponents of market culture tend to treat the market as God, for Sirico it is God's chosen instrument. From this perspective, there is no intrinsic conflict between traditional morality, as expressed in Christian faith, and market culture. The institution of the market preserves human dignity and freedom, allowing people to settle their differences peacefully, without resort to violence, and market self-interest promotes the welfare of all by promoting economic development and wealth creation. Entrepreneurs succeed by serving others, and when they succeed they use their profits to help others by charitable donations—clear evidence that their market self-interest is, in reality, an expression of worthy selflessness.

Of course, not all Christians would agree. In Britain the clergy, if not their parishioners, tend to the political left and see markets, not the state, as the corrosive force in contemporary society. But for many Christian entrepreneurs—and many Americans—Sirico's arguments are almost self-evident. So what is going on here? Are the conflicts of the bimoral society an illusion, born out of a misunderstanding of the nature of markets? Or are the Christian defenders of market culture themselves under an illusion?

To answer these questions we need to recognize the tensions between three social institutions: market, state, and church. The liberal tradition of the Enlightenment, from which both free market and social welfare liberalism are descended, was based on the marriage, exemplified in the works of Adam Smith, between free market economics and traditional moral restraint. Originally, that moral restraint was religiously based. As religion and the authority of the church declined, however, the state took on the role of moral guardian, and as the inherent tensions between market self-interest and traditional morality heightened, so liberals had in effect to choose between the self-interest of the market and the moral duties of the state.[21] For the large sector of contemporary society for whom the church is no longer relevant, this choice presents itself as a straightforward (if ultimately impossible) choice between traditional and economic moralities. For the committed Christian, though, the situation is more complicated. One on hand, the values of traditional morality are not in question. On the other hand, however, the proper source of those values is belief in God, and not a Godless secular state. In continental Europe, the tendency has been to emphasize the virtue of compassion and to side with the state. In America, where hierarchy has always been treated with suspicion, the Christian churches still command majority support and religious attitudes (even in the Catholic and Episcopal churches) are much more individualistic, the tendency has been to trust in faith and to side with the market.

In seeking to marry market self-interest with an individualistic brand of traditional morality informed by religious faith, the Christian advocates of market culture are following a long-standing American tradition, and in the context of their beliefs their position is perfectly consistent. The problem is that from a wider perspective these beliefs seem outdated and anachronistic. To rely on one's own religious convictions to supply a traditionally moral foundation for one's own market enterprise is perfectly reasonable. To rely, in the twenty-first century, on a more widespread religious belief for the moral regulation of markets in general seems dangerously naive.

## The morality of power

A common feature of the views from the right, and of the storyline of the triumph of reason more generally, is the emphasis on individual freedom, embodied in free markets, as a supreme good. The critics of these views argue, however, and with some justification, that this emphasis skips over an important point, namely that the free market culture does not, in fact, produce free markets. The missing element here is power. For a successful entrepreneur the ideal free market is not like a theoretical economist's free market, with infinitely many buyers and sellers and transparent prices. Rather, it is a market in which the entrepreneur is free from regulation and restrictions, but in which he is also 'free' to exploit that situation by gaining a dominant market share and imposing his power on others. This ambiguity in the meaning of freedom is a central feature of contemporary attitudes to business and society, and we shall return to it in the next chapter, but in the context of the crisis of morality debate it is the concept of power that is key. Perhaps because they tend to represent the more powerful groups in our society, commentators from the right rarely make any mention of power, but for those from the left it is crucial.

The link between morality and power in a hierarchical culture is complex. At a very basic level morality is a function of power. For a young child in a family or school setting, for example, to be good is quite simply to do what you are told. But it is also a limitation on power. Those at the top of a hierarchical system have a moral duty to use their power for the collective good, not for their individual self-interest, and traditional moral values are all associated with a restraint on power. As Richard Stivers notes, 'Ethical meaning arises in the limitations placed on power. The values of freedom, justice, love, and equality all place limits on acting out of individual or collective self-interest.'[22]

For commentators such as David Korten, whose views on the triumph of greed we encountered in Chapter 3, the crisis of morality arises from the fact that in contemporary society the power of one group of actors, businesses and financial institutions, is no longer constrained. Corrupted by their power these 'once beneficial' institutions have succumbed to financial greed and self-interest and created a world in which only the selfish can survive.[23] For sociologists such as Stivers, however, the effects of power are much more insidious.

In *The Culture of Cynicism*, Stivers begins from the observation that traditional morality is in decline, but rejects attempts to explain or remedy this in terms of political changes, the rise of big business, or the failure of moral authority.[24] The problem, he argues, is deeper than that, for it is morality itself, as practised in contemporary American society, that is encouraging self-serving behaviour. For Stivers, who draws heavily on the ideas of the French sociologist and theologian Jacques Ellul, the key feature of contemporary society is not the rise of market culture but the domination and worship of technology: 'The new lived morality and its mythological justification flow from this fundamental experience—that technology as ultimate power is the solution to all problems.'[25]

Technology, broadly understood to include everything from machines and communications to bureaucratic procedures and psychological techniques, promises us success, survival, happiness, and health, and it these which have become the core values of the new morality. The traditional morality of obliga- tion is still with us but only as what Stivers calls moral custom, a morality of the past that lives on as nostalgia, but has all but disappeared from practice and become subservient to the dominant lived morality, which is the morality of technology. The problem is that whereas traditional morality placed con- straints on power and emphasized the responsibility of individual choice, the morality of technology, which is expressed in bureaucratic rules and in the norms of media-generated public opinion, is itself all-powerful and leaves no room for choice. It is, in this sense, 'an anti-morality':[26]

That is, every traditional morality has placed some limitations on the exercise of power—political and personal. Because of our fascination with technology, indeed our tacit adoration of it, we do not perceive the need to limit its growth and expansion into every sphere of human existence. Technology is at bottom nothing more than an expres- sion of power: it is the most efficacious and efficient means of acting. My thesis is that technical and bureaucratic rules are the 'morality' of technology. Never has any society been hemmed in by so many rules and regulations.

Stivers identifies two main expressions of technology in our society: bureau- cracy, or organizational technique, and psychological technique. Whereas tra- ditional moral norms are context dependent and symbolically interdependent, bureaucratic rules are general and abstract. Their meaning is fixed, and what- ever ends they were originally designed to serve are eclipsed by the means devised to achieve these. The result, and the intention, is to maximize effi- ciency by controlling behaviour: in an effective bureaucracy people follow the rules without question. A classic illustration of this is provided by Stanley Milgram's famous experiments in which a majority of volunteers in a scientific experiment on learning, in fact a mock experiment, readily gave subjects what they believed to be painful and even fatal electric shocks on the instructions of a white-coated 'scientist'. In a technological setting, their everyday moral beliefs were ditched in favour of obedience to technical rules. The same phenomenon is also central to sociologist Zygmunt Bauman's account of the Nazi Holocaust. The Holocaust, according to Bauman, was possible only because of the effectiveness of a bureaucratic routine that neutralized moral behaviour: 'Men are easily induced to contribute to collective and co-ordinated endeavours the outcomes of which they would find repulsive and unbearable in the context of morally significant relationships.'[27]

The thousands of people involved in rounding up, transporting, and killing the Jews were not all evil; they were simply following bureaucratic rules. Put another way, while violent passions have often caused mass killings, only a modern technocratic civilization could accomplish genocide on this scale, for 'the civilizing process is, among other things, a process of divesting the use and employment of violence from moral calculus, and of emancipating the desiderata of rationality from interference of ethical norms or moral inhibitions.'[28] For Bauman, as for Stivers, 'bureaucracy's double feat is the moralization of technology, coupled with the denial of the moral significance of non-technical issues.'[29]

Psychological technique embraces everything from advertising and PR to therapy and self-help. It involves the technical manipulation of oneself and of others and, according to Stivers, has effectively supplanted traditional manners and morality. Technology provides answers for all our problems and what were traditionally the core problems of moral practice—how should I live my life, how should I respond to the needs of others—have been replaced in modern society by the purely technical problems of therapeutic technique and image manipulation. Life itself has been 'transformed into a never-ending series of technical problems'.[30]

On this version of history, bureaucratic and market cultures are not opposing forces, but the twin products of the Enlightenment. Big business, global capital markets, the consumer society, and the bureaucratic state are all products of technological modernity. All promise an illusory freedom—the freedom of markets, the freedom of consumer choice, the freedom of the ballot box—but all work together to exercise technological power and enslave the people. The rise of market culture, on this account, simply represents a shift in power from one source of oppression to another, from the bureaucratic state to the big business enterprise.

This perspective, in which human freedom and moral choice have been destroyed by the oppressive power of technology and its commercial and bureaucratic manifestations, dates back to the mid-twentieth century and is characteristic of the European school of critical social thinking. The basic themes can be found in different forms both in the writings of Michel Foucault and in those of the Frankfurt School (Herbert Marcuse, Max Horkheimer, Theodore Adorno, Jürgen Habermas). Its great strengths lie in its passionate defence of humanity and in its ability to probe beneath the surface of things and uncover the powerful forces at play in seemingly innocuous situations. Its weakness, perhaps, lies in its tendency to see oppression everywhere. This means that the distinctions of contemporary society, the distinctions we have described in terms of the bimoral society, tend to get elided. If all the facets of modern society conspire to act in the same direction, then there is not much point in trying to steer a path through them. Every organized response to the problems we face, whether in politics or in management, is immediately suspect, and productive practical debate becomes almost impossible. So for Richard Stivers, a political solution to moral decline is impossible: Politics is too laden with technique, too corrupted by technology, to do anything other than advance the morality of technology. All we can do is fight the system at the personal level of individual rebellion, rediscovering moral meaning by living out an individual ethic of love and non-power.[31]

## Morality and indifference

A rather different view of the crisis of morality, but one that draws on the same general body of ideas, attributes it not so much to power, though that is indirectly implicated, as to indifference. In *Moral Culture*, Keith Tester explores contemporary morality through the medium of massacre.[32] Through a study of the massacre by American soldiers at My Lai during the Vietnam War, he tries to understand 'how good Westerners can commit atrocities and slaughter and yet believe themselves to be quite innocent of blame'.[33] And he explores what underlies the Western responses, or more accurately the absence of any Western responses, to well-documented instances of massacre and genocide elsewhere—in Cambodia, Bosnia, and Rwanda. His account is complex. Indeed, he is at pains to point out that the evidence resists any simple characterization of morality under the conditions of modernity. But it highlights three important and interrelated features of the treatment of moral issues in contemporary society.

First, Tester points to the institutionalization and monetarization of society, which places a barrier between moral perception and moral action. Drawing on observations by Michael Ignatieff,[34] he notes that if we perceive a moral wrong we no longer act ourselves (like volunteering to be nurses or going to fight in the Spanish Civil War) but pay professionals to act instead. We donate to charities, for example. Or if, as is often the case, we have not the faintest idea *what* should be done, we simply demand that *something* be done and leave it to the politicians, the aid agencies, and human rights observers to formulate an appropriate response. But just as institutional constraints prevent us from acting ourselves, or even from imagining acting ourselves, so bureaucratic constraints disempower the institutions we pay to act for us. And as politics itself has become institutionalized and economized, becoming dominated by issues of resource allocation and efficiency, so the political process has become ethically indifferent and moral conscience has ceased to be politically effective.

Second, Tester points to the commodification of morality. Whereas our perceptions of moral wrong and the need to rectify it were once limited to our own community, television and the media now present us with an effective infinity of moral problems. All of these are identical in the sense that they can be treated only by a donation of money, and only a few of them—an arbitrary few—can in practice be selected for consideration. Donating money to a moral cause is, of course, a form of consumption—in some cases, using Veblen's phrase, of conspicuous consumption, undertaken to lend distinction to or otherwise enhance the reputation of the donor—and it is governed by the same rules as govern other forms of consumption in a consumer society.[35] We follow the dictates of fashion and donate to feed our self-image. As in a shopping mall, we are attracted to what is novel, but presented with so many buying opportunities even novelty loses the power to shock.

Third, drawing on the ideas of critical theorist Herbert Marcuse, Tester points to the more general effects of consumer society and the mediation of reality by television. In *One Dimensional Man*, Marcuse argued that in contemporary society everything becomes captured by the world of consumption. Any attempt to rebel against the illusions of freedom or the idea that everything is perfect immediately gets packaged itself into yet another consumer product, that further extends the range of consumer choice. Art becomes domesticated and loses its power to assert that things could be different. Violence becomes an entertaining spectacle. Moral conscience is subsumed by a state of contentment, by what he calls a 'Happy Consciousness'.[36] Marcuse was writing in a world not yet dominated by television, but in contemporary society television is clearly implicated. As Tester puts it,[37]

It could well be argued that the television news broadcasts which make us aware of the contemporary genocides are also the mechanisms of the avoidance of moral self-reflexion. It could be argued that the broadcasts themselves assist in the avoidance of moral guilt precisely because they tell us that although some things are dreadful at least the Croatians can still drink Coke and eat pizza (so things cannot be that bad really); that admittedly it is awful that a girl has been raped in front of her mother but the company just down the road is closing, and I might be the next to be made redundant.

Perhaps television still has some power to shock. The pictures of hijacked airliners crashing into the twin towers of the World Trade Center in September 2001 made for a truly awful spectacle that few Americans—and few Britons—will ever forget. But the force of those images came largely from the unbelievable, unimaginable nature of what they portrayed, and from the almost unique way in which they really did bring the horrors of terrorism closer. Most moral atrocities take place a long way from the comfortable living rooms of affluent Westerners and television keeps them there. We know that genocide still happens, and we know that the world is full of smaller-scale happenings that go against the traditional morality we profess. But in the very act of drawing attention to these, television both distances us from them and slots them into a world of countless everyday occurrences. On one hand, we feel powerless to act. On the other hand, we feel no need to act. We can simply flick over from genocide on one channel to a ball game on another; from a real life case of domestic cruelty, infidelity, or neglect on one channel to a fictional case on another. Everything is relativized and everything is reduced to entertainment. We donate to charity and settle for the consolations of the Happy Consciousness. At the moral level, indifference reigns.

Tester's story is suggestive and insightful. It is also depressing, because there is no obvious way of overcoming indifference, other perhaps than through the direct experience of disaster. Tester himself, retreating to the objective ground of sociological description and questioning the morality of pretending to be able, from the sociological perspective, to go beyond that, offers no answers to the questions he raises and no cause for optimism.[38]

## Morality and reason

In the quotations from Zygmunt Bauman in the section on the morality of power, the eclipse of traditional morality was attributed both to technology, as in Stivers's account, and to rationality. The two are, of course, intimately related, for technology, especially in the forms identified by Stivers, is essentially a product of rationality, but they are not the same thing and the last account of the demoralization of contemporary society on which we shall focus looks to reason itself, rather than its manifestations, as the primary cause of moral decline. As Bauman explains at the end of his classic book on *Postmodern Ethics*,[39]

Morality is not safe in the hands of reason, though this is exactly what spokesmen of reason promise . . . [M]orality can be 'rationalized' only at the cost of self-denial and self-attrition. From that reason-assisted self-denial, the self emerges morally disarmed, unable (and unwilling) to face up to the multitude of moral challenges and cacophony of ethical prescriptions. At the far end of the long march of reason, moral nihilism waits: that moral nihilism which in its deepest essence means not the denial of binding ethical code, and not the blunders of relativistic theory—but the loss of ability to be moral.

Baumann is drawing here on the ideas of the French philosopher Emmanuel Levinas, for whom the self can only be defined in terms of the other and for whom all rationalization, by turning the self and others into objects, essentially erodes the human condition. Other critics of modernity, however, coming from very different philosophical perspectives, would agree with his conclusion. For the conservative philosopher and advocate of communitarianism, Alasdair MacIntyre, for example, the demoralization of society can be traced back to the Enlightenment attempts, by Kant and the utilitarian philosophers, to replace traditional virtues with rationally constructed ethics in which what was good or right was deduced logically from some kind of first principles.[40] For Ralph Fevre, whose ideas we encountered in Chapter 4, it is a product of the extraordinary success of common sense reasoning. Morality, for Fevre, is a product of belief and the emotions, but with the development of an advanced capitalist society in which our waking hours are taken up more and more by observations of common sense (through television) and actions that call for common sense decisions (like working, shopping, entertainment choices, even trading shares), we have become overwhelmed by common sense rationality and have lost touch, for the time being, with the moral world of emotions and beliefs.[41]

The association of morality with emotions and beliefs is controversial. Greed and hatred are, after all, as much products of the emotions as love and duty, and religious belief has probably spilt far more blood than cold calculation. Many people would argue that sound moral judgement, especially in difficult or complex situations, relies heavily on rational analysis and control of the emotions. But Fevre would probably not dispute this. The distinction he is making is between sense-based reasoning and feeling-based reasoning rather than between reason and non-reason, and his point is that in contemporary society one particular type of rationality has eclipsed others. Looking at it another way, we might say that traditional moral judgements are rational, but that they rely on the feelings for their motivation. Emotions and beliefs may be unreliable as guides to moral analysis, but unless our concern is emotionally engaged, we will never get around to the moral analysis in the first place. Here Fevre's perspective links with Tester's, for a prominent feature of a world dominated by common sense is a lack of moral engagement. At the emotional level, indifference reigns.

A curious feature about both Fevre's account and Bauman's is that they remain optimistic for the future of traditional morality. For Bauman, who attributes the eclipse of morality to the dominance of bureaucratic technology and technologically based forms of rationality, the fragmentation of the postmodern world is positive. From his existentialist perspective a morality determined by authority is no morality at all, and the breakdown of the institutions of moral authority that has characterized the last few decades is an opportunity for individual moral creativity as well as for self-interest. His left-wing European politics of emancipation, thus, brings him to a rather similar conclusion to that produced by the right-wing American politics of self-reliance, in which bureaucracy is also condemned as removing moral choice. For Fevre, very much as for Fukuyama, our present situation is a temporary disruption. Unlike Fukuyama, he takes the view that existing beliefs and moral sentiments have run their course, but he is confident that through human creativity, ingenuity, and imagination we will be able to fill the sense-making gaps they have left, just as we have in earlier phases of our history. As we struggle to make sense of the changing world, we will inevitably find new things to believe in and a reinvented morality (as an example, though not as a proposal, he suggests the possibility of an eco-morality) with which to repair our fractured understanding of the world. De-moralization will be followed by remoralization.

Fevre's optimism is heartening, but difficult to follow in practice. Focusing on domestic relationships, his account leaves out completely the potential of our present situation for disaster on a grand scale. And focusing on eventual solutions it tells us nothing about to handle the situation now. The injunction to go and find something new to believe in may be a good way of preparing for the twenty-second or twenty-third century, but it does not tell us how to get from here to 2030 and stay in one piece.

## SUMMARY AND REVIEW

It would be relatively easy to dismiss the whole idea of a crisis of morality as a typical bit of *fin de siècle* agonizing. There seems, after all, to have been something of a crisis of morality at the end of the eighteenth century and again, according to Durkheim at least, at the end of the nineteenth. The fact that this particular turn of a century is also the turn of a millennium is, perhaps, another reason for scepticism. The previous millennium was notable for its prophecies of doom. It would certainly be a great mistake to think that moral values have collapsed completely, or that there was some golden age of morality in times past, in which the ideas of duty and obligation reigned supreme, greed was universally condemned, and self-interest was kept firmly in its place or else was uniformly beneficent. It would be a mistake, too, to think that the religious belief structures of earlier Christian cultures made them significantly more moral in practice than contemporary secular ones; that moral indifference was unknown before the advent of television; or that people did not find ways of avoiding moral choice before the development of the modern bureaucracy. The various developments discussed in this and earlier chapters have all to be kept in perspective. Having said, that, however, it is hard to deny that the moral culture of our society has been changing, or that this change has reached some kind of critical phase, presenting us with situations and challenges that are significantly different from those to which we have been accustomed. The question is: how can we best understand this change, and the challenges it has brought?

In the light of our earlier analysis, the view from the right, which seeks to marry market individualism with Christian belief and traditional moral values and which attributes the contemporary decline of those values to the rise of the welfare state, seems altogether too glib and out of touch with historical reality. It is certainly a useful corrective (especially for those of us brought up in Europe) to the equally idealized visions of a socialist welfare state as some kind of universal panacea. There is value in self-reliance. But it seems almost completely blind to the cultural changes of the last 300 years. What has happened in the last few decades is not just a temporary blip, a short-term product of structural economic changes (as for Fukuyama) or of misguided social policies (as for the religious right), but part and parcel of a much longer-term, and much deeper, set of changes. For better or worse, society has developed and moved on. Our knowledge, our skills, our beliefs, and our attitudes to authority have all changed, and we cannot simply revert to an earlier stage of development.

The views from the left are, on the whole, more sensitive to these changes. Although we have characterized them in terms of their political leanings they are not, in fact, marked by particularly strong political ideologies and are written by and for academics rather than for popular or political consumption. Their historical and sociological analyses are both rich and insightful. They still tend, however, to be rather narrow and specific in their focus. Television and the media are so pervasive that their effects on moral culture cannot be ignored, but Tester's focus on attitudes to distant events allows him to say little about the moral culture of work and home. Bureaucracy and its technologies may well be associated with an emphasis on instrumental technique and a dulling of moral sensibilities, but bureaucracy is not the cause of our present predicaments, any more than the welfare state is. Nor will the end of bureaucracy solve our problems, any more than the withdrawal of a drug can solve the psychological problems that lead someone to addiction—though to pursue the analogy it might well be what forces us to confront them.[42]

The most compelling of the accounts is probably Fevre's analysis of common sense reasoning, but this too has its limitations. We have already noted some of these, but the most significant from our present perspective are, first, his insistence that the application of common sense reasoning to moral problems is not appropriate or not proper; and second, his failure to explore the dynamic relationship between the two kinds of reasoning. The first of these is common to most writers on the crisis of morality and is easy to sympathize with. I share his prejudice and probably would not be writing this book if I did not. But it is a prejudice and if other people are, in fact, comfortable with common sense or economic approaches to moral issues we have to take that fact seriously. The second limitation is related to the first. Fevre presents moral or feeling-based reasoning and common sense reasoning, from a cognitive perspective, as alternative modes of thinking applicable to different situations. He documents the extent to which the form of reasoning appropriate to one set of situations has come to be used in another, but he always keeps them in separate compartments. He does not address what it means to live in a world where both forms of reasoning, which often lead to very different conclusions, are available and understood, and in which they are routinely combined. In the remainder of this chapter we shall argue that the present crisis of morality is characterized not so much by a situation in which traditional moral reasoning and values have given way to economic or common sense reasoning and economic values, as by one in which both types of reasoning and both sets of values are treated as socially legitimate and are regularly employed to address the same situations. We do not live in a demoralized society so much as in a bimoral one.

## THE BIMORAL SOCIETY

Contemporary society is characterized, much as previous societies have been, by a combination of moral obligation and market self-interest, but it no longer makes sense in today's world to separate out the realms of traditional morality and markets. The weakening of traditional moral constraints and the simultaneous growth of a market culture with its characteristic morality of self-interest have resulted in an effectively bimoral society. They have resulted, that is, in a society in which the morality of obligation and the morality of self-interest both have face legitimacy, and in which there are no clear rules determining which one should be applied in any particular circumstances. We shall look at how this situation is manifested in the world of management in Chapter 7. In this section we shall introduce the bimoral society and the tensions that characterize it by looking at its more private manifestations, in conceptions of the self and in the experience of interpersonal relationships.

## Conceptions of the self

In *The Fall of Public Man*, written in the 1970s, sociologist and historian Richard Sennett wrote of an 'intimate society' that had developed in response to the dislocations of industrial capitalism and secularization in the nineteenth century and that had come to characterize contemporary society.[43] In this society the sense of what he called 'group ego interest', historically expressed as class interest, a sense of the needs, wants, or demands of a social group as a whole, had been suspended in favour of a narcissistic approach to social relationships as mirroring the concerns of inner psychology. Community was seen not as arising from the social interactions of *different* people but from the sharing of a *collective* personality, and in particular of revealed motives and intentions. The effect of this was to exclude from a person's effective community those who were in any way different, those with whom there was no basis for the shared intimacy of narcissistic absorption, and so to reduce the community in which a person engaged from that of a social class or society at large to that of the family and other intimates. Social life continued, and continued to make public demands on people; but these demands were increasingly in conflict with the equation of authenticity and inner experience, with the notion that the authentic self (and the moral self) was a psychic not a social phenomenon. 'Often against our own knowledge', Sennett suggested, 'we are caught up in a war between the demands of social existence and the belief that we develop as human beings only through contrary modes of intimate psychic experience'.[44] On one hand an obligation to 'perform' in society, to contribute to public life; on the other hand, a concern to protect the self and an identification of that self-protection with moral integrity.

This conflict is amply evidenced in Robert Bellah and associates' large-scale empirical study of American values published in 1985, *Habits of the Heart*.[45] They found tensions, for example, between a traditional perception of love as commitment, resting on binding obligations, and a psychologically centred perception of love as a sympathy of feeling between authentic selves; between marriage as a form of social tie and marriage as a form of psychological gratification. Even in their most intimate relationships, the people they interviewed were 'caught between the ideals of obligation and freedom'.[46] They still held to traditional moral values, but instead of grounding those values in the constraints of society they sought to ground them in the freedom of a 'therapeutic self', detached from any social context and defined instead in terms of subjective feelings and preferences.[47]

According to this therapeutic attitude, which the researchers found to be almost universally present, each self in effect constituted its own moral universe in which subjective feelings were the only moral guide. Though rooted in feeling rather than in economic reason, morality rested in effect on perceived self-interest, and the moral community was reduced to the range of empathetic communication.[48] Indeed, positive references to community were not to traditional communities of diversity at all but to lifestyle enclaves of like-minded individuals (like-minded within the limited extent of their interactions, that is, sharing the same lifestyle), where what was celebrated was the narcissism of similarity. Of course, people did not see it that way. They talked the language of traditional moral virtues, and glossed over the narrowing of moral focus. In prioritizing the demands of the private self and transferring the basis of moral authority from the social to the private realm, they were not consciously seeking to escape from traditional moral obligations: mostly, indeed, they saw no conflict between the obligations of citizenship and the interests of the self. But they inevitably opened up the possibility of such a conflict.

To explore this possibility a bit further, we can go back to the work of Richard Sennett. One of Sennett's core concerns was with the psychologization of social oppression, and in *The Hidden Injuries of Class*, written with Jonathan Cobb at the beginning of the 1970s, he explored the impact of this on working class Americans.[49] In the individualistic meritocracy of American society, the status of the blue-collar worker had come to be seen by the workers who were interviewed not as a consequence of class oppression or failed opportunity, but as one of character defect. For these people the public realm seemed almost non-existent— to the people around them they were nobodies—and the private realm of family relationships was marked by a deep sense of personal inadequacy. The only way they could maintain their sense of dignity or inner worth was by sacrificing their lives for their children, by working and saving so that their children might get to college and become better people than they were themselves. Here, the concern for the self found expression in a traditional ethic of sacrificial work. The social arena in which people lived their moral lives was dramatically reduced, as everything was referred to the intimate realm of the immediate family, but within that realm a very traditional morality held sway. By the time Sennett returned to his theme in the 1990s, however, in *The Corrosion of Character*, the flexible structures and short-termism of the new flexible economy had removed the basis for that particular solution.[50] In an uncertain world, long-term sacrifice had become meaningless as a basis for identity. The social demands of ever-changing jobs and changing team roles might perhaps have been accommodated by a well-developed socially constructed personality, but they provided no stable basis for the development of such a personality. Burdened with a psychic model of the self, people were forced into an ethic of self-interest, putting on whatever mask was needed to survive, at whatever cost to those around them.

Another view of how the tensions of a bimoral society are experienced at a psychological level can be found in the work of psychoanalyst Erich Fromm. In the mid-1970s, building on his earlier work on personality and ethics, Fromm identified two modes of existence, which he called 'having' and 'being', and which are most clearly captured in our everyday language.[51] Imagine, he said, a patient going to a psychoanalyst: 'Doctor, I *have* a problem; I *have* insomnia. Although I *have* a beautiful house, nice children and a happy marriage, I *have* many worries.' In an earlier period the patient would not have used this language at all but would have said 'I *am* troubled', 'I *cannot* sleep', 'I *live* in a nice house', 'I *am* happily married', and so on. Nouns had replaced verbs. Possession had replaced experience. Having had replaced being. In the same way many students, at school or university, now expect to be given knowledge rather than to learn or defend their opinions as if they were possessions. They want to have taken and so to possess a programme and degree, rather than to engage in an educational process. Their teachers, meanwhile, take a similar view. Deeply possessive of their time, they see their classes as hours to be given up, rather than as opportunities for serving the student's learning needs. And do we not all, from time to time, seek to have read a book rather than to read it, to have been somewhere rather than to be there, to have authority rather than to act authoritatively, to have wisdom rather than to be wise?

Fromm's point is that having is not something that sits alongside being but, from a psychological perspective, an alternative to it. Being is one mode of existence, a mode according to Fromm in which we engage actively in the social realm. Having is another mode of existence, which he roots in what we have called here the market culture, and which he relates to consumption:[52]

[T]o consume is one form of having, and perhaps the most important one for today's affluent societies. Consuming has ambiguous qualities: It relieves anxiety, because what one has cannot be taken away; but it also requires one to consume ever more, because previous consumption soon loses its satisfactory character. Modern consumers may identify themselves by the formula: I *am* = *what I have and what I consume.*

As we noted earlier in the book, the culture of consumption can be traced back at least to the seventeenth century. There is a long history of people using possessions to display their (public) identities, through dress, address, and other forms of conspicuous consumption. In the twentieth century, advertisers of consumer products have increasingly manipulated people's self-perceptions by emphasizing the link between personality and consumption, even where that consumption is invisible.[53] People wear a particular brand of lingerie not as an earlier age wore clothes, to denote a social identity, but to reinforce a psychological one. Even with visible products such as cars or designer labels the appeal is not to consumers' desire to express their outward, socially connected selves, but to their desire to communicate something 'authentic' about their intimate selves. In the psychology of having, the economic self-interest of market transactions and the emotional self-interest of the narcissistic self come together.

In Fromm's view, 'having' had almost completely eclipsed 'being' in modern society and had taken the world to the brink of catastrophe. That surely overstates the changes: having has certainly become deeply pervasive, but there is no evidence that it has destroyed people's capacity for being. The tension between the two modes of existence is, however, a vivid example at the psychological level of the tensions of the bimoral society.

## Interpersonal relationships

Moral culture impacts on society at every level, from the self-conception of the individual to the politics of the state, but the central arena for moral action is that of interpersonal relationships. We have already seen how in contemporary society this arena has shrunk. People tend more and more to live in suburban isolation, avoiding any relationships that might impose commitments, any encounters that might prove uncomfortable, any situations that might make moral demands upon them. The communities in which they are morally engaged are no longer those of a neighbourhood, with its extended families, close neighbours, shopkeepers, municipal workers, and assorted 'characters', but are typically reduced to their chosen friends and close families, together perhaps with a few individuals whom fate from time to time throws into their paths. The arena of moral action has been reduced. But what about people's behaviour within that arena? They may engage in fewer moral relationships, but is their practical approach to the relationships they do engage in any less moral, in a traditional sense, than it used to be?

Outside areas of particular social concern, such as domestic violence, I know of no significant research into this area, into how people behave as opposed to what they profess. But informal observation would suggest that when people do engage in relationships they still tend to do so for the most part in a traditionally moral way. Some people are more dutiful, more caring, and more morally responsive than others. Some people are more circumspect, more protective of their time, their money, their privacy, or their emotional commitment. Different people respond differently to different situations—perhaps giving time but not money or vice versa. But in their everyday actions most people take account of the needs of others. In an accident or emergency they respond altruistically, often with minimal regard for their own safety. They help their friends and family and in social situations they take pains to avoid causing hurt. Because many of our social institutions have been weakened or redefined, the context of behaviour has changed and this can create an impression of immorality. People are much more ready to quit on their marriages, for example. But to some extent duties are defined by institutions rather than the other way around, so when the institutions change the duties associated with them also change. It could be argued that the duties associated with cohabitation are actually stronger than they used to be, since it is now perceived as a legitimate alternative to marriage rather than as an arrangement entered into specifically to avoid the obligations of marriage.

Overall people do not appear to act significantly less morally now from how they did a generation, or even a century ago. Moreover, it is evident from their responses to literature, television, and film that they can associate with and respond to the same moral concerns that exercised previous generations. The popularity of televised versions of the novels of Jane Austen or Charles Dickens may owe something to period costumes, but people also respond to the moral issues raised. C. S. Lewis's overt Christian proselytizing may grate somewhat today, but the underlying morals still arouse people's sympathy. The massive popularity amongst both children and adults of J. K. Rowling's *Harry Potter* stories, which are as traditionally moral as you can get, suggests that people's moral instincts are still very much alive.

What has changed dramatically is the way in which these moral instincts are contextualized, even in the intimate setting of the immediate family. In a large-scale study of people's normative perceptions of family obligations carried out in the mid-1980s, Janet Finch and Jennifer Mason found ample evidence of the weakening of family ties we noted in Chapter 5.[54] Presenting people with a wide range of situations in which family members needed or wanted support of various kinds (time, money, accommodation, and so on) they found a very marked lack of consensus as to what should be provided, especially by parents to grown up children or by children to older parents. For many people the moral obligations of kinship were evidently still very strong, but for others they were very much weaker than traditionally assumed. Underlying this disagreement, however, Finch and Mason found significant consensus on underlying moral norms. Whatever conclusions they reached in particular instances, people tended to argue in traditional moral terms.

Three points can be made here. First, it is apparent that for most of the respondents, the traditional moral obligations of family were no longer absolute. The self-interest of the person whose duty was being appealed to was also treated as a legitimate consideration. Second, it seems evident that at a time when self-interest had still not acquired quite the social legitimacy it enjoys now, people were to some extent rationalizing their invocation of self-interest in overtly moral terms. Third, however, and allowing for this, even when self-interest was a major consideration it qualified traditional moral duty rather than replacing it. So it was not a question of whether someone should act on the basis of self-interest or of traditional moral duty but of how they should balance a legitimate self-interest against a legitimate obligation to help others in need.

The research approach adopted by Finch and Mason meant that the responses they received were apt to be thought out rather than instinctive. Also, although the situations they described in their survey questionnaires might arise in any family, they were essentially exceptional situations: typically, a parent or grown-up child needing financial support or temporary accommodation. In the more common situations of everyday life, traditional morality is less likely to be applied consciously, through reference to general principles or authorities, and more likely to be applied unconsciously, as a matter of habit. If asked to do so, we could give reasons for our behaviour, but most of the time we just behave habitually.

As Giddens, Bourdieu, and other social theorists have pointed out, this habitual behaviour is crucial not only to our day-to-day survival (we simply could not cope either with the practicalities of thinking out all our actions from scratch or with the insecurity of holding everything to doubt) but also to the recursive maintenance of stable social structures.[55] Established institutions or social structures (in terms of cultural theory, the classification structures of the hierarchy) dictate our unconscious behaviour and that behaviour in turn reinforces the structures on which it is based. The very fact that habits are unconscious gives them enormous power. Habits, as they say, die hard. But just how resilient, in this period of great social change, are our traditional moral habits? Perhaps the most unsettling feature of the bimoral society is that we are beginning to question traditional moral prescriptions not only in the exceptional cases that demand explicit, conscious attention but also, albeit to a more limited extent, in the routine cases of everyday life. Again it is not a question simply of replacing traditional obligation with self-interest, but of balancing the two. People used habitually to give up their seats on a bus or train to someone evidently discomforted by having to stand. (Men also used to give them up to women, children to adults, and everybody to people of a certain age, but apart from notions of respect or gallantry these conventions were also carriers of a more general moral rule, obviating the need for judgements of discomfort and so facilitating the habitual behaviour.) Some people continue to do this. Others do not even consider it. But for many people the situation now demands active consideration, taking account both of traditional moral obligation and of self-interest: how great is that person's need, how much discomfort will standing cause me (how many stops before I get off), how does the weighting of needs stand up against the rule of first come first served?

At first sight this example is not at all disturbing. What is happening, after all, is that blind obedience to authority is being replaced by reason. From the perspective of utilitarian moral philosophy, it is perfectly proper to take account of the interests of the actor as well as those acted upon, and seek a solution that maximizes their overall welfare. The problem is that the 'reasoning' in such situations is intensely subjective. As the Finch and Mason study showed, different people applying the same reasoning to the same problem are apt to come to completely opposite conclusions. To some extent it might be possible to increase the level of consensus through dialogue, and we shall return to this possibility in a later chapter. However, that can only work in practice, if it can work at all, on the level of general moral rules. The moment we break away from general rules of moral obligation and admit the legitimacy of self-interest as a part determinant of moral practice, we implicitly transfer moral authority to the subjective judgement of the individual. Whether it is a question of giving up my seat on the bus, helping someone in trouble, spending time with a lonely neighbour, settling the debts of my children, or providing a home for my parents, it's up to me to make the calculation and decide for myself the extent of my obligation.

The legitimacy of self-interest is most apparent in the sphere of 'positive' moral acts, such as helping out in the ways we have described, but it also applies increasingly to 'negative' acts, such as promise-breaking, plagiarism, or deceiving a partner. No one defends these as morally right, but there is a far greater preparedness than there was to excuse them on the grounds of the legitimate self-interest of the perpetrator. Harm might be done, but in the bimoral society that harm is not necessarily wrongful in itself. It is simply a factor to be taken into account. Moreover, individual interests are readily extended to group interests. The recent arguments in Britain over immigration and asylum seekers are interesting in this respect, for whereas traditional opposition to immigration was based on denying the rights of foreigners, current arguments are based more on asserting the interests of taxpayers and the unemployed. On traditional moral grounds, the case against the current British policy on asylum seekers is exceptionally strong. These are people in very serious need, looking for help from a country that can well afford to give it, in a world in which migration is commonplace. Many people, however, feel that helping in this case might go against their own economic self-interest, and they can confidently assert this concern as a reason for not helping.

Returning to the level of individual actions and relationships, people can always choose, and many still do choose, to stick by the old rules, but as the bimoral society becomes more firmly established this becomes progressively harder to do. In the first place those rules, no longer enforced by moral authority, are no longer backed up by social sanctions. If I do not give up my seat, no one is likely to tell me off or subject me to a critical glare. They may blame me secretly, but in contemporary society that, so to speak, is their problem, not mine. Shame loses its power and so, in due course, does guilt. I may initially break a rule accidentally, but if it goes unpunished or un-remarked upon, and the feeling of guilt that might have been anticipated does not arise, the temptation will be there to break it again. In the second place, if other people break the rule with impunity I may well find myself exploited or taken advantage of. To take a very mundane example, if I stick to the moral code of queuing for a bus when other people break it, I may never get on a bus at all. If I help people in need when others find reason not to I will soon get imposed upon. However reluctant I am to impose my self-interest, I may well find myself forced to assert it in self-defence.

## CONCLUSION

It would be wrong to overdramatize the changes described above. They are relatively subtle and have taken place gradually over a period of decades. They pose new challenges, but by and large people get along. Most people manage to maintain a social as well as a psychological identity, to be citizens as well as consumers, to balance their own interests with those of others. Moreover, alongside the constant blurring and dismantling of moral boundaries runs a parallel process of redefinition. We may be uncertain, in many situations, what is morally right, but to some extent the weakening of moral authority has been compensated for by a strengthening of the law, as areas that were previously left to people's moral judgement are brought into legislation. Laws on harassment and on the physical punishment of children, for example, are much more restrictive than the moral practices they have replaced.

Having said that, however, it would also be wrong to underplay the changes, to suggest that nothing fundamentally has changed or to argue, as some people do, that the tightening of legislation is an indication of strengthening moral standards. There is certainly a sense in which our moral awareness has continued to advance, even while the authorities underlying it have declined. We are far more prepared now than we ever have been to see all people, and even some animals, as moral creatures, entitled to our respect and concern. We are also far more aware of the ways in which we might unwittingly cause harm, through pollution, social disruption, or mental cruelty, for example. The attention now being given to the ethical aspects of business, medicine, and science is quite without precedent. But still the fact remains: Despite all these developments we now live in an effectively bimoral society, in which the conduct of interpersonal relationships is based not just on traditional moral duty but also, at the same time, on a socially legitimate self-interest. Living in such a bimoral society we have repeatedly to find a balance between obligation and self-interest, and this balance is inherently subjective. In a world without rules, morality inevitably becomes relativized to some extent: It is up to each individual to decide, in each situation, what is the 'right' way to behave.

# 7

# The Moral Tensions of Management

## MANAGEMENT, MORALITY, AND THE
## NEW CORPORATE CULTURE

In social life we have a clear choice as to how far we allow our self-interest to compromise our sense of traditional moral obligations. It is still more or less possible, in most situations, to stick by the rules of traditional morality. It may require much more self-discipline than it used to, and we may well get exploited in the process, but the choice is ours to make. As the philosopher Alasdair MacIntyre has expressed it, morality is democratized.[1] At work, however, and especially for a manager in a business corporation, things are very different. We are still faced with the same kinds of issues, but in the market culture of flexible business organizations it is simply not possible to escape from the dictates of self-interest.

There is a common stereotype of the manager as an entirely amoral creature, turning the handles of a bureaucratic machine or engineering the working of an organization for maximum efficiency or effectiveness. MacIntyre casts the manager with the therapist and the rich aesthete as one of the three dominant 'characters' (one might say archetypes) of modern culture and the one that most characterizes the Western culture of the mid–late twentieth century, and he notes that[2]

Managers themselves and most writers about management conceive of themselves as morally neutral characters whose skills enable them to devise the most efficient means of achieving whatever end is proposed. Whether a given manager is effective or not is on the dominant view a quite different question from that of the morality of the ends which his effectiveness serves or fails to serve.

Others have made the same point, and there is certainly a lot in it. From the 'scientific management' of the early twentieth century through the post-war O&M (organizations and methods) and work-study movements to the business process re-engineering of the 1990s, there has been a continued strong emphasis on the technical engineering aspects of management.[3] Business schools and management teachers seek, for their own reasons, to present management as a professional activity built on a body of knowledge and associated skills and techniques rooted in economics and the social sciences. And there can be little doubt that the business culture does tend to suppress difficult questions of values. Thus, while the purpose of the corporation and its role in society may be an appropriate concern for the board of directors, for shareholders, or for the political institutions of society, it is not the concern of ordinary managers. Business leaders want their managers to get on with the job in hand, not to worry all the time about why they are doing it, and so managers are held responsible only for the means by which corporate goals are to be achieved, not for the goals themselves. As the sociologist Stanley Deetz has observed, this tends to lock managers into a form of purely instrumental, means-oriented reasoning with the result that all questions of values, whether the values of the corporation or the values associated with personal, family, or community interests, get shut out. The means become ends in themselves.[4]

Deetz also observes that one of the principal components of the management task is the management of conflicting interests through forms of mediation. Management is characteristically concerned with choosing between alternative options, selecting and rejecting staff, allocating resources between competing projects, resolving differences of judgement or opinion. In each case some interests are inevitably favoured, while others lose out. Many of these conflicts arise from differences of values, which would most naturally be resolved through the consideration of values: through judgements that take account not only of technical but also of moral dimensions. But the way the managerial role is defined gives no place to values, or to the emotions that go with them. The interests of the manager therefore lie in the process of mediation rather than in its specific outcomes, and in particular in a process which can be seen to be rational and 'objective' or value-neutral, and which eliminates or disguises any continuing value-based conflict.

In this way, managers are led to routinize or mechanize, as far as possible, the process of mediation, and so to avoid the value conflicts and emotional crises that would emerge if issues were treated individually. They are also led to disguise these conflicts by translating them into forms that can be expressed and mediated through value-neutral language and mechanisms. Where conflicts cannot be disguised in this way, they have either to be suppressed and denied or else to be referred elsewhere. Thus, internal goal conflicts are typically denied, while conflicts between work and home, which are partially outside managerial control, get pushed back to the home for resolution.

The value-neutral (or supposedly value-neutral) language in which conflicts are reframed and resolved is, of course, that of economics, and the most powerful form of mediation is pricing. Within the corporate setting, the means can always be defined in terms of economic efficiency, and all negotiations can be reduced to questions of money. If a conflict cannot be resolved by economic mechanisms, then within the construction of managerialism it is the conflict, not the mechanism, that is anomalous. It may be attributed to external factors beyond the control of the system (such as personal or situational problems), or to technical glitches, or it may just be denied altogether. What is paramount is that the integrity of the managerial system is protected.

There is no doubt, then, that the forces pushing managers toward an assumed amorality are, and always have been, very powerful. But in traditional bureaucratic organizations there was also another side to the story. In Chapter 2, we discussed Melville Dalton's pioneering study of management in an industrial bureaucracy, noting how the restrictions of bureaucracy forced managers into using immoral means (subterfuge, deception) in order to achieve moral ends.[5] This might at first sound very like what Deetz is describing, but a striking feature of Dalton's account is the extent to which his managers recognized a moral aspect to their work. The performance of the business may have been their top priority, but achieving that was itself seen as a traditionally moral duty and other things were also important: for example, that decent people who were ill-suited to the jobs in which they were placed were treated decently. The managers inhabited a business world of moral conflicts, not a world of amorality. Moreover, they responded to these conflicts by engaging their social moral selves. There were myriad ties between the firms Dalton studied and their local communities, and these ties did not just counter the potentially dehumanizing effects of the bureaucracy but also provided settings outside the firm in which managers could address the moral aspects of their work.

Traditional business organizations may have been devoted to largely economic ends, but they were structured on the same hierarchical principles as the societies in which they operated and were based on the same traditional morality of obligation. If managers did devote themselves to purely instrumental goals, it was largely because that was what their moral duty to the company required. And in practice the requirements for efficiency or effectiveness were rarely absolute. It was accepted, for example, that senior managers had a responsibility to look after those who reported to them, and that once someone had joined the management of a corporation they should not be removed. Traditional organizations were as much exercised by the problem of finding the right job for the person as they were by that of finding the right person for the job.

Most of the time, this made sense economically as well as morally. In a stable competitive environment in which competitive advantage was based primarily on the economies of experience, it was important to have a strong cadre of loyal and experienced managers who knew the industry, the business, and each other well, who would be willing to carry that knowledge wherever it was needed and who could, above all, be relied upon not to make mistakes, not to let the side down. A strong supportive culture, in which the business looked after its employees and encouraged them to look after each other, was a good way of achieving this, so the maintenance of traditional moral values served the self-interest of the business and its shareholders well. The self-interest of the manger was also satisfied, as whatever its demands on time or family (and in international businesses especially these could be considerable) the firm provided both a stable social identity and the financial and emotional security of a long-term career.

## The new corporate culture

This changed when, as we saw in Chapter 4, competition intensified, new technologies destroyed the traditional sources of competitive advantage, and the moral compact of the traditional corporation fell apart. The first effects of this process can be seen in Robert Jackall's empirical study of organizational ethics in the early 1980s, *Moral Mazes*.[6] The organizations studied by Jackall were traditional large industrial bureaucracies, in mature industries, but those industries were in decline and the bureaucracies could neither cope with this nor respond to it. The managerial workforce had become less a source of competitive advantage, and more a source of superfluous costs. Careers were under threat and for many of the middle-aged managers who had grown up in the firm and the industry the chances of re-employment were slight. Even in this environment, some kind of traditional morality remained, but it was very narrowly focused and little more than an expression of self-interest: people were loyal to their buddies. The close linkages between the business and its community, the sense of moral responsibility to the business, and the sense of responsibility to anyone who was not a buddy had all gone. Self-interested survival was the name of the game.

Jackall's organizations are best seen as pathological examples. Though presented as typical bureaucracies they tell us more about what happens when bureaucracy fails to function. They are, however, typical of their age, because in the 1980s industrial bureaucracy was failing to function on a grand scale. By the 1990s, it was giving way to the new kind of organizing based on market principles that we discussed in Chapter 4.

Built as they are around a need for flexibility, mobility, and short-term economic performance, new-style 'post-bureaucratic', 'flexible', or 'network' organizations have little room for the stable moral relationships of traditional bureaucracy.[7] With manufacturing exported and managers moving from project to project and from location to location, they are not embedded in local communities, nor do they generate stable communities internally. For staff employed as temps or on short-term contracts, assessed and rewarded according to economic performance and economic performance alone, and expected to act self-interestedly, there is little to be gained from being loyal to the firm and much to be lost from being loyal to colleagues.

One effect of this is to accentuate the tendencies toward managerial instrumentalism identified by Stanley Deetz. Faced with the inevitable value-laden conflicts of organizational life, managers are not pushed to resolve them but to ignore, explain away, suppress, or convert them into economic pseudo-conflicts. Even when they rise to the top of the system and take on board-level responsibilities, they are pushed by the culture and incentive structures to take their instrumentalism with them. Accustomed to instrumental rather than end-oriented reasoning, and to placing business needs above individual morality, they simply replace the authority of 'the business' by that of 'the market'. The ends or purposes of the business become the means of meeting the market's needs, so that even at this level the discourse of values is replaced by that of efficiency.

In a pure market culture these pressures might not cause any problems, but we do not live—and most people still do not want to live—in a pure market culture. Moreover, today's business organizations are not purely market structures. To some extent people *can* treat management as an amoral activity, leaving their moral concerns at home and treating business as a game, with no implications beyond the numbers on the bottom line. But only to some extent, for managers are at root ordinary people, with ordinary moral values and sensibilities. Most of them do care what good or harm their businesses do. They do care, above all, about the welfare of their colleagues and of the staff who report to them and for whom they are still in some hierarchical sense responsible. And just as the legitimacy of self-interest introduces complications into our treatment of the traditional moral demands of everyday life, so the persistence of traditional morality introduces complications into our treatment of the economic demands of management life. In a bimoral society, managers have to deal with a whole new range of stresses on the relationships in which they engage. In the sections that follow we shall look in turn at the vertical and horizontal relationships of management life and at the relationship between work and home.

## THE MANAGER AS BOSS

### Hiring and firing

As we noted earlier, contemporary business organizations are still bureaucracies in at least one crucial respect. However de-layered they may be, they still retain the vertical dimension of hierarchy. Every manager has a boss, and every manager is a boss, giving instructions and making sure they are carried out satisfactorily. In particular, most managers have some responsibility, either directly or through their recommendations, for hiring and firing: for recruiting people into the organization or, within the organization into departments, projects, and teams; for promoting or not promoting them; for renewing or not renewing their contracts; and when things do not work out for firing them.

In some ways hiring and firing are much easier now than they used to be. In a flexible economy of short-term contracts there is less at stake on both sides. But for many managers firing people, or even declining to renew their contracts, is still one of the most difficult things that they have to do and it is worth asking why, in a market context, this should be. Why should ceasing to employ someone be any more difficult than ceasing to use any other supplier? The answer, of course, is the one we have already given. Despite the dominance of the market culture in business, we live in a bimoral culture, not a purely market one, and the relationships between managers and their reports are relationships between traditionally moral human beings as well as between economic agents. This has a number of consequences worth noting.

In the first place, managers develop friendships. I am not thinking here of particularly close or intimate friendships. Working for an organization has always required people to keep their work lives apart from such intimacies and to make sure that they do not bias professional judgements or otherwise compromise the interests of the organization. I am thinking, rather, of ordinary working friendships, confined to the office (and perhaps the pub or bar), such as characterize any group of people working together. It is inevitable that managers will like some of their reports more than others, and desirable that they should guard against favouritism, but it is also natural that they should feel some human concern for all of their reports. Indeed, this is an important part of good management. Treating reports with sympathy and concern brings out the best in their work. It encourages and facilitates communication and sensitizes the manager to their unrealized potentials and development needs. It helps the manager identify if things are going wrong, and makes it easier to take remedial action. All this is of positive value to the business, even within contemporary business cultures. A manager who shied away from friendship and kept people at arm's length would simply not be able to do her job. In traditional bureaucratic organizations it caused no conflict. Managers were expected to develop their staff; they were not normally expected to fire them. But in contemporary organizations it is a source of considerable tension, for if a manager is doing her job properly she will have routinely to terminate or not renew the contracts of people of whom she is fond, for whom she has a genuine concern.

This is particularly difficult where the reports concerned are above a certain age and joined the company with expectations of secure employment. Young people today set out on life knowing that there's no such thing as job security, and they order their commitments on that basis. The generation who joined the workforce in the 1960s and 1970s, especially in clerical, professional, or management positions, did so under a different implied contract. The deal was that they would be loyal to their employers, work hard, and perform to their best of their ability; their employers in turn would be loyal to them. They ordered their commitments accordingly, not only in practical terms—wives devoting themselves to the household, for example, rather than maintaining their own earning capacity—but also in psychological terms. The (typically male) employee invested much of his identity in his company and, most critically, in the status of employment.

For people from this generation, who have given their lives to their companies, dismissal comes very hard. In 1999 the press carried the story of a manager of the Japanese Bridgestone tyre company who had been made redundant when his firm faced up to the pressures of international

competition and the falling yen. Breaking with a tradition of lifetime employment, the firm had introduced a compulsory early retirement programme
covering half its general managers. One of the victims was Mashiro Nonaka,
who had worked for Bridgestone since graduating from university in the mid-
1960s. On 22nd May 1999 he committed hara-kiri in the Chief Executive Officer's
office. The letter he left was reported as saying

Since entering Bridgestone I have devoted my entire life to the company; for over thirty
years I have neglected my private life and family . . . The recent restructuring, and especially the management retirement programme, is like an act of betrayal . . . The best
thing for me now is to die in the presence of Umisaki [the CEO]. I do hara-kiri to protest.
I love Bridgestone and always will, therefore I need to act now.

The tradition of lifetime employment is far more deeply embedded in
Japanese society than it ever was in the West, public face is far more important,
and suicide carries less negative connotations. But while the example is extreme
it makes a point. Being sacked in middle age, after working dutifully for a company for twenty years or more, is not just about the cash. For people who are
unlikely to find another job (though the more resourceful might find part-time
work among the army of self-employed consultants), it is about status, face, and
self-esteem. Pulling children out of private education, moving to a cheaper
house, and retiring on a smaller pension destroy the ends to which a life has been
devoted. The senior managers of a company can easily decide, on economic
grounds, that jobs need cutting. But for the middle managers who have to decide
who is to be cut, and who know those people personally, it is far more difficult.

   Part of this difficulty may lie, as we have already noted, in friendship, but part
also lies in a recognition of the traditional moral obligations attending any sustained relationship. Managers and their reports do not engage in arms length
market transactions but in continuing relationships, out of which obligations
develop in both directions. These obligations—to treat each other fairly and
decently, to avoid nasty surprises, and so on—are indeed the basis of the
mutual trust upon which all forms of cooperative activity depend. In a contemporary organization there may be no obligation on a boss to keep someone
in employment when the demands of the business suggest otherwise, but it is
difficult to build up a trusting management relationship without giving the
impression, however unintentionally, of some such obligation. The termination of a contract is almost always an unpleasant surprise and is almost always
accompanied by a feeling of betrayal and a sense, on both sides, of unfairness.

   A further problem in this context is that while the moral obligations of a relationship work both ways, they are not normally symmetrical. A central feature
of traditional morality is that power carries with it responsibility, so that if one
party in a relationship has more power than the other she has correspondingly
greater obligations. The theory of new economy organizations is that the
relationships between employees and their companies, or more immediately
their bosses, are market relationships in which each party contracts freely. The

reality, however, is that there are substantial power imbalances. The political power of an employee is inherently weaker than that of her boss and this power imbalance is manifest precisely in the process of dismissal, which one can do to the other but not vice versa. The economic power of a large company is massively greater than that of an employee, especially in a de-unionized world.

Traditional organizations recognized these imbalances and the obligations they implied, and managers' duties to the company were not placed in conflict with their duties to employees, or with their own self-interest. According to the rhetoric of the new economy, the power imbalance between company and employee is also recognized in part, as most companies undertake to provide their staff with training and development so that if they are forced to leave the company and re-enter the job market they are better equipped to get another job than they were when they started. The standard line is that companies no longer provide secure employment, but do provide the transferable skills for people to secure their own employment. This, if true, would take some of the tensions out of the manager's task, but in fact it is rarely true, at least for professional and managerial employees. Companies as a whole spend no more on general training and skills development of their professionals and middle managers than they used to, and the companies that spend most are the ones least likely to fire people, either because they retain some traditional moral values or because they are particularly successful. Writing in the mid-1990s, John Storey and his colleagues noted that for British companies management development had become a second order activity, chopping and changing to meet the short-term market needs of the company rather than the longer-term needs of its employees.[8] When things get difficult, the training budget and, especially, the time allocated to training are among the first things to go.

In practice, managers have to sink or swim, learning for themselves as they go. The rhetoric of employability is often little more than a public relations exercise designed on one hand to attract recruits and on the other hand to salve consciences. But because it creates promises that are not kept (and that could never be seen by dismissed employees as having been kept, even if they had been) it just makes the manager's task even harder. In contemporary organizations both the manager's self-interest (in preserving her own job) and her obligations to the company, whether these are seen as contractual or traditionally moral, require her to act routinely in breach of the normal moral obligations of power.

## Stewardship and agency

A particular manifestation of the tensions of management in a bimoral society is in the peculiar job of a Chief Executive or CEO. In traditional bureaucratic corporations the CEO occupied one of two roles. Either he was a representative of controlling family interests, in which case his organizational role was that of a patron, or he was himself a management employee, in which case he was no more than the first among equals within the management structure. Either way, his management task was essentially that of a steward, looking after the corporation in the interests of its owners and the stakeholders to whom they felt responsible, and his legitimacy was derived from his stewardship. If he was an employee he may have been better paid than the other managers, but the difference was not great and was more than accounted for, in their eyes and in those of the outside world, by the extra responsibility he bore. Even if his style of leadership was distant, he was united with the other members of the hierarchy—at least with those in the managerial ranks—by a common purpose and a common paymaster. If he was a patron, he had obvious benefits and privileges that were denied to the rest of the management, but he was also responsible to the family in a way that they were not, and the family in turn was responsible to the organization and employees.

The assumption underlying this system was the assumption underlying all role-structured cultures, namely that provided people are treated decently and with respect they are motivated to perform the roles assigned to them, honestly and to the best of their abilities. The CEO of a corporation was employed to do the best for the corporation and its stakeholders; that is what he took as his task, and that is what everyone assumed he did. In our bimoral society, this perception of top management as stewards still persists. Indeed, it is still dominant in much of Europe, in Japan, and in many privately owned corporations around the world. But even in these contexts it can no longer be taken for granted, and in the context of the publicly quoted British or American corporation it has been overshadowed by perceptions of agency and self-interest.

In general terms, the widespread perception that CEOs are motivated primarily by self-interest (in the popular British press the terms 'CEO' and 'fat cat' have become virtually synonymous) can probably be seen as part of the reaction of a traditionally moral society to the incursion of economic values. The CEO, with his large, publicly declared pay packet, is a convenient symbol of a market culture and the inequalities that brings. Investment bankers earn far more, and have far fewer responsibilities, and top lawyers and surgeons earn similar amounts, but they are less in the public eye and do not head up organizations that employ, or make redundant, large numbers of poorly paid workers. The perception also has more specific origins, however, for the dramatic technological and political changes that opened up global competition in the 1980s were accompanied by changes in the capital markets, which came to be dominated by increasingly powerful and sophisticated institutional investors. So the profits of established corporations came under pressure just as their shareholders were growing more demanding and less forgiving.[9]

Through all this the chief executives and their top management teams continued, by and large, to act and be treated as stewards, but even hierarchical role-structured cultures need someone to blame when things go wrong. Mediocrity in a bureaucracy can be tolerated, but failure cannot. Moreover, while mediocrity can be attributed to limited competence, failure cannot easily be attributed to incompetence, for the simple reason that the incompetence of one person casts doubt on the competence of the others who placed him in position. When CEOs failed to meet shareholder demands it was generally because they were trying to cope with situations for which they were unprepared, using structures and systems that were inappropriate to the task. They tried their best, and they simply were not up to it. But being not up to it was not a sufficient excuse—to 'save' the system they also had to be considered in some way negligent, in breach of the trust that had been placed in them.

When hierarchies fail, the market intervenes. The change of perception of the chief executive from a trusted steward to one who could not necessarily be trusted opened the door to new perceptions taken from agency theory and its model of economic man. From the perspective of agency theory, stewardship is an illusion. Everybody acts in his or her own self-interest, and CEOs behave as stewards only if it is in their interests to do so.

Today, the agency theory of corporate governance dominates the academic literature on the subject and exerts a strong influence on public, professional, and practitioner perspectives. According to this theory there is really only one stakeholder in the corporation and that is its shareholders, all of whom are assumed to have essentially the same interest in maximizing economic performance. To achieve their aims, they engage an agent, the CEO, to whom they necessarily relinquish some discretionary power. Since the agent is by definition self-interested, however, the shareholders are faced with a classical agency problem. How can they tie in the agent's behaviour, over which they have no direct control, to their own interests? In economic terms, how can they minimize the 'agency costs' arising from the delegation of control?[10]

Agency theory is not concerned with managerial incompetence. Indeed, it assumes that the agents are perfectly competent and that they are blessed, like all economic agents, with rational minds untroubled by emotion or stress, and with a complete knowledge of the consequences of their actions. If they wanted to deliver maximum economic performance for the shareholders they could. The problem is that as self-interested agents they are tempted to do otherwise. They may invest, for example, in projects that will increase their power and prestige or provide them with interesting challenges, when these are not optimal from a shareholder perspective. Conversely, they may under-invest in projects that promise good returns but are boring or out of line with their self-image. They may sacrifice opportunities for the sake of a peaceful job, a happy marriage, or an enjoyable social life. They may structure the organization as a pleasant work environment rather than as a demanding one. They may spend more on luxury offices and corporate jets than can be strictly justified by the demands of corporate performance. And they may manipulate their reports so as to give an incomplete or misleading account to shareholders of what is going on.

The language used by agency economists is fairly dramatic and raises the hackles of those who believe in the values of honest stewardship. CEOs as agents engage, it is said, in shirking and wilful deception. But if the words sound alarming, the behaviours they are used to describe are scarcely out of the ordinary. We know that firms that are structured to provide rewarding and cooperative working environments for their senior managers generate on average lower financial returns than those which are structured round individual accountability. Industries that are comfortable to work in seem to be less profitable, on average, than those that are not. And all the evidence on diversification suggests that it is driven more by management ambition than by any real prospect of shareholder returns. In other words, the agency perspective may be one-sided, but it is not entirely unreasonable.

To resolve the agency problem of corporate governance, the theorists offer three possible solutions. One is to closely monitor the behaviour of the CEO, so as to reduce the scope for self-seeking. This is fine in theory, but difficult to do much about in practice. In Germany and Japan the need for consensus imposes some constraints, and the prevalence of debt keeps the banks informed, if no one else; but the British and American systems rely almost entirely upon published accounts and these reflect past rather than current behaviour. For quoted companies, a system of twice yearly or quarterly reporting and stock market announcements when companies know that analysts' predictions are likely to be significantly awry keeps shareholders informed of current performance, but current performance reflects past management actions. Shareholders cannot effectively monitor the real-time behaviour of the CEO, and it is not clear what the effects would be if they could. Close monitoring could maybe put a cap on deception and self-seeking, and eliminate gross mistakes, but it could also damage motivation and reduce overall performance levels. If people are to flourish and perform well, they need to be left to some extent to get on with things.

The second proposed solution is to rely on the market for corporate control and the discipline engendered by the constant threat of takeover. This works in the long term, but from the perspective of the shareholders it looks more like a way of cutting their losses than of maximizing their profits. The third and most popular solution is to tie the CEO's own interests into those of the shareholders, through an appropriate remuneration package. Theoretically, the idea is to transfer some of the risk of the enterprise from the shareholders to the CEO by constructing a pay package that rewards him for shareholder gains and penalises him for shareholder losses. This costs money. On the assumption that they work for the cash as well as the kicks, and do not have so much invested as to make their remuneration a financial irrelevance, most CEOs must be risk averse. This means that they would not in their right minds trade in a contract paying, let us say, a flat rate salary of $1 million for one that offered them an expected average return of that, with the possibility of much more but with a risk of something much smaller. They will expect to be paid to take on such a risk, raising the expected remuneration, and significantly raising what will have to be paid if they perform above expectations. From the shareholders' perspective, however, the extra remuneration costs may be a small price to pay compared with the returns they can expect if the incentive works.

In 1990 the *Harvard Business Review* published an article by two of the academic pioneers of the agency theory of corporate governance,

Michael Jensen and Kevin Murphy, under the title 'CEO pay—it's not how much you pay but how'.[11] This article drew attention to the fact that American CEOs were being remunerated not just through their basic salaries, as had once been the case, but also through a wide range of performance related bonuses and stock options. It noted that while the sensitivity of CEO remuneration to corporate performance varied enormously from corporation to corporation, there was a consistently positive correlation between them. And it drew on agency theory as a possible explanation of what was happening. Shareholders were using performance related compensation packages to align the interests of the naturally self-interested CEOs with their own. The story was a good one. Jensen and Murphy actually suggested that the observed sensitivity of CEO pay to performance was statistically too low to be satisfactorily explained by agency theory, but the implication of this was that performance-related pay elements should be increased. Ever since their article the subject of CEO pay has been inseparably linked with agency theory in the popular as well as the academic mind. In Britain as well as in America, CEOs are now very highly remunerated (the typical total remuneration for a top company CEO in Britain is now over £1 million, that for a top American company CEO very much higher: Indeed, it has been estimated that the managers of US corporations have now given themselves over 10 per cent of the total outstanding US equity stock in the form of stock options), with the greater part of this being performance related pay: a bonus based on current results, stock options that will rise in value with the share price, and the benefits of long-term incentive plans linked to financial or share price performance over a two- to five-year period. French and German companies, which traditionally paid their CEOs more modestly and only introduced performance related pay in the 1990s, are now rapidly moving over to the same kinds of packages and same overall pay levels as in the UK.[12] The justification usually given for CEO pay packages is that the amounts are necessary to attract the best candidates and the structure provides a necessary incentive to perform: CEOs are rewarded in the way they are, and have to be rewarded in this way, because they are self-interested agents whose interests need to be tied to those of the shareholders.[13]

This perception of self-interest is heightened by the observation that while the theory of performance related play is that the CEO should share both upside and downside risk with shareholders, the typical CEO pay package has little downside. Even though the most blatant performance-related pay shams such as 'guaranteed bonuses' have largely been phased out, most CEOs enjoy very comfortable basic salaries and very generous pension provisions: If they got nothing from the performance-related aspects of their pay, they would still be very well paid. Many incentive schemes are relatively undemanding and are kept that way, to the extent of repricing stock options when share prices fall. The perception is also heightened by the way CEOs in America have responded to public scrutiny, lobbying to ensure that their enormous share options are not recorded as expenses in the company accounts.[14]

If we look only at their remuneration packages, the perception that CEOs are driven by self-interest is entirely understandable, but in most cases the pay tells only one half of the story. In the first place, the downside risk is not in the pay package. Nowadays, if performance disappoints, even on a short-term basis, the CEO pays with his job. The average tenure of top 100 company CEOs in Britain was reckoned in 2001 to be about four years and declining. Of course, losing your job as a top company CEO is not like losing your job as a coalminer or production line worker. Sacked CEOs may have difficulty getting another CEO position, at least in the short term, but given their experience and ability, they can usually get very well-paid part-time work as chairmen, directors, or consultants. Even without any further earnings, moreover, most CEOs have enough set by and in their pension plans to be financially set up for life. We should certainly not feel too sorry for them. But losing a job is not just about money, as we noted earlier, and what most CEOs fear is not the financial loss but the damage to their self-esteem and, especially, the effects of the inevitably wounding press comments on their partners and children.

In the second place, despite what their pay packages might suggest, most CEOs still see themselves as stewards and still act as stewards. Indeed one justification often given for accepting a generous pay deal is that by removing financial worry it leaves the CEO free to escape the distractions of his self-interest and concentrate all his energies on managing the company as best he can. Most CEOs are driven by performance and achievement. The money is a scorecard, and a compensation for the families they never see, but if there is one person in the company who does not need an incentive to deliver shareholder value it is the CEO. Informed commentators on business recognize this and see most CEOs as honest stewards. Variations in performance tend to be attributed largely, and probably correctly, to external forces beyond management's control, and where blame is attached, poor performance is attributed simply to incompetence and good performance to ability. Nine times out of ten, the assumption is that the CEO is committed to his job, that he is not a self-seeking agent at all (at least outside of his pay negotiations), but an honest and devoted steward.

In the third place, the presuppositions of agency theory are not shared even by shareholders. For while they remunerate CEOs on the basis that they are legitimately self-interested, they also expect them to be morally dutiful—dutiful, that is, to the shareholders.

CEOs, then, are for the most part stewards, who are guided by traditional moral obligations: a primary obligation to their shareholders, and secondary obligations to their employees, suppliers, communities, and other stakeholders. The public, by and large, think that they *should* be stewards, serving a complex of stakeholder interests, and the shareholders also think they should be stewards, in the rather narrower sense of serving the shareholders' interests. But both groups also see them as self-interested economic agents, who are rewarded as agents, and justly punished as agents when things go wrong—for even if poor performance is not their fault it is recognized that, like football managers, they will have to take the blame and resign.

As long as things are going well, this confusion does not cause the CEO any real problems. The press coverage can be irritating, but it goes with the job. When things are going badly, however, the CEO finds himself in a curious position. In a recession, for example, the interests of the shareholders may be best met by severe downsizing and plant closures. Because his pay and, more critically, his job are tied to performance, the CEO's self-interest will be met in the same way. But as a steward he also has responsibilities to employees and communities, who would suffer from the closures. If he were simply a steward working in a traditionally moral culture, he would weigh the interests of the different parties, taking account of their circumstances and considering what obligations had been created by previous agreements, and reach an honourable and defensible, if difficult, decision. If he were simply an agent working in a market culture, he would act in his own (and thereby the share-holders') interests, and within that culture his decision would again be easily defensible. But in a bimoral society in which self-interest is seen as legitimate but only up to an undefined point, he is in a lose–lose situation. If he goes ahead with the closures he will be condemned not only by the employees but also by the public as failing in his moral duty and serving his own selfish inter-ests. If he does not go ahead with them he will be condemned by shareholders on exactly the same grounds—for putting his own psychological self-interest, served by avoiding unpleasantness and guilt, ahead of his duty to them.

A similar dynamic applies to many areas of business ethics, where senior man-agers are torn between a contractual and economically self-interested regard for the profits of the company and a traditional moral regard for its responsibilities. It is often argued that 'ethics pay' in business, and in the long term they probably do. Ethical companies limit their downside risk and build reputations that attract both customers and employees. In the short term, however, there can be little doubt that ethics cost, and in times of severe competition—especially in emerg-ing or saturated markets—the very existence of a long term is conditional upon short-term performance.[15] In times of excess capacity, high employment or safety standards, or standards that are higher than those of benchmark competi-tors, impose additional costs that can be unsustainable at the margin. In fast developing product markets, dubious selling practices or reduced product test-ing may be the only way to steal a march on competitors. For managers faced with these circumstances the practical choice can be that between failing to meet obligations of traditional moral care (with the consequent potential for environ-mental or human disasters) and failing to meet obligations to maximize performance (with the consequent potential for the collapse of the company).

Issues of this kind affect managers at all relatively senior levels, but when decisions get difficult they often fall on the CEO. The successful CEO is a heroic leader in the entrepreneurial mode. He is self-interested and well paid, but no one begrudges him that, because it is what prosperity is made of and he is, anyway, morally upright and responsible. If the corporation is booming he can afford to be. No stakeholders need lose out; there are no difficult decisions to be made. His responsible stewardship does not go against the shareholder interests but adds value to the corporation, building reputation, and attracting first-rate staff. The failed CEO, in contrast, is an evil exploiter, interested only in his own pay packet. His attempts at broad-minded stewardship make a mockery of his accountability to shareholders. His self-interest and his public insistence on shareholder value above all else are morally despicable. (He is, remember, a significant shareholder himself.) With the corporation in trouble, every decision becomes a conflict of interest that he can never satisfactorily resolve. His negligence is matched only by his incompetence; and as any CEO will tell you, the difference between success and failure is a hair's breadth.

## THE MANAGER AS COLLEAGUE: THE ETHICS OF TEAMWORK

As with any leadership position, being a CEO can be very lonely. Every company has a 'top team' but in most cases, as teamwork guru Jon Katzenbach has pointed out, that term is a misnomer.[16] Senior executives work together, but the top of the business organization remains essentially bureaucratic with each executive having a set of well-defined formal areas of responsibility. The CEO consults his 'team', but in the end the decisions are his, and in most governance systems he is held individually accountable for the results. Lower down the organization, however, teamwork structures have taken over from bureaucratic offices as the main basis of organizing, and for most junior and middle managers they have become a central feature of working life.

Teamwork is not a new phenomenon. Its benefits have long been apparent and have long been exploited on the sports field, in music, and in the theatre. In business, too, teamwork has always played a fundamental part in those smaller, younger organizations for which constant innovation is a necessity, particularly those in high-tech or the arts. The introduction of teamwork to larger corporations is much more recent, however. In a traditional hierarchical culture, the fear of loss of control makes it extraordinarily difficult to give teams the freedom and autonomy they need to perform. As we saw in Chapter 4, the first attempts to capture the benefits of team working in the 1970s took the form of matrix organizations in which instead of being freed from reporting along hierarchical lines, the teams effectively had to report along multiple lines, to all the divisions from which their members were drawn. As the pressures for performance and innovation continued to build, however, the matrix structures gradually gave way to project teams, which still had limited autonomy but in which the team members were at least freed from their functional or divisional responsibilities. Then, as the corporations began to shift away from the values of hierarchy and towards those of the market, these in turn gave way to the self-organizing teams we see today.

The advantages of teamwork in the competitive context of the flexible economy are evident. Cutting across traditional management levels and traditional functional boundaries, teams are more flexible and responsive than their more traditional bureaucratic alternatives. Put together on an ad hoc basis for specific tasks, they can quickly pull together the skills and capabilities needed. By co-opting new members they can respond to changing needs as a task unfolds or the environment changes. The sharing of tasks and targets provides for improved communication, which again facilitates rapid and effective responses. Psychologically, teamwork enables the participants in the team to build up mutual trust and confidence, reinforce each other's commitment and motivation, develop a shared sense of direction, and respond to change as an opportunity, not a threat. The result, when it works, is faster and more creative problem solving, more robust decision outcomes, and improved productivity and performance.

The difficult bit is making it work.[17] The best teams work by using the excitement and challenge of a shared project, with shared accountability, a common purpose, and ambitious performance targets, to capture the commitment and energies of their members. The results can be exceptional and the experience exhilarating, but in a bimoral society even these success stories run into problems, especially with regard to work–home relationships. (We shall return to these problems in the next section.) Moreover, the success stories are relatively rare. In most teamwork situations, one or more of the ingredients necessary for success is missing. It can be difficult to generate excitement out of relatively mundane tasks, and without it high performance targets can become demotivating rather than motivating. It can be especially difficult in a market culture, with its emphasis on individual advancement, to get the shared commitment and accountability on which teams depend.

Young graduates working in investment banks work eighty plus hours a week, and have to maintain contact almost hourly, by mobile telephone or email, whenever they are not working. After two or three years many of them are thrown out, exhausted. But for these youngsters an extraordinary level of commitment is a reasonable price to pay for the opportunity of entering a lucrative market. It's part of the initiation process of becoming a 'Big Man' in the market society, a form of trial which few survive but many willingly undertake, a way of matching supply and demand. They have no other commitments, they are very well paid, and they have every reason to be loyal to their teams and their employers out of pure self-interest. In most companies and for most managers, however, these conditions do not apply.

The core problem is that while teamwork has provided an effective response to the need for change and flexibility, it is really no more suited to a market culture, with its emphasis on individual self-interest, than it was to a hierarchical culture, with its emphasis on well-defined roles and responsibilities. Underlying this is a more fundamental problem still, namely that in a market culture organizations themselves are out of place. The essence of organizations is that they achieve things that could not be achieved by free market exchanges between contracting individuals. They coordinate in ways that markets, even today's highly sophisticated and information-rich markets, cannot, and they achieve this coordination by evoking people's personal qualities of trust, loyalty, and obligation. Working in an organization may serve someone's self-interest in many ways—providing financial security and stability, and a congenial working environment, for example—but if the organization is to function effectively it also requires a suppression of that self-interest. Teamwork is a compromise between the demands of the market culture and the need for organization, and as such it captures all the tensions of the bimoral society.[10]

These tensions are especially visible in blue-collar teams, where the tasks remain relatively mundane and repetitive and it is hard to maintain any kind of project excitement. The rhetoric surrounding these teams is of self-organizing, empowerment, and shared accountability, but what this tends to mean in practice is that supervision is replaced by mutual surveillance (with pay dependent on team performance, every colleague is a potential liability and team members monitor each other) and comradeship by protective self-interest. Richard Sennett, drawing on ethnographic accounts of blue-collar teamwork by Charles Darrah, Laurie Graham, and Gideon Kunda, as well as on his own less formal observations, has characterized teamwork as 'the group practice of demeaning superficiality'.[19] Teams require a mask of cooperativeness, but with power no longer constrained by authority they are really arenas for competition. What matters is not getting the job done, as it used to be in the old bureaucracies, but keeping your place on the team.

In the management context, where teamwork is project based, where the team outcomes cannot normally be easily measured, and where pay is for the most part worked out individually, there is a slightly different dynamic. There is still an element of mutual surveillance, as reputation depends on performance and pay and advancement depend on reputation. But it is not keeping your place on the team that matters so much as getting a place on the next team. One evident route to management success in contemporary business is to network your way from one team to another through the organization (or organizations), always appearing to cooperate but avidly looking after your own self-interest, constantly reinventing yourself, taking credit for successful projects, and avoiding blame for failures. There is a constant tension between legitimate self-interest and an obligation to fellow team members.

Like the tensions inherent in managing vertical relationships, the tensions of teamwork come to the fore when things are not going well, when it becomes clear that, for whatever reason, the project outcome will not match up to the hopes or expectations of senior managers. In these circumstances, traditional morality suggests that you see the project out and share responsibility with your colleagues. But self-interest suggests that you jump ship, find yourself a new team, and leave others to finish the project. In a bimoral society either course can be seen as legitimate.

## THE MANAGER AS EMPLOYEE: BETWEEN WORK AND HOME

As we noted above, the other tension generated by teamwork, and especially by successful teamwork, is a tension between work and home. The fundamental reason why teams can be so effective is because in a team situation the team objectives take control. The shared commitment to achieving those objectives overcomes the barriers of communication and reticence that limit the effectiveness of mere groups, and overrides the constraints under which people normally operate—constraints of work, but also of home. The peer pressure of the team forces its members to 'carry their weight', which means working extra hours, staying in contact through their mobile telephones (an essential component of the technological environment that has brought team-working to prominence), and flexing their hours to meet the needs of team meetings. Even for those who embrace teamwork willingly or enthusiastically, this carries the danger of uncontrolled, escalating commitments. The task gradually takes over and people simply fail to notice, perhaps until it is too late, just how little they are seeing of their children, how much they are landing on their spouses, how unresponsive they are becoming to the needs of other family and close friends. Moreover, good teams, as their proponents never cease to emphasize, have fun, which means socializing as well as working together, giving up the time, commitment, and energy that might otherwise be devoted to family and friends. This is fine if it is what people want and if they can structure their lives accordingly, but not everyone lives to work. Some people also work to live, and many seek to balance the joys of work with other of life's joys.

When managers do realize how much their teamwork is impinging on their home life and try to draw a line, this poses problems for everyone concerned. For the individual manager it is a question of how to balance three sets of obligations: obligations to the team, obligations to the family, and obligations to the self (which might act in either direction). For the other team members the question is how far to make allowances. One of the most common moral dilemmas reported by managers is how to respond to the needs of a team member whose work commitments are constrained by family demands—typically, the demands on the mother of a small child or of a sick child, or the demands on a single parent. Most colleagues feel it is right to make allowances for such circumstances, and will happily do so for a short period. But there soon comes a point when they begin to feel exploited and see their colleague resentfully as a 'free rider'. Neither the needs of the colleague nor their recognition of those needs have changed, but their self-interest asserts itself and finds support in a feeling of moral indignation, based on a notion of fair contributions within the team.

Teamwork exacerbates the problems of reconciling work with home, but it's not their only source. In an increasingly competitive business world, and with increasingly competitive labour markets, contemporary business organizations look for more from their managers and give less than they used to. Whether in teams or not, the managers work longer hours than they used to. Their hours away from work are less well protected and firms, despite a lot of rhetoric to the contrary, are less willing or less able to make allowances for domestic circumstances. Meanwhile, families themselves have become more difficult to manage, as traditional patterns of family life have been eroded.

In the mid- to late-1990s, Tony Watson and Pauline Harris carried out an interview-based study of 'emergent managers' in Britain.[20] These were people who had recently been appointed to managerial positions, at different ages, from different backgrounds, and in a wide variety of organizations. Not surprisingly, their experiences varied widely, but there were some common factors. Most of the managers worked very long hours, with ten- or even twelve-hour days not uncommon. Though they tried not to, many also worked at weekends. In part this reflected the demands of the job. Managerial work in contemporary organizations is not about doing this or that but about doing 'whatever it takes' to get performance results. In part it reflected the dominant culture of the organizations in which they worked, which required not only commitment but also visible commitment. In some companies people felt compelled to work late even if they had nothing to do. In most they had to be seen to be committed and, moreover, to be coping well with the pressures that that created.

Starting out on their managerial careers, most of these people felt a need to prove themselves to their bosses. Many clearly hoped that the pressures would ease as they established themselves. But it is not clear that they had any rational justification for this hope. In business today, a hard-earned long-term reputation counts for little. What matter are current perceptions and the latest performance figures, and it is evident that the pressures experienced by these junior managers are experienced by their seniors as well. In a bimoral society, the commitment expected by the company is loaded with moral overtones, but the managers interviewed by Watson and Harris clearly recognized that the requirement for commitment was not a moral one. It was imposed on them by a company that, however powerless it might be in its own economic markets, had significant power over their lives. If they wanted to survive and succeed, they had to do whatever was asked of them, regardless of the impact on home and family.

This impact was clearly significant, and not just in terms of the hours worked, though this was important. Many of the managers interviewed talked about the impact promotion to management had had on their social lives, with evenings out a thing of the past. They also talked of the difficulty of switching off, and the tendency to take their work concerns home with them. This was not necessarily a question of taking home problems. Managerial work is challenging and absorbing and can be very enjoyable and rewarding. Most of the managers were clearly very positive and genuinely enthusiastic about their jobs. But that could be very hard on partners, as even when not working they were still preoccupied by work, with limited time or attention for their loved ones. When the work became less enjoyable, infused with anger or frustration if things went badly, with the stresses of organizational politics, or with sheer exhaustion, the impact on home life was still more severe. The managers talked of relying on their partners to keep them human, but also of how unfair this was on the partners, some of whom had work stresses of their own to cope with. Indeed, for some of the managers, managing the boundaries between work and home—the balance between conflicting priorities and expectations—was evidently more stressful than management in the narrower sense of what they did at work.

These problems are not new. Managerial work has always impinged on families. They have been greatly magnified, however, by the increased demands of contemporary business and, indeed, public sector organizations. They have also been affected by changes in the family. Fifty years ago, the majority of families (with or without children) were based on an earning husband and a homemaking wife. Today only a small minority of households (15 per cent in 1990s America) follow this pattern.[21] Changing social values and improved birth control have made it easier and more acceptable for women to enter the workforce, while changing earning patterns have made it necessary that they do so. A generation ago, a typical male manager could legitimate his commitment to work in terms of a stable and secure salary, and rely on his non-working wife for domestic and emotional support. As we shall see shortly, these role models still carry considerable force, but in today's world the male manager can no longer guarantee financial security and his partner (if he has one) is likely to have her (or his) own job and work stresses. (We shall come back to the situation facing the female manager.)

It is characteristic of the bimoral society that this profound social change is itself marked by conflicting demands. On one hand, our culture still attaches great importance to the family and to traditional family obligations. 'Family values' are still lauded. On the other hand, it legitimates the economic demands of business that prevent people from fulfilling those obligations. The men in Watson and Harris's study talked of wanting to do the best for their families, but of being unable to deliver, given the demands placed on them by their work. They tried to balance the demands of work and home, but the economic pressures meant that work always won out. As Kathleen Gerson has noted, the situation is made worse by the persistence of work patterns based on the traditional assumption of the male earner.[22] Although in some areas work patterns have become more flexible, the flexibility has served the company's interests more than the employee's, and at the management level it is minimal. At all levels the demands of partners and children are effectively invisible to the organization, and parenting desires are harshly penalized.

If this is a problem for men, it is far more of one for women. To listen to corporate rhetoric, you would think that the prospects for women managers had improved dramatically over the last ten years. Whereas taking a career break, or even the possibility that one might, as a woman, take a career break, used to mark the end of any promotion hopes, now everybody is treated equally, regardless of gender or of family responsibilities. The problem is that this change has not come about through firms allowing for the responsibilities of motherhood but through them ignoring them. So a woman manager will be treated just like a man, but she will also be expected to perform just like a man, and in particular to work the same long and antisocial hours that male managers work. If that causes difficulties, that is her problem, not the firm's.

Meanwhile, however, back in the home, the woman is still expected to be the homemaker. Even when men and women work the same hours, the domestic burdens of family life, such as shopping, cooking, cleaning, and child care, still seem to be borne disproportionately by the women. Women also continue to do most of the 'emotion work' that holds partnerships and families together and helps to manage the stresses produced by working lives.[23] One of the women interviewed by Watson and Harris talked revealingly of how her boss tried to be sympathetic, telling her to work from home if she had problems with child care. 'I don't think he really thinks about what that means . . . if I'm looking after my baby . . . I'm not going to be able to do any work . . . when he works from home he goes and sits in his study and shuts the door.' Moreover, '[his sympathy] doesn't stop him from giving you loads of work to do . . . I think he still expects you to do over and above your working week, which we all do.'[24]

Interestingly, the women managers in this study did not expect any help from their organizations when it came to the demands of child care. They knew that any compromises necessary to make work and home compatible would have to come from them. The American working women studied by Kathleen Gerson, also in the 1990s, took the same pragmatic view. Most were committed to making the combination of work and motherhood work, but they recognized that in contemporary culture they could expect little help from their employers, and little support from society.[25] In a bimoral society, women managers are criticized if they give anything less than total commitment to their employers and work colleagues, and criticized equally if they give less than total commitment to their families. They are also criticized, moreover, if they do not work at all.

## THE PARADOX OF FREEDOM

It is important not to lose a sense of perspective on what has been happening in the world of management. While the pressures on business to cut corners and shave costs have been growing, so too have the regulatory requirements for health and safety. While senior line managers may find it hard to look beyond the economic imperatives of the company, they are humans too. The higher up the organization you go, the more likely you are to find traditional family arrangements. At the very top, almost all CEOs (who are almost all men) have traditional families with homemaking wives. This is partly a generational thing, and partly a reflection of the type of character and work commitment needed to succeed in business. Most women know what they are marrying and what the implications will be. But successful management also requires an understanding of people, and even CEOs are aware of the pressures facing their managers. Most senior and middle managers are sympathetic to the conflicts faced by the people who report to them, even if they feel unable to do much about them. Human resource managers are stuck in a battle of their own, trying to gain organizational credibility by stressing their strategic role and focusing on performance, but they would never have become human resource managers if they did not believe that people are important, in themselves as well as for their companies. Indeed the field of human resource management (HRM), both professional and academic, has never been concerned with issues of ethics and organizational responsibility as much as in the last few years. Business ethics and the social responsibility of business receive far more attention from researchers, teachers, and corporate image-makers than they ever did in the past. But while these concerns reflect the tensions of a bimoral society, they are more a reaction to the changes taking place than a driving force in their own right. Any management student naive enough to think that the issues and concerns reflected in a business ethics or HRM textbook are indicative of the priorities of contemporary business is in for a very rude awakening.

A key word in the rhetoric by which contemporary business practices are advanced and defended is 'freedom'. We have already noted, in discussing 'free' markets and the relationship between freedom and power in earlier chapters, that freedom can be a mixed blessing, and this is nowhere more evident than in the world of work and employment. From a market perspective, the flexibility introduced by short-term contracts and the working arrangements that go with them is an unqualified benefit. It not only leaves companies 'free' to compete without the artificial constraints of traditional career obligations. It also leaves people 'free' to manage their own working lives, to take charge of their own careers. But what does freedom really mean, in this context?

The word 'freedom' (like its synonym 'liberty') has always had overwhelmingly positive connotations. We think historically of freedom from oppression by authoritarian regimes, freedom from the control of imperial powers, or freedom from the institution of slavery. We think of freedom from torture or from religious or ethnic persecution, the freedom to vote, freedom of conscience, free speech, or the freedom of the press. We take pride and reassurance in the fact that we live in a free society. As critical thinkers from Marcuse onwards have repeatedly reminded us, however, freedom is not always what it appears. In particular, the freedom to choose is contingent on the choices available and in most case what we have is a choice between certain well-defined options that serve to prohibit as much as to enable. This is most obvious in the area of consumer choices, where we typically choose between a wide range of near-identical products, and where the illusion of the 'free' consumer masks a situation in which consumers are effectively in the thrall of the large corporations who not only supply their needs but effectively create those needs as well. As the sociologist Zygmunt Bauman has put it: 'The market feeds on the unhappiness it generates: the fears, anxieties and sufferings of personal inadequacy it induces release the consumer behaviour indispensable to its continuation.'[26]

The intensity of the competition and the sheer variety of goods available give an appearance of unprecedented choice, but in an age of mass communication and increasingly sophisticated advertising techniques, the companies are in control and, to quote Bauman again, 'It is no more clear what (who) is the object of consumption, who (what) is the consumer.'[27]

As we noted earlier in Chapter 4, a similar situation pertains in politics, where political choices are effectively limited to the political products on offer from the major parties. It also pertains, to some extent, in intellectual life. Herbert Marcuse, writing nearly forty years ago, pointed out that in a society dominated by mass media, intellectual freedom had to be seen as the freedom to choose between alternative expressions of public opinion and not as a freedom to think for oneself. Whether in the economic, political, or intellectual domain, he suggested, 'With technical progress as its instrument, unfreedom . . . is perpetuated and intensified in the form of many liberties and comforts.'[28]

Allowing that these critiques come from the political left, from a tradition that is inherently suspicious of capitalism and its products, it is hard to deny that there is some truth in them. In today's society, which is supposedly more free than any that has preceded it, consumer corporations and the mass media dictate and limit our options to a remarkable degree and true freedom of thought, action, or voice can be very difficult to achieve. This is not the aspect of freedom that most concerns people, however, if only because most people are blissfully unaware of the constraints under which they think and act. Of far more pressing concern is the fact that the freedom of the market culture cuts two ways. To put it very bluntly, the freedom to compete is also the freedom to lose.

Going back to the freedom of the new careers, the freedom of people to make their own life decisions instead of having them made for them by a paternalistic bureaucracy, both the positive and the negative aspects are clearly visible. On the positive side this freedom does in some sense serve the individual as well as the company. Just as the breaking down of national trade boundaries has allowed entrepreneurial corporations to flourish in the new economy, so the breaking down of the organizational boundaries that have traditionally enclosed careers has allowed entrepreneurial individuals to flourish. 'Boundaryless careers', as they have often been called, or 'intelligent careers', 'portfolio careers', 'post-corporate careers', or 'entrepreneurial careers', create opportunities not just for entrepreneurial gain but also for learning and self-fulfilment.[29]

Research carried out in New Zealand in the 1990s, by Michael Arthur, Kerr Inkson, and Judith Pringle, suggests that many people have reacted to the end of traditional careers very positively.[30] They really have taken control of their working lives, proactively exploring possibilities that would previously have been closed to them, acquiring skills and knowledge, and structuring career patterns in multiple organizations to suit their changing needs. The freedom to experiment has enabled people to find out what they want from work, and to find effective ways of combining work with leisure interests or family commitments, resulting in more suitable and considered working choices. Moreover the challenges of new jobs and new organizations have given people fresh energy.

Not everyone in this study responded so positively, however, and for many people the flexibility of new working arrangements is marked not by challenges and opportunities but by the threat of redundancy and unemployment. The freedom to take control of their own careers is the freedom to be left not only without a career but also without a job and all that implies in terms of financial and emotional security. This is partly a question of generation. Adaptation to such a different world is much easier for the young than it is for older workers, whose lives have taught them the skills to cope with stability rather than those to cope with change and flexibility. It is also a question of temperament, confidence, and ability. Whereas some people find uncertainty exciting and challenging, others find it threatening and disabling. Some people are naturally good at reinventing and marketing themselves and negotiating their way through the new career jungle, while others are too shy to do this successfully, even though their performative skills may be considerable. The well educated, generally, have transferable skills that can be adapted to a variety of situations. The less well educated rely more on the training that is no longer available.

For many sectors of the population, the end of traditional careers is deeply unsettling, a source of disabling insecurity rather than of enabling freedom. And in the bimoral society, this insecurity is heightened by two further considerations. The first is the prospect of the end not only of careers, but also, and far more fundamentally, of jobs. The second is the prospect of the collapse, or at least the weakening, of the welfare state.

For some sectors of the population, 'the end of work', to use Jeremy Rifkin's now famous expression, is already a reality. Rapid developments in information technology and the export of low-grade manufacturing jobs to developing countries have left whole communities of unskilled workers without any prospect of getting a job. Semi-skilled, clerical, and administrative workers are also fast becoming redundant. Where all this is going is still a matter for hot debate. Rifkin and others present a scenario of technological development in which there is less and less demand for human work, even at the highly skilled end of the spectrum.[31] Others see a world of self-employment, or a world segregated into workers and non-workers in the same way that Athenian society was segregated into citizens and slaves.[32] What is evident is that many people who lose their jobs, even in the prime of their working lives, are unlikely to find others, and that for some people even getting a job at all may now be impossible.

In the long term, perhaps we shall learn to live without jobs, or even without work, but we are a very long way away from that. As we noted above, a job or occupation confers a social identity. It channels people's energies and gives meaning to their lives. It gives people dignity.[33] When somebody is faced with the possibility of a life without work, or with only scraps of part-time work, it can be difficult—especially in the absence of strong communities or strong religious beliefs—to find a purpose for living, and all too easy to degenerate into a life of despondency. Young people setting out on life with no prospect of a job turn to drugs or crime, or drugs (to relieve the boredom) *then* crime (to pay for the drugs). According to sociologist William J. Wilson, who has spent much of his career studying the black communities of America's inner cities, there are now many black neighbourhoods in which the unemployed out-number the employed, and the effects of joblessness are even more serious than the more recognized effects of poverty. Work provides an anchor for daily life, for both individuals and communities. Without it, both disintegrate.[34]

The conflict between the end of jobs and the need for work is not an overtly moral one, but it is intimately related to the tensions of the bimoral society. In a traditional hierarchical society, one's job or occupation defines one's position in the social 'grid' or classification structure, which in turn defines one's socially constructed identity. To have a job or occupation is, in a very real sense, to be a member of the moral community that makes up the society. In a market soci-ety, in contrast, status comes from employing others, from being successfully self-employed, or at least from being able to dictate the terms of one's (con-tracted) employment. To simply have a job is to be subservient to a 'Big Man' entrepreneur and so to be excluded from the primary moral community.

The conflicts associated with welfare are more overtly moral. The leading world economies vary in their provision of welfare and health care support, with northern European countries providing far more generous support than, say, the United States; but in all cases the support that is provided is under threat. According to the ideology of market culture, this is progress. Support of this kind is not something provided out of a duty to look after the less fortunate members of society, but a distortion of free markets that acts *against* the inter-ests of the individuals affected. Just as old-fashioned planned careers are said to remove the freedom of individuals to take control of their own careers, so welfare is said to constrain people within a web of dependency and take away their opportunity for self-improvement. Of course, the idea that giving to the poor prevents them from looking after themselves is not new. It has always pro-vided an excuse for the wealthy not to part with their wealth and has always been a mainstay of conservative thinking. But it has been strongly reinforced in recent years both by the rise of market ideology and by the practical realization that existing policies may prove unsustainable. With the amount of work avail-able in the Western economies apparently in long-term decline, and with rap-idly ageing populations increasing the demands for health care and pensions, it is becoming hard to see how existing levels of support can be maintained with-out unacceptably high taxation levels. So managers or workers facing the loss of their jobs are having to confront not just the freedom to manage their own careers, but also the freedom to live within existing levels of state support, in poverty and ill-health.

For German sociologist Ulrich Beck, both the fear of the end of work and the fear of the end of welfare are characteristic of a political economy of insecurity, which has much wider manifestations.[35] For Beck, the development of tech-nology has not only left us without any assurance of jobs but has also led to incalculable environmental and ecological risks. The distribution of wealth is replaced as the key feature of social order by the distribution of risk, and insecurity replaces poverty as the key problem facing society.[36] Moreover, while the sources of insecurity, in the form of the technological and financial capital that drive the world economy, are global in nature and growing in power, the defences against insecurity, in the form of work, welfare, family, and community, are local and in decline. The collapse of work, the fragmentation of social identity, the inability of governments to pay welfare costs, the expectation of poverty in old age, and the exposure of people to unseen technological risks are all manifestations of a collapse of the established structures of modern society, the central feature of which is a redistribution of risk from society to the individual.

In our own terms, this redistribution of risk can be seen as a shift from a risk-averse hierarchical society, in which each individual devotes herself to and places herself in the care of the collectivity, to a market society in which it is every man for himself and in which taking risks is the only way to get returns. In the process of the shift, the security and stability of the hierarchy give way to the endemic insecurity and change potential of the market. This change is happening, however, much faster than we can accommodate to it, and at a time when we have grown more appreciative of the comforts of security than ever before. Despite their ideals, traditionally moral societies have not always been able to deliver very high levels of security, but over the last century the middle classes, in particular, have grown used to a world in which employment, employability, and a certain level of income could be pretty well guaranteed. In the last fifty years, a period marked first by high employment and then by well-funded welfare systems, and throughout by an absence of major wars, the working classes too have grown used to a relatively secure existence. For most people, these gains have been tremendously valuable, and security remains both socially and psychologically important. The choice between security and freedom is not one we are ready to make.

# 8

# The Challenge of Contemporary Management

Although 'flexible' or 'post-bureaucratic' organizations are still a relative novelty, some aspects of their operation are already well understood. The need to encourage and reward individual enterprise, for example, is widely appreciated, and a lot of work has gone into defining the reporting- evaluation-, and incentive-based remuneration systems needed to achieve this. A lot of attention has also been paid to the development of information systems able to distribute knowledge rapidly to the points at which it is needed, without either locking it up in bureaucratized compartments or creating information overload. In business schools there is a new focus on career management, and entrepreneurship has moved from being a minority option to being the core of the MBA programme. A generation of young managers has responded well to the challenge of taking responsibility for their own learning and careers, displaying a drive and independence, a competitiveness, and a degree of self-confidence that many of their parents' generation lacked. In all the enthusiasm for enterprise and autonomy, however, very little attention has been paid to the core of the new management challenge, which is not how to foster market values—that is the easy bit—but how to combine these with the traditionally moral concerns and behaviours that are still necessary if the newly empowered self-interest is to be made to work for the communities in which it operates— the companies themselves, the local communities in which they are sited, and society at large. Durkheim may have been overstating things when he suggested a century ago that entrepreneurial self-interest was in danger of undermining the whole moral fabric and stability of society, but he nevertheless had a point.[1] One of the lessons we can draw from the Enron affair is that self-interest, if unchecked by moral restraint, *can* get the better of people and lead to situations that serve the interests of no one.

Where this moral restraint will come from, in a world in which traditional moral authorities no longer have credibility, will in the end be a problem for society. We shall look at this problem in the next chapter. Meanwhile, though, the immediate challenge facing managers is not so much how to legitimate traditional moral values as how to express and enact them, and so secure the collective interests that ultimately depend on them, in the absence of a traditionally rule-based or strongly hierarchical organizational culture. In this chapter we shall explore three separate aspects of this challenge. The first is a challenge of leadership, as top executives are called on to ensure that the individual entrepreneurial energies set free in flexible organizations are directed, synchronized, and employed constructively in the service of the organizations and their stakeholders. The focus here is on strategy and direction rather than on morality as such, but as we shall see the challenge nevertheless has a significant moral dimension. The second challenge is more explicitly moral. In a flexible organization, managers at all levels need to create and sustain the sense of moral community that is necessary if the damaging excesses of self-interest are to be avoided and if people are to work together in effective, trusting relationships. The third challenge is more general: in a bimoral society we must somehow learn to manage, and teach other people to manage, in a world without rules, or at least in a world in which rules are there to be broken.

## HOLDING IT ALL TOGETHER: THE CHALLENGE OF LEADERSHIP

### The problem

Flexible ways of organizing have brought great benefits, combining efficiency with responsiveness and releasing the entrepreneurial energies of their members. They have also brought new challenges. Old-fashioned bureaucracies may have made poor use of the energies and inventiveness of their staff. They were certainly slow moving and resistant to change. But the moral compact on which they were based secured a high level of organizational commitment and this, and the rules and guidelines within which jobs were framed, enabled them to direct people's efforts towards a common purpose. In flexible organizations, with their fixed-term contracts, job insecurity, and looser forms of control, there is no obvious basis for organizational commitment or for ensuring that everyone is pulling in the same direction. Incentive schemes can reward desired outcomes, but in the fast-moving competitive arenas of the flexible economy it is not always clear in advance what the desired outcomes will be, or how they should be formulated, and as researchers have repeatedly shown incentive pay is full of pitfalls. By encouraging people's self-interest it encourages them to play the system, discouraging cooperative behaviours and focusing people on the rewards available rather than on the task at hand. Researchers have found that people on incentive pay are less likely to help their co-workers; that hospital surgeons whose pay was adjusted to counter fears of high mortality rates responded by refusing to treat high-risk patients; that executives adjust reported earnings to maximize their bonuses. In one case an

American football team coach was worried that his quarterback was throwing too many interceptions, and adjusted his contract to discourage this. He promptly stopped throwing the ball, even when the play suggested he should.[2]

When companies began to move over to more flexible forms of organizing, the problem of directing people's divergent self-interests so that they contributed constructively to the aims of the company as a whole was not at first apparent. On the contrary, while companies adopted the principles of market culture and cut back heavily on their commitments to employees, they did not lessen their demand for dedication and commitment on the employees' part. They sought to have things both ways, combining all the benefits of hierarchical control with all the benefits of market freedom, and to a large extent they succeeded. Old habits die hard, and managers who had been used to working within a traditional hierarchical culture—and who came, for the most part, from the middle-class stratum of society in which traditional moral values were most deeply embedded—maintained their sense of moral commitment long after their employers had broken with theirs. These managers were also concerned for their own and their families' security, and were acutely conscious of the power disparity between the individual and the corporation. They felt in no position to do anything other than what was demanded of them.

The power of the corporation over its employees is one thing that has not changed in the flexible economy. In most cases, the threat to the individual of being fired is still far greater than the threat to the company of someone resigning. As we saw in the last chapter, the more subtle expressions of corporate power discussed by Stanley Deetz are also largely unaffected, as yet, by the change of organizational form. Because the problems arising from the asymmetry of commitment are problems of values rather than of technique, and because they manifest themselves as problems for the individual rather than as problems for the organization, they are not considered a proper subject for organizational debate and cannot easily be challenged. They can, however, be ignored, and to some extent they are being ignored by a new generation of entrepreneurial managers brought up in the ways of market culture and the flexible economy. The core skill for these managers is not the ability to manage, though many of them have strong business skills, but the ability to sell themselves, and part of what they sell, in a market that demands it, is the impression of commitment. If their companies want commitment they will talk commitment, but since their real commitment is to themselves they will not necessarily give it. They will give enough to advance their careers, and move on before they are moved on.

The power of the new generation to dictate terms to their employers is still very limited. Even if they are not worried about job security (and some are more worried than they will admit) they suffer like anyone else from the long working hours and work–home conflicts that characterize contemporary management. Superficially at least, their behaviour can be controlled. But given that each is focused on a different, personal end, and not on the ends of the company, directing and focusing their efforts is another matter. As they increasingly replace the older generation—and teach that generation new ways of thinking—simply demanding commitment will no longer work: companies and their top managers will have to find new means of direction and coordination.

Not everyone accepts that this is a problem. Inspired by the recent development of mathematical theories of non-hierarchical self-organizing systems and self-organizing networks, some observers have tried to cast flexible or 'network' organizations in these terms. They have extolled the virtues of 'self-organizing teams' and argued that by adopting the principles of self-organization it is possible to eliminate hierarchy altogether. The trouble with this argument is that self-organizing systems in general, and self-organizing teams in particular, are not in themselves purposeful. The mechanism at work is essentially one of mutual adaptation and this enables them to organize around a given purpose, and as such to substitute for some aspects of hierarchy. Self-organizing teams can also respond adaptively to changing environments, in a way that hierarchies cannot, and they can resolve differences between the individual aims and objectives of their members. But unless they are directed they will simply evolve in their own way, adapting to environmental stimuli and to different personal agendas, but without any necessary reference to the needs or purpose of the corporation.[3]

Self-organization seems to work well in small bounded communities with clear needs: for the maintenance of social order, for example, or for simple survival. In terms of the cultural theory discussed in Chapter 2, it is most naturally associated with sects, where the primary aim is survival or maintenance of a religious ideal, rather than with markets or hierarchies. The complex objectives of all business organizations and the rapidly changing membership of contemporary network organizations and the teams within them make the sect a singularly inappropriate model. Having said that, however, the strong group characteristic of the sect has evident attractions for senior managers who can no longer rely on hierarchical forms of control. One early response to the problem of direction and coordination in flexible organizations was the 1990s enthusiasm for 'corporate vision', and this can be seen as an attempt to create artificially some of the strong group characteristics of the sect.

Vision used to be associated mainly with the leadership of an individual, a 'visionary leader', but in the 1990s it became depersonalized as corporations sought to have in place a 'strategic vision' or 'corporate vision' that was effectively independent of their leadership. Sometimes this was a pretty bland affair, another set of words for the catchall mission statement: 'Our vision is to be one of the best companies in the areas in which we operate.' But the aim was to generate something richer, more symbolically powerful, with which the organizational members could identify and to which they could rally. The idea was that if the employees could be sold a vision of the corporation and its future to which they could subscribe, they would take that vision as their goal and work cooperatively and unselfishly towards it, even while the company was treating them quite selfishly, according to the rules of the market. In a sense it was a form of organizational brainwashing.

The vision approach may have worked, up to a point, but it was always going to impact more effectively on those employees who were already committed to the company than on those with their own personal agendas. For the older generation of managers, the future was often dominated by a sense of insecurity and a fear of lost jobs and lost prosperity; commitment to a corporate vision may well have helped to block out this fear. Younger managers, however, appear to have been more inclined to see the vision for what it was, repeating the mantra but not being significantly affected by it.[4] In the 2000s, corporate visions still exist, but they seem to be much more closely tied to leadership.

## The role of leadership

In his 1990 book *A Force for Change*, leadership guru John Kotter described the leadership function in terms of three processes of direction, alignment, and motivation:[5]

1. Establishing direction—developing a vision of the future, often the distant future, along with strategies for producing the changes needed to achieve that vision.
2. Aligning people—communicating the direction to those whose cooperation may be needed so as to create coalitions that understand the vision and that are committed to its achievement.
3. Motivating and inspiring—keeping people moving in the right direction despite major political, bureaucratic, and resource barriers to change by appealing to very basic, but often untapped, human needs, values, and emotions.

As is apparent, Kotter's main focus was on the role of leadership in organizational change. The context in which he was writing was the failure of large bureaucratic organizations to achieve the strategic changes that were evidently required in the 1980s, and he attributed this failure to the fact that the so-called leaders, the top executives of American corporations, were not, in fact, leading but managing. They were planning, budgeting, organizing, staffing, and controlling, maintaining the functionality of the hierarchical machine, but without changing the machine itself to cope with new circumstances. Other commentators of the period made similar distinctions, between managing for stability and leading for change, between managing the day-to-day routine of a business and questioning and changing that routine. As Warren Bennis famously put it, 'Leaders are people who do the right thing; managers are people who do things right.'[6] Both were necessary, but in hierarchical organizations, while the management function was well developed, the leadership function was not.

From the perspective we have taken here, the inability of large bureaucratic organizations to change appears more as an inherent property of hierarchical cultures than as something that can be blamed on their leaders. In contemporary corporate cultures with their strong market elements, change is rather less of a problem. But the distinction Kotter drew is still important, for the very processes he described as essential for change leadership in bureaucracies are also essential in flexible organizations, not only for directing and focusing their change processes but also for maintaining their stability. While the requirements of management may have changed, those of leadership have not. The top managers of flexible organizations need to develop, and to keep developing, directions and strategies for their organizations; to communicate those directions and align people with them; and to motivate and inspire people to maintain that alignment and contribute productively to the organizational objectives. In some ways the loosening of bureaucratic structures has removed the obstacles to these processes, but in others it has made them still more challenging. Leadership is now needed in times of stability as well as in times of change. In the absence of bureaucratic structures and controls, aligning people is massively more difficult and so, in the absence of the moral compact of bureaucracy, is motivating and inspiring them.

These challenges not only enhance the demands of business leadership, they also require a particular type of leadership. A common distinction in leadership studies is that between autocratic or boss-centred and democratic or subordinate-centred leadership styles. A more complex version of this typology distinguishes between authoritarian, participative, empowering, and servant leadership. Authoritarian leaders take responsibility for setting strategy and goals, and implement these through top-down control. Participative leaders retain control but involve their employees, at least superficially, in the decision-making and implementation processes, using this involvement as a means of aligning and motivating them. Empowering leaders give up a significant amount of control in order to release the creative energies of their employees, enabling them work out for themselves how best, and even in what direction to proceed. In a sense they are not leaders at all, but facilitators. 'Servant leaders', to use the phrase coined by Robert Greenleaf, or 'transforming leaders' as William Torbert calls them, take this further by suspending their own self-interest and putting themselves in the service of the organization and its members.[7]

Although many writers on leadership have tended to favour more democratic leadership styles, at least implicitly, an authoritarian style was often the most effective in a hierarchical context. Hierarchical cultures favour well-defined roles, and leadership, in the traditional authoritarian sense, is such a role. The staff of old-fashioned business bureaucracies expected to be told what to do and looked to their leaders to tell them. However, authoritarian leadership relies heavily on the structures of the hierarchy: on the moral commitment of employees, the control mechanisms of status, and the predictability of bureaucratic mechanisms. In flexible organizations, in which these are present to a much smaller extent, it is much less appropriate. Based as they are on individual freedom and autonomy, the organizing principles of these organizations almost inevitably call for more democratic leadership styles. The question is, how democratic?

Attractive as the notions of empowering or servant leadership are, in a business context they are not sufficient for at least two reasons. In the first place, business organizations combine considerable complexity with a need for rapid decision making and implementation. Empowered employees can respond effectively at a local level, but ensuring that that response is consistent with the needs of other parts of the organization is much more difficult. The coordinating processes of an organization with an effective empowering leader should be faster and more effective than those of a purely self-organizing system, but in a competitive business environment there will, nevertheless, be times when they have to be short-circuited in the interests of speed. In the second place, leading a business is not just about serving the needs of a community of employees. It is also about serving the interests of other stakeholders, above all shareholders. At times, these interests will be complementary, and what is right for the employees will also be right for the shareholders, but at other times they may diverge. A key task of the business leader is to balance and where necessary adjudicate between the interests of different stakeholders, and that cannot be done by handing control to employees.

These considerations suggest that the basic leadership style for today's business organizations should be a participative one, in which autonomy is balanced with control. If the benefits of flexible forms of organizing are to be gained, however, the autonomy will have to be genuine. It will not be enough, as in a hierarchical organization, to give people the illusion of autonomy so as to win their support. Employees will have to be given a real freedom to act. This means that while leaders will need to maintain control, they will have to do so by being aware of and building on the aims of their employees, which means that they will also have to adopt some of the characteristics of empowering or servant leadership.

## The Chief Executive Officer's job

To explore these implications further, we need to look more closely at the work of a contemporary Chief Executive Officer (CEO). In 2001–2 I interviewed the CEOs of forty of the UK FTSE 100 companies. They came from different generations, with ages ranging from 40 to 65, and from a range of different backgrounds. They had been in post for periods ranging from a few months to fifteen years, and embodied a range of styles and approaches. Some of their companies were still run on more or less traditional bureaucratic lines, some used highly flexible market structures. Most were somewhere in between, relatively flexible team-based organizations but with significant elements of hierarchical structure.[8]

The majority of these CEOs described their work in terms of three core elements, which corresponded roughly to the three sub-processes of leadership described by Kotter: strategy, communications, and people management. Strategy was a central concern for most of them, in a way it was not for the CEOs of a decade ago, and in describing it they placed themselves very firmly in the role of the strategist. Some of them distinguished explicitly between the strategic analyses offered by consultants and 'real strategy', which was their job, and a far more intuitive process concerned with creatively finding a direction for the business. The strategy processes they described were mostly participative, involving at least one and sometimes two tiers of management, and appeared to be more actively participative the more flexible the organization. Certainly the only exceptions, where strategy formation was a top-down process, were in the older-style bureaucracies.

The strategy processes described by the CEOs were also conceived very personally, even possessively. However participatively the direction and strategy might be determined, the CEOs treated them in some sense as their personal property. They felt that the onus was very clearly on them, and no one else, to decide on a vision and direction for the company and on a strategy by which to achieve it, and to take personal responsibility for these. If things did not work out they would have to accept the consequences and go; there was no one else they could blame. Again, the sense of ownership seems to have been stronger in the more flexible organizations, and to be lacking only in a couple of the old bureaucracies, where strategy was seen as a staff planning process and the CEO was concerned more with operating efficiency—with management, in Kotter's terms, rather than with leadership. Moreover, within eighteen months of the interviews, the CEOs who took this approach had both 'resigned'.

If direction and strategy are the central preoccupation of the CEOs—what they spend their time thinking about—communications dominate their day-to-day work. The CEOs of large public companies spend a lot of their time, a day a week or more, on their communications with external constituencies—investors, analysts, and the media—but they spend even more time on internal communications, visiting sites, talking with employees, getting across the vision and strategy they have formulated. Talking about their communications role the CEOs interviewed repeatedly brought to mind Kotter's description of the alignment process as 'delivering a complex message to a large, diverse and skeptical audience', a process that requires not only great clarity and convincing examples, but also endless and completely consistent repetition. With the exception, again, of some of the older style bureaucracies, most of the CEOs saw communicating vision and strategy as the crux of their job. They were well aware of its difficulty as well as of its importance, and many of them pointed to it as something that had changed in the course of their careers. Twenty years ago, they observed, CEOs did not need to be great communicators. Now they do, and the people who are finding their way into the top corporate jobs are increasingly people with particularly strong communications skills, or more exceptionally people prepared to learn and be trained in those skills.

The other side of communication is listening. In general, the listening skills of the CEOs interviewed appeared to be less well developed than their outward communication skills, but more than any other characteristic the ability to listen did seem to distinguish the most successful CEOs from the rest. Those who most impressed, both at interview and in terms of their performance record, were not only able to communicate the directions of their companies with great clarity, but also had an exceptional grasp on what key constituencies—shareholders, managers, employees—felt about those directions. Listening, and listening first, so as to empathize before communicating, is a key element of transforming or servant leadership, and it seems to be an important part of the leadership profile in flexible organizations.

The third prominent aspect of the CEO's job is leadership of the top management team. Part of this is succession management, but much of it is team building, motivating and inspiring the group of managers with whom the CEO is in regular face-to-face contact. In a contemporary business, these managers are all on incentive pay of some kind and are all competing with each other for one of the top jobs, or for the recognition that will help them land a top job elsewhere. They would not have got as far as they have if they were not highly competitive, but in many companies the majority are now headed for early retirement, to make way for a new batch of would-be chief executives. For the business to succeed they have to be motivated and inspired to put the company's interests ahead of their own, and keep pulling in the same direction. Not all the CEOs interviewed claimed particular skills in this area, but as several of them observed, if they couldn't do it, no one else could. Like their communications role, it could not be delegated.

While they actively managed their top teams, however, most of the CEOs did not see themselves as part of the team. Many described the CEO's job as a lonely one, the burdens of which could not be shared. This points to another important aspect of the leadership challenge in more flexible organizations. Contemporary CEOs are very powerful, but they are also very vulnerable. They are vulnerable, as we noted in Chapter 7, to the criticism that goes with multiple accountabilities in a bimoral society, and they have very little job security. Rather like football managers, the buck stops with them, and if they make a wrong call—or more accurately, perhaps, *when* they make a wrong call—they pay with their jobs. This combination of pressures can be very isolating, especially in a competitive corporate culture in which the people with whom a CEO might share his problems are either people he has defeated for the top job or people who are waiting for the opportunity to succeed him.

CEOs respond to these pressures in different ways. A very few of those interviewed were simply arrogant. Supremely confident in the knowledge of their own superiority they ignored any criticism and ran their companies autocratically. As we have already noted, however, this style of leadership is only possible in a strong hierarchy. Most of the CEOs adopted more participative styles, and were more conscious both of their limitations and of their vulnerabilities. In the majority of cases, however, there was still a certain air of hubris. Most of the CEOs were proud of what they had achieved, and rightly so—they were a group of exceptional achievers, with outstanding abilities. But there was also a sense, fuelled by their high public profile and by the isolation of their job, that this achievement somehow made them into a different class of being. They had made it to the top, they could take the pressures, and they were going to keep on winning, which meant lasting longer in the job than other CEOs, or making a bigger difference, by growing or reshaping the company. In a sense these people gave themselves completely to their companies: they lived and breathed their jobs, seven days a week, fifty-two weeks a year. But in a sense, their companies became part vehicles for their own personal ambitions.

A few of the CEOs, in contrast, and a few of the most successful, seemed to take a rather different view. They were no less competitive, but they reacted differently to reaching the top. They had made it, and were proud of that, but in doing so they had accumulated more than enough money to live on, and they knew that the next stage in their careers was as likely to be the sack as an orderly retirement or progression to chairman. In a complex competitive environment, no one was infallible, and the best they could hope for was to get it right more often than not. So rather than pursuing their personal ambitions they decided to use their time at the top by putting themselves at the service of their companies. This did not mean relinquishing control, but it did mean adopting some of the psychological attitude of servant leadership, of exercising control for the benefit of others. It meant approaching the job with a certain humility. It meant listening carefully to and empathizing with what the various stakeholders in the business had to say, and making value-based judgements about which interests should dominate and when. It also meant creating, or at least trying to create, a purposeful environment in which groups of employees could be trusted and empowered to steer their own paths in a world of conflicting demands and divergent interests.

Just as very few of the CEOs interviewed were outrageously arrogant or self-interested, so very few were exceedingly humble or strongly other-oriented. Most were somewhere in the middle. But where there was an element of humility it appeared to have interesting effects. Most significantly, a greater degree of humility appeared to be linked to a greater readiness to work as part of a team, letting other people influence or take decisions while taking full and sole responsibility for any failures. This raises the difficult but interesting question as to whether leadership in flexible organizations should, in some sense, be a team rather than an individual function.

## Individuals and teams

As Kotter has pointed out, the leadership functions in larger organizations are almost inevitably spread across a number of people. A CEO cannot be everywhere, and actively aligning people with the vision and strategy of the organization, and motivating and inspiring them to keep focusing on that vision and direction, may require leadership contributions from a variety of people at different times and in different circumstances.[9] When we talk of leadership, however, we almost invariably think of individual leadership, and this is the dominant model in business today. Even in highly flexible team-based network organizations, the 'top management team' tends not to be a team at all, but a bureaucratic hierarchy, with members filling well-defined functional roles (finance director, human resources director, etc.) and one person, usually the CEO, acting as leader.[10] The CEO may not be the only person who directs, motivates, and inspires, but in a truly hierarchical fashion he directs, motivates, and inspires the division heads or project leaders whose role it is to direct, motivate, and inspire others.

From a cultural perspective, this is scarcely surprising, since both market and hierarchical cultures work through individual leadership and, where organizations are involved, hierarchical structures. Today's business organizations and our thinking and theorizing about them have grown out of a bureaucratic context, and our discussion in this section has been framed by that context. Our concern has been with how the leadership role, hierarchically defined, is affected by the removal of the control structures and moral compact of bureaucracy. We could also have looked at things from the opposite perspective, however. In market cultures, 'Big Men' compete self-interestedly for power and resources, and as market behaviours have become socially legitimated so businesses and their leaders have come to act and be seen more and more in 'Big Man' terms. Given the continuing influence of traditional moral values, however, they cannot act as they would in a true market culture. In a true market culture, organizations are not merely hierarchical (using the word here in an informal sense and without its cultural implications) but very strongly, even violently, autocratic. They have to be so, because if they were not, if market competition were allowed to thrive freely within the organization, the leader would risk losing control. Criminal organizations provide a good example of this. They have scope for competition, for people to prove themselves and bid for leadership positions, and their leadership is ultimately decided by a form of market competition, but to protect their positions incumbent leaders rule, and need to rule, with a rod of iron.

To the extent, then, that businesses are market organizations, the challenge of leadership is one of how to keep control, in a culture in which there are moral limits on the exercise of power. An effective response to this challenge will inevitably rely on much the same processes as we have already discussed, but it will also entail enhancing as far as possible the mystique of the leader (even at the cost of being held personally accountable by shareholders); retaining personal control as far as possible of the key strategic and communications functions; and managing the threat of succession by a careful division of power and knowledge at the top of the organization, a task that is made significantly easier by the preservation of a functional bureaucracy in top management, such that only the CEO has an overall perspective of the business.

For slightly different reasons, both hierarchical and market cultures favour a model of individual leadership and well-defined top management roles, and quite apart from the fact that the leadership functions are most naturally conceived of and enacted as individual functions it is no surprise that that model has endured. It is embedded in existing bureaucratic practice. It suits the CEOs in their competitive big men personae. It also suits the institutional shareholders in the form of their fund managers, who operate in a very competitive individualistic culture themselves and look for an individual to take responsibility if the business should go downhill.

Against this, the prevailing model does run up against a number of problems. First, it places almost impossible demands upon the CEO, especially in a large company. This is partly a question of skills. Inspirational leaders who are also good strategists and good judges of people are in pretty short supply. It is partly just a question of time. Because the communications functions of the leader—communicating externally and aligning, motivating, and inspiring people internally—are both immensely time-consuming and essential for short-term survival, the core function of setting a vision and strategy tends to get pushed out. A new CEO may put quite a lot of work into this, but once a course is set it is very difficult to find the time and energy to revisit it. Indeed, even the best CEOs of large companies are apt to 'burn out' and lose their effectiveness relatively quickly. Second, and related to this, are difficulties arising from a lack of continuity. Without the time or the skills to do everything required of an individual leader, CEOs inevitably make mistakes. These mistakes lead to changes in the leadership, but with so much concentrated in one person a smooth transition is inherently difficult and the new leader, whether appointed from inside or outside the organization, has to start again from the beginning and build up both his knowledge and his reputation from scratch. Third, an individualized style of leadership and the lack of a genuine team at the top make it much harder to motivate people further down the organization to suppress their own competitive instincts to work together in teams.

More generally, the pressures that have pushed business organizations into adopting flexible team-based structures would appear to apply just as much at the top of the organization as elsewhere. We noted earlier that teams are not a natural organizing device in *either* markets *or* hierarchies, but that does not mean they are not an appropriate response to the compromises required in a bimoral society. For all their difficulties they seem, at present, to be the most effective way we know to engage individual interests in the service of a common interest, and this is precisely what business leadership requires.

Given the individual interests at stake, the power currently invested in the CEO, the advantages to the CEO of that power, and the advantages to others of having an individual to blame when things go wrong, we are unlikely to see a rapid movement towards team-based leadership. The challenge is there, however, and the more leaders are willing to let go of their self-interest, giving up their power without giving up their responsibility, and sharing their leadership with their colleagues, the more we shall learn about how businesses might effectively be led in the future.

## MAINTAINING A MORAL COMMUNITY: THE CHALLENGE OF MANAGEMENT

### Moral leadership and business performance

The leadership challenge discussed in the last section is essentially strategic. It is about finding and implementing a direction for the business that will bring it success in a competitive marketplace. But leadership also has an explicitly moral dimension. This is most clearly apparent in discussions of servant leadership, but it is not restricted to that context. Studies of what makes for effective business leadership, or of what people look for in a leader, consistently emphasize the importance of ethics. Researchers have found, for example, that employee commitment is higher in ethical cultures, and when CEOs demonstrate high ethical standards and ethical awareness.[11] When Joseph Badaracco and Richard Ellis asked a group of American business leaders what personal traits had helped them lead their corporations to success, and what advice they would give to would-be CEOs, the response they got was dominated by the advocacy of a strong set of personal ethical standards.[12] A report of the Business Roundtable, a group of America's top CEOs, similarly noted that to achieve results a CEO needed to be 'openly and strongly committed to ethical conduct'.[13] There is an undeniable element here of image promotion, of leaders advancing their own interests by selling an ethical image of themselves to both their workers and the wider public. The same leaders who harp on about personal ethical standards may be quite capable of setting those standards aside when they get in the way of performance targets, and of putting strong pressure on their employees to do the same. But there is more to it than that. The attitudes, beliefs, and, especially, actions of a CEO set the tone for a company's organizational culture, and the ethical integrity or otherwise of that culture can impact significantly on economic performance and on the tasks and processes of strategic leadership.[14]

Ethical leadership and an ethical culture can impact on organizational performance in at least three ways. They can reduce the cost of unethical personal conduct, such as cheating and fraud; they can reduce the risk of events such as major accidents or misguided business decisions that might damage the company's reputation. And they can enhance the effectiveness of organizational processes.

Workplace fraud and cheating on a small scale are extraordinarily common, with a majority of UK employees in a recent survey admitting to transgressions of one kind or another—taking home office stationery, abusing telephone or email facilities, fiddling travel expenses, and so on.[15] Much of this is effectively condoned and carries no moral stigma. Providing it stays within bounds it is considered as legitimate 'perks' and probably does little or no harm. It is important, however, that it stays within bounds. In a traditional hierarchical context, this is relatively easy to ensure. The detailed rules of the hierarchy limit access to corporate resources, the moral basis of the organization is clearly understood, and the organizational structure ensures close and regular supervision. Excessive departmentalization can occasionally lead to situations in which an employee is able to cook the books or run a remote department for his personal gain, but in general such behaviours are quickly spotted and appropriate disciplinary actions taken.

A slightly more serious problem for hierarchies, especially in a business context, is the risk of approved transgressions that start as one-off responses to situations that cannot be addressed within the formal constraints of bureaucracy and end up being institutionalized. One of the interesting features of Melville Dalton's study of 1950s bureaucracies, discussed in earlier chapters, was the way in which moral transgressions arose from the need to get things done—from changing or unexpected circumstances that the bureaucratic machine could not cope with. For example, unable to solve a production problem or to meet customer demands within the normal operating rules, a manager might resort to some form of informal remuneration in kind for a key operative. Considerations of fairness might then lead to this being extended to others and becoming viewed as a right, while at the same time the formal requirements of the bureaucracy meant that it could only be continued by subterfuge. With the passage of time an honest attempt to meet the needs of the corporation became transformed into a form of institutionalized theft.[16] Even in these circumstances, however, the culture of the hierarchy, and the way in which it was morally embedded in society at large, seem to have ensured that the situation was kept under reasonable control.

In organizations with a more market orientation, in which self-interest rather than duty becomes the accepted starting point for business decisions, this control is much more difficult. In the first place, managers guided by self-interest will inevitably respond differently to opportunities to gain at a firm's expense than will those guided by duty. Gerald Mars's ethnographic study of *Cheats at Work*, based on research carried out in the 1970s, pre-dated the move to flexible organizations but focused on groups of people with jobs in which they effectively worked for themselves rather than as part of a corporate community.[17] These people knew full well that their fiddling, pilfering, and other cheats were immoral in the eyes of society, but they justified them in terms of a legitimate self-interest. Their employers (or, in the case of small business entrepreneurs, the state) were not looking after their interests, so they had to look after their own. In the second place, an organization cannot give its employees the freedom to act entrepreneurially, in the hope of gaining thereby, without at the same time exposing itself to the risk that that freedom will be abused.

Contemporary flexible organizations are as reliant on good ethical conduct as any other, but they are effective precisely because they dispense with the constraints of traditional bureaucracies. They have neither the hierarchical control systems to monitor and prevent unethical conduct nor the cultural values to constrain self-interest, and they cannot introduce these without compromising the very foundations of their success. In order to achieve the ethical conduct they need, leaders must, therefore, turn to more positive methods, inspiring and motivating people to act ethically rather than constraining them to do so.

The second way in which ethical leadership can impact upon performance is by reducing the risk of events or decisions that might lead to reputational damage. As we discussed in Chapter 6, bureaucracy has its own problems here, as the compartmentalization of roles and responsibilities and the routinization of behaviour can prevent people from registering or responding to significant moral risks. The technology, in the form of rules and routines, is left to do all the moral work. The Challenger space shuttle explosion of 1986 can be seen as a failure of bureaucracy, and so can the 1984 disaster at the Union Carbide chemical plant in Bhopal, India, which claimed 2,500 lives and brought long-term disease and suffering to up to 300,000 more.[18] In the latter case the financial cost to Union Carbide and the cost to its reputation pale into insignificance when compared with the scale of the human tragedy, but they were, nevertheless, substantial.

In the contemporary context of the flexible economy the risks are different, but still severe. The central problem is that flexible organizations are designed to maximize short-term performance and as part of that to encourage the kind of individual risk-taking that bureaucracies abhor. There is little doubt that in the long run traditional ethics pay, for all the reasons we are discussing here, but there is little doubt either that in terms of short-term performance they can cost. This is particularly apparent in fast-moving technology-based industries, and in mature and declining industries. In technology-based industries time is of the essence, as the speed with which a product can be got to market and a consumer brand or technological standard established is critical for building market share. In these circumstances the temptation is to keep up with or get ahead of competitors by taking short cuts with product testing or other aspects of product safety. In mature and declining industries it is the cost base that is critical, as failing to match competitors on cost can make the company vulnerable to price competition. Here, the temptation is to gain cost advantage by exploitative labour practices or by skimping on environmental or health and safety standards.

Although it is more strongly felt in some areas than in others, this tension between performance and ethics affects all businesses, and has been the root cause of some of the most notable failures of business ethics. To cite just two examples, Ford's decision to use and to keep on using fuel tanks carrying a high risk of explosion in the Pinto car in the 1970s was based very clearly on cost considerations. And the scandal surrounding mis-selling at the Sears Auto Centers in the early 1990s resulted directly from the need to cut losses in a mature market with surplus capacity. The tension is particularly acute, however, in more flexible organizations. These organizations are very good at responding to performance pressures, but their typically strong emphasis on performance, the autonomy they give to employees, and their characteristic legitimation of self-interest all carry ethical risks. The fact that clothing companies Nike and Gap got into far more trouble in the late 1990s than some of their competitors did over the unethical behaviours of their subcontractors in South-east Asia, for example, cannot be separated from the fact that they were also the least bureaucratic, most responsive, and most market-oriented companies in the industry. Other notable examples come from the world of finance, in which flexible forms of organizing have long been the norm. The government bond dealing scandal that almost brought down the Wall Street investment bankers Salomon Brothers in 1991 was the product of an aggressive performance-based market culture, in which teams of traders with highly geared performance-based remuneration packages worked with a high degree of autonomy and under minimal hierarchical constraints. A few years later similar organizational conditions allowed a 'rogue dealer', Nick Leeson, to run up losses that did bring down the old London banking house of Barings.[19]

The third, and arguably the most important, way in which ethical leadership can contribute to performance is much more positive. By building organizational cultures in which there is a high, and high-level, commitment to honesty and fairness, and in which compassion, sensitivity, and awareness of the needs of others are highly valued, leaders can not only enhance employee commitment but also build an environment of trust and mutual respect. These are important qualities even in hierarchies, but in flexible organizations they are pivotal. If senior managers are to empower and give autonomy to employees, they need to trust them. They need to be open with information and they need to let people make their own judgements and take their own decisions. If employees at all levels are to commit themselves to the business without the job security found in more traditional organizations, they need at least to be confident that their contributions will be fairly evaluated and that they will be treated with justice and respect. If teams are to function effectively, their members have to trust and respect each other, sharing knowledge and ideas and relying on each other's contributions. In short, trust and respect provide the glue that enables flexible organizations to be flexible, and to gain all the performance benefits of that flexibility, without falling apart.[20] Trust and respect depend in their turn on the traditional moral values of fairness, honesty, and compassion, and the most effective way of implanting those, especially in the absence of traditional authority structures, is through ethical leadership. This is why the ideas of servant leadership, transforming leadership, and values-based leadership, traditionally associated with religious or political figures such as Jesus, Ghandi, Mother Teresa, or Pope John XXIII, have recently come to the fore in business. The ethical leadership heroes of the business world—people like Robert Haas of Levi Strauss, James Burke of Johnson & Johnson, Jean Riboud of Schlumberger, or Aaron Feuerstein of Malden Mills—are not saints, and we probably would not want them to be so. Business is an instrumental activity and the first requirement of its leaders must be that they turn a profit, and enable the business to prosper. But in the businesses of our bimoral society some element of servant leadership seems to be essential.

## Morality and management

Unfortunately, business organizations cannot always rely on their leaders for the ethical basis they need. Business attracts enterprise and the most enterprising are often the least scrupulous. The history of business is littered with examples of unethical leadership, from the robber barons of nineteenth-century American industry through to late twentieth-century figures such as Robert Maxwell and Asil Nadir. Most recently, the fraudulent accounting practices that led to the collapse of the giant Enron Corporation in 2002 were initiated by the leaders of the company and sanctioned by its board. The misrepresentation of profits at telecoms giant Worldcom, revealed shortly after the Enron collapse, also came from the top. In both companies the root of the problem lay in the failure of flexible market-based organizations to control costs and manage the risks associated with entrepreneurial ambition, but far from providing the ethical leadership needed to overcome this, their leaders were the worst culprits. The other corporate horror stories of 2001–2 also stemmed predominantly from problems of leadership—the excessive risk-taking by the CEO and finance director at Marconi, the CEO's tax evasion and possible fraud at Tyco, the alleged insider dealing by Martha Smith, and so on.

Moreover, even when leaders are not morally culpable, they can find it very difficult to instil moral values. We have already noted that that the personal ambition and competitiveness that drive successful management careers sit uneasily with the humility and other-orientation required for servant leadership, but even an ethically oriented leader may be hampered by circumstances. Few CEOs nowadays have the luxury of taking over a business in which improving short-term performance is not an urgent priority. CEO succession used to be an orderly affair. Now CEOs are more likely to resign than to retire, leaving their successors to face whatever set of problems it was that brought about their resignation. Ethical values are most effectively communicated through actions rather than words and communicating honesty and fairness and building trust all take time, which many CEOs simply do not have. This is especially so in large corporations, where the great majority of employees may never even meet their CEO, and where patterns of trust and fair dealing may take years to filter through the entire organization. By the time they have filtered through, the leadership may well have changed again, throwing everything into question.

For these reasons, the creation and maintenance of a moral environment cannot simply be left to the CEO. Nor, for reasons we shall explore in the next section, can it be left to an ethical code of conduct. It must, therefore, become the responsibility of ordinary managers. Indeed, we can go further and say that in flexible organizations it must become the core function of management: morality, in today's world, is what management is all about.

This last statement may at first seem strange. As we discussed in Chapter 7, management has in the past been characterized as a peculiarly *amoral*, instrumental activity, and business organizations of all kinds have tended to reinforce this. Managers are expected to concern themselves with means, not ends, and held accountable for the means they employ to choose between different options they are pushed towards 'objective' economic measures of costs and benefits. Issues of values have to be either organizationally suppressed (buried and ignored, or thrown back onto the individual to deal with at a personal level) or translated into value-neutral economic terms. Countless managers have agonized about the moral justice of their decisions at home, sharing their concerns with family and close friends, but have been unable to air those concerns at work.

This pattern was characteristic of bureaucratic organizations, in which the moral emphasis was on authority and rules rather than individual choice, and in some sense it was appropriate there. That is not to say that it could not be damaging and oppressive, but the moral basis of hierarchical culture normally ensured that moral issues were well covered. Managers did not need to take responsibility for traditional ethical values, because they were built into the structure and culture of the organization. In flexible organizations the enhancement of economic values and market thinking has tended if anything to reinforce the pattern, increasing the emphasis on instrumental analysis and pushing traditional moral considerations still further underground. One view that has been put forward is that this is also appropriate, but a closer examination suggests otherwise.

Contemporary theories of the firm, heavily influenced by the ideology of economics, typically describe it as a 'nexus of contracts'. The firm, according to this model, is a legal entity that exists only insofar as it is party to a set of formal or informal contractual economic relationships, and the interactions of the different parties are defined in terms of these contractual relationships.[21] Thus, suppliers are economic actors who enter into contracts to supply goods and services at a given price and employees, similarly, are economic actors who contract to supply their labour in return for wages. Because people are motivated, on this model, primarily by self-interest, any element of discretion in a contract is likely to be exploited and the central problem of business organization is how to ensure that this does not happen. So a core function of the labour provided by managers is to monitor the contractual relationships of suppliers and employees. But since managers are also self-interested employees themselves, junior managers have to be monitored by senior managers and so on. At the centre of the firm the CEO enters into a contractual relationship with the company's owners or shareholders to manage the firm as their agents. The board, which is technically appointed by the shareholders, monitors the CEO.

If we accept this economic model of the firm, then it is natural to conclude that the discretion of managers should be minimized and that moral judgements, which cannot be objectively evaluated by monitors, should be prohibited. In his 1998 presidential address to the Society of Business Ethics, a leading business ethics academic, John Boatright, made precisely this argument, suggesting that the moral interests of society would be best served by minimizing the moral discretion of managers.[22] In contemporary society, he argued, managers were best seen as self-interested economic actors, acting and thinking like market participants, striving to get the best deal. Rather than promoting the ideals of moral management, which was doomed to failure and would only give people the discretionary space for immoral behaviour, we should accept the market culture of management and control its morality as we would that of any other economic market, through regulation.

If we were living in a purely market culture, Boatright's line of argument might hold up, but in a bimoral society things are much more complex, and the economic model of the firm is, like most economic models, a gross simplification. People are not just economic contractors but human beings and the relationships in which they engage almost always transcend the economic dimension. In particular, they are always specific to the people and circumstances involved. A company may have exactly the same contractual relationships with two of its employees, but while one might shirk and do whatever she can get away with the other might consistently exceed her contractual obligations, coming in when sick and working all hours to help out in a crisis, or providing emotional support to colleagues with problems and helping them to do a better job. Or one might be struggling to bring up a child as a single parent, or to look after an ageing parent of her own, while another is free from outside obligations. Moreover, people's circumstances are always changing. A person who is normally a committed team member may become distracted by personal problems and unable temporarily to contribute her share. For anybody with family responsibilities the amount of time and effort that can be devoted to a job will inevitably vary as the needs of children vary, even though the contract remains the same. From a purely economic perspective these differences do not matter: they are simply factors that affect people's interests and it is the resulting behaviour that has to be controlled, whether by monitoring and regulation or by financial incentives. In a bimoral society, however, they do matter, and they have to be managed.

Giving managers moral discretion may not make sense in either a hierarchical or a market culture, but then nor does organizing through teams. And just as the operating needs of flexible organizations have led to the new organizing device of teams, even though these fit naturally into neither hierarchical nor market cultures, they also point to an entirely new role for managers. In flexible organizations, managers are no longer needed to make economically objective decisions, the routine resource selection and allocation decisions that were the staple of the old managerial role. That can now be done perfectly well by market mechanisms, and the whole point of flexible organizations is to enable these mechanisms to operate. What managers are needed for now is precisely to call the moral shots, and in so doing to maintain the environment of mutual trust, mutual respect, sympathy, awareness, and compassion within which teams can function effectively and the interests of their members can be productively engaged.

This 'moral' management role can be divided into three parts: supporting and enhancing the moral leadership of the firm; maintaining ethical standards (even when the leaders do not); and creating and maintaining a moral community within the manager's own areas of responsibility.

The first part of the role needs little further discussion. It consists of ensuring that the value judgements made by the organizational leadership are effectively communicated so as to direct and align the energies and efforts of employees. Most obviously, this involves balancing the interests of different stakeholders—shareholders, customers, suppliers, local communities, the employees themselves—in the day-to-day activities of the firm, and ensuring that commitments made or owed to particular groups are honoured.

The second part of the role is the most explicitly ethical. It consists primarily of identifying and responding effectively to any potential disasters or ethical malpractices that may occur within the organization. This does not necessarily mean managers becoming amateur philosophers, conducting Kantian analyses of potentially problematic practices to determine whether they are ethical or not. Although business does throw up complex problems that can only be resolved by very careful analysis, most ethical breaches—and certainly most serious ethical breaches—are pretty obviously so. And even with the recent decline of traditional moral authority most people still have a pretty good sense of right and wrong. The difficulty lies in engaging that sense of right and wrong, maintaining a sense of moral awareness in an environment characterized by the instrumental reasoning of the market, the moral indifference described by Keith Tester, and the emotionally unengaged 'common-sense' reasoning analysed by Ralph Fevre.[23] There is no easy solution to this, but what managers can do is to legitimate moral discussion and debate within their teams and work groups and so create a climate in which engagement is at least possible.

The third part of the 'moral' management role, and that which is most critical for the functioning of flexible organizations, is ensuring that the groups and teams of employees for whom a manager is responsible act as moral communities. This involves balancing the divergent interests of individual employees and ensuring that their specific circumstances, needs, and commitments are given appropriate consideration. It involves acting with transparent honesty and fairness, and encouraging others to do likewise. It involves providing people with support and encouragement, helping them to learn and grow, and enhancing their own capacity for moral judgement. And it also involves building an environment of mutual trust, in which trusting relationships are valued and honoured.

We have been discussing trust in this chapter as if it were a straightforward concept, but it is actually a particularly difficult one, for two main reasons. In the first place, it has two distinct and yet inseparable elements. On one hand, there is a kind of unconditional trust. In a religious context we are asked to put our trust in God, and in a similar sense we trust those we love or who are close to us.[24] On the other hand there is a kind of calculated trust. We decide to trust people, up to a certain point (and no further) on the basis that we are taking a risk, but calculate the risk to be worthwhile in serving our own ends.[25] In the second place, trust is specific to relationships rather than individuals. So whereas we can talk straightforwardly of an individual manager being honest or fair, we can only talk of someone being trusting or trusted in a qualified sense—trusting of certain people, or trusted by certain people. There is an individual quality associated with trust. 'Trustworthiness' is a central concept in Confucianism, for example, and in other Eastern ethical systems, but it is not objectively measurable. Somebody can strive to be trustworthy but trustworthiness, like beauty, is ultimately in the eye of the beholder.[26]

These features of trust can easily generate confusion and much of the writing about it, especially in the management literature, is indeed deeply confused as people talk about 'levels of trust' without distinguishing between the trusting and the trusted.[27] In general, when we say that trust is a good thing, that it is socially desirable or economically beneficial, what we mean is that trustworthiness is good. If people can be trusted then all sorts of things become possible that are not possible if they cannot be trusted. Since trustworthiness is not objectively measurable, however, it can never be taken for granted and so too much trusting exposes us to the risks of misplaced trust and is not, normally, beneficial.[28]

In traditional society, these complications were not particularly problematic as there was a relatively clear distinction between the communities and circumstances in which trusting relationships were the norm and those in which they were not. Within the core community of a hierarchical culture, trust is institutionalized rather than personalized, but it is generally interpreted in an unconditional sense and trustworthiness is assumed.[29] This assumption is open to exploitation, of course, and safeguards are needed to prevent that, but by and large people trust in each other's honesty and good intentions and question or withdraw that trust only if there are specific reasons for doing so. Strangers, on the other hand, are not to be trusted, so any trust afforded to people outside the core community is of the calculated kind, and the same is true within any market subcultures.

Similarly in hierarchical business organizations, in which a traditional morality of obligation prevailed, trust was more or less assumed. In market environments, however, it is calculated and restricted. A basic level of trust is needed for markets to operate, at least if they are sophisticated enough to include credit, but the underlying assumption is that people are to be trusted only so far as it is in their own economic self-interest to be trustworthy.

In flexible organizations, which carry elements of both hierarchical and market cultures, these two approaches to trust collide and the management of trust becomes much more difficult. If people are to work together in organizations, trusting relationships are essential, and this is more than ever the case when the basic organizing structure is the team. In a bureaucracy the clear job definitions and organizational rules do much of the trust work: even if you cannot trust in the individual you can trust in the system. But in flexible team-based organizations the relationships are much more personal, and to work effectively you have to be able to trust the members of your team *as individuals*. At the very same time, however, you have to recognize that these individuals are primarily motivated, as you may be, by a legitimate self-interest and cannot necessarily be trusted other than in a calculated fashion. Indeed, the market ideas that now dominate management thinking positively encourage distrust, treating honest incompetence as if it were shirking and moral duties to others (to your children, for example, or others outside the organization) as expressions of self-interest. Common sense (in Fevre's use of the phrase, which we discussed in Chapter 4) tells us that people are not to be trusted. We hear gossip and read in the newspapers of countless cases in which employees rip off their organizations or betray their colleagues, but we never read stories about how trusting attitudes are repaid in kind.

For teams to operate effectively in these conditions requires something that goes beyond either the calculating trust of the market or the institutionalized trust of the hierarchy. It requires the development of an interpersonal trustworthiness, based on mutual understanding and empathy, and a mutual recognition of each other's interests and needs. The challenge for the manager, here, is both to lead this process, applying some of the principles of servant leadership to the group of employees for whom she is responsible, and to foster the relationships within this group so that it becomes a genuine moral community. Of course, not all the relationships will work out, and not all the trust will be repaid. There will be difficult decisions when managers have to arbitrate between conflicting team members, or draw the line (often a very fine line) between personal interests that should be viewed with tolerance and supportive understanding and those that make unreasonable demands on colleagues and the organization. But decisions like these, which are ultimately moral decisions, are at the core of the managerial role in flexible organizations, as it is the way in which they are made that will ultimately determine the success or failure of the enterprise.

## MANAGING WITHOUT RULES: THE CHALLENGE OF LEARNING

A common thread running through this chapter has been the need to replace the structured rules and relationships of bureaucracy with more immediate and more personal kinds of engagement. We have talked for example of the need for managers to empathize with and become aware of the needs of others, to generate interpersonal trust and trustworthiness, and to make moral judgements—to call the moral shots. These needs are not always appreciated, however, and an instructive example of this is the way in which companies, in pursuit of business ethics, have been placing increasing faith in codes of conduct: in detailed rulebooks to guide and control managerial decision making in areas of ethical sensitivity.[30]

This is a natural and quite understandable bureaucratic response to the risks of market culture, but it is a quintessentially bureaucratic response, which relies heavily on the assumptions of hierarchical culture. It assumes, for example, that the environment is predictable enough for moral risks to be identified and specified in advance, and that ethical conventions are clear enough for rules to be devised to meet all possible situations. Neither of these is true in a typical business environment. More fundamentally, it assumes that authority will be obeyed and rules will be followed. Neither of these can be assumed in a flexible organization, where creativity and enterprise are core values and competitive advantage is achieved by changing the rules and finding new ways of doing things.

This line of argument should not, of course, be taken too far. In practice, even markets operate within rules. To be effective, however, these rules must meet at least two requirements. First, they must be seen to be in the self-interests of the market participants, including the most powerful among them, whose power gives them the ability to break the rules if they wish. In a market culture legitimacy derives from self-interest. Second, they must be clear and unambiguous, so that entrepreneurial activity is focused on competing within them rather than on gaining advantage by reinterpreting them. In a flexible organization, with its mixture of market and hierarchical elements, there is some room for compromise on these requirements. A leader can still exert some authority, and good leadership can direct people's energies and create a culture of common interest, but the second requirement in particular is still very important. If clear rules can be established—as they may be for health and safety requirements (hard hats must be worn in area X) or environmental standards (exposure must be limited to an accurately measurable dose of Y)— there is a reasonable chance of making them hold. But if the rules are in any way ambiguous, subjective, or unquantifiable, they are likely to be at best taken as challenges and at worst ignored.

Ethical rules can sometimes meet this test. Many companies, for instance, impose strict limits on the values of gifts employees may accept and forbid outright various forms of gift giving. But in general ethics is not an exact science and ethical codes of conduct tend in practice either to be so vague as to be banal or, if they are more specific, to be narrowly over-prescriptive and self-contradictory.[31] Even in traditional bureaucracies this creates the danger that they will do more harm than good by creating a false sense of complacency, enhancing the tendency of bureaucracy to suppress moral awareness and imagination. In more flexible organizations, where the pressures for performance are typically stronger, self-interest is allowed to flourish and people are encouraged to be more creative in their problem solving, any looseness or contradictions within the ethical code, and any conflicts between the demands of the code and the demands of performance, are likely to be exploited.

Ethical codes have their place. They can help protect people from harassment or discrimination, for example, and they can reinforce the point that in our bimoral society traditional morality still has a value, in business as well as in society. Their very existence makes a statement both to employees and to the outside world, and by publishing its code a company makes itself publicly accountable. But in flexible organizations, the effective management of ethics cannot be achieved through codes of conduct alone. As we have already discussed, it also requires something much more personal: inspiring moral leadership and a carefully nurtured culture of moral awareness and concern for the other.

The same principle holds for management in general. Despite the continuing tendencies of business organizations to control their managers by mechanizing and devaluing their work, management is at its core a discretionary function. Indeed, what has always distinguished the role of management from other roles in the organization is a level of discretion to make judgements and act upon them that other employees do not have. In traditional bureaucratic organizations, this discretion was controlled by rules. One set of formal rules specified in detail the limits of discretion associated with each managerial role: What decisions the manager could take herself and what had to be referred to a superior. Another set of less formal rules followed from established precedents as to how certain situations should be handled, both in terms of communications procedures and in terms of general principles or paradigms of behaviour. When it came to approving loans, for example, the branch manager of a traditional bank had considerable discretion within the formally laid down constraints, but precedent and the culture of the bank more generally ensured that certain kinds of loans were in practice avoided, and certain kinds of customers favoured over others.[32]

When traditional bureaucracy began to fail as an effective organizing principle for business, one of the first responses was to reduce managerial discretion still further by mechanizing the managerial role. The business process re-engineering movement of the 1990s brought much-needed radical surgery to expensive bureaucratic systems that no longer served any useful purpose, but it also sought to minimize discretion by replacing managerial judgements wherever possible with expert systems.[33] To pursue our earlier example, the discretion of the bank manager in lending decisions was largely replaced by computer-based evaluation systems. It soon became apparent, however, that the main problem lay with the constraints rather than with the discretion and a key aspect of flexible organizations is that managers should be freed from the straitjacket of rules. Flexible organizations still need to control inappropriate use or abuse of discretion but they do it through the dialogue of interpersonal relationships—the mutual surveillance and dialogue of the team, the listening and questioning of a manager—rather than by either explicit rules or established routines and procedures. Rules are still used for many of the unimportant things, such as the processing of expenses, where an explicit standard causes no problems and saves everybody time and hassle. But for the more important things, such as the development of markets and products, or the development of people, rules have become a hindrance. The consequence is that managers must now learn to manage without rules. In the process, they must also manage to learn without rules.

## Managing learning

Learning is critical if businesses are to survive and prosper, and over the last twenty years organizational learning has quite rightly received increasing attention from management scholars, consultants, and practitioners. In this time, though, our understanding of what constitutes learning, and especially organizational learning, has changed considerably. The first important step in this respect was the recognition that we use the word 'learning' to describe two rather different processes, which Chris Argyris and Donald Schön christened single loop and double loop learning. Single loop learning can be described in terms of a simple mechanical feedback mechanism in which the learner monitors the difference between the existing and desired performance and modifies her behaviour incrementally to correct this. When we learn to catch a ball, for instance, we gradually refine our hand–eye coordination and the use of our hands and fingers. Each attempt provides new information and we gradually converge on an 'ideal' catching behaviour that, once reached, remains unchanged. Double loop learning, in contrast, is divergent and exploratory; it comes into play when the simple single loop feedback mechanism does not work and we have to question and change the feedback mechanism itself. Crudely put, single loop learning is the process by which we learn to perfect something we are already doing, modifying our responses to the same, repeated stimuli so as to perform more effectively. Double loop learning is the process by which we learn to do something new, changing our behaviour in response to new or changing stimuli.[34]

In their pioneering study, Argyris and Schön argued that organizations, like people, needed both single and double loop learning but that also like people they were much better at the former than at the latter. They were very good at refining their routines and operating procedures so as to optimize their responses to a stable environment, but much less good at changing those routines and procedures when changes in the environment rendered them inappropriate or redundant. Like early farmers responding to reduced crop yields by perfecting their ploughing and sowing techniques and intensifying their land use, when what was needed was to let land lie fallow or introduce crop rotations, they could respond to performance downturns by perfecting their existing routines but could not question and change those routines. They could not get out of the loop of single loop learning to reflect on and unlearn or 'unfreeze' the practices that had been successful in the past.[35]

The organizations with which Argyris and Schön and other early writers on organizational learning were concerned were essentially bureaucratic, and this strongly conditioned the problems they faced. In the first place, in bureaucracies, organizational knowledge, in the sense of procedural knowledge or know-how, is stored either in the organization's formal operating procedures, rules, and routines, or in its culturally embedded paradigms and practices. Learning is therefore a question of creating, perfecting, and when necessary changing these procedures, rules, routines, and practices, and up until the early 1990s studies of organizational learning were conceived in essentially these terms.[36] In flexible organizations, however, know-how is stored in other ways and the problem of learning is, therefore, rather different. In the second place, as we have already noted in earlier chapters, hierarchical cultures in general and bureaucratic organizations in particular are especially good at developing, refining, and perfecting reliable operating procedures, rules, routines, and culturally embedded practices. They are, in other words, especially good at single loop learning. But they are also especially bad at changing these, or at double loop learning. In flexible organizations double loop learning is still a significant problem, but because market cultures are generally much better at responding creatively to changing circumstances it is less of a problem than it was. In the absence of stable rules and routines, however, single loop learning also becomes a problem.

In a flexible economy in which many of the processes that used to be carried on inside a business are outsourced and in which physical assets are more of an encumbrance than a source of competitive advantage, it is widely recognized that the most important resource possessed by a firm is its knowledge. Strategic advantage comes from the way in which this knowledge is developed, managed, and exploited, and learning occupies centre stage.[37] Every business organization today aspires to be a learning organization. But as people have just recently begun to recognize, the knowledge that is critical here is not what people usually mean when they talk about knowledge. Explicit, codified knowledge, such as that which can be held in databases or formal systems and procedures, is necessary, of course. Firms must have effective ways not only of acquiring and storing this kind of knowledge, but also of distributing it to the various points at which it is needed. But with current advances in information systems this is not particularly problematic. Nor, given the ease with which it can be copied and disseminated, is this kind of codified knowledge a particularly strong or sustainable source of competitive advantage. What is both more important and more problematic is a different kind of implicit, 'tacit' knowledge, and especially tacit know-how, which remains unarticulated and operates at an intuitive level.[38]

In order to add value to an organization, this tacit know-how must, in some way, be held by the organization, and not just by the individuals within it; but since it cannot be codified the only way in which it can be organizationally held is as a kind of shared understanding, based on interpersonal relationships and experiences. In a stable bureaucracy, this understanding is stored in the stories, myths, and informal practices that are built up as part of the single loop learning process of the organization and communicated from one member to another in a process of cultural acclimatization. It makes a significant contribution to the firm's competitive advantage, but is also a significant barrier to double loop learning and change. Fast moving flexible organizations can neither generate such deeply embedded cultural know-how nor afford the risks associated with it. They must, therefore, manage their know-how more actively.

The consequence of this is that managers in flexible organizations have to actively manage an interpersonal learning process based on tacit know-how, and with elements of both single loop and double loop learning. Because the know-how is tacit it cannot be explicitly taught. Indeed the manager may well be a step behind the teams reporting to her, and learning from them as much as the other way around. If the learning is to be captured by the organization, however, she must learn from her teams, which means that she must participate actively enough in the team processes to share the tacit understanding that they generate. At the same time, she must also communicate the understanding she has gained from other teams, including those of which she has been a part herself, but without taking away from the autonomy of the team, or constraining its creativity. Finally, she must also develop, in herself and in others, the critical questioning and reflection that are necessary to identify and expose aspects of tacit knowledge that are unproductive or no longer productive—tacit assumptions and attitudes that are inappropriate in the current competitive environment or that get in the way of effective working relationships.

This is a tall order, but the skills it requires from the manager are completely consistent with those we have already identified. She must be good at listening to people and at empathizing with them, and at creating an environment in which they listen to and empathize with each other. She must be good at trusting people and at gaining their trust, and at creating an environment in which they grow to trust each other. She must be good at questioning, herself as well as others, in a way that exposes hidden prejudices and assumptions; that opens up possibilities rather than closing them down; and that empowers rather than threatens. She must be good at sharing her own knowledge and experience, not in a calculated way, as one might impart bits and pieces of explicit knowledge, because she may not know herself what it is of value that she knows, but by openly living it.

In managing the learning process, the manager in a flexible organization needs in effect to become a kind of teacher, but one who teaches by opening minds rather than by closing them, and by living example and personal engagement rather than by communicating facts. As the philosopher and theologian Martin Buber, himself a great teacher, used to observe, it is not so much what a teacher (or, in our terms, a manager) says that matters, but how she acts, and especially how she interacts with her students.[39]

## Learning to manage

This analogy between managers and teachers raises one final question, namely, who teaches the teachers, or to put it another way, how do managers learn to manage the learning process? The dominant route to management learning in the last twenty or thirty years has been the MBA or senior executive programme, but can business schools and their programmes teach the kinds of advanced interpersonal skills we have been talking about?

The short answer is that the best way to learn to manage is by experience: by engaging, if you are lucky, with other managers who have already moved up the learning curve, or otherwise by trial, error, and reflection. As the flexible economy develops and the management skills it calls for come to be more widely recognized, reputations will be built and it will become possible to build a 'learning career' by working with and learning from particular managers and groups of managers, in much the same way as people in the past built a career by working in different functional roles. Meanwhile, the best you can do is to maintain your own reflective stance and accumulate experience, learning from whatever relationships work throws up.

Business schools can, however, provide a valuable foundation for this learning, in at least two important respects. First, while competitive advantage in the new economy comes mainly from tacit knowledge, more explicit forms of knowledge are still absolutely essential to any business. The core techniques of financial, strategic, and marketing analysis are not only as relevant and important for business success now as they ever were, but also much more widely needed. Whereas in the past financial analysis would be done by finance specialists, marketing by a marketing specialists, and so on, in flexible, team-based organizations all managers—and many non-managers—need a sound understanding of how businesses work and prosper. Only once these technical aspects of business are fully grasped, moreover, can a manager devote the energy and attention necessary to successfully managing. A loose analogy might be with musical or dramatic performance, where the success of the performance depends critically upon the interpersonal relationships and learning processes within the group, but these processes themselves depend upon a shared core of technical expertise. Even if it cannot teach managers to manage, an MBA can give them valuable technical skills, the absence of which would get in the way of their later experiential learning.

Second, however, an MBA can in a relatively modest way teach people some of the skills of managing. As Charles Handy has pointed out, 'managing' is not restricted to the workplace, but occurs wherever people with different interests are required to cooperate in pursuit of some common purpose: in families, in communities, in sport, and, potentially, in school or college.[40] Many MBA programmes already offer basic listening and communications skills development and provide a relatively safe environment in which people can learn how to work effectively with each other in study groups. A few programmes have gone much further, building their courses around practical team-based projects, helping students to recognize and explore the personal, professional, and cultural biases and presumptions they bring to these projects, and helping them to articulate, reflect upon, and learn from their teamwork experiences.[41]

As in management itself, a lot depends on the teacher, and especially on her ability to listen, empathize, nurture, and give openly and with complete commitment of herself, so earning the trust of the students to engage themselves, to question, and to open themselves up to the possibility of learning. Indeed, because of the specific role of the teacher in an educational establishment and the responsibilities associated with that, the moral aspect becomes even more important. In practice, many business school teachers go out of their way to avoid any moral engagement. Instead of giving of themselves they hide their real selves behind their 'expert' personae. But every business school I have known also has on its staff teachers who take the opposite view, who are committed personally to their students, and who are prepared to engage with their needs and concerns. Not all are particularly gifted teachers, but they all contribute in some way to the learning process.

# 9

# The Challenge for Contemporary Society

Success in contemporary business requires an extraordinary combination of skills. On one hand, there are the individualistic skills needed for entrepreneurship: intense competitiveness and a single-minded and stubborn determination to succeed. On the other hand, there are the interpersonal skills needed for management: the ability to listen, to trust, and to inspire trustworthiness, and a genuine concern for others. Without being able to resort to autocratic styles of leadership, the entrepreneur who lacks the skills of management can get far, but only so far. With no bureaucratic culture to protect her, the manager who lacks the skills of entrepreneurship is unlikely to get anywhere at all, or at least to last long, in the competitive world of business. Learning to combine the two sets of skills can be extraordinarily rewarding, but it is always going to be challenging. It is especially challenging in a society that has still not found a satisfactory way of expressing its bimoral nature, of relating self-interest to obligation.

Very few people would argue with the fact that the traditional morality of obligation is not merely socially legitimate, but absolutely essential for the survival of a cohesive and peaceful society. Indeed, while publicly asserting a strong moral position on a particular issue has become relatively rare, denying the general importance of morality remains taboo. At the same time, while they might not advocate the position in public, few people today would deny that individual self-interest is also quite normal and acceptable, or that we would be significantly less prosperous without it. In other words, both obligation and self-interest are seen as both necessary and socially legitimate. But we have not yet found a satisfactory way of combining or balancing them, either conceptually or institutionally. Indeed, while we cannot avoid thinking about them together and weighing them against each other in our private decision making, we largely avoid talking about them together. We justify our actions in ways that refer to one or the other ('I got what I wanted'; 'it wasn't in my interests'; 'I had to help') but not to both.

This failure can be seen quite clearly in recent attempts to forge a political 'Third Way' between or beyond socialism and conservatism. These attempts have numerous origins and there are in consequence numerous Third Ways, but the term is most commonly associated with the 'New Labour' government of Tony Blair in Britain, and with the political philosophy of Anthony Giddens.[1] Giddens does not concern himself greatly with the tension between self-interest and obligation. Like Ulrich Beck, many of whose ideas he shares, he is more concerned with ecological issues, with the changing nature of risk, and with the new problematic of a post-scarcity society. At the centre of his argument, however, is a conception of society that is similar to (and indeed one of the sources of) that presented here: a globalized post-traditional society in which obedience to authority is replaced by reflexive discourse and the legitimate pursuit of individual interests, and in which politics is shaped by personal interdependence. Politically, this leads him towards what he calls a dialogic democracy, a generalization of what other writers have called deliberative democracy. The focus of such a political system should not be on counting votes so as to determine and then act upon the will of the people, because that is recognized as being practically impossible, but on creating open public debate on the basis of which reasonable judgements can be made. The emphasis of government, whether local, national, or international, should not be on controlling behaviour, but on enabling individuals and groups to determine and live out their own priorities. The emphasis of the welfare state should not be on covering the risks of poverty or ill-health by rescuing people after the event but on providing the support necessary to enable them to minimize those risks in the first place. More immediately, welfare should continue to provide people with security when things go wrong, but its focus should be on enabling them to look after their own interests.

Giddens's Third Way seeks a balance between individual autonomy and social interdependence, but explicitly dissociates these from self-interest on the one hand and duty (with its authoritarian associations) on the other. Giddens recognizes that excessive commercial self-interest poses a threat to society in the short term, but argues that in the longer term it will destroy itself, as capitalism runs up against the limits posed by the environment and by its own creation of manufactured risk. Self-interest simply will not work and nor in a post-traditional society will blind duty. The political and moral future lies rather in notions of individual and collective responsibility, which will emerge naturally from increased global interdependence and which, he suggests, 'are able to override divisions of interest'.[2]

We shall, in fact, reach much the same conclusion, but the jump from here to there is not quite so easy. Commercial self-interest may ultimately fail to work, but if allowed to run its course unchecked it could well bring down society with it. Meanwhile it is working well enough for those who espouse it to be inseparable in practice from autonomy, so that encouraging autonomy remains tantamount to encouraging self-interest. We are also a long way from having worked out a consensus of responsibility that can carry the moral weight necessary to counter and restrain that self-interest. In contemporary political dialogue, most notably in the language of communitarianism, 'responsibility' is always someone else's responsibility: It is a duty imposed upon them, not, as in Giddens's conception, an emergent property of interdependence.

These become real issues as soon as one moves from political philosophy to practical politics. The practical version of the Third Way espoused by New Labour has much in common with the theoretical version, especially in its view of welfare, but it has of necessity to deal with the society we are rather than the society we may be becoming. In this context, it combines the advocacy of free market capitalism and the associated values of self-reliance and an entrepreneurial self-interest with a very traditional moral insistence on duty and obligation. It goes along, to a large extent, with the view from the right that we discussed in Chapter 6, but draws a line at the right's critique of the welfare state. It concedes to the right that the welfare state should be reduced and the burden of care shifted from the state back to the individual—through an insistence on the responsibilities of families, for example, or through personal pension provision—but it does so on largely pragmatic rather than ideological grounds and insists that people's duty to look after themselves is matched by a duty of society to look after those in need, and indeed to address and reduce material inequalities. It welcomes and endorses the market culture but insists, at the same time, on a responsibility for and moral duty to others.

At first sight this position would seem a perfect match for the needs of the bimoral society. The problem is that the sense of duty or obligation on which it relies is still grounded in traditional authority. For Tony Blair and other senior members of the government it is grounded in Christianity, specifically, and in religious authority, more generally. For a religiously disinterested public, it is effectively grounded in little more than the moral authority of Tony Blair. The consequence is that for all the good words and good intentions, the Third Way in practice places few, if any, constraints on economic self-interest.

A similar problem faces managers, who are even more bound by the practical realities of the present than are politicians. We suggested in Chapter 8 that managing the tensions between entrepreneurial self-interest and the common good in flexible organizations called for a kind of interpersonal moral management that might well be captured by Giddens's notion of responsibility rather than duty: open dialogue, trustworthiness, an active engagement with and concern for the other, building mutual trust and respect. Since there is still no well worked out social consensus as to what this notion of responsibility entails and on what it is based, however, there is no social resource on which managers can draw (as they could once draw on a hierarchical conception of duty) to explain and support their position. They can, and must, lead by example, but if self-interested employees choose not to follow that example, there is little they can do about it.

The same lack of a post-traditional moral consensus also bedevils the relationship between business and society. Unable to find any common conceptual ground on which to debate the moral aspects of international business, the leaders of business and finance on one hand and the environmentalist and anti-globalization lobbies on the other speak past each other in mutual incomprehension. Exasperated by their failure to communicate their reasonable concerns, the critics of business resort to ever more exaggerated tales of business evils and even to physical violence, thus reducing rather than increasing the chances of constructive dialogue. Meanwhile debates on corporate governance, which should properly focus on the constructive relationship between business enterprise and the public interest, become mired in the language of agency and self-interest and reduced to a competition between the financial interests of corporate management and the financial interests of their institutional shareholders. At the level of world politics, too, self-interest is alive and well, but moral consensus seems almost entirely lacking. Not surprisingly in this context, the international regulation of business and finance remains virtually nonexistent.

To address these issues fully would take us well beyond the scope of this book, but their importance for business is such that they cannot be ignored entirely. In this chapter we shall, therefore, look briefly at two questions. The first asks on what commonly acceptable principles a morality of obligation appropriate to the bimoral society of the twenty-first century might be based. We have already suggested that this is likely to take the form of a morality of interpersonal relationships, in which the obligation is to act with responsibility and positive concern for the other, rather than a morality of social order based on specific proscriptions. But on what basis might we build the kind of consensus that would make such a morality effective? Our second question asks how the new moral consensus might be institutionalized so as provide for the effective regulation and governance of international business and finance, ensuring that they serve the public as well as private interests. In order to establish the context in which these questions need to be addressed, we shall begin by looking more explicitly than we have done so far at the issue of globalization.

## GLOBALIZATION AND ITS PROBLEMS

So far in the book we have used the term 'globalization' quite loosely, as a way of describing familiar processes: the growth of international trade and international financial systems, of multinational or transnational corporations and global brands, of international travel and communications. We have linked these processes both with the rise of business power and with the decline of traditional moral authority, and it has been implicit in our discussion that if a new moral consensus is to be effective as a counterbalance to economic self-interest it will have to be in some sense a global moral consensus. In academic circles, however, the nature and extent of globalization has been a highly contentious issue, with some commentators writing as if the nation state and its activities had already been superseded by a global economy and global society, while others contend that globalization is little more than a myth, and that in economic terms, especially, the world is no more globalized now than it was in the early twentieth century, before the onset of the First World War.[3] As always, the truth lies somewhere between the two extremes, but before proceeding we need to be clearer about some of the ways in which globalization is impacting on society.

Anthony Giddens has defined globalization as 'action at a distance',[4] or more usefully as 'the intensification of worldwide social relations which link distant realities in such a way that local happenings are shaped by events occurring many miles away and vice-versa'.[5] What is critical about what is happening now, in other words, is the global interconnectedness of economic and cultural activity. The nation state has not disappeared and is not likely to, at least in the short or medium term. Political systems rely for their effectiveness on some perception of shared identity, and nationality remains by far the most effective conferrer of such identity.[6] Nation states are, however, losing some of their traditional power to control their own destinies, as both the price and availability of economic goods and the availability of conceptual goods (ideas, beliefs, ambitions, and aspirations) are increasingly influenced by events occurring elsewhere.

This interconnectedness has many aspects but one of the most important is that associated with the globalization of environmental risk. In his seminal book *Risk Society*, the German sociologist Ulrich Beck highlighted the growth and dissemination in contemporary society of technologically produced risk.[7] The risks attendant on an earlier industrial age—of mining or factory accidents, for example, or coal pollution—were both visible and localized. The production of technological risk could be seen as a marginal side effect of industrialization. The risks produced by contemporary technology, in contrast, are invisible and far-reaching, often global, in their effects. Environmental damage is not limited to a factory or the visibly polluted river into which it discharges, but affects people far away from the source of the damage. Acid rain or radioactive clouds, generated on one continent, fall invisibly on another. Carbon dioxide and carbon monoxide emissions and the destruction of the rainforests lead to climate change on a global scale. As food is shipped around the world, so are the toxins that may or may not be in it. The technologies of nuclear, chemical, and biological warfare threaten us all, endangering not just bits of life but all of it. Moreover, because many of these risks are invisible, intangible, and known only in theory (as 'safe' levels of toxins or statistical risks of cancers, for example) they are open to social definition and construction. Whether injured by them physically or not (and we may never know), we still suffer the anxiety, the psychological injury, associated with them.

This aspect of global interconnectedness is particularly important for two reasons. The first is that it is inescapably global. Some environmental effects arise from a simple overspill of pollution from the region in which it is produced to other regions. They are global only in the sense that they spread around parts of the globe. But others, such as global warming, arise from the properties, in particular the finitude, of the globe itself. Through much of modernity mankind has been concerned with conquering nature and exploiting its seemingly endless resources. In certain critical respects, however, that project has reached its limits and our efforts are being reflected, both physically from the upper atmosphere and psychologically through the creation of insecurity, back upon us.[8] The second reason why it is important is that it highlights the inadequacy of a world political system that depends only on the nation state and has no means of governing the activities of business internationally. Culturally, and even economically, it is still possible for nations to insulate themselves to *some* extent from what is happening elsewhere. Environmentally, it is not.

Another aspect of global interconnectedness that is particularly important in our present context is the economic interconnectedness arising from global financial markets. George Soros is an international financier turned philanthropist. As arguably the world's most successful ever financial speculator, he is also an expert on the operation of financial markets and especially on the speculative cycles that characterize these, and he has written about these in a number of books.[9] In *The Crisis of Global Capitalism* he defines the global capitalist system in terms of economic interconnectedness as a system:[10]

that is characterised not only by free trade in goods and services but even more by the free movement of capital. Interest rates, exchange rates, and stock prices in various countries are intimately interrelated and global financial markets exert tremendous influence on economic conditions . . . The system is very favourable to financial capital, which is free to go where it is best rewarded, which in turn has led to the rapid growth of global financial markets. The result is a gigantic circulatory system, sucking up capital into the financial markets and institutions at the centre and then pumping it out into the periphery either directly in the form of credits and portfolio investments or indirectly through multinational corporations.

This system is not only global. It is also, like the 'system' of environmental risks analysed by Beck, inherently unstable and beyond any political control. Its instabilities arise from three of its core features: money, individualism, and credit. Money is the dominant value of the system. Since, in a world deprived of tradition, we do not know what we want (and since those at the centre of the system already have the *things* they might want anyway) the whole system is focused on the pursuit of money. Money is also the basis of the entire system: whether people are dealing in currencies or bonds or shares or derivatives, it is money, not goods, that changes hands. But money has no intrinsic value, and things that have no intrinsic value are prone to speculative bubbles. In pursuit of money, a currency, a bond, or a share is worth precisely what the next person is prepared to pay for it: as Keynes observed, investment becomes all about guessing how other people guess how other people guess. So, for example, in the recent boom in Internet stocks, a bias in favour of such stocks pushed up their price. As people noticed the trend of rising prices so they sought to cash in by buying more of the stocks, reinforcing both the bias in their favour and the upward trend in prices—and so on, until enough companies went bust to push people into the reverse behaviour, which was also self-reinforcing. These tendencies are amplified by trend-following behaviours by the financial institutions, whose managers are typically paid according to how they perform relative to a peer group, rather than in absolute terms. This means that as a particular investment or a particular market rises in value so the institutions seek to increase their allocation of funds to it, pushing up values further and so on.[11]

The instability inherent in monetary markets is also amplified by the heavy dependence of those markets on credit. Credit, and the leverage it provides, is essential to the system, and to the optimal allocation of resources. But credit is also, in Soros's terms, a reflexive phenomenon. The ability to borrow depends on the value of collateral, typically real estate, but the value of real estate also depends on what people are prepared to lend against it. Similarly, the ability of a developing country to borrow depends on its prosperity, but its prosperity also depends on its ability to borrow.

Individualism, and the pursuit of individual self-interest, are behaviours on which free markets depend, but again they have a destabilizing effect. For example, individual institutional investors manage their own risk by various forms of hedging and by stop loss control devices that force people to close their positions by selling their investments if losses reach a certain level. These limit the risks at the individual level, but they increase the instability of the system as a whole. When prices go down, the institutions sell, sending prices further down and so on.

These examples could be multiplied, but they are not, for Soros, the cause of the problem. Financial markets will always correct themselves eventually, even if the process is rather painful. Of greater concern is the way in which the global financial system interacts with the political system, which is still based on the nation state. The point here is that while the global financial system exerts a very strong influence on the political systems of nation states, the only ways in which the political systems can affect the financial system are ways that add to the self-reinforcing properties of that system and so magnify its instability. All countries, even the most powerful, find their political choices determined to some extent by the financial system. They have to compete for international capital, they are at the mercy of currency movements, and they have to frame their fiscal and economic policies accordingly. Developing countries, at the periphery of the system, are almost completely at its mercy. The richer countries have more influence, but they can exert that influence only through domestic policies and are bound to exert it primarily in their own domestic interests. As in the case of institutional investors discussed above, they seek to manage their own risks, responding to developing country problems by pulling out their capital, but this only adds to the problems, increasing instability. Meanwhile, because national political systems can never control the international financial system but only, at best, mitigate some of its effects, the political process appears inadequate and loses credibility. This enhances the case for free market fundamentalism as an alternative to government control, strengthening the financial system further, and limiting still further the effectiveness of political processes.

The analysis of global environmental risks and the analysis of global financial risks both point to the urgent need for some kind of supranational governance and regulation of business and finance. Such governance and regulation will only be possible, however, if there is a moral consensus on which to base it. In time, such a consensus might be based on the cultural homogeneity of a world in which social and cultural interconnectedness have significantly eroded national difference—or perhaps in which American hegemony has successfully imposed American values on the rest of the world. At present, however, these forms of interconnectedness are serving mainly to illuminate national (and indeed sub-national) differences and so emphasizing the heterogeneity rather than the homogeneity of cultural values. And while American business and media are powerful vehicles for the spread of market values, America's attempts to exercise a power based on traditional moral values, especially in the Middle East, are landing it in cultural isolation. Any form of moral consensus must therefore be based, as Anthony Giddens, John Gray, and others have argued, upon cultural pluralism and the need to establish a modus vivendi between different cultural norms.[12]

## RIGHTS, HUMANITY, AND THE FOUNDATIONS OF MORAL CONSENSUS

### Universal human rights

The most obvious foundation for a global moral consensus is the idea of individual human rights. The philosophy of rights is rooted in law rather than in ethics and the historic American Bill of Rights and French Declaration of the Rights of Man and Citizen, both of which were published in 1789, were much more concerned with the protection of the individual from state oppression than with a moral foundation for society.[13] However, the Universal Declaration of Human Rights, drafted by an international commission of the United Nations and published in 1948, is much more strongly moral in emphasis. It has also come to command almost universal support across the world, forming the basis of regional and international treaties such as the European Convention on Human Rights (incorporated into British law by the 1998 Human Rights Act) as well as of a multitude of national bills of rights.[14]

This widespread support for the concept of human rights embodied in the Universal Declaration can be attributed to a number of factors. First and most obviously, rights are desirable. The moral codes of society have traditionally been expressed as constraints, usually of a negative kind: do not do this, do not do that. Even where the language has been more positive, specifying duties of worship or care for example, the effect has been similarly constraining. Such constraints are the foundation of a hierarchical culture, but they are accepted on the basis of legitimate authority, rather than because people want to be constrained. New constraints, or the imposition of constraints from outside a society, have always been resisted. A universal declaration of constraints would be a complete non-starter. Rights on the other hand, even though they might on more careful consideration imply constraints, are most immediately associated with freedom from constraints. And whatever we may think about other people being unconstrained we welcome such freedom for ourselves. Accepting rights, so long as the concomitant duties are not too closely spelled out, is easy.

This is especially the case at a time when traditional moral authorities, and by implication the constraints they have imposed, are coming into question. The classic expressions of rights in the eighteenth century Enlightenment were associated with movements of liberation and the rejection of established hierarchies, with the French Revolution and the American Declaration of Independence. The Universal Declaration of Human Rights was written in the wake of the Nazi terrors and at the dawn of colonial disintegration, and it has flourished in a world in which hierarchy has increasingly been viewed with suspicion rather than respect.

Because they are positively rather than negatively framed, rights are also much easier than duties or constraints to reconcile across cultures. The Universal Declaration of Human Rights is, in fact, full of culturally specific quirks. It includes, for example, the right to own property, as well as intellectual property rights; the right to 'periodic holidays with pay'; and the right of parents to choose the kind of education given to their children. It establishes the family as the 'the natural and fundamental group unit of society' and although its rights to work and an adequate standard of living are expressed as rights pertaining to 'everyone', references back to this person are to 'himself and his family'. It also includes rights that, fifty years later, many countries still cannot or will not deliver: the right to free and fair elections with universal suffrage; to a standard of living adequate for food, housing, and medical care; to welfare provision in old age or in the case of unemployment, sickness, disability, or (another cultural quirk) widowhood; to 'technical and professional' as well as elementary education; and to free movement across all borders. None of this, however, has prevented countries from signing up to its provisions, which, being positive, can always be seen as aspirational in a way that negative constraints never could. Indeed, this aspect of a system of rights is apparent not only in the reception of the declaration, but also in its formulation, the process of which was essentially additive. The members of the commission each sought to add the rights appropriate to their own countries' circumstances and by and large seem to have accepted each other's additions. When members tried to add in detailed lists of duties, however, the opposite process seems to have occurred, as people effectively vetoed duties they did not wish to be bound by.[15] It is far, far easier to accept other people's aspirations than it is to accept their constraints.

One particular outcome of this process is that the Universal Declaration makes no mention of God (the traditional basis of hierarchical authority) but is founded instead on a notion of human dignity: 'the inherent dignity . . . of all members of the human family'. This appears to have been critical in enabling commissioners from a wide variety of religious backgrounds to find common ground, and it has been critical since in ensuring the widespread acceptance of the declaration. The concept of human dignity can be found in some form in all of the world's main religions and ethical systems, and its central role in the declaration has helped people from different cultures to establish a connection between universal human rights and their own particular moral traditions. It gives the system of rights real moral substance, which it would otherwise lack, but without tying it to any particular moral authority.

## The limits of rights

As witnessed by recent British legislation and the discussion that has surrounded it, as well as by developments in other countries across the world, there is a growing acceptance of the idea that individual human rights might act as a basis for morality. They certainly seem to provide the most promising basis, at present, for an institutionalized global morality of obligation. If this is to be more fully developed, however, a number of issues will need to be addressed.

The first of these issues concerns the politics of recognition and the question of how best to balance individual rights against the collective rights claimed by particular social groupings or communities in a pluralistic society: women's rights, gay rights, aboriginal rights, black rights, Muslim rights, and so on. At first sight this does not seem to be a problem. What these different communities are asking for is after all to be treated with equal respect and dignity, and in theory this should be covered perfectly well by individual rights. The problem is that we cannot ignore the weight of history and prejudice, which rebounds on the self-perceptions of those prejudiced against and disadvantages certain groups even when they are treated with notional equality. In this context, it is argued, practical morality requires that we not only afford respect but also build it, going beyond a tolerance of pluralism to positively affirm cultural differences and so help previously disadvantaged groups to build up new narrative identities. In the process, collective rights are claimed—rights to positive discrimination, affirmative action, or compulsory education—that impact on the individual rights of others.[16] In a deliberative democracy, in which most people will inevitably participate through the spokespersons of the groups with which they most closely identify rather than as individual voices, these tensions should in principle be resolvable, but conflicts between rights cannot be resolved by reference to rights, so some other moral principles will be needed.

A second issue that will need to be addressed is that of property rights. In the Universal Declaration of Human Rights the right to own property is just one right among many, but it was a focal point of the historical development of a philosophy of rights and still occupies a central position in rights-based American liberalism. The problem with the right to property is not so much its culturally specific origin—other rights share that—as the fact that it can be so easily adapted to serve the cause of self-interest. Other rights of an economic nature are normally limited by need. The Universal Declaration, for example, includes the rights to 'just and favourable remuneration ensuring . . . an existence worthy of human dignity' and to 'a standard of living adequate for the health and well-being of himself and his family, including food, clothing, housing and medical care and necessary social services'. In each case there is a qualification. The right to property, however, is unqualified, and in practice it is a right most volubly claimed by those who already have property aplenty and are driven by greed and acquisitiveness. Historically, Americans used the right to property to protect their 'right' to slave ownership. Nowadays it is used to provide a moral buttress to unseemly wealth and to defend the wealthy against the tax demands that would follow from comprehensive social security programmes, of precisely the kind implied by the Universal Declaration.

A related issue is that of corporate rights. As we noted earlier, American corporations are legal persons with all the rights and benefits of personhood, and they assert some of those rights, in particular the rights to property and free speech, strongly. While claiming the rights of individuals, however, they are much wealthier and much more powerful than any individual. Their right to free speech is used not merely to state their case in the face of criticism but to forcefully advance their self-interest, drowning any attempts at criticism and dominating public discourse.

The issues of property rights and corporate rights do not relate to anything inherently problematic in the Universal Declaration of Human Rights, but to the fact that rights are currently seen in two different ways, which can easily be confused. Especially in America, but also to a lesser extent elsewhere, they are still seen, as in the Enlightenment conception, as providing a legal protection against interference by the state, as well as in the more modern way as providing an expression of human dignity and basic moral standards. If the latter conception is to be effective, it needs to be clearly separated from the former,

In addition to the issues already discussed, an ethics of rights also faces two much more fundamental problems. One of these is that most of the rights people claim, and most of the rights set out in the Universal Declaration, are not absolute. Different rights can conflict with each other, and perceptions of rights vary both across time and between and within cultures. This is a problem inherent in the determination of ethical priorities in any pluralistic or evolving society, and is not peculiar to a system of rights. Indeed, as we have already noted, it is somewhat less of a problem reconciling rights, which can be read as aspirations, than it would be reconciling moral constraints, which cannot. In a dialogic or deliberative political system competing aspirations can be debated and compared and judgements reached as to the most appropriate compromises for that particular society at that particular time. Some moral basis is needed to guide that debate, however, just as it is to guide a debate on individual and collective rights.

The other fundamental problem with individual human rights is that most, if not all of them, are effectively meaningless without the existence of corresponding duties or obligations, many of which go well beyond the relatively passive obligations of a respect for life or privacy. This is true of most rights, but is most obviously true of 'welfare rights' such as the right to an adequate standard of living, the right to medical care, or the right to education. In these cases, it is no good people just respecting the rights. Someone has to deliver the paid work or social security, the doctors and medicines, the teachers and schools. Moreover since this delivery cannot be an obligation on every, or indeed any, individual, it requires an institutional framework by which the obligation can be broken up and allocated—a framework, for example, in which some obligations are placed on families, employers, or local communities and some on the society as a whole, and in which taxation is levied on the population to pay for services needed to fulfil the latter, and for their administration.

This is a philosophical point,[17] but it has also been the source of more practical concerns about the moral integrity of systems of rights. Moral conservatives have criticized an emphasis on rights as offering more to criminals than to their victims and as legitimating behaviours that used to be morally prohibited. Church leaders, both Christian and Jewish, have condemned the modern emphasis on human rights on more general grounds as being all take and no give, and have suggested that rather than contributing to a moral society it actively undermines morality by focusing on what we can claim from others rather than on what we owe others.[18] Tony Blair, in a speech made shortly before the passage of the Human Rights Act, asserted, 'a decent society is not actually based on rights. It is based on duty',[19] and in a pamphlet on the Third Way he noted that 'The rights we enjoy reflect the duties we owe; rights and opportunity without responsibility are engines of selfishness and greed.'[20] Of course, church leaders have little option but to defend tradition. They have a lot riding on the systems of constraints that a system of rights might supersede. Blair's statements may also be seen as a reflection of his Christian commitment, as well as a rebuttal to critics of the Human Rights Act. But if rights *are* all take and no give, the cross-cultural consensus they are able to support will ultimately be fruitless.

## Humanity and moral concern

All these considerations lead us to the same general point. A system of individual human rights may provide a good basis for a global moral consensus, but it cannot do all the moral work that will be required if that consensus is to provide an effective restraint on self-interest. In addition to the rights themselves we shall also need principles for determining, through dialogue and debate, which rights are to be included and which are to be given priority at any time and in any circumstance; how they are to be interpreted and applied; and above all how they should be delivered in practice. These principles will need, moreover, to be powerful enough to engage our active moral concern, but sufficiently free of the trappings of tradition to act effectively across cultures.

Reference to duties, or even to duty in the abstract, fails the latter part of this test. It smacks of authority and tradition. The principle of human dignity that informs the Universal Declaration of Human Rights, on the other hand, 'the inherent dignity . . . of all members of the human family', fails the former part. It is worthy and commands universal assent, but it does not engage us emotionally. The concept of responsibility, as used by Anthony Giddens, is more promising. It suggests something coming from one's position in a community, or even from inside oneself, rather than something imposed, and it carries the imperative force necessary for a foundational moral principle. But it is both too strong and too weak. In Giddens's own writing it carries connotations of its use by the sociologist and social philosopher Zygmunt Bauman for whom, following the French philosopher Emmanuel Levinas, the human condition is characterized by a primal and unconditional responsibility to the other.[21] In this sense, our responsibility to others is utter and complete. The demand made is awesome. In more common usage, however, the question of responsible for what, and to what extent, is left open. We may accept some responsibilities but duck or shy away from others, and we may be responsible to differing degrees: the demand is unspecified, and so relatively light.

The Universal Declaration of Human Rights makes very few references to obligations of any sort. The final article refers to 'duties to the community', but this seems to be almost an afterthought and contains no suggestion as to what form the duties might take. The very first article, however, calls for something rather different: 'All humans are born free and equal in dignity and rights. They are endowed with reason and conscience and *should act towards one another in a spirit of brotherhood* [emphasis added].'

Acting in a spirit of brotherhood is not just acting out of duty or some vague sense of responsibility. Nor, though it comes much closer to this, is it acting out of responsibility in Bauman's sense of total commitment. What it comes closest to is the attitude expressed by the cardinal virtues of charity in the Christian sense, or loving-kindness in Judaism and Buddhism, or by the quality of human-heartedness or humaneness (*ren*) that underlies Confucian ethics. Although it finds different expressions in different cultural traditions, this attitude translates fairly easily across cultures, and being positive it can, like the concept of rights, provide the basis for a constructive cross-cultural dialogue and consensus. It is powerful enough emotionally to engage people's moral concern, and connects directly to the positive moral aspirations of all the major religious traditions. As its central place in the entirely secular and, in its time, strongly post-traditional system of Confucianism shows, however, it is in no way dependent on such traditions.[22] Whether it will, in fact, form the basis of a global moral consensus we can only speculate, but something like it will be needed to give moral force to a system of rights and it seems on the face of it to be a strong candidate for the role.

## REGULATION AND CORPORATE GOVERNANCE

Our discussion of the foundations of a moral consensus may appear to have taken us a long way from our central concern with business and management, but in fact it is of immediate relevance. Respect for human dignity and an attitude of human-heartedness are at the core of management as well as of life more generally, and we shall suggest in this section that they will also be a necessary component of any effective system of corporate governance and regulation.

### The problem of regulation

The first question to ask here is whether regulation, in the sense of externally imposed rules and procedures, is needed at all. We have already argued in Chapter 8 that bureaucratic rules and regulations are unlikely to be effective in the flexible organizations of a bimoral society, and observations of contemporary governmental regulation might well seem to reinforce that. One of the great ironies of our time is that just as rules and regulations are losing their effectiveness they are also proliferating as never before. Even as they have introduced market principles to the management of their own departments and agencies, contemporary governments have gone into bureaucratic overdrive, subjecting both the public and the private sectors to a regime of ever more burdensome micro-regulation and bureaucratic audit. Burdensome though it is, however, much of the regulation introduced in recent years is largely irrelevant to the problems faced by contemporary society. For the most part it is classic bureaucratic red tape, requiring forms to be filled in to classify actions in prescribed ways, and further forms to be filled in to classify the ways in which the first set of forms were filled in. In the public sector, where government also controls the purse strings, this can be severely disabling. It has arguably been a source of significant demotivation in public sector services such as health, education, and the police.[23] In business, however, though it can be deeply irritating, it is really no more than an added cost, and so long as the cost is borne by everyone it is seen as a relatively small price to pay for the economic freedom that has resulted from the much more significant deregulation of markets over the last few decades. But it can scarcely be called productive.

As we noted in Chapter 8, in the context of ethical codes of conduct, such a surge of bureaucratization is not really surprising. Increasing regulation is the natural response of any hierarchy threatened by a loss of control, and most of our institutions, including those of business, still have a strong hierarchical element. Government, which is primarily concerned with the establishment and enforcement of law, cannot be anything other than hierarchical, and cannot operate other than through legal and regulatory frameworks. Societies cannot be governed as organizations can be governed, by individual leadership and interpersonal relationships. Contemporary societies are both massively larger than organizations and inherently pluralistic, and they need a framework of law.[24] The fact that governments have recently gone overboard with trivial regulations should not blind us to the fact they have an important regulatory role to play.

But do they have such a role to play in business? It is hard to deny that the deregulation of markets over the last twenty years has been extremely productive economically, and it is short step from that observation to the suggestion that economic markets should be left to regulate themselves, with minimal state inference. This is certainly what some of their participants would prefer, but it runs into serious problems. For one thing, the mutual interests of the market participants are not the same as the interests of society as a whole. For another, markets by their very nature produce winners and losers, and it is only by regulating them from outside that the power of the winners can be curbed.

Any argument for self-regulation is always based on the assumption, implicit or explicit, that the people who will draw up the regulations are 'decent people', who will take the public interest into account and work within the moral norms of society. Where business is concerned, this assumption has always been suspect. In contemporary society, in which self-interest is a given a freer licence than ever before, in which the traditional expressions of moral constraint are losing their force, and in which a new moral consensus is still being shaped, it is inherently implausible. Most business leaders are decent people, but they are also self-interested entrepreneurs and their principal focus, in matters of business, is on profit. Allowing self-regulation is tantamount to allowing the competitors in the market to regulate it on the basis of their mutual self-interest, and this can be very different from the public interest.

This can be illustrated through two types of examples. The first is that of the 'closed shop'. In some areas of business, notably finance, accounting, and the law, self-regulation has long been the norm, and in some respects it has effectively maintained standards. But it has also had the effects of excluding people on grounds other than ability, of limiting competition and so raising prices, and more generally of perpetuating practices that most people would not consider to be in the public interest. The other type of example concerns markets where the effects of competitive action are felt far beyond the market itself. One example here would be that of the international financial markets discussed earlier in this chapter, where the actions of market participants, for example currency traders, can have massive impacts on the populations of developing countries, impacts that would be most unlikely to be prevented by a system of self-regulation. Closer to home, the investment banks and fund management houses of the City of London, which is predominantly self-regulating, have been affected only slightly by the stock market boom and bust of the last few years. But the beneficiaries of the company pension funds they manage have suffered enormously. To take some more obvious examples, putting the environmental regulation of oil and gas extraction into the hands of the world's oil companies, or allowing companies generally to determine their own reporting standards, would be unlikely to lead to an outcome in the public interest.

The other major problem with self-regulation stems from the basic fact that markets are competitive. They produce winners and losers, and when people win they do not usually want to bend over backwards to make things easier for the losers. They want to win more, to be even more successful, to make themselves even richer. Winning, like the money that is usually its measure, is addictive. The problem is that winning also brings considerable power, including the power, in a self-regulated market, to change the rules. However decent a person Bill Gates is, we probably would not want Microsoft to determine the regulations for the software industry—indeed the American government has been fighting in court for the past few years precisely to prevent that from happening. Nor would we necessarily want Monsanto to be responsible for regulating genetically engineered crops.

External regulation *is* needed. Moreover, globalization is making this need both greater and more difficult to achieve. Take for example the areas of Health and Safety and Food and Drugs testing. In these areas the existing regulatory systems of Europe and the United States of America appear to work reasonably well. There is a clearly identified threat to the public interest and a social consensus on the need to counter it. Regulators are able to set specific, usually quantitative standards that businesses are willing to accept as providing protection, removing uncertainty, and stipulating rules within which competition can take place. These standards are not globally recognized, however, and extending them globally may not be straightforward. No product and process can ever be totally safe, and establishing safety standards requires a careful trade-off between the risks involved and the costs of reducing them, a trade-off that is critically dependent on the urgency of the desire for economic advancement. A single country like the United States or a group of similar countries, like the European Union, can agree on standards appropriate to them, but countries in different circumstances may see things differently. Less affluent and disease-ridden nations may rightly resent having pollution dumped on them by rich multinational companies, but left to themselves they might also prefer to have much less onerous standards (enabling more employment and greater growth) and take much greater risks (e.g. with an untested drug) than the richer nations.[25]

Environmental regulation faces a similar situation, but with two complications. First, as we have noted, environmental damage often occurs outside the country in which it is 'produced', so the need for global regulation is greater. Second, the costs of reducing environmental damage are massive, and the combination of the power of the industry lobby and the short-term emphasis of politics has almost certainly resulted in much looser regulations, even in the advanced economies, than a true consideration of the public interest would imply. Here, there is a challenge not only to provide a global system of regulation, but also to increase the effect of regulation everywhere. Another challenge arises from the need to regulate the social impact of industry. Pollution effects can in general be easily quantified and objectively measured. Even though the limits set may not be very onerous, the more responsible of the extraction companies now have well-documented and well-understood procedures for limiting environmental damage. Social damage is much harder to measure, and so much harder to control, whether voluntarily or through regulation.[26]

In other areas, such as finance, where as we have already noted there is an urgent need for international regulation, the tenuous nature of the link between cause and effect causes different problems. In cement manufacture or food treatment the link between what a firm does and the risk or harm that results is either apparent or can at least be investigated by scientific research, and regulators have direct remedies on which they can draw. They can ban products or processes, limit emissions levels, or prescribe testing programmes. Finance cannot be regulated in this way. Any system of regulation has, therefore, to be based on more general considerations of prudence that will always be subjective. To some extent corporate governance falls into the same category. It is possible to regulate a firm on specific dimensions, such as environmental performance, but not to regulate directly the moral integrity of its officers. Corporate governance regulations, thus, take the form of standards of disclosure (accounting standards) and procedural codes of board conduct. The former are undoubtedly effective to some extent, but are always open to creative evasion. The latter are easily dismissed as inappropriate interference or bureaucratic meddling that gets in the way of performance while doing little or nothing to enhance integrity. Many of the UK corporate governance reforms of the last decade have been criticized by business people as simply creating unnecessary bureaucracy.

In all these areas, regulation presents problems, even with strong governments. The problems are exacerbated by the fact that governments are no longer as strong as they once were. It is not that their laws are completely flouted or ignored. Their peculiar hierarchical role is generally recognized. But with the general weakening of hierarchical culture their authority is inevitably questioned. If national governments have difficulties in asserting their authority, moreover, these are nothing as compared to the difficulties that will face any attempts at global regulation, where there is still no credible political authority at all. If systems of corporate governance and the regulation of business and finance are to be effective, both nationally and especially globally, they will have to be built on dialogue rather than on authority, and that dialogue will in turn have to be built upon a foundation that can command a common consensus.

## Trust and control

In the light of our earlier discussion, the most obvious basis for the global regulation of business would be the framework of the Universal Declaration of Human Rights, and some moves have indeed been made in this direction. The United Nations has recently called on businesses to build human rights values into their mission statements, and the World Bank has incorporated respect for individual human rights into its commercial lending requirements.[27] Human rights considerations have also influenced the Organization for Economic Cooperation and Development guidelines for multinationals, while international non-governmental organizations, such as the International Labor Organization, Amnesty International, and various church groupings, have also pressed a human rights agenda upon business.[28] If we are to develop a regulatory system based on human rights, however, we shall face all the difficulties discussed earlier in this chapter. We shall also face one further difficulty. For as well as needing moral consensus at the social level we shall also need to find a way of carrying that consensus into the more market-oriented culture of business. A literal observance of human rights regulations might eliminate some of the harmful effects of business self-interest. It might, for instance, give some protection to employees, or to communities whose lives are affected by a polluting business. But so long as businesses act without positive moral obligations, respect for rights can only take us so far. For rights-based regulation to be truly effective in business, businesses and their managers would have to take on the same kind of moral obligations, exhibit the same kind of human-heartedness, as people acting in an individual capacity.[29]

This brings us back to the need for moral management and to the issues of trust and trustworthiness discussed in Chapter 8. Whereas self-regulation arguably suffers from the problem of too much trust—the gentlemen's club syndrome in which all participants are assumed to be decent, moral people—contemporary approaches to corporate governance and externally imposed financial regulation suffer from too little trust. Strongly influenced by economic thinking, they are based on the agency theory principle of mistrust. They assume, in other words, that people are inherently self-interested and entirely untrustworthy, and try and devise mechanisms that will contain this self-interest. These include the 'market for corporate control', or takeover market, which acts as a disciplinary mechanism to deter managers from underperforming; incentive pay packages for Chief Executive Officers which seek to tie their personal interests to the financial interests of their shareholders; and reporting requirements designed to monitor managerial performance on a quarterly or half-yearly basis. In the wake of the Enron collapse, American CEOs are being asked to commit themselves personally to the accuracy of these accounts.

As John Roberts has recently emphasized, a common feature of these disciplinary mechanisms is that they control managerial behaviour 'by creating a narcissistic preoccupation with how the self and its activities will be seen and judged'.[30] By putting managers in the spotlight, they force them to take account of how their performance is seen by others, but they also isolate them from their surroundings. In Roberts's terms, the processes of corporate governance are 'individualising' processes, generating 'a sense of self as essentially independent and autonomous with only an external and instrumental relationship to others'.[31] They are not only responses to perceived self-interest, but actually produce and reproduce that self-interest, destroying trust and actively exacerbating the governance problem.

An alternative approach much more in tune with the needs we have identified in this book would be to develop what Roberts calls 'socialising' processes of accountability, based on face-to-face interpersonal relationships, in which trust and trustworthiness are positively developed. Instead of seeking to prevent business and its managers from doing harm by putting them under a spotlight and isolating them from the rest of society, protecting society from their assumed self-interest, the aim here would be to develop their moral awareness, moral imagination, and moral concern, or human-heartedness, by connecting them as closely as possible with the rest of society, and by engaging them in explicitly moral dialogue. This would tie in both with the needs of management and leadership, as discussed in the last chapter, and with the more general needs of a pluralistic society discussed in this. Just as the needs of our society appear to call for political processes that are deliberative or dialogic in nature, so too in corporate governance dialogic processes will be needed to establish and maintain a modus vivendi between the interests of a business and the broader and more pluralistic interests of the society in which it operates.

It is not yet clear how such a system of corporate governance might be achieved, but the obvious starting point is the board of directors. In the current Anglo-American system of corporate governance, the board plays a largely economic role. Non-executive directors, appointed to act on behalf of shareholders, oversee the performance of the executive team and appoint or, where necessary, dismiss the CEO. In cases of theft or corruption a CEO may be dismissed on ethical grounds, but these cases are seen as exceptional and the primary concern of the board is with financial performance. Their positive contributions to the company, in terms of feedback, advice, or personal contacts, are also directed to the same ends. In the alternative German system, the remit of the supervisory board is slightly wider. Employee interests are explicitly represented and partly because of this German boards have traditionally recognized the interests of local communities and society at large. But as competitive pressures have escalated in the last twenty years these interests have increasingly taken a back seat. Boards could, however, take on a broader role. If company law were changed so as to make at least some of the non-executive directors of a company appointed to serve in the public interest, rather than in the specific interests of shareholders or employees, the board's regular face-to-face meetings between relative equals might provide the opportunity for deliberative processes of moral engagement, through which business executives could be kept in touch with the moral concerns of society at large.

It would be naive to suggest that a governance system of this kind would be proof against abuse. There would always be a danger that the public representatives would be co-opted to the narrow interests of the firm or its management, and there will always be charismatic entrepreneurs who can gull people into thinking that they are moral when they are not. The boards of Enron, Tyco, and Robert Maxwell's Mirror Group were stuffed full of people who should have known better than to trust the rogues who ran those companies. They were, however, people chosen by the chairmen and chief executives concerned—and chosen, we must presume, precisely because they were gullible. A system that required executives to engage directly, and on moral grounds, with directors not of their own choosing, would not be impossible to manipulate, but it might be harder.

The same general reasoning might also be applied to the regulation of industries and financial markets. Many sectoral regulators are, like boards, concerned primarily with economic issues. Others are concerned mainly with ensuring fair competition and, in some cases, protecting the interests of customers. In both cases, the preferred method of regulation is regulation at a distance, setting standards and procedures and monitoring their enforcement. A few regulators have, however, been prepared to engage their regulatees in face-to-face discourse on matters of the public interest and there is no reason why promotion of the public interest, through direct personal engagement and moral dialogue, should not become a core duty of regulators, both nationally and internationally. Indeed, in areas of international business and finance where global standards might be hard to establish, such a dialogic engagement might well be a necessary first step on the path to global regulation.

## A social contract for business

An essential feature of socializing or dialogic forms of corporate governance or regulation is that while they might need to be backed up by legal sanctions, including where necessary the imposition of formal controls, they should not depend on such sanctions for their effectiveness. A dialogue conducted under the shadow of authority will not be a genuine dialogue, and will not produce the effects desired. So why should business and financial leaders engage willingly in a moral dialogue such as we have envisaged, and not just assert the legitimacy of their self-interest? Is there anything about deliberative governance and regulation that will make it more acceptable to the business community than the existing systems? I think there is. In a bimoral society, most business people are not immoral or even amoral. They are human beings, just like anyone else, and what they object to is not the intrusion of moral concerns but the enforcement of a supposedly moral compact, in terms that they do not recognize and over which they have no influence, and in a way that implies they have no moral concerns of their own. They also recognize that, despite their growing power, they still depend on society for a licence to operate, but working in a market culture they distrust hierarchical authority and expect to be able to negotiate the terms of that licence, not to have them dictated to them. They object to being told what to do, but they are much more open to the idea of a negotiated social contract.

The idea of a social contract, in which people informally accept certain social or moral obligations as the 'price' of certain individual benefits, carries heavy philosophical connotations. It can be traced back in different forms to the philosophies of Hobbes and Rousseau, it underlies the influential twentieth-century political philosophy of John Rawls, and in the hands of Thomas Donaldson and Thomas Dunfee it has recently been used to develop a philosophy of international business ethics.[32] Rawls's concern is with the theoretical argument as to what kind of social contract people should rationally agree to, under certain ideal conditions.[33] Donaldson and Dunfee combine this approach with recognition of the obligations people do in fact accept, but their aim is still to develop guidelines as to how businesses should behave. In every-day language, however, people talk of a social contract much more prosaically to describe a set of obligations that is actually entered into (or that one party thought the other had entered into) and it is in this sense that the term is appropriate here. Business people are interested in real contracts, not ideal ones, and in a deliberative democracy it is real compromises, not ideal solutions, that matter.

We noted earlier in the book that the benefits of incorporation have come to be treated as rights rather than privileges. Limited liability, for example, is seen as a legal measure to enhance economic growth, to which all companies are entitled, and not as a socially conferred privilege. While business practitioners may not see themselves as particularly privileged, however, they do see themselves as part of society, and in some kind of contractual relationship with it. The idea that the benefits of incorporation (not only limited liability but also corporate personhood and a measure of legal protection for a company's officers when things go badly wrong) and the freedom to trade have to be bought at some price, and that that price should be negotiated, is one that they can understand and accept. If society can accept on its part that a negotiated consensus is likely to be more productive than imposed constraints, and moral engagement more valuable than bureaucratic compliance, the idea of a social contract might be one on which corporate governance and regulation can build.

The arguments of this chapter are necessarily tentative. In political terms, our society is still struggling to cope with pluralism, never mind globalization, while attitudes to corporate governance are still locked into an outmoded framework of agency and control. We can speculate on the way forward, but we cannot predict it with any confidence. The speculations we have put forward are, however, consistent with the emerging picture of management portrayed in the last chapter. In a bimoral society, the morality of obligation, whether in society, in business, or in the processes by which the two are linked, cannot be imposed by traditional authorities, but must be built upon interpersonal relationships and the moral feelings these engender. Unlike the bureaucratic constraints of an earlier age, an attitude of moral concern, or human-heartedness, need not be a hindrance to the pursuit of enterprise; but it might just prevent that enterprise from being self-destructive.

# 10

# Conclusion

The argument of this book builds on an essentially historical thesis. The main points of this thesis, which is set out in detail in the first half of the book, can be summarized as follows:

1. Civilized societies have always been characterized by the co-presence of two contrasting sets of principles governing how people live their lives. One of these is associated with traditional morality, or the morality of obligation, and the other with self-interest. Traditional moral principles allow for a modicum of self-interest, but their emphasis is on people's obligations and duties to others: duties of honesty and respect, fairness and equity, care and assistance. The principles of what I have called market morality, or the morality of self-interest, also impose some obligations, but these are relatively limited. The emphasis of the principles is competitive rather than cooperative, on advancing one's own interests rather than on meeting the needs of others.

2. From the dawn of civilization until relatively recently in history, the principles of traditional morality were clearly dominant. Social behaviour was regulated by dominant institutions of church, state, and community, all of which acted as traditional moral authorities. Even businesses were structured as traditional moral communities, with the obligations of managers, whether in a family firm or in a modern bureaucratic business organization, mirroring those of citizens in society at large. Behaviour according to the morality of the market was accepted as necessary for the economic growth and development of a society, but it was also seen as a potential threat to the traditional moral order and was permitted only under licence, so to speak, in carefully circumscribed arenas and subject to a range of regulatory safeguards.

3. Over the last twenty to thirty years, in the latter part of the twentieth century, this dominance of traditional moral principles was severely eroded. Freed from many of the constraints of both domestic and global regulation, the institutions of business and finance grew massively in power and influence, while the traditional moral authorities of church,

state, family, community, and education were all seriously weakened. Changing lifestyles weakened people's traditional moral ties, while television played havoc with traditional moral sense making. Economic and instrumental 'common-sense' forms of reasoning, rooted in the ideology of market culture and based on the principles of self-interest, were applied to areas that had previously been the preserve of moral feelings and beliefs.

4. As a result of these and other, related developments, the morality of self-interest has acquired a social legitimacy to match that of traditional morality. Traditional moral principles are still very important and still govern people's lives, both directly and indirectly, through custom and the law, in all sorts of ways. But in a wide range of situations they are no longer binding. Where once people followed authority, they must now become their own moral authorities, weighing the principles of traditional morality as best they can against those of a legitimate self-interest. To put it another way, the two sets of principles by which people govern their lives are no longer confined to separate, well-defined arenas. Their ranges of application overlap significantly, and in many situations it is no longer apparent which should take precedence.

5. Although these changes have come about very recently and very quickly, and are at least partly attributable to recent advances in media and communications technologies, they have deep historical roots. What we have seen over the last few decades is not something that has arisen out of the blue, but an acceleration of processes that have been under way at least since the Enlightenment of the eighteenth century. It is unlikely to be a temporary blip, of merely transient significance.

If it is not just a temporary blip, though, what is it? Here, history runs out on us. My own reading would be that that we are going through a process of globalization in which the different cultures of the world and the moralities associated with them are jostling with each other for supremacy; and that if we do not destroy ourselves in the process, this is likely to lead ultimately to the emergence of a single dominant world culture, and quite possibly to that of a common global expression of traditional moral principles. This reading can readily be contested, however, and not just by those who challenge the extent of contemporary economic globalization or the decline of traditional moral authority. The effects of religion, for example, are quite impossible to predict. I have argued that the decline of Christianity in the developed world, which has been gathering pace for centuries, is unlikely to be suddenly reversed, but the religious instinct is deeply embedded in the human psyche and anything is possible. World politics are also inherently unpredictable. In early 2003, a bellicose American administration, determined to wage pre-emptive wars in Iraq and elsewhere, was using language and expressing sentiments that had lain dormant for half a century. The United Nations was in tatters and the political stability of the world seemed threatened in a way that could not have been envisaged just five years earlier. A retreat to the nation state was by no means inconceivable.

Even if my reading is basically correct, moreover, it leaves important questions unanswered. It is impossible to predict how stable a bimoral society will be, how long it will survive, or where it will lead. It may simply mark an historic transition from one traditionally moral era, dominated by the nation state and the existing world religions, to another, dominated by new religions or yet to be created global institutions. Or it may mark a different kind of transition, from order to chaos. Pessimists can look to the decline of the Roman Empire and suggest that a society that becomes absorbed in pleasure and undermined by self-interest can easily collapse altogether. Such a regression is almost impossible to imagine, but it has happened before and it could no doubt happen again. Our capacity for destructive self-interest, whether through environmental pollution, through weapons of mass destruction, or through a mass exodus from social responsibility to the delights of virtual reality, far exceeds that of the Romans. On the other hand, it may be that with sufficiently developed business and market institutions a society dominated by self-interest *is* actually viable, and that the bimoral society marks a period of transition from one dominant kind of morality to another. Or it may be that the bimoral society is not transitional at all, but a model for the long-term future of society.

Whatever the long-term prospects, however, they do not seem to me to affect the short- and medium-term reality. The bimoral society is here, and it is here for the foreseeable future. On the timescale of business organizations, management careers, and personal life-projects it is effectively here to stay. It also matters. In describing the bimoral orientation of contemporary society I have inevitably omitted to describe much else that is important. I have focused on just one feature of the social world and described it in just one way. There are other features on which I could have focused, and there are other ways in which this particular feature could have been described and analysed. In the complex world of human affairs there is always more than one way of looking at things, and any description is a distortion. I do believe, though, that the perspective I have chosen here is both valuable and productive, and in the second half of the book I have tried to show how.

My main focus has been on the implications of the bimoral society for management. As the moral culture of society has changed, so has the structure of business organizations. Business has always been marked by market culture and directed by self-interest, but in the business bureaucracies of the post-war era these characteristics were well hidden. The route to competitive success was through large-scale coordination, long-term relationships, and accumulated experience, all of which were well served by an organizational culture in which loyal service was rewarded and traditional moral obligations prevailed. Neither the interests of the business and its shareholders nor those of its managers needed to be asserted, as both could be achieved by the observance of traditional moral principles.

As the competitive environment changed and heavy bureaucratic structures began to hinder rather than to enhance competitiveness, this communion of interests began to break down. Companies continued to demand loyalty from their employees, but they could no longer afford to give it in return. Employees continued to profess loyalty and commitment, but with their security shattered they were increasingly forced to look after their own interests in a competitive struggle for survival. Deprived of the traditional moral compact that had been their great strength, old-fashioned bureaucracies collapsed under their own weight, and new organizational forms emerged.

Contemporary business organizations take a wide range of forms, from the highly rigid and bureaucratic to the highly flexible and, to use Henry Mintzberg's evocative term, adhocratic. In cultural and moral terms, however, most are hybrid forms in which the tensions of the bimoral society are clearly reflected. On one hand, most business organizations today retain significant elements of bureaucracy, in particular a strong vertical dimension. Apart from the Chief Executive Officer, every manager has a boss, and every manager is a boss. The vertical relationships that ensue are marked, as they always have been, by significant power differentials, and because they are relationships between people, living in a society that recognizes and values the prin ciples of traditional morality, these power differentials carry perceived moral obligations. Most managers still feel a moral duty to serve their employers and support their bosses, by working hard and to the best of their ability. They also feel a duty to look after, as best they can, the employees who report to them, people for whom they are morally as well as financially responsible.

On the other hand, these same business organizations are also structured according to the rules of the market. Self-interest is expected and even encouraged. People are expected, in particular, to look after their own careers and are employed on contracts that offer little or no security. The dominant ideology presented by the corporation is that of the free market, with employees treated as free agents, and on this view of things the power differentials carry no moral obligations. Employees are free to change their jobs, and employers are free to change their staff. It all comes down to supply and demand.

Linking these two cultural elements are organizational devices that fit properly into neither: teams and networks. Many contemporary businesses still look from the outside rather like traditional bureaucracies, but most are no longer structured round the tightly defined 'offices', each responsible for a specific task (and located, symbolically, in a separate room), and rigid reporting lines of classical bureaucracy. Job definitions are now much broader and more flexible, channels of communication take the form of extended networks, and the core operating structure is the team. For teams to work effectively, they need high levels of freedom, autonomy, and flexibility, all of which are anathema to traditional bureaucracy. They also need to operate as traditional moral communities with high levels of mutual trust, loyalty, and commitment, all of which is anathema to market culture. In the right cultural context they can be extraordinarily effective, and it is no accident that they have flourished in the context of the bimoral society, but they are also inherently vulnerable to the tensions of that society.

In this context management, or being a manager, is beset by moral tensions. Managers today are responsible, as managers always have been, to their immediate superiors. But whereas other responsibilities could once be subsumed under that, they are now quite separate, and pulling in different directions. Contemporary managers are responsible directly for the company's performance, of which they are constantly aware, and on the basis of which they are paid. They are responsible to the team members with whom they work, who rely on their contributions and high level of commitment; and to the employees who report to them and rely on their support. They have responsibilities to their families and to others who rely on their friendship or care, and they are responsible for looking after their own interests—for developing their careers and for building and sustaining their incomes.

Perhaps the most obvious tension in all this is between work and home, between the needs of the family and the demands of the job. Managers today work exceptionally long hours and are always on call. The job demands it, and the insecurity of the job demands it. In many ways, being a manager now carries all the costs of being self-employed, but with few of the benefits. This creates tensions for men, who report feelings of guilt, as their families do not get the time and attention they need. It is far more difficult for women with families, who are likely to be criticized for working or for not working, and who just have to compromise as best they can in an impossible situation. In the bimoral society women can compete with men for managerial advancement on a completely equal footing, but they are expected to give an equal commitment. If they choose to be mothers as well, that is their free choice, and they must take the consequences.

The work–home tensions can also be seen in teams, when one of the team members hits difficulties at home (a sick child, spouse, or parent, for example) that impact on the working of the team. Team members are both colleagues and competitors. As colleagues they have traditional moral relationships, which make allowance for circumstance. As competitors, seeking promotion or advancement or networking their ways to new teams and new possibilities, they act through self-interest and cannot afford to make allowances if these impact upon performance. There is also a tension in contemporary management teamwork between the achievement of solid results and the need to manage impressions. When a project does not work out, the traditionally moral thing to do is to see it through and take the blame. The smart thing to do is to network avidly and move on fast, leaving others to pick up the pieces.

As well as being employees and team workers, managers are also bosses. They have to manage teams and they have, crucially, to hire, promote, and fire, or not renew the contracts of, employees. In theory this is easier in a market culture, where there is no future commitment beyond the terms of the contract, but that easiness disappears when we take account of the power differentials and the reality of human relationships. Managers have to ask their reports for loyalty and commitment, even though they cannot offer it in return. They can give friendship and support, and create a trusting relationship. Indeed, if they are to get the most out of their employees, they must do this. It is what management is all about. But they must do it knowing that they may have to take hard, market-based decisions and to renege on the implicit moral contract; that they will not be able to give help and support if and when it is really needed.

At the top of the organization, these tensions are compounded by others, as senior managers have to take responsibility for other stakeholders as well as for shareholder performance, and to live out the curious role of the contemporary CEO. They must act as their predecessors acted, as stewards of the corporation, but in doing so their judgement is constrained. The market culture, which gives priority to shareholder returns, requires them to take very hard decisions, many of which go against traditional moral principles. Their pay is structured such that these decisions are handsomely rewarded, but that only heightens the tension. Make 1,000 people redundant, enhance performance, and get paid a few million pounds extra for that performance, and they are castigated by the popular press as self-interested and, in traditional terms, immoral. Look after their employees and the communities that depend on them, and they are also castigated, this time by the financial institutions, as self-interested and as failing in their traditionally moral commitment to shareholders. In a pure market culture, of course, self-interest is moral, not immoral, so the latter criticism is inherently unfair; but in a bimoral society it is what they get. Like football managers, they also get the sack when performance falters, whether or not they are at fault.

Managing all these tensions presents numerous challenges, not all of which have yet been fully recognised. There is now widespread recognition of the need for the development of entrepreneurial and career self-management skills alongside the traditional functional and technical skills of management. Important as these are, however, they are not at the core of the new management challenge. The core of the challenge is to combine enterprise with humanity, to channel and direct the entrepreneurial energies that are now being released so as to serve both the needs of the company—which is a challenge in itself—and, beyond that, the needs of society at large.

Part of this is a challenge of leadership. The demands of business leadership have not changed. Leaders still need, in John Kotter's formulation, to provide direction, including a vision for the company and a strategy for achieving it; to communicate that direction and align people behind it; and to motivate and inspire people to keep moving in that direction, despite all the barriers and distractions that get in their way. Whereas in the past leadership was needed only for change, however, it is now needed for stability as well. Provided that it was going in the right direction an old-fashioned bureaucracy needed little leadership; it was change that was the problem. In more flexible organizations, where entrepreneurial self-interest pushes people in their own directions and where moral tensions pull them in multiple directions, just holding the organization together is a leadership challenge.

The nature of the organization also impacts on the kinds of leadership that are effective. Both bureaucratic and market cultures tend to favour strong individual leadership and those who reach the top of contemporary business tend to be highly competitive individuals. Once at the top, they are held personally to account in a way that isolates them further from their colleagues, and pushes them towards autocratic styles of leadership. The effectiveness of flexible organizations, however, depends critically on the freedom and autonomy that they give their employees, and attempts at autocratic leadership are apt to be counter-productive. At the other end of the leadership spectrum, empowering styles of leadership can be tremendously effective for small organizations, and for the leadership of communities where the interests of those being empowered are of paramount importance. But a business is not just a community. It has objectives to meet, and these will not always correspond to the interests of its employees. Moreover, achieving consensus by mutual adjustment is too slow a mechanism to respond effectively to rapidly changing competitive environments in large, complex companies.

Contemporary business leaders have to find ways of combining genuine autonomy with control, and empowerment with clear direction. In practice, this means following the dictates of empowering or servant leadership, listening to people, understanding them, and building on their own individual aims and objectives; treating them openly to build up trust and trustworthiness. But it does not mean following their wishes. Business leaders have in the end to call the shots, and to take responsibility for their calls.

Another part of the management challenge is explicitly moral, in the traditional sense. It has become commonplace to see managers as morally neutral technicians engaged in a world of rational problem solving in the pursuit of economic efficiency. This is the conception advanced by business schools, by management consultants, and by managers themselves, keen to emphasize their technical expertise. As critical sociologists have pointed out, it is also a product of the disciplinary forces of bureaucratic business organizations, which disable people's moral faculties. Questions of moral values are either distorted and translated into purely economic terms, or suppressed altogether and thrown back onto individuals to cope with as best they can in the private realm outside their management roles. Contemporary business organizations do not so much disable people's moral faculties as crowd them out. In amongst all their other responsibilities, managers are now held explicitly responsible for upholding traditional moral standards in the business, for what is usually called 'business ethics'. But the disciplinary forces are still present and in a society in which moral engagement is getting progressively more difficult, in a business culture in which self-interest is ardently promoted, and in jobs in which the immediate, instrumental demands are manifold and all absorbing, finding space for the traditionally moral is incredibly difficult.

In a central and critically important sense, however, morality is now what management is all about. In contemporary organizations, the technical problem solving and pursuit of efficiency that dominate existing conceptions of managerial work are carried out primarily through IT-based market mechanisms. To be effective these mechanisms need the support of skilled technicians. They also need to be regulated. But the discretionary skills of technical managerial problem solving are fast becoming redundant. And with the technical side taken care of, the task of the manager becomes precisely that which was previously forbidden: the political and moral task of determining purposes and priorities, reconciling divergent interests, and nurturing interpersonal relationships. The economic advantages of flexible organizations come from giving people the freedom to act as entrepreneurial agents, but these advantages can only be realized and sustained if they are set in the context of a traditionally moral community based on mutual trust and respect, active moral awareness and concern, the recognition of diverse needs and interests, and the fair treatment of those needs and interests. In old-fashioned bureaucracies, traditional moral duties and obligations were built into the rulebook, but contemporary management is all about breaking the rules, and finding new ways of doing things. The moral dimension has to be managed directly, by managers, through the medium of personal relationships.

At the heart of this new model of management is the building of trust, or more accurately of trustworthiness. Only if people trust each other will they share their knowledge and insights and so learn from each other, allowing the organization to capture the benefits of their individual enterprise. In a knowledge-based economy, the ability to learn is the ultimate source of sustainable competitive advantage and managing learning is a third key component of the contemporary management challenge. In bureaucracies, knowledge was stored in the structure and culture of the organization and passed easily from one generation to another. Unlearning was the problem. In more flexible organizations, knowledge is held by transient individuals and in temporary teams, and learning needs much more active management. Part of this can be done through distributed information systems. Because the knowledge that counts tends to be tacit know-how rather than codified information, however, both learning and unlearning also have to be managed directly, through the management of personal relationships. Fortunately, the skills required are much the same as those required to meet the challenges of leadership and moral management: listening, empathy, personal engagement, open and honest communications, and demonstrable trust and trustworthiness.

If the bimoral society presents challenges for management, it presents even greater challenges for society. One of these is an educational challenge. The traditional elements of a business school education are still necessary. In a flexible organization skills cannot be neatly partitioned and managers probably need financial and accounting, marketing, and strategic skills more today than they ever have done. But they also need something else. They need grounding in the messy realities of the human condition, an understanding of politics and culture, and an awareness of the historical forces that have shaped the world in which we live. They also need advanced listening and interpersonal skills and critical self-knowledge; and they need role models from whom to learn. Business schools could provide some of this, but few yet do so.

Another challenge for society is the challenge of corporate governance, of regulating business so as to ensure that it serves the needs of society and not just the self-interest of its principals. An extraordinary amount of attention has been paid to this issue in recent years, but much of it seems to have been counter-productive. The supreme irony of contemporary society is that at a time when bureaucratic rules and regulations are losing their effectiveness, they are proliferating as never before. This is a natural response to the changes we are experiencing. When authorities begin to lose their power they try all the harder to exert it, and when bureaucracies lose their effectiveness they respond in the only way they can, by tightening and adding to their regulations. At best, however, this just adds to the cost of doing business. Companies make sure that the forms are ticked and the regulations observed (or the fines paid, if that works out cheaper) and get on with their business. At worst it reproduces the very behaviours it is intended to curtail. By focusing attention on the presentation of the company it encourages instrumental impression management and reduces genuine moral engagement. Starting out from the assumption of corporate self-interest, it feeds that self-interest and destroys the trust between business and society.

In governance as in management, the key to managing the tensions of the bimoral society lies in building relationships of trust. In a high trust environment, a plurality of interests can be recognized and enterprise can be allowed to flourish. The question is how to create such an environment. Political theorists of the Third Way, recognizing the globalized and post-traditional nature of our society, have written of the need for dialogic or deliberative forms of democracy in which the public interest is served by a modus vivendi built on open dialogue, rather than by the imposition of authority. These remain a long way off in practice, if only because we have yet to develop a post-traditional moral consensus on which the dialogue could be based, but they surely point in the right direction. We have no need to curtail business and blunt the forces of enterprise by disciplinary forms of governance. But we do need to trust businesses to be open and honest about their interests and activities, and we do need them to engage in constructive dialogue around the relationship between those interests and the interests of society at large.

# NOTES

## CHAPTER 1

1. Traffic and litter laws, for example, and laws requiring the disclosure or earnings for taxation purposes, are all routinely flouted in the pursuit of self-interest.
2. In particular, I am not advocating here a position of moral relativism, a position that cannot, in my view, be either proved or disproved.
3. I recognize that there is potential for confusion here, but alternative uses of language seem on balance to be even more confusing. Sociologists and anthropologists of morals, almost all of whom encounter difficulties in this respect, tend to use the word 'morality' in much the same ways as I do, but slide silently between one meaning and the other without making any clear distinctions.
4. The term 'bimoral' is not in common usage, but it was used, in the hyphenated form 'bi-moral', by Van Ness Myers, (1933). *History as Past Ethics: An Introduction to the History of Morals*, 380, who wrote of 'a sort of bi-moral code made up of rules and practices mutually inconsistent and irreconcilable'. His reference was to war ethics rather than to market ethics, but the usage is otherwise similar to that I intend. I am grateful to the staff of the *Oxford English Dictionary* for this reference.
5. This case is argued very powerfully, from a historical perspective, by Landes, David (1999). *The Wealth and Poverty of Nations* (London: Abacus).
6. This point was first stressed by Emile Durkheim, who drew attention to the differences in moral structure between what he called 'traditional' (we might say 'primitive') and modern societies (Durkheim, Emile (1933). *The Division of Labour in Society* (New York: Free Press)). It is made most tellingly, in the context of modern societies, by Michel Foucault and Alasdair MacIntyre. In his *History of Sexuality*, Foucault explores the way in which not only specific ethics but the nature of the ethical itself has changed from one social context to another. See Foucault, Michel (1978–86). *The History of Sexuality* (New York: Pantheon), especially the preface to Volume 2. MacIntyre's focus is on the social context of moral philosophy and how views of justice and moral reason presented by philosophers as having absolute truth can be seen historically as being tightly bound up with (and, he would say, understandable only in terms of) the specific social contexts within which they wrote. See MacIntyre, Alasdair (1967). *A Short History of Ethics* (London: Routledge & Kegan Paul); idem (1988). *Whose Justice? Which Rationality?* (London: Duckworth).

7. There is an analogy here with the philosophy of science and with Karl Popper's absolutist response to Thomas Kuhn's relativistic and sociological conception of science in his *The Structure of Scientific Revolutions*. Kuhn argued that science was not a 'purely' rational activity as earlier philosophers had assumed, but was constrained and conditioned by the prevailing norms of a particular scientific community. Popper's response, in effect, was to say maybe it is, but if so that is a failing of the scientists. He was prepared, in other words, to concede the relativism of practice, but not that of truth. See Kuhn, Thomas S. (1970). *The Structure of Scientific Revolutions*, 2nd edn. (Chicago: University of Chicago Press); Popper, Karl R. (1970). 'Normal science and its dangers', in Imre Lakatos and Alan Musgrave (eds.), *Criticism and the Growth of Knowledge* (Cambridge: Cambridge University Press), 51–8. The analogy between the philosophies of science and morals is quite a general one, as those who have taken a particular stance in one context have generally taken a similar one in the other. The most influential of all modern philosophers, Immanuel Kant, sought in the eighteenth century to establish both morality and scientific truth upon the absolute grounds of reason, and this programme has been at the heart of academic philosophy since. When it has been challenged, as by the French sociologist Emile Durkheim or the American pragmatists William James and John Dewey at the turn of the twentieth century, or by continental philosophers of the late twentieth century, the challenge has often applied equally to science and to ethics. Kuhn's work was concerned only with science, and there is as yet no equivalent in the sociology of ethics to the sociological 'science studies' that have grown up in its wake, but there are evident parallels between Kuhn's sociology of science and Alasdair MacIntyre's socially contextualized philosophy of ethics.

# CHAPTER 2

1. The classic treatment of cooperative game theory is Axelrod, Robert (1984). *The Evolution of Cooperation* (New York: Basic Books); updated in idem (1997). *The Complexity of Cooperation* (Princeton: Princeton University Press). For evolutionary advocates of self-interest as the foundation for cooperation see, for example, Alexander, Richard D. (1987). *The Biology of Moral Systems* (New York: de Gruyter); Wilson, Edward O. (1975). *Sociobiology: the New Synthesis* (Cambridge, MA: Harvard University Press); idem (1978). *On Human Nature* (Cambridge, MA: Harvard University Press); Ridley, Matt (1997). *The Origins of Virtue: Human Instinct and the Evolution of Cooperation* (New York: Viking). For a critique of that view see Singer, Peter (1997). *How are we to Live: Ethics in an Age of Self-Interest* (Oxford: Oxford University Press); and Rose, Hilary and Rose, Steven (eds.), (2000). *Alas, Poor Darwin: Arguments Against Evolutionary Psychology* (New York: Harmony).

2. For 'ultimatum game' experiments, in which one player allocates money between herself and another, see Camerer, Colin and Thaler, Richard H. (1995). 'Ultimatums, dictators, and manner', *Journal of Economic Perspectives*, 9, 209–19; and Henrich, Robert et al. (2001). 'In search of homo economicus: behavioral experiments in small scale societies', *American Economic Review*, 91, 73–8. For more complex public goods experiments, see Fehr, Scott A. and Gachter, Simon (2000). 'Cooperation and punishment in public goods experiments', *American Economic Review*, 90, 980–94.

3. The classic argument to this effect is Durkheim's: Durkheim, Emile (1973). *Moral Education* (New York: Free Press); idem 'The dualism of human nature and its social conditions', in Kurt H. Wolff (ed.) (1960). *Emile Durkheim, 1858–1917* (Columbus: Ohio State University Press), 325–41; Edel, M. and Edel, A. (1959). Anthropology and Ethics (Springfield IL: Charles C. Thomas).

4. The classic psychological treatment is in Kohlberg, Lawrence (1981). *Essays on Moral Development* (San Francisco); see also Piaget, Jean (1971). *Biology and Knowledge* (Chicago: University of Chicago Press); Rest, James R. (1986). *Moral Development: Advances in Research and Theory* (New York: Praeger); and, for a sociological perspective, Sennett, Richard (1977). *The Fall of Public Man* (New York: Knopf); idem (1998). *The Corrosion of Character* (New York: Norton).

5. See Bellah, Robert N., Madsen, Richard, Sullivan, William M., Swidler, Ann, and Tipton, Steven M. (1985). *Habits of the Heart: Individualism and Commitment in American Life* (Berkeley: University of California Press).

6. For a discussion of this see Edel and Edel, *Anthropology and Ethics*; Howell, Signe (1997). 'Introduction' to *The Ethnography of Moralities* (London: Routledge); Firth, Raymond William (1964). *Essays on Social Organization and Values* (London: London School of Economics).

7. Howell, 'Introduction'; Geertz, Clifford (ed.) (2000). 'Anti-anti-relativism', in his *Available Light: Anthropological Reflections on Philosophical Topics* (Princeton: Princeton University Press); Hatch, Elvin (1983). *Culture and Morality: The Relativity of Values in Anthropology* (New York: Columbia University Press).

8. Douglas, Mary (1996). *Natural Symbols: Explorations in Cosmology* (London: Routledge), p. xii.

9. Wittgenstein, Ludwig (1958). *Philosophical Investigations* (Oxford: Blackwell).

10. The types were first described in Douglas, Mary (1970). *Natural Symbols: Explorations in Cosmology* (London: Barrie & Rockliff), and the labels attached in 'Cultural bias' (1978). Occasional paper 35 of the Royal Anthropological Institute.

11. Douglas, *Natural Symbols*, 1996 edn., xix *ff.*

12. For Williamson, the 'market' is in effect a spot market and market and hierarchy are simply different types of market contractual arrangement. See, for example, Williamson, Oliver E. (1975). *Markets and Hierarchies: Analysis and Anti-Trust Implications* (New York: Free Press); idem (1993).'Transaction cost economics and organization theory', *Industrial and Corporate Change*, 2, 107–56. As Ghoshal and Moran have noted, the ethics and institutions of hierarchical societies and organizations (in the sociological sense) are completely alien to the transaction cost perspective: Ghoshal, Sumantra and Moran, Peter (1996). 'Bad for practice: a critique of the transaction cost theory', *Academy of Management Review*, 21, 13–47. The confusion over the two versions of the market–hierarchy distinction is, however, a common feature of the management literature: see, for example, Ouchi, William (1980). 'Markets, bureaucracies and clans', *Administrative Science Quarterly*, 25, 129–41; Boisot, Max (1995). *Information Space: A Framework for learning in Organizations, Institutions and Culture* (London: Routledge).

13. Douglas, *Natural Symbols* (1973 and 1996 edns.). The categories of grid and group were developed from contemporary work on speech systems by Bernstein, Basil (1964). 'Social class and psychotherapy', *British Journal of Sociology*, 15, 54–64; idem (1971). *Class, Codes and Control, Volume 1: Theoretical Studies towards a Sociology of Language* (London: Routledge & Kegan Paul), and were introduced in the first, 1970 edn. of *Natural Symbols*. The revised version of the theory presented here comes from

the revised, 1973 edn. of the book. The theory was later simplified and reworked as a theory of ideal types, in which the grid and group variables were redefined in terms of social structure rather than their effect upon individuals and the grid–group space was replaced by a simple 2 × 2 matrix. In this form it provided the basis for a number of subsequent variations. See Douglas, 'Cultural bias'; Douglas Mary (ed.) (1982). *Essays in the Sociology of Perception* (London: Routledge & Kegan Paul); idem (1992). 'The normative debate and the origins of culture', in her *Risk and Blame: Essays in Cultural Theory* (London: Routledge). Most of the applications of the theory, by Douglas and others, have been based upon this simple version of the theory, but the version presented here is both closer to the original empirical evidence and better suited to issues of cultural pluralism and change, which is what we are interested in here. For further discussion see Hendry, John (1999). 'Cultural theory and contemporary management organization', *Human Relations*, 52, 557–77.

14. We can, of course, imagine somebody being constrained by some aspects of the classification system but not by others, or being dominated by the group in some ways but dominating in others.

15. In later versions of the theory, this dual nature of markets was sacrificed in the cause of simplicity and the oppressed masses were more or less forgotten. As we shall see, there are some good reasons for this, but in the context of primitive societies the duality is important.

16. Giddens, Anthony (1979). *Central Problems in Social Theory* (London: Macmillan); idem (1984). *The Constitution of Society* (Cambridge: Polity).

17. For a theorist of social practice such as Anthony Giddens, the self-reproducing nature of social structures would seem to rule out almost any change other than very gradual incremental changes or changes imposed from outside the society. The restriction of such theories, however, is that they have no place for individual variations: their societies and cultures are effectively homogeneous and, in consequence, effectively static. See Giddens, *The Constitution of Society*, especially 244 *ff.*

18. Douglas, Mary, 'Institutions of the third kind', in her *Risk and Blame*, 167–86.

19. See, for example, Strathern, Marilyn, 'Double standards' in Howell, *The Ethnography of Moralities*, 127–51.

20. This point is stressed by Durkheim, Emile (1933). *The Division of Labour in Society* (London: Macmillan).

21. For discussions of bureaucracy and markets in early civilizations see, for example, Knapp, A. Bernard (1988). *The History and Culture of Ancient Western Asia and Egypt* (Belmont, CA: Wadsworth); Postgate, J. Nicholas (1992). *Early Mesopotania: Society and Economy at the Dawn of History* (London: Routledge); (1970–75). *The Cambridge Ancient History, Volumes I and II* (Cambridge: Cambridge University Press).

22. The relationship between war, politics, and finance has been explored for the modern period by Ferguson, Niall (2001). *The Cash Nexus: Money and Power in the Modern World*, 1700–2000 (London: Penguin). For earlier periods see Bonney, Richard (ed.) (1995). *Economic Systems and State Finance* (Oxford: Oxford University Press), especially the chapters on 'Expenditure' and 'Public credit' by Martin Körner; idem (1999). *The Rise of the Fiscal State in Europe, c.* 1200–1815 (Oxford: Oxford University Press). As Körner shows, the recourse of monarchs to private borrowing from internationally operating merchant bankers can be traced back to the thirteenth century, and grew rapidly thereafter. Körner also estimates the costs of government for various European states in the medieval and early modern periods and finds that the costs of war typically account for between 40% and 50% of the total, with the proportion rising over time.

23. See, for example, Pliny to Maecilius Nepos in Radice, Betty (ed.) (1969). *The Letters of the Younger Pliny* (Harmondsworth: Penguin), 170. For a contemporary sociological analysis of the political process see Bourdieu, Pierre (1991). *Language and Symbolic Power* (Cambridge: Polity).

24. See Mintzberg, Henry (1979). *The Structuring of Organizations* (Englewood Cliffs, NJ: Prentice Hall); Peters, Tom and Waterman, Robert (1982). *In Search of Excellence* (New York: Harper & Row); Lloyd, Tom (1984). *Dinosaur & Co.: Studies in Corporate Evolution* (Harmondsworth: Penguin); Kanter, Rosabeth Moss (1989). *When Giants Learn to Dance* (London: Simon & Schuster).

25. Balazs, Etienne. *La bureaucratie céleste: recherches sur l'économie et la société de la Chine traditionelle*, as quoted in Landes, David (1999). *The Wealth and Poverty of Nations* (London: Abacus), 57. I have used 'bother' in place of Landes' 'harassment' as capturing better the sense of the French 'tracasserie'.

26. See Peyrefitte, Alain (1992). *The Immobile Empire* (New York: Knopf); Hall, John A. (1985). *Powers and Liberties: The Causes and Consequences of the Rise of the West* (Oxford: Oxford University Press); and, for a version tainted only slightly by free market ideology, Landes, *The Wealth and Poverty of Nations*, 335–49.

27. For some historians, economic activity was the defining characteristic of the Roman Empire in the late first and second centuries: See, for example, Rostovtzeff, Mikhail I. (1971). *A History of the Ancient World, Volume II—Rome* (Westport, CT: Greenwood). Contemporary views downplay the importance of the economic as against the political and military aspects of Roman society, and emphasize that for all its advances the society was not like a modern one, but they do not change the overall picture of a society of relatively free enterprise and general prosperity: see (2000). *The Cambridge Ancient History Volume XI* (Cambridge: Cambridge University Press), 736–40.

28. See Boxer, Charles R. (1990). *The Dutch Seaborne Empire*, 1600–1800 (London: Penguin); Braudel, Fernand (1982). *Civilization and Capitalism, 15th–18th Century. Volume II: The Wheels of Commerce* (London: Collins). The most vivid account of Dutch business and society in the fifteenth century is to be found not in a formal history, but in the work of an (exceptionally scholarly and historically reliable) historical novelist: Dorothy Dunnett's *House of Niccolo* series.

29. Quoted by Porter, Roy (1991). *English Society in the Eighteenth Century* (London: Penguin), 186.

30. See Porter, Roy *English Society in the Eighteenth Century*; idem (2000). *Enlightenment: Britain and the Making of the Modern World* (London: Penguin); Berg, Maxine (1994). *The Age of Manufactures, 1700–1820: Industry, Innovation and Work in Britain* (London: Routledge); and, for the origins of consumerism, Weatherill, Lorna (1996). *Consumer Behaviour and Material Culture in Britain, 1660–1760*, 2nd edn. (London: Routledge); McKendrick, Neil, Brewer, John, and Plumb, J. H. (1982). *The Birth of a Consumer Society: The Commericalisation of Eighteenth Century England* (London: Europa); and Brewer, John and Porter, Roy (eds.). (1993). *Consumption and the World of Goods* (London: Routledge).

31. The best account of this collapse is still Gibbon, Edward (1994). *The History of the Decline and Fall of the Roman Empire* (London: Penguin).

32. For the decline of Holland see Israel, Jonathan I. (1995). *The Dutch Republic: Its Rise, Greatness, and Fall*, 1487–1806 (Oxford: Clarendon Press); and Aymard, Maurice (ed.) (1982). *Dutch Capitalism and World Capitalism* (Cambridge: Cambridge University Press); for England see Christie, Ian R. (1984). *Stress and Stability in Late Eighteenth*

*Century Britain* (Oxford: Clarendon Press); Evans, Eric J. (1983). *The Forging of the Modern State: Early Industrial Britain*, 1783–1870 (London: Longman); and Thompson, F. M. L. (2001). *Gentrification and the Enterprise Culture: Britain 1780–1980* (Oxford: Oxford University Press).

33. Most large societies also harbour sects, but while they can be problematic these are of limited significance. The reason they can be problematic is because the strong group demands of sect membership can destabilize other institutions of which people are, perforce, members. In a civilized society it can be difficult for sects to isolate themselves completely from other groupings. Their members are subject to the laws of the land and may, for example, be conscripted into the army. They may also need to earn a living and end up working in hierarchical organizations. In either case their rejection of the authority structure of the hierarchy means that their commitment to its processes cannot be relied upon, and their presence makes the system vulnerable to malfunction as well as open to the intrusion of subversive ideas. Similarly, in a market context the presence of sect members, for whom allegiance to the sect is paramount, can subvert the principles of open markets and free bargaining on which society depends. To some extent, however, this allegiance ensures that the interactions between sects and other cultural forms are self-limiting. So, as we noted earlier, is their size. The result is that they tend to be a marginal nuisance, rather than a serious concern.

34. We might also include scientists and inventors, but for our purposes here they can be considered as a subset of artists.

35. On China see Balazs, *La Bureaucratie Céleste*; on the Soviet Union see McCauley, Martin (1993). *The Soviet Union, 1917–1991* (London: Longman).

36. Redondi, Pietro (1988). *Galileo Heretic* (London: Penguin), provides a penetrating analysis of the way in which Galileo's works threatened the stability of the culture in which he lived.

37. This is particularly apparent in the case of the Jews, but is historically much more widespread. In the early sixteenth century, for example, England allowed the immigration of persecuted religious minorities from the continent, but required that the immigrants live in specified districts and restricted their activities to specified trades: see Cunningham, William (1969). *Alien Immigrants in England* (London: Cass). It was also until recently commonplace for travellers to more rigidly structured societies to be required to stay in specific areas or hotels, and to be allowed to travel only with an official escort.

38. Durkheim, Emile (1996). *Professional Ethics and Civil Morals* (London: Routledge), quote from p. 10.

39. See (1992). *The Cambridge Ancient History, Volume V* (Cambridge: Cambridge University Press), 287–305; and Whitehead, David (1977). *The Ideology of the Athenian Metic* (Cambridge: Cambridge Philosophical Society).

40. On usury see Nelson, Benjamin (1949). *The Idea of Usury, from Tribal Brotherhood to Universal Otherhood* (Princeton: Princeton University Press); and, for an insightful study based around the English Usury Statute in the late sixteenth and early seventeenth centuries, Jones, Norman (1989). *God and the Moneylenders: Usury and Law in Early Modern England* (Oxford: Blackwell). In modern times usury has become acceptable in Christian societies, but it is still forbidden by Islamic law, so in modern Islamic states it is often the Christians who are the moneylenders.

41. See Landes, *The Wealth and Poverty of Nations*, for detailed references to early European imperialism, capitalism, and the slave trade.

42. This account is based on those offered by Hall, *Powers and Liberties*; and Mann, Michael (1986). *The Sources of Social Power. Volume 1: A History of Power from the*

*Beginning to 1760* A.D. (Cambridge: Cambridge University Press); see also Bechler, Jean (1975). *The Origins of Capitalism* (Oxford: Oxford University Press); Jones, Eric L. (1981). *The European Miracle: Environments, Economies and Geopolitics in the History of Europe and Asia* (Cambridge: Cambridge University Press); and, for a range of interpretations, Bechler, Jean, Hall, John A., and Mann, Michael (eds.) (1988). *Europe and the Rise of Capitalism* (Oxford: Basil Blackwell).

43. Landes, *The Wealth and Poverty of Nations*, 42.
44. Mackenney, Richard (1987). *Tradesmen and Traders: the World of the Guilds in Venice and Europe c.1250–c.1650* (London: Croom Helm). On monetarization see Kaye, Joel (1998). *Economy and Nature in the Fourteenth Century: Money, Market Exchange and the Emergence of Scientific Thought* (Cambridge: Cambridge University Press).
45. See Bonney, *Economics Systems* and *Rise of the Fiscal State*. For the early modern period see also Neal, Larry (1990). *The Rise of Financial Capitalism: International Capital Markets in the Age of Reason* (Cambridge: Cambridge University Press).
46. Boxer, *The Dutch Seaborne Empire*; Masselman, George (1963). *The Cradle of Colonialism* (New Haven: Yale University Press); Chaudhuri, K. N. (1978). *The Trading World of Asia and the English East India Company, 1660–1760* (Cambridge: Cambridge University Press); Landes, *The Wealth and Poverty of Nations*.
47. Neal, *Rise of Financial Capitalism*.
48. The story of the Royal African Company is a fascinating one from all sorts of perspectives. It is told in Kiern, Tim (1995). 'Monopoly, economic thought and the Royal African company', in John Brewer and Susan Staves (eds.), *Early Modern Conceptions of Property* (London: Routledge), 427–66.
49. See Michie, Ranald C. (1999). *The London Stock Exchange: A History* (Oxford: Oxford University Press); Ferguson, *Cash Nexus*.
50. Ferguson, *Cash Nexus*, 113–20.
51. This section is based heavily on Porter, *English Society in the Eighteenth Century*.
52. Ibid., 258.
53. Smith, Adam (1976). *The Wealth of Nations* (Oxford: Oxford University Press), 26.
54. Smith, Adam (1976). *The Theory of Moral Sentiments* (Oxford: Oxford University Press), 308; Bernard Mandeville, (1970). *The Fable of the Bees, or, Private Vices, Public Benefits* (Harmondsworth: Penguin).
55. For good treatments of Smith's writing see Werhane, Patricia (1991). *Adam Smith and his Legacy for Modern Capitalism* (Oxford: Oxford University Press); Fitzgibbons, Athol (1995). *Adam Smith's System of Liberty, Wealth and Virtue: The Moral and Political Foundations of The Wealth of Nations* (Oxford: Clarendon Press); Griswold, Charles L. (1999). *Adam Smith and Virtues of Enlightenment* (Cambridge: Cambridge University Press); and Rothschild, Emma (2001). *Economic Sentiments: Adam Smith, Condorcet and the Enlightenment* (Cambridge, MA: Harvard University Press).
56. The quotation is from the introduction to Balzac's *Scènes de la Vie Parisienne*, quoted in Fanger's translation by Sennett, *The Fall of Public Man*, 158.
57. Marx, Karl and Engels, Friedrich (1998). *The Communist Manifesto* (Oxford: Oxford University Press), originally published in German in 1848.
58. The shock spurred him to write. *The Way we Live Now*, published in 1875; see John Sutherland's (1982) introduction to the *World's Classics* edition (Oxford: Oxford University Press). The world of finance and its excesses was also the subject of Emile Zola's novel *L'Argent*.
59. For discussions of nineteenth century morality from three very different perspectives see Sennett, *The Fall of Public Man*; Himmelfarb, Gertrude (1991). *Poverty and Compassion: The Moral Imagination of the Late Victorians*

(New York: Knopf); idem (1995). *The De-Moralization of Society* (New York: Alfred Knopf); and Foucault, Michel (1990). *The History of Sexuality, Volume 1: The Will to Knowledge* (London: Penguin); see also Thompson, F. M. L. (1988). *The Rise of Respectable Society: A Social History of Victorian Britain, 1830–1900* (London: Fontana) and *Gentrification and the Enterprise Culture*. To rely on novelists to give an accurate portrayal of social values and practices, as Sennett to some extent relies on Balzac, is precarious at best, but when reviewing business it is especially so. Novelists and business practitioners live in very different worlds, and this is reflected in the scarcity of business references in literature. Geoffrey Carnall, reviewing representations of business in early nineteenth-century English literature, refers to the 'sheer invisibility of serious business activity in the literature'. There are more references later in the century but they are still caricatured, inconclusive, and relatively rare. Businessmen appear both as moral heroes and as moral villains, but the prevailing attitudes to and of business remain elusive. See Pollard, Arthur (ed.) (2000). *The Representation of Business in English Literature* (London: Institute of Economic Affairs), quote by Carnall on p. 48.

60. See, for example, Spencer, Herbert (1851/1996). *Social Statics* (London, Routledge), and *idem* (1879/1996). *The Data of Ethics* (London: Routledge).
61. Spencer, *The Data of Ethics*, 187 *ff.* and 210–16.
62. Note 50 above.
63. Durkheim, *Professional Ethics and Civil Morals*.
64. Cottrell, P. L. (1980). *Industrial Finance, 1830–1914: The Finance and Organisation of English Manufacturing Industry*. (London: Methuen); Michie, *London Stock Exchange*.
65. Geisst, Charles R. (1997). *Wall Street* (New York: Oxford University Press).
66. For the history of this process see Chandler, Alfred D. (1977). *The Visible Hand: The Managerial Revolution in American Business* (Cambridge, MA: Harvard University Press) and (1962). *Strategy and Structure* (Cambridge, MA: MIT Press); Chandler, Alfred D. and Daems, Herman (eds.) (1980). *Managerial Hierarchies* (Cambridge, MA: Harvard University Press); and Channon, Derek (1973). *The Strategy and Structure of British Enterprise* (Boston: Harvard Business School).
67. Dalton, Melville (1959). *Men who Manage: Fusions of Feeling and Theory in Administration* (New York: Wiley). Dalton observed three factories and one department store, but his main insights came from the factories.
68. Jackall, Robert (1988). *Moral Mazes: The World of Corporate Managers* (New York: Oxford University Press).
69. The quotation actually appeared twice on the book and once on the dust jacket: Jackall, *Moral Mazes*, 6, 109.
70. For the history of financial markets see Michie, *The London Stock Exchange*; Ferguson, *Cash Nexus*; Geisst, *Wall Street*. For American labour market regulation see Kaufman, Allen, Zacharias, Lawrence, and Karson, Marvin (1995). *Managers vs. Owners: The Struggle for Corporate Control in American Democracy*.
71. Luttwak, Edward (1998). *Turbo-Capitalism: Winners and Losers in the Global Economy* (London: Weidenfeld & Nicolson), 27 *ff.*

# CHAPTER 3

1. This section draws heavily on Cottrell, P. L. (1980). *Industrial Finance 1830–1914: The Finance and Organisation of English Manufacturing Industry* (London: Methuen); and also on Mathias, Peter and Postan, M. M. (eds.) (1978). *The Cambridge Economic*

*History of Europe, Volume VII. The Industrial Economies: Capital, Labour and Enterprise* (in two parts) (Cambridge: Cambridge University Press). There was a third form of business, the incorporated company. Originally designed to get around the Bubble Act, this was a form of large partnership established under trust deeds, which allowed some private trading of partnership shares and while bearing unlimited liability afforded some protection to individual partners. It seems to have been used mainly for community-based ventures such as insurance and utilities companies, which did not receive charters but which were able to attract relatively large numbers of local investors.

2. See Mathias and Postan, *The Industrial Economies, Part I (Britain, France, Germany and Scandinavia)*.

3. For the early development of business regulation in America see Nelson, William E. (1982). *The Roots of American Bureaucracy, 1830–1900* (Cambridge, MA: Harvard University Press); and Mathias and Postan, *The Industrial Economies, Part II*.

4. For the history and culture of Wall Street see Geisst, Charles R. (1997). *Wall Street: A History* (New York: Oxford University Press: *The World's Banker 1849–1998 (New York: Penguin)*); see also Carosso, Vincent (1970). *Investment Banking in America* (Cambridge, MA: Harvard University Press); for the City of London see Kynaston, David (1994). *The City of London. Volume I: A World of its Own, 1815–1890* (London: Chatto & Windus) and (1997). *Volume 2: Golden Years, 1890–1914*; Michie, Ranald C. (1999). *The London Stock Exchange: A History* (Oxford: Oxford University Press). There are also histories of most of the individual banking houses: see, for example, Ferguson, Niall (1998). *The House of Rothschild*.

5. See Bratton, Walter J. Jr. (1994). 'The new economic theory of the firm: critical perspectives from history' in S. Wheeler (ed.), *The Law of Business Enterprise* (New York: Oxford University Press); Hurst, James W. (1970). *The Legitimacy of the Business Corporation in the Law of the United States 1780–1970* (Charleston: University Press of Virginia); Payne, Peter L. 'Industrial entrepreneurship and management in Great Britain' in Mathias and Postan, *The Industrial Economies, Part I*, 180–230 and 664–89.

6. Cottrell, *Industrial Finance*, 45 *ff*.

7. About ten years before the Union Pacific scandal became public, in the early 1860s, not long before he was assassinated, Abraham Lincoln observed that 'Corporations have been enthroned . . . An era of corruption in high places will follow and the money power will endeavour to prolong its reign by working on the prejudices of the people . . . until wealth is aggregated in a few hands . . .' In the short term, at least, he was right on all counts. The observation is quoted by Wasserman, Henry (1983). *America Born and Reborn* (New York: Collier), 89; and again by Korten, David C. (1995). *When Corporations Rule the World* (London: Earthscan), 58.

8. Geisst, *Wall Street*, 66 *ff*.

9. See Hurst, *The Legitimacy of the Business Corporation*; George, Peter (1982). *The Emergence of Industrial America: Strategic Factors in American Economic Growth since 1870* (Albany: SUNY Press); Chandler, Alfred D. (1977). *The Visible Hand: The Managerial Revolution in American Business* (Cambridge, MA: Harvard University Press).

10. See Fohlen, Claude, 'Entrepreneurship and management in France in the nineteenth century', in Mathias and Postan, *The Industrial Economies, Part I*, 347–81; and Kocka Jürgen, T. R., 'Entrepreneurs and managers in German industrialization', ibid., 492–89.

11. Remember that the egalitarianism of the sect is bounded by the membership of the sect; in American culture we find both a belief in the equality of all men (where, as in

the Constitution, egalitarianism becomes merged with hierarchical obligation) and a belief in the equality of some men (e.g. whites, or protestants, or Mormons).

12. Chandler, *Visible Hand*; and see also Lazonick, William (1991). *Business Organization and the Myth of the Market Economy* (Cambridge: Cambridge University Press). In order to get around state incorporation laws prohibiting one company from holding shares in another, the mergers were initially organized as 'trusts' in which companies effectively pooled their interests to gain scale and monopoly advantages. Later, as state laws were relaxed, they were organized as holding companies, and later still as fully integrated companies, but the term trust continued to be used to describe a monopoly, hence the American term 'anti-trust' for monopolies and mergers legislation.

13. Geisst, *Wall Street*; Roe, Mark J. (1994). *Strong Managers, Weak Owners: The Political Roots of American Corporate Finance* (Princeton: Princeton University Press). Roe suggests that the limitations imposed on commercial banks were themselves rooted in local politics, as proprietors influenced legislatures to protect their local monopoly positions. For a slightly different interpretation see Coffee, John C. Jr. (2001). 'The rise of dispersed ownership: the roles of law and the state in the separation of ownership and control', *Yale Law Journal*, 111, 1–78.

14. Roe, Mark J. (1997). 'The political roots of American corporate finance', *Journal of Applied Corporate Finance*, 9(4), 8–22; see also Chandler, *Visible Hand*; Roe, *Strong Managers, Weak Owners*; Coffee, 'The rise of dispersed ownership'; Berle, Adolf A. Jr and Means, Gardiner C. (1932). *The Modern Corporation and Private Property* (New York: Macmillan). The corporation with diversified share ownership is often referred to by scholars as a Berle–Means corporation, following their classic analysis.

15. The rate of change of British business has been hotly debated. See, for example, Hannah, Leslie (1976). *The Rise of the Corporate Economy*, 2nd edn (London: Macmillan); Kennedy, William P. (1994). *Industrial Structure, Capital Markets and the Origins of British Economic Decline* (Cambridge: Cambridge University Press); Chandler, Alfred D. (1976). 'The development of the modern management structure in the US and the UK', in Leslie Hannah (ed.), *Management Strategy and Business Development: An Historical and Comparative Analysis* (London: Macmillan), 24–51; Scott, John (1990). 'Corporate control and corporate rule: Britain in an international perspective', *British Journal of Sociology*, 41, 351–73; van Helten, Jean-Jacques and Cassis, Youssef (eds.) (1990). *Capitalism in a Mature Economy: Financial Institutions, Capital Exports and British Industry, 1870–1939* (Aldershot: Gower). For current data on ownership structures internationally see Porta, Rafael L., Lopez-de-Silanes, Florencio, and Shleifer, Andrei (1999). 'Corporate ownership around the world', *Journal of Finance*, 54, 471–517.

16. See Scott, John (1997). *Corporate Business and Capitalist Classes* (Oxford: Oxford University Press); Charkham, Jonathan (1994). *Keeping Good Company: A Study of Corporate Governance in Five Countries* (Oxford: Oxford University Press); Coffee, 'The rise of dispersed ownership'.

17. Coffee, 'The rise of dispersed ownership'.

18. Geisst, *Wall Street*; Chandler, Alfred D. (1962). *Strategy and Structure* (Cambridge, MA: MIT Press).

19. Chandler, 'Development of Modern Management structure'; Kennedy, *Industrial Structure*; Wiener, Martin J. (1981). *English Culture and the Decline of the Industrial Spirit, 1850–1980* (Cambridge: Cambridge University Press).

20. Hurst, *Legitimacy of the Business Corporation*.

21. Robertson, Ross M. and Walton, Gary M. (1979). *History of the American Economy* (New York: Harcourt Brace Jovanovich).

22. Hurst, *Legitimacy of the Business Corporation*; Wasserman, *American Born and Reborn*; Grossman, Richard L. and Adams, Frank T. (1993). *Taking Care of Business: Citizenship and the Charter of Incorporation* (Cambridge, MA: Charter).

23. Berle and Means, *Modern Corporation*; Berle, Adolf A. Jr. (1931). 'Corporate powers as powers in trust', *Harvard Law Review*, 44, 1049 and (1932). 'For whom are corporate managers trustees: A note', *Harvard Law Review*, 45, 1365–72.

24. Dodd, E. Merrick Jr. (1932). 'For whom are corporate managers trustees?', *Harvard Law Review*, 45, 1145–63.

25. Some business ethicists have sought to demonstrate that the corporation *is* a moral person, but their logical demonstrations fall apart in the face of Lord Thurlow's common sense observation. See, for example, French, Peter (1979). 'The corporation as a moral person', *American Philosophical Quarterly*, 16, 207–15.

26. Poynder, J. (ed.) (1884). *Literary Extracts*, vol. 1 (New York), 268.

27. This is not to deny that that there are people even in England who break the law with impunity and get away with it. But they do this through corruption, whereas companies can do it openly and legitimately.

28. We should also note that while social attitudes change relatively slowly, the rise of big business through the merger wave of 1895–1905 happened extraordinarily quickly.

29. Marchand, Roland (1998). *Creating the Corporate Soul: The Rise of Public Relations and Corporate Imagery in American Big Business* (Berkeley: University of California Press). The Heinz advertisement is shown on p. 35. For Cadburys see Dellheim, Charles (1987). 'The creation of a company culture: Cadburys, 1861–1931', *American Historical Review*, 92, 13–44.

30. Marchand, *Creating the Corporate Soul*, gives a superb scholarly account of American public relations in the first half of the twentieth century.

31. For other stories of corporations presenting public images directly opposed to reality see Hawken, Paul (1993). *The Ecology of Commerce: A Declaration of Sustainability* (New York: Harper).

32. Korten, David C. (1995). *When Corporations Rule the World* (London: Earthscan), 152–3.

33. For classical critical studies see Marcuse, Herbert (1961, 1994). *One Dimensional Man. Studies in the Ideology of Advanced Industrial Society* (London: Routledge); Fromm, Erich (1978). *To Have or to Be* (New York: Jonathan Cape).

34. Or do not normally have. In the 2001 New York mayoral election the winning candidate was reported to have spent $68 million, nearly $10 per registered voter, of his own money.

35. Ferguson, Niall (2001). *The Cash Nexus: Money and Power in the Modern World, 1700–2000* (London: Penguin), 265; Hertz, Noreena (2001). *The Silent Takeover* (London: Heinemann), 120.

36. Hertz, *The Silent Takeover*, 109 ff.

37. Ibid., 124.

38. See, for example, Bryce, Robert (2002). *Pipe Dreams: Greed, Ego, Jealousy, and the Death of Enron* (London: Public Affairs); and Fox, Loren (2002). *The Rise and Fall of Enron* (New York: Wiley).

39. Monbiot, George (2000). *Captive State* (London: Macmillan).

40. For a careful sociological analysis of the political activities of business in the 1960s and 1970s see Useem, Michael (1984). *The Inner Circle: Large Corporations and the Rise of Business Political Activity in the US and UK* (Oxford: Oxford University Press). For more recent, more general, and somewhat less objective accounts see, for example, Korten, *When Corporations Rule the World*; Megalli, Mark and

Friedman, Andy (1991). *Masks of Deception: Corporate Front Groups in America* (Washington, DC: Essential Information); Alliance for Justice (1993). *Justice for Sale* (Washington, DC: Alliance for Justice); Greider, William (1992). *Who Will Tell the People? The Betrayal of American Democracy* (New York: Simon and Schuster); Schiller, Herbert I. (1996). 'Information deprivation in an information-rich society', in George Gerbner, Hamid Mowlana, and Herbert I. Schiller (eds.), *Invisible Crises: What Conglomerate Control of Media means for America and the World* (Boulder: Westview).

41. For a comprehensive study of the industry and its campaigns see Miles, Robert H. and Cameron, Kim S. (1982). *Coffin Nails and Corporate Strategy* (Englewood Cliffs, NJ: Prentice Hall). Information on the companies' research findings first came out during court cases in the early 1990s. See Zitkin, Richard and Langford, Carol M. (1999). *The Moral Compass of the American Lawyer* (Ballantine); see also Levin, Myron (1998). 'Years of immunity and arrogance up in smoke', *Los Angeles Times*, 10 May.

42. See, for example, Pollard, Sidney (1984). *The Wasting of the British Economy* (London: Croom Helm). See also Wiener, *English Culture* and, for a counter view, Thompson, F. M. L. (2001). *Gentrification and the Enterprise Culture: Britain, 1780–1980* (Oxford: Oxford University Press).

43. See, for example, the case studies in Monbiot, *Captive State*.

44. At the time of writing, fifteen of the UK top 100 companies are the products of the 1980s and 1990s privatization process.

45. The PFI also seems to have created considerable scope for political influence, and for practices not far removed from corruption. See Monbiot, *Captive State*.

46. See Monbiot, *Captive State*, 332 *ff.* Examples from America include the American Coal Federation teaching pack maintaining 'the earth could benefit rather than be harmed from increased carbon dioxide' and a Mobil Corporation pack on freedom of the press suggesting that the First Amendment guaranteed free market capitalism. In Britain a pack provided by British Nuclear Fuels contains the marvellous teaching point: 'Accidents happen all the time. Can you think of some accidents that have happened in school . . .'

47. Luttwak, Edward (1998). *Turbo-Capitalism: Winners and Losers in the Global Economy* (London: Weidenfeld & Nicolson). For a detailed account of the employment legislation that was at the heart of the British changes see Davies, Paul and Freedland, Mark (1993). *Labour Legislation and Public Policy* (Oxford: Oxford University Press).

48. For analyses of the relative power of global corporations and nation states see Strange, Susan (1996). *The Retreat of the State: The Diffusion of Power in the World Economy* (Cambridge: Cambridge University Press), and Hertz, *The Silent Takeover*. The issues surrounding globalization are, however, contentious. They will be reviewed later in the book.

49. Data collated from UN and World Bank publications.

50. Korten, *When Corporations Rule the World*, quote from p. 12.

51. Korten, *When Corporations Rule the World*; Stiglitz, Joseph E. (2002). *Globalization and its Discontents* (London: Penguin).

52. See, for example, Dollar, David and Collier, Paul (2001). *Globalization, Growth, and Poverty: Building an Inclusive World* (New York: Oxford University Press and World Bank). It would be fair to say that many of the economic researchers employed by the World Bank are both well aware of these measurement problems and careful not to claim more than their data allow. In doing their best to draw what conclusions they

can on the basis of what can be measured, however, they almost inevitably overemphasize the measurable. For further discussion of this problem see Chapter 4.

53. Stiglitz, *Globalization and its Discontents*.
54. Bales, Kevin (1999). *Disposable People: New Slavery in the Global Economy* (Berkeley: University of California Press).
55. Hendry, John (2000). 'Just do it—Nike in Asia', European Case Clearing House; see also Greider, William (1997). *One World, Ready or Not: The Manic Logic of Global Capitalism* (New York: Simon Schuster).
56. This story was documented in the 'Modern Times' series on BBC television, 1998.
57. *Washington Post*, 19 June 1994, pp. H1, H7.
58. See Monbiot, *Captive State*, and Stiglitz, *Globalization and its Discontents*.
59. See, for example, the *UNCTAD World Investment Report 2002* (United Nations).
60. Korten, *When Corporations Rule the World*, 12.
61. Kynaston, David (1999). *The City of London. Volume III: Illusions of Gold, 1914–1945* (London: Chatto & Windus) and (2001). *Volume IV: A Club no More, 1945–2000* (London: Chatto & Windus).
62. For America see Kaufman, Allen, Zacharias, Lawrence, and Karson, Marvin (1995). *Managers vs. Owners: The Struggle for Corporate Control in American Democracy* (New York: Oxford University Press); also Geisst, *Wall Street*; for Britain see Michie, *London Stock Exchange*; Kynaston, *The City of London IV*. Hostile takeover activity began to be a feature of the stock markets in the early 1960s and the phrase 'market for corporate control' was coined in 1965, but the aggressors then were business entrepreneurs building up conglomerates rather than the financial entrepreneurs who came to the fore in the 1980s.
63. Soros, George (1998). *The Crisis of Global Capitalism: Open Society Endangered* (London: Little Brown & Co).
64. Stiglitz, *Globalization and its Discontents*, 94 ff.
65. A story going the rounds in 1999 was of a young girl, the daughter of an investment banker, who came home from school one day with a mongrel puppy and a request that her father write out a cheque for £2,000, which was what she had agreed to pay for it. In response to the inevitable exclamations she explained that it was quite all right, because she anticipated a buyer at £2,500.
66. At the time of writing, in late 2002, the City is just beginning to feel the pinch, as the hedge fund market is becoming saturated and the business corporations are reigning in their advisory fees.
67. See Porta et al., 'Corporate ownership around the world'; Monks, Robert A. G. and Minow, Nell (2001). *Corporate Governance* 2nd edn. (Oxford: Blackwell); Lazonick, William and O'Sullivan, Mary (2000). 'Maximizing shareholder value: a new ideology for corporate governance', *Economy and Society*, 29, 13–35; and, for a detailed study of the rise of institutional shareholder activism, Useem, Michael (1996). *Investor capitalism: How Money Managers are Changing the Face of Corporate America* (New York: Basic Books). For the influence of shareholder capitalism in France and Germany see Morin, François (2000). 'A transformation in the French model of shareholding and management', and Jürgens, Ulrich, Naumann, Katrin, and Rupp, Joachim (2000). 'Shareholder value in an adverse environment: The German case', *Economy and Society*, 29, 36–53, and 54–79, respectively.

## CHAPTER 4

1. For a general history of economics and economists see Galbraith, John Kenneth (1987). *A History of Economics* (London: Hamish Hamilton); for the history of economic theory see Hodgson, Geoffrey (1988). *Institutions and Economics* (Cambridge: Polity).
2. See, for example, Friedman, Milton (1962). *Capitalism and Freedom* (Chicago: University of Chicago Press); Becker, Gary S. (1976). *The Economic Approach to Human Behavior* (Chicago: University of Chicago Press); Williamson, Oliver E. (1975). *Markets and Hierarchies* (New York: Free Press); and for alternative approaches Hodgson, *Institutions and Economics*; and Lazonick, William (1991). *Business Organization and the Myth of the Market Economy* (Cambridge: Cambridge University Press).
3. It is only fair to note that many institutional economists would disagree with this observation, in some cases quite strongly. They would agree, broadly speaking, with the characterization of the economic mindset that follows, but deny that it applies to them. In response I would say only that while many of them are indeed trying to break out of this mindset their attempts seem, at least from the perspective of an outsider looking in, to be markedly unsuccessful, both in terms of their influence and in terms of their achievement. A possible exception to this is Etzioni, Amitai (1988). *The Moral Dimension: Towards a New Economics* (New York: Free Press)—but then few economists would accept Etzioni as one of their own. Sen, Amartya (1986). *On Ethics and Economics* (Oxford: Basil Blackwell), has been more influential, but his critique is far more restricted.
4. For an authoritative account of contemporary economics see, for example, Milgrom, Paul and Roberts, John (1992). *Economics, Organization and Management* (Englewood Cliffs, NJ: Prentice Hall). I have analysed the linked assumptions of self-interest and rational competence in Hendry, John (2002). 'The principal's other problems: honest incompetence and the specification of contracts', *Academy of Management Review*, 27, 98–113.
5. See the discussion at the beginning of Chapter 2 and, for a review of the academic arguments here, Hendry, 'The principal's other problems'.
6. Marshall, Alfred (1920). *Principles of Economics*, 8th edn. (London: Macmillan), vol. 1, p. 1.
7. For a perceptive contemporary analysis see Galbraith, John Kenneth (1967). *The New Industrial State* (London: Hamish Hamilton).
8. See Ashcroft, Richard (1986). *Revolutionary Politics and Locke's Two Treatises of Government* (Princeton: Princeton University Press).
9. For a recent historical account of the role of property in American culture see Linklater, Andro (2002). *Measuring America: How the Greatest Land Sale in History Shaped the United States* (New York: HarperCollins).
10. I have intentionally used the male pronoun for economists, not because they are all men but because as Deirdre McCloskey has argued persuasively, many of their methods and assumptions do seem to be characteristically masculine. Professor McCloskey's insight came about rather unusually, as the experience of a gender change (she used to be called Donald) prompted her to relate what she had been uncomfortable about in herself to what she had been uncomfortable about in her academic discipline. See McCloskey, Deirdre (1997) 'Economists get out of the

sandpit now!', *The Times Higher*, 28 March, and McCloskey, Donald (1983). 'The rhetoric of economics', *Journal of Economic Literature*, 21, 481–517.

11. Coase, Ronald H. (1937). 'The nature of the firm', *Economica*, 4, 386–405; Schumpeter, Joseph (1939). *Business Cycles* (New York: McGraw Hill).

12. The classic study of market versus organizational forms is Williamson, *Markets and Hierarchies*. On the relationship between economic theory and reality see Lazonick, *Business Organization and the Myth of the Market Economy*. On the relationship between organizations and self-interest see Ghoshal, Sumantra and Moran, Peter (1996). 'Bad for practice: a critique of the transaction cost theory', *Academy of Management Review*, 21, 13–47.

13. See Coates, A. A. Bob (1993). *The Sociology and Professionalization of Economics, British and American Essays Volume II* (London: Routledge).

14. Escobar, Arturo (1995). *Encountering development: The Making and Unmaking of the Third World, 1945–1992* (Princeton: Princeton University Press).

15. Banerjee, Subhabrata Bobby (2003). 'Who sustains whose development? Sustainable development and the reinvention of nature', *Organization Studies*, 24, 143–80.

16. McNaghten, Phil and Urry, John (1998). *Contested Natures* (London: Sage).

17. Friedman, *Capitalism and Freedom*; and Friedman, Milton (1970). 'The social responsibility of business is to increase its profits', *New York Times*, 30 September. Like Smith and Spencer before him, Friedman is often misunderstood. He is quite clear of the view, for example, that laws and well-established norms should be honoured. But he also maintains unequivocally that while business people should operate within these basic constraints any kind of altruism is irresponsible.

18. *Columbia World Quotations*, 1996. On leaving a federal court the following year he still maintained that 'greed is alright—everybody should be a little bit greedy'.

19. Hoenig, Jonathan (1999). *Greed is Good: The Capitalist Pig Guide to Investing* (New York: Harper).

20. 'Greed: is it necessarily bad?', Princeton: Films for the Humanities and Sciences, FSH9251, 2000. The trickle down effect is often cited as a social justification for free market economic policies, but the evidence of America in the 1980s and 1990s suggests that this effect is a long-term one at best. In a period of considerable economic growth, while the rich got immensely richer, the poor and middling actually got poorer in real terms; see Galbraith, John Kenneth (1992). *The Culture of Contentment* (New York: Houghton Mifflin); and Luttwak, Edward (1998). *Turbo-Capitalism: Winners and Losers in the Global Economy* (London: Weidenfeld & Nicolson).

21. Luttwak, *Turbo-Capitalism*.

22. Wolfe, Alan (1989). *Whose Keeper? Social Science and Moral Obligation* (Berkeley: University of California Press), 29.

23. Galbraith, *Culture of Contentment*. As Galbraith and others noted, spending on welfare, health, and education declined in the 1980s, minimum wages failed to keep up with inflation, and the gap between rich and poor increased markedly. See, for example, Herzenberg, Stephen A., Alic, John A., and Wial, Howard (1998). *New Rules for a New Economy: Employment and Opportunity in Post-Industrial America* (New York: ILR Press).

24. See, for example, Postrel, Virginia (1998). *The Future and its Enemies: The Growing Conflict over Creativity, Enterprise and Progress* (New York: Free Press). This market populism, which is also present in a more subdued form in Britain, is described by Frank, Thomas (2000). *One Market Under God: Extreme Capitalism, Market Populism and the End of Economic Democracy* (New York: Doubleday). As the title suggests,

Franks seems somewhat paranoid about the phenomenon and his claims should not always be taken at face value. A judicious checking of his sources is strongly advised. The book is, nevertheless, valuable for drawing attention to what is a real tendency in contemporary thinking.

25. Cox, Harvey (1999). 'The market as God', *The Atlantic Monthly* (March), 18–23.

26. These data and others are collected by Putnam, Robert D. (2000). *Bowling Alone: The Collapse and Revival of American Community* (New York: Simon & Schuster), ch. 14.

27. Lyotard, Jean-François (1984). *The Postmodern Condition: A Report on Knowledge* (Manchester: Manchester University Press), 76.

28. Chandler, Alfred D. (1977). *The Visible Hand: The Managerial Revolution in American Business* (Cambridge, MA: Harvard University Press).

29. Chandler, Alfred D. (1962). *Strategy and Structure* (Cambridge, MA: MIT Press).

30. Douglas, Mary (1992). 'Muffled ears', in her *Risk and Blame: Essays in Cultural Theory* (London: Routledge).

31. Peters, Tom and Waterman, Richard (1982). *In Search of Excellence* (New York: Harper & Row).

32. Douglas, Mary (1996). *Natural Symbols: Explanations in Cosmology*, 3rd edn. (London: Routledge).

33. For discussions of the contradictions of the 'corporate culture' movement see Pascale, Richard T. (1985). 'The paradox of 'corporate culture': reconciling ourselves to socialization', *California Management Review*, 27, 26–41; Hendry, John and Hope, Veronica (1994). 'Cultural change and competitive performance', *European Management Journal*, 12, 401–6.

34. du Gay, Paul (1996). *Consumption and Identity at Work* (London: Sage), 56.

35. Richard Sennett, one of the most perceptive observers of the flexible economy, argues that what we are witnessing is a new form of bureaucracy rather than its replacement: Sennett, Richard (1998). *The Corrosion of Character* (New York: Norton). For a constructive critique of du Gay's arguments see Fournier, Valerie and Grey, Christopher (1999). 'Too much, too little and too often: a critique of du Gay's analysis of enterprise', *Organization*, 6, 107–28. For an argument to the effect that bureaucracy is the only way to manage large organizations see Jaques, Elliot (1990). 'In praise of hierarchy', *Harvard Business Review*, 68, January–February, 127–33.

36. Mary Douglas, 'The normative debate and the origins of culture' in her *Risk and Blame*.

37. Mintzberg, Henry (1996). 'Managing government, governing management', *Harvard Business Review*, 74, May–June, 75–83.

38. For positive accounts of these developments see Barzelay, Michael (2001). *The New Public Management* (Berkeley: University of California Press); Lane, Jan-Erik (2000). *New Public Management* (London: Routledge); for a critique see du Gay, Paul (1993). 'Entrepreneurial management in the public sector', *Work, Employment and Society*, 7, 643–8. A more balanced view is given in Ferlie, Ewan, Pettigrew, Andrew, Ashburner, Lynn, and Fitzgerald, Louise, *The New Public Management in Action* (Oxford: Oxford University Press, 1996).

39. Bourdieu, Pierre (1991). 'Political representation: elements for a theory of the political field', in his *Language and Symbolic Power* (Cambridge: Polity), 171–202, quote on p. 172. The market of politics is not, of course, a perfect one. The process of representation leads inexorably to an oligopoly structure, in which the behaviour of the consumer is characterized by an enforced brand loyalty, as she is effectively forced to use the same brand (party) for all products (issues).

40. Hertz, Noreena (2001). *The Silent Takeover* (London: Heinemann).
41. Bourdieu, 'Political representation'. Bourdieu's analysis suggests that outside times of crisis the power of the political elite to set the terms of the political agenda, independent of the concerns of the mass of people, is extreme. See also Deetz, Stanley (1992). *Democracy in an Age of Corporate Colonization* (Albany: SUNY Press).
42. Fevre, Ralph W. (2000). *The Demoralization of Western Culture: Social Theory and the Dilemmas of Modern Living* (London: Continuum).
43. Fevre, *Demoralization of Western Culture*, 18.
44. Ibid., 15.
45. Meštrović, Stjepan (1997). *Post-Emotional Society* (London: Sage).
46. For an excellent account of the role of witnesses in early modern science see Shapin, Steve (1994). *A Social History of Truth: Civility and Science in Seventeenth Century England* (Chicago: Chicago University Press).
47. Fevre, *Demoralization of Western Culture*, 56 *ff.*
48. Ibid., 207–8.

# CHAPTER 5

1. Fukuyama, Francis (1999). *The Great Disruption* (New York: Free Press), 5. As will become clear in Chapters 6 and 9 later, I disagree quite strongly with aspects of Fukuyama's interpretation of this Great Disruption, but his careful analysis of the statistical evidence is exemplary and I shall rely heavily on it in this section.
2. Himmelfarb, Gertrude (1995). *The De-Moralization of Society. From Victorian Virtues to Modern Values* (New York: Knopf).
3. *The Sunday Times*, 9 February 2003.
4. Luttwak, Edward (1998). *Turbo-Capitalism: Winners and Losers in the Global Economy* (London: Weidenfeld & Nicolson), 55.
5. On the other hand, the American figures cited owe much to the criminalization of cannabis possession (Luttwak, *Turbo-Capitalism*). Because of under-reporting to and by the police, changing priorities in law enforcement and changing definitions of what is or is not a criminal offence, crime statistics are notoriously difficult to interpret. However, the changes in the second half of the twentieth century are so enormous, and of such a different magnitude from anything that went before, that it is impossible to dismiss them. The UK figures given here are based on official statistics as reported in Himmelfarb, *De-Moralization of Society*. Fukuyama, *The Great Disruption*, gives figures for the period 1950–98 for both violent crimes and theft in fifteen different developed countries.
6. Figures for 1950 onwards from Fukuyama, *The Great Disruption*, and, for the earlier period, from Himmelfarb, *The De-Moralization of Society*.
7. Frank, Thomas (2000). *One Market Under God: Extreme Capitalism, Market Populism and the End of Economic Democracy* (New York: Doubleday), 6.
8. Fukuyama, *The Great Disruption*, 28.
9. These figures are cited in Hall, Peter A. (2002). 'Great Britain: The role of government and the distribution of social capital', in Robert D. Putnam (ed.), *Democracies in Flux. The Evolution of Social Capital in Contemporary Society* (New York: Oxford University Press), 21–58 on p. 46.

10. Putnam, Robert D. (2000). *Bowling Alone. The Collapse and Revival of American Community* (New York: Simon & Schuster), 134–47.

11. For discussions of a range of different countries see Putnam, *Democracies in Flux*.

12. On the Enlightenment project see Gay, Peter (1977). *The Enlightenment: An Interpretation. The Science of Freedom* (New York: Norton).

13. See Gay, *Enlightenment*; and MacIntyre, Alasdair (1988). *Whose Justice? Which Rationality* (London: Duckworth).

14. Kant, Immanuel, *Critique of Pure Reason* (orig. 1781, trans. ed. Norman Kemp Smith, London: Macmillan 1956) and *Critique of Practical Reason* (orig. 1788, trans. ed. Lewis White Beck, Indianapolis: Bobbs-Merrill, 1956). For Kant's moral philosophy in application see his *The Metaphysics of Morals* (orig. 1797, trans. ed. Mary Gregor, Cambridge: Cambridge University Press, 1991).

15. Beiser, Frederick C. (1987). *The Fate of Reason: German Philosophy from Kant to Fichte* (Cambridge, MA: Harvard University Press). Kant himself had strong religious beliefs, and his moral philosophy was predicated on a belief in God and immortality. See MacIntyre, Alasdair (1967). *A Short History of Ethics* (London: Routledge); and Sullivan, Roger J. (1989). *Immanuel Kant's Moral Theory* (Cambridge: Cambridge University Press).

16. See Schama, Simon (1989). *Citizens: A Chronicle of the French Revolution* (New York: Viking).

17. For discussion of liberal–communitarian differences see Delaney, C. F. (ed.) (1994). *The Liberalism-Communitarianism Debate* (Lanham, MD: Rowman & Littlefield); and, for particularly acute analyses of the assumptions of the rival camps, Taylor, Charles (1995). 'Cross-purposes: the liberal-communitarian debate', in his *Philosophical Arguments* (Cambridge, MA: Harvard University Press), 181–203; and Wolfe, Alan (1989). *Whose Keeper? Social Science and Moral Obligation* (Berkeley: University of California Press).

18. Gay, *Enlightenment*, 167 ff.

19. Interpreting 'official' figures for church membership or even for the census is a hazardous activity. For a summary of the figures see Evans, Eric J. (1983). *The Forging of the Modern State: Early Industrial Britain, 1783–1870* (London: Longman), and for a detailed analysis of the census, Snell, K. D. M. and Ell, Paul S. (2001). *Rival Jerusalems: The Geography of Victorian Religion* (Cambridge: Cambridge University Press).

20. The figure for those saying religion was important comes from a Pew Research Centre survey reported in *Prospect*, March 2003, p. 7.

21. See Putnam, *Democracies in Flux*, 409.

22. See note 20 above.

23. Putnam, *Bowling Alone*, 69 ff.

24. Worms, Jean-Pierre (2002). 'Old and new civic social ties in France', in Putnam, *Democracies in Flux*, 137–188, 179.

25. Jung, Carl Gustav (1988). 'Psychotherapists or the clergy', in his *Psychology and Western Religion* (London: Routledge), 195–216, 201.

26. For a well-balanced analysis of this issue see Ruse, Michael (2000). *Can a Darwinian be a Christian? The Relationship between Science and Religion* (Cambridge: Cambridge University Press).

27. See Giddens, Anthony (1994). *Beyond Left and Right: The Future of Radical Politics* (Cambridge: Polity).

28. For a discussion of changing perspectives of political probity and evidence of increasing disrespect for politicians see Ferguson, Niall (2001). *The Cash Nexus: Money*

*and Power in the Modern World, 1700–2000* (London: Penguin), 265–6. For more detailed statistics on a range of countries see Putnam, *Democracies in Flux.*

29. Gilligan, Carol (1982). *In a Different Voice: Psychological Theory and Women's Development* (Cambridge, MA: Harvard University Press); see also Noddings, Nel (1978). *Caring: A Feminine Approach to Ethics and Education* (Berkeley: University of California Press); and Koehn, Daryl (1998). *Rethinking Feminist Ethics: Care, Trust and Empathy* (London: Routledge). We should note here that feminist writers on ethics often see the institutions of hierarchical culture (bureaucracy, rules) as typically male (or at least part of the male subjugation of women) and so set themselves against these. The values advocated by these writers are, however, far more at odds with those of a market than with those of a hierarchy.

30. Powell, Arthur G., Farrar, Eleanor, and Cohen, David K. (1986). *The Shopping Mall High School* (Boston: Houghton Mifflin), 56, quoted in Wolfe, *Whose Keeper?*, 74.

31. For the hype (the Internet as source of world freedom, unlimited wealth creation, etc.) see, for example, *Wired,* January 1998; and for a harsh critique see Frank, *One Market Under God.*

32. UNCTAD (2002). *World Investment Report 2002* (Geneva: United Nations); idem (2001). *Trade and Development Report 2001* (Geneva: United Nations).

33. De George, Richard T. (1993). *Competing with Integrity in International Business* (New York: Oxford University Press).

34. For American figures see Putnam, *Bowling Alone, 222 ff.* For China see Lull, James (1991). *China Turned On: Television, Reform and Resistance* (London: Routledge). For global data see Herman, Edward and McChesney, Robert (1997). *The Global Media: The New Missionaries of Corporate Capitalism* (London: Cassell).

35. Bales, in a study of contemporary slavery in the developing world, reports families as selling their daughters into bonded labour as prostitutes in order to pay for television sets: Bales, Kevin (1999). *Disposable People: New Slavery in the Global Economy* (Berkeley: University of California Press). On the globalization of the media see Herman and McChesney, *The Global Media*; and Thompson, John B. (1995). *The Media and Modernity* (Cambridge: Polity).

36. In America, opinion polls have consistently shown around 80% of people saying that TV violence is harmful and favouring its regulation. Yet violence is what people watch. It sells well and it sells globally. Over half the major characters in prime time TV series are involved in violence, and heavy TV viewers are statistically more likely to overestimate the occurrence of violence in the real world. The reason for all this violence, of course, is that it holds people attention, which is good for advertising revenues. See Gerbner, George (1996). 'The hidden side of television violence'; and Bagdikian, Ben H. 'Brave new world minus 400', in George Gerbner, Hamid Mowlana, and Herbert I. Schiller (eds.), *Invisible Crises: What Conglomerate Control of Media Means for America and the World* (Boulder: Westview).

37. Stivers, Richard (1994). *The Culture of Cynicism* (Oxford: Blackwell), 139 *ff.* See also Meyrowitz, Joshua (1985). *No Sense of Place* (New York: Oxford University Press).

38. For the changing nature of armed conflict see Von Crefeld, Martin (1999). *The Rise and Decline of the State* (Cambridge: Cambridge University Press).

39. Baumgartner, M. P. (1988). *The Moral Order of a Suburb* (New York: Oxford University Press); Wolfe, Alan (1988). *One Nation After All* (New York: Viking).

40. Baumgartner, *Moral Order of a Suburb,* 127.

41. Ibid.; and see also Jackson, Kenneth T. (1985). *Crabgrass Frontier: The Suburbanization of the United States* (Oxford: Oxford University Press). These qualitative observations are reflected in statistics on political and community involvement, mobility, vehicle usage, etc. See Putnam, *Bowling Alone*, ch. 12 for a recent summary of the data.
42. Wolfe, *One Nation After All*, 4.
43. Ibid., 250 *ff.*

# CHAPTER 6

1. The image of the coin is not accidental. The two sides of a coin typically show the monarch's head, representing hierarchical authority, and a monetary value, representing market exchange.
2. Rorty, Richard (1998). *Contingency, Irony, and Solidarity* (Cambridge: Cambridge University Press).
3. For a substantial discussion of these issues and their possible outcomes see Galbraith, John Kenneth (1992). *The Culture of Contentment* (New York: Houghton Mifflin).
4. Fukuyama, Francis (1999). *The Great Disruption: Human Nature and the Reconstitution of Social Order* (New York: The Free Press).
5. Fukuyama, *The Great Disruption*, 250. At the time Fukuyama was writing, serious crime rates in New York and some other American cities were falling.
6. Ibid., 278–9.
7. Friedman, Milton (1962). *Capitalism and Freedom* (Chicago: University of Chicago Press) and (1970). 'The social responsibility of business is to increase its profits', *New York Times Magazine*, September 13, 32–3, quotation from p. 32.
8. Barry, Norman (2001), 'Ethics, conventions and capitalism', in Brian Griffiths, Robert A. Sirico, Norman Barry, and Frank Field (eds.), *Capitalism, Morality and Markets* (London: IEA), 57–77, 77.
9. Ibid., 60.
10. Novak, Michael (1998). 'The crisis of social democracy', in Michael Novak and others, *Is There a Third Way? Essays on the Changing Direction of Socialist Thought* (London: IEA), 1–22; Bork, R. (1996). *Slouching toward Gommorah* (New York: Harper Collins).
11. Himmelfarb, Gertrude (1995). *The De-moralization of Society. From Victorian Virtues to Modern Values* (New York: Knopf), 125 *ff.*
12. Emerson, Ralph Waldo (1983). *Essays and Lectures* (New York: Library of America).
13. See Himmelfarb, *The De-Moralization of Society*.
14. Ibid., 252.
15. Ibid., 241.
16. Ibid., 240.
17. Novak, 'The crisis of social democracy', quotation from p. 11.
18. Kristol, Irving (1997). 'The spiritual crisis of the welfare state', *Wall Street Journal*, 3 February.
19. Or, their opponents might say, by economic thinking, with its emphasis on short-term monetary benefits.
20. Sirico, Robert A. (2001). 'The culture of virtue, the culture of the market', in Griffiths et al. (eds). *Capitalism, Morality and Markets*, 41–56.

21. See Wolfe, Alan (1987). *Whose Keeper? Social Science and Moral Obligation* (Berkeley: University of California Press), 108.

22. Stivers, Richard (1994). *The Culture of Cynicism. American Morality in Decline* (Oxford: Blackwell), 175.

23. Korten, David C. (1995). *When Corporations Rule the World* (London: Earthscan).

24. Stivers, *Culture of Cynicism*.

25. Ibid., 9.

26. Ibid., p. ix.

27. Bauman, Zygmunt (1990). 'Effacing the face: on the social management of moral proximity', *Theory, Culture and Society*, 7, 5–38, quotation from p. 34.

28. Bauman, Zygmunt (1989). *Modernity and the Holocaust* (Cambridge: Polity), 28, italicized in original.

29. Ibid., 160, italicized in original.

30. Stivers, *Culture of Cynicism*, 103.

31. Ibid., 181.

32. Keith Tester, *Moral Culture* (London: Sage, 1997).

33. Ibid., 18.

34. Ignatieff, Michael (1995). 'The seductiveness of moral disgust', *Social Research*, 62, 77–97.

35. See Veblen, Thorstein (1953). *The Theory of the Leisure Class: An Economic Study of Institutions* (New York: Mentor Books).

36. Marcuse, Herbert (1961, 1994). *One Dimensional Man: Studies in the Ideology of Advanced Industrial Society* (London: Routledge).

37. Tester, *Moral Culture*, 5.

38. As will be apparent, this position of Tester's seems to me to be disingenuous. If we are to understand the situation we are in, then we must indeed try to keep our analysis separate from our preferences. Here, the free market proponents of a return to Christianity evidently fall down. But quite apart from the fact that an objective view of human affairs is, in the end, impossible, there is little point in providing a description if we are not prepared to act on it. In the grand scheme of things the suggestions of one person (especially, one might say, of an academic!) may make very little difference to the world, but that is no excuse for not trying.

39. Bauman, Zygmunt (1993). *Postmodern Ethics* (Oxford: Blackwell), 247–8.

40. MacIntyre, Alasdair (1985). *After Virtue: A Study in Moral Theory*, 2nd edn. (London: Duckworth) and (1990). *Whose Justice? Which Rationality?* (London: Duckworth).

41. Fevre, Ralph W. (2000). *The Demoralization of Western Culture: Social Theory and the Dilemmas of Modern Living* (London: Continuum).

42. Paul du Gay has recently elaborated an argument opposed to that of Baumann and Stivers, associating ethics with bureaucracy and attributing a demoralization of contemporary work, especially in the public sector, to a replacement of bureaucratic by enterprise cultures: du Gay, Paul (2000). *In Praise of Bureaucracy* (London: Sage). In some respects du Gay's analysis is very much in line with my own general argument for an association of traditional concepts of moral obligation with a hierarchical as opposed to a market culture. However, his defence of the morality of bureaucracy appears to suffer from much the same problems as his earlier attack on enterprise, discussed in Chapter 4 earlier, as theoretical commitments overshadow empirical reality and the shades of grey that characterize all human activity become lost in an argument that recognizes only black and white.

43. Sennett, Richard (1977). *The Fall of Public Man* (New York: Knopf ). It should be noted that Sennett's analysis in this book is rich and multifaceted, and the use I have made of it here does not begin to do it justice.

44. Sennett, (1993). *Fall of Public Man*, 263.

45. Bellah, Robert, Madsen, Richard, Sullivan, William M., Swidler, Ann, and Tipton, Steven M. (1985). *Habits of the Heart: Individualism and Commitment in American Life* (Berkeley: University of California Press).

46. Bellah et al., *Habits of the Heart*, 102.

47. Other research suggests that this tension is highly gendered, in that while women tend to see love and marriage as, ideally, empathetic, based on a sharing of selves, men are much less inclined to share their feelings. In contemporary society, however, both sexes seem to see marriage primarily as meeting their particular psychological (and in men's case sexual) needs, and only secondarily as a social arrangement. See, for example, Duncombe, Jean and Marsden, Dennis (1993). 'Love and intimacy: the gender division of emotion and "emotion work": a neglected aspect of sociological discussion of heterosexual relationships', *Sociology*, 27, 221–41.

48. For a parallel analysis of changing measures of 'success' in American life see Stivers, *Culture of Cynicism*, 21–2.

49. Sennett, Richard and Cobb, Jonathan (1972). *The Hidden Injuries of Class* (New York: Knopf).

50. Sennett, Richard (1998). *The Corrosion of Character* (New York: Norton).

51. Fromm, Erich (1976). *To Have or to Be?* (New York: Harper & Row).

52. Ibid., 36.

53. For explorations of these issues see, for example, Miles, Steven (1998). *Consumerism as a Way of Life* (London: Sage); Edgell, Stephen, Hetherington, Kevin, and Warde, Alan (eds.) (1996). *Consumption Matters: The Production and Experience of Consumption* (Oxford: Blackwell); Barnard, Malcolm (1996). *Fashion as Communication* (London: Routledge); and Davis, Fred (1992). *Fashion, Culture and Identity* (Chicago: Chicago University Press).

54. Finch, Janet and Mason, Jennifer (1993). *Negotiating Family Responsibilities* (London: Routledge). For similar evidence from America see Kornhaber, Arthur (1985). 'Grandparenthood and the "New Social Contract" ', in Vern L. Bengton and Joan F. Robertson (eds.), *Grandparenthood* (Beverley Hills: Sage).

55. See, for example, Giddens, Anthony (1984). *The Constitution of Society* (Cambridge: Polity, 1984); Bourdieu, Pierre (1990). *The Logic of Practice* (Cambridge: Polity). The idea that morality, in particular, is essentially habitual goes back to the pragmatist philosophy of John Dewey.

# CHAPTER 7

1. MacIntyre, Alasdair (1985). *After Virtue: A Study in Moral Theory*, 2nd edn. (London: Duckworth), 32.

2. Ibid., 74. MacIntyre goes on to question the moral neutrality of managerial effectiveness by casting effectiveness in terms of manipulative power rather than expertise, but it his representation of the 'dominant view' that is of interest here.

3. The pioneer of scientific management was Taylor, Frederick W. (1911). *The Principles of Scientific Management* (New York: Harper & Row). For influential accounts of business process re-engineering see Davenport, Thomas H. (1993). *Process Innovation* (Boston: Harvard Business School Press); and Hammer, Michael (July–August 1993). 'Re-engineering work: don't automate, obliterate', *Harvard Business Review*, 104–12. For a critical review of this tradition see Hendry, John (1995). 'Process reengineering and the dynamic balance of the organisation', *European Management Journal*, 13, 52–7.

4. Deetz, Stanley (1992). *Democracy in an Age of Corporate Colonization* (Albany SUNY Press). Deetz approaches managerialism from a critical perspective rooted in the writings of Foucault and Habermas, and inclines to slightly stronger conclusions than we shall draw here. His basic observations, however, seem thoroughly sound.

5. Dalton, Melville (1959). *Men who Manage: Fusions of Feeling and Theory in Administration* (New York: Wiley).

6. Jackall, Robert (1988). *Moral Mazes: The World of Corporate Managers* (New York: Oxford University Press).

7. Hecksher, Charles C. and Donnellon, Anne (eds.) (1994). *The Post-Bureaucratic Organization: New Perspectives on Organizational Change* (Thousand Oaks, CA: Sage); Grey, Chris and Garsten, Christine (2001). 'Trust, control and post-bureaucracy', *Organization Studies*, 22, 229–250.

8. Storey, John, Edwards, Peter, and Sisson, Keith (1997). *Managers in the Making: Development and Control in Corporate Britain and Japan* (London: Sage).

9. See Useem, Michael (1996). *Investor Capitalism: How Money Managers are Changing the Face of Corporate America* (New York: Basic Books).

10. The classic statements of the agency problem are by Ross, Stephen (1973). 'The economic theory of agency: the principal's problem', *American Economic Review*, 62, 134–9; and, in the corporate governance context, Jensen, Michael C. and Meckling, William H. (1976). 'Theory of the firm: managerial behavior, agency costs, and ownership structure', *Journal of Financial Economics*, 3, 305–60. For a critical review that addresses issues of incompetence as well as self-interest see Hendry, John (2002), 'The principal's other problem: honest incompetence and the specification of objectives', *Academy of Management Review*, 27, 98–113.

11. Jensen, Michael C. and Murphy, Kevin J. (May–June 1990). 'CEO pay—it's not how much you pay but how', *Harvard Business Review*, 158–83.

12. The Towers Perrin 2001–2 Worldwide Total Remuneration Study of top management pay (www.towers.com) showed that the top executives of large European companies (turnover of about US$0.5 billion or more) were taking home between £400,000 (Sweden) and £700,000 (UK) with between 35% (Sweden) and 44% (Germany) of this being in the form of bonuses and long-term incentives. The figures for the United States of America were £1.9 million, of which 68% was bonuses and incentives.

13. For a review of the theory of CEO pay see Gomez-Mejia, Luis R. and Wiseman, Robert M. (1997). 'Reframing executive compensation: an assessment and outlook', *Journal of Management*, 23, 291–374.

14. The logic is that the costs are not incurred until the options are exercised, but as investor Warren Buffet reportedly observed, 'If options aren't a form of compensation, what are they? If compensation isn't an expense, what is it? And if expenses shouldn't go into the calculation of earnings, where in the world should they go?'

15. For some good examples of the tensions between ethics and short-term performance see the cases collected in Paine, Lynn Sharpe (1996). *Cases in Leadership, Ethics, and Organizational Integrity: A Strategic Perspective* (New York: McGraw-Hill).

16. Katzenbach, Jon R. (1997). 'The myth of the top management team', *Harvard Business Review*, 75 (November–December) 83–91.
17. For a best-selling account of how teams do and do not work see Katzenbach, Jon R. and Smith, Douglas K. (1993). *The Wisdom of Teams: Creating the High-Performance Organization* (New York: McGraw Hill). For a more analytical review see Dunphy, D. and Bryant, B. (1996). 'Teams: panaceas or prescriptions for improved performance?', *Human Relations*, 49, 677–99.
18. It might be thought that, in the terms of cultural theory, teams would be more like sects than like markets or hierarchies, but corporate teams need internal structure and need to be open, as sects are not, to changing memberships, changing circumstances, and the changing needs of the corporation. Sects can generate tremendous loyalty, but if a management team turns into a sect it is doomed to failure.
19. Sennett, Richard (1998). *The Corrosion of Character* (New York: Norton), 99. See also Darrah, Charles N. (1996). *Learning and Work: An Exploration of Industrial Ethnography* (New York: Garland); Graham, Laurie (1995). *On the Line at Subaru-Isuzu* (Ithaca: Cornell University Press); Kunda, Gideon (1992). *Engineering Culture: Control and Commitment in a High-Tech Corporation* (Philadelphia: Temple University Press).
20. Watson, Tony and Harris, Pauline (1997). *The Emergent Manager* (London: Sage).
21. See Gerson, Kathleen (1998). 'Gender and the future of the family', in Dana Vannoy and Paula J. Dubeck (eds.), *Challenges for Work and Family in the Twenty-First Century* (Hawthorne, NY: Aldine de Gruyter), 11–22.
22. Gerson, 'Gender and the future of the family'.
23. On emotion work see Duncombe, Jean and Marsden, Dennis (1993). 'Love and intimacy: the gender division of emotion and "emotion work": a neglected aspect of sociological discussion of heterosexual relationships', *Sociology*, 27, 221–41; on cooking, shopping, and child care see Charles, Nickie and Kerr, Marion (1988). *Women, Food and Families* (Manchester: Manchester University Press). It seems likely that the sharing of work has changed somewhat since this study, but unlikely that it has changed significantly.
24. Watson and Harris, *The Emergent Manager*, 217.
25. Gerson, 'Gender and the future of the family'.
26. Bauman, Zygmunt (1989). *Legislators and Interpreters* (Cambridge: Polity Press), 189.
27. Bauman, Zygmunt (1993). *Postmodern Ethics* (Oxford: Blackwell), 174.
28. Marcuse, Herbert (1961). *One Dimensional Man: Studies in the Ideology of Advanced Industrial Society* (London: Routledge and Kegan Paul), quotation from 2nd (1994) edn. 33.
29. For reviews of these developments see Arthur, Michael B., Inkson, Kerr, and Pringle, Judith K. (1999). *The New Careers: Individual Action and Economic Change* (London: Sage); and Peiperl, Maury, Arthur, Michael B., Goffee, Rob, and Morris, Tim (eds.), (2000). *Career Frontiers: New Conceptions of Working Lives* (Oxford: Oxford University Press).
30. Arthur et al., *The New Careers*.
31. Rifkin, Jeremy (1995). *The End of Work* (New York: Putnam); and see also, for example, Bridges, William (1995). *Jobshift: How to Prosper in a Workplace without Jobs* (London: Nicholas Brealey).
32. For a review of the various scenarios that have been put forward see Beck, Ulrich (2000). *The Brave New World of Work* (London: Polity).
33. For an accessible exploration of the significance of work and review of related literatures see Gini, Al (2000). *My Job, My Self: Work and the Creation of the Modern Individual* (New York: Routledge).

34. Wilson, William J. (1996). *When Work Disappears: The World of the New Urban Poor* (New York: Knopf).
35. Beck, *The Brave New World of Work.*
36. Beck, Ulrich (1992). *Risk Society: Towards a New Modernity* (London: Sage).

# CHAPTER 8

1. Durkheim, Emile (1933). *The Division of Labour in Society* (New York: Free Press); idem (1957). *Professional Ethics and Civic Morals* (London: Routledge). I have discussed Durkheim's position in more detail in Hendry, John (2001). 'After Durkheim: an agenda for the sociology of business ethics', *Journal of Business Ethics, 34,* 209–18.
2. For a review of this literature see Prendergast, Canice (1999). 'The provision of incentives in firms.' *Journal of Economic Literature, 37,* 7–63.
3. For a discussion of the limits of self-organization in the broader context of social and economic order see Fukuyama, Francis (1999). *The Great Disruption: Human Nature and the Reconstitution of Social Order* (New York: Free Press), especially chs. 11–13.
4. These observations are based on discussions with participants on MBA and executive courses rather than on any formal research, but they tie in with research observations on responses to culture change programmes. See, for example, Hope, Veronica, and Hendry, John (1995). 'Corporate culture change: is it still relevant for organisations in the 1990s?', *Human Resource Management Journal, 5*(4), 61–73.
5. Kotter, John P. (1990). *A Force for Change: How Leadership Differs from Management* (New York: Free Press), 5.
6. Bennis, Warren (1990). *Why Leaders Can't Lead: The Unconscious Conspiracy Continues* (San Francisco: Jossey-Bass), 18.
7. There are many versions of these typologies, but this account is based on that given by Daft, Richard L. (1999). *Leadership: Theory and Practice* (Fort Worth: Dryden Press); see also Greenleaf, Robert K. (1977). *Servant Leadership: A Journey into the Nature of Legitimate Power and Greatness* (Mahwah, NJ: Paulist Press); Torbert, William R. (1991). *The Power of Balance: Transforming Self, Society and Scientific Inquiry* (Newbury Park, CA: Sage). The term 'transforming leadership' derives from the work of James McGregor Burns, who contrasted it with 'transactional leadership', one being values-driven and the other incentives-driven. See Burns, James McGregor (1978). *Leadership* (New York: Harper & Row). Torbert builds on this idea but enhances its moral and developmental aspects, bringing it close to Greenleaf's servant leader concept.
8. This research is still ongoing and the details have not yet been published.
9. Kotter, *A Force for Change.*
10. Katzenbach, Jon R. (1997). 'The myth of the top management team', *Harvard Business Review, 75* (November–December), 83–91.
11. Treviño, Linda Klebe, and Nelson, Katherine A. (1999). *Managing Business Ethics: Straight Talk about How to do it Right,* 2nd edn (New York: Wiley).
12. Badaracco, Joseph L. Jr., and Ellis, Richard R. (1989). *Leadership and the Quest for Integrity* (Boston: Harvard Business School Press).

13. Business Roundtable, *Corporate Ethics: A Prime Business Asset* (New York: Business Roundtable, 1988), quoted by Treviño and Nelson, *Managing Business Ethics*, 210.
14. For a classic discussion of leadership and organizational culture see Schein, Edgar H. (1985). *Organizational Culture and Leadership* (San Francisco: Jossey-Bass).
15. *The Sunday Times*, 1 September 2002.
16. Dalton, Melville (1959). *Men who Manage: Fusions of Feeling and Theory in Administration* (New York: Wiley).
17. Mars, Gerald (1982). *Cheats at Work* (London: Allen & Unwin).
18. The Bhopal accident is described in de George, Richard T. (1993). *Competing with Integrity in International Business* (New York: Oxford University Press), and the Challenger disaster in Werhane, Patricia H. (1999). *Moral Imagination and Management Decision-making* (New York: Oxford University Press). Patricia Werhane argues very persuasively for the need for managers to engage a kind of moral imagination alongside moral reasoning, if unethical decision-making is to be avoided, and she focuses on this rather than on the bureaucratic context. As we discussed in Chapter 6, however, other writers have argued that one of the central problems with bureaucracy is precisely that it stifles such a moral imagination.
19. These cases and others have been written up in various places. A good collection of short summaries can be found in Treviño and Nelson, *Managing Business Ethics*, and of full-length cases in Paine, Lynn Sharpe (1996). *Cases in Leadership, Ethics, and Organizational Integrity: A Strategic Perspective* (New York: McGraw-Hill).
20. See, for example, Miles, Raymond E. and Snow, Charles C. (1992). 'Causes of failure in network organizations', *California Management Review* (Summer), 73–92; Gambetta, Diego (1988). *Trust: Making and Breaking Cooperative Relations* (Oxford: Blackwell); Jones, Gareth R. and George, Jennifer M. (1988). 'The experience and evolution of trust: implications for cooperation and teamwork', *Academy of Management Review*, 23, 531–6.
21. The nexus of contracts model of the firm is due to Alchian, Armen A. and Demsetz, Harold (1972) 'Production, information costs, and economic organization', *The American Economic Review*, 62, 777–95, and was developed as an agency model by Jensen, Michael C. and Meckling, William H. (1976). 'Theory of the firm: managerial behavior, agency costs, and ownership structure', *Journal of Financial Economics*, 3, 305–60. For these and other key contributions to the economic theory of the firm see Putterman, Louis and Kroszner, Randall S. (eds.) (1996). *The Economic Nature of the Firm*. Second Edition (Cambridge: Cambridge University Press).
22. Boatright, John R. (1999). 'Presidential address: does business ethics rest on a mistake?', *Business Ethics Quarterly*, 9, 583–92.
23. See Chapters 4 and 6 for discussions of Fevre's and Tester's analyses.
24. For trust in this sense see, for example, Baier, Annette C. (1994). *Moral Prejudices* (Cambridge, MA: Harvard University Press); and Becker, Lawrence C. (1996). 'Trust as noncognitive security about motives', *Ethics*, 107, 43–61.
25. For a clear exposition of trust in this sense see Williamson, Oliver E. (1993). 'Calculativeness, trust and economic organization', *Journal of Law and Economics*, 30, 131–45. See also Barney, Jay B. and Hansen, M. H. (1994). 'Trustworthiness as a source of competitive advantage', *Strategic Management Journal*, 15, 175–90.
26. For an excellent discussion of trustworthiness in the writings of Confucius and the Japanese philosopher Tesura Watsuji and their relevance to a business context, see Koehn, Daryl (2001). *Local Insights, Global Ethics for Business* (Amsterdam: Rodopi).

27. For surveys of the management literature on trust see Kramer, R. M. and Tyler, T. R. (eds.) (1996). *Trust in Organisations: Frontiers of Theory and Research* (Thousand Oaks, CA: Sage); (1998). *Academy of Management Review*, 23(3) (special issue).

28. See, for example, Wicks, Andrew C., Berman Shawn, L. and Jones, Thomas M. (1999). 'The structure of optimal trust: moral and strategic implications', *Academy of Management Review*, 24, 99–116.

29. For explorations of institutionalised trust see, for example, North, Douglass C. (1990). *Institutions, Institutional Change and Economic Performance* (New York: Cambridge University Press); and Fukuyama, Francis (1995). *Trust: The Social Virtues and the Creation of Prosperity* (New York: Free Press).

30. For a recent UK survey see Le Jeune, Martin and Webley, Simon (2002). *Ethical Business–Corporate Uses of Codes of Conduct* (London: Institute of Business Ethics).

31. For a general critique of ethical codes see Sorell, Tom and Hendry, John (1994). *Business Ethics* (Oxford: Butterworth-Heinemann).

32. For a discussion of these cultural mechanisms of control see Johnson, Gerry (1987). *Strategic Change and the Management Process* (Oxford: Blackwell) and (1992). 'Managing strategic change: strategy, culture and action', *Long Range Planning*, 25, 28–36.

33. For the principles of business process reengineering see Hammer, Michael (1993). 'Re-engineering work: don't automate, obliterate', *Harvard Business Review*, 71 (July–August), 104–12; and Davenport, Thomas H. (1993). *Process Innovation* (Boston: Harvard Business School Press). For a critical review see Hendry, John (1995). 'Process re-engineering and the dynamic balance of the organisation', *European Management Journal*, 13, 52–7.

34. Argyris, Chris and Schön, Donald A. (1978). *Organizational Learning: A Theory of Action Perspective* (Reading, MA: Addison-Wesley) and (1996). *Organizational Learning II: Theory, Method and Practice* (Reading, MA: Addison-Wesley).

35. The term 'unfreezing' comes from the work of Lewin, Kurt (1951). *Field Theory in Social Science* (New York: Harper & Row).

36. See, for example, Levitt, Barbara and March, James G. (1988). 'Organizational learning', *Annual Review of Sociology*, 14, 319–40; Huber, George P. (1991). 'Organizational leanring: the contributing processes and literatures', *Organization Science*, 2, 88–115; and Dodgson, Mark (1993). 'Organizational learning: a review of some literatures', *Organization Studies*, 14, 375–94.

37. See Nonaka, Ikujiro and Takeuchi, Hirotaka (1995). *The Knowledge Creating Company* (New York: Oxford University Press); Grant, Robert M. (1996). 'Toward a knowledge-based theory of the firm', *Strategic Management Journal*, 17 (Winter Special Issue), 109–22; Spender, J.-C. (1996). 'Making knowledge the basis of a dynamic theory of the firm', *Strategic Management Journal*, 17 (Winter Special Issue), 45–62.

38. The concept of tacit knowledge is due to Polanyi, Michael (1962). *Personal Knowledge: Towards a Post-Critical Philosophy* (New York: Harper) and (1966). *The Tacit Dimension* (New York: Anchor Day Books). The difference between tacit and explicit knowledge was recognized by writers such as Nonaka and Takeuchi, in *The Knowledge Creating Company*, but its peculiar importance for flexible organizations has only been noted more recently. See, for example, Lam, Alice (2000). 'Tacit knowledge, organizational learning and societal institutions: an integrated framework', *Organization Studies*, 21, 487–513; and von Krogh, Georg (1998). 'Care in knowledge creation', *California Management Review*, 40, (Summer), 133–53. See also Wenger,

Etienne (1998). *Communities of Practice: Learning, Meaning and Identity* (New York: Oxford University Press). For an exploration of the complex relationships between different kinds of organizational knowledge see Boisot, Max (1995). *Information Space: A Framework for Learning in Organizations, Institutions and Culture* (London: Routledge).

39. Buber, Martin (1975). 'Education' and 'The education of character', in *Between Man and Man* (London: Fontana). See also Hodges, Anthony (1975). *An Encounter with Martin Buber* (London: Penguin), 135 *ff.*

40. Handy, Charles B. (1997). *Understanding Organizations* (London: Penguin).

41. One example of this is the University of Cambridge MBA, which I was lucky enough to direct from its inception in 1990 until 1998. A key influence on this programme was Charles Handy, with whom I had worked earlier at the London Business School, but the principal architect and builder of the learning experience we created was my colleague John Roberts who has written about the programme in Roberts, John D. (1996). 'Management education and the limits of technical rationality', in Robert French and Christopher Grey (eds.), *Rethinking Management Education* (London: Sage), 54–75.

## CHAPTER 9

1. See for example Giddens, Anthony (1995). *Beyond Left and Right: The Future of Radical Politics* (Cambridge: Polity) and idem (1998). *The Third Way: The Renewal of Social Democracy* (Cambridge: Polity).

2. Giddens, *Beyond Left and Right*, 21.

3. For opposing views see, for example, Ohmae, Kenichi (1995). *The End of the Nation State* (London: HarperCollins); and Hirst, Paul and Thompson, Graham, (1996). *Globalization in Question* (Cambridge: Polity). These and other positions are critically reviewed in Held, David, McGrew, Anthony, Goldblatt, David, and Perraton, Jonathan (1999). *Global Transformations: Politics, Economics and Culture* (Cambridge: Polity).

4. Giddens, *Beyond Left and Right*, 4.

5. Giddens, Anthony (1990). *The Consequences of Modernity* (Cambridge: Polity), 64.

6. For a defence of the nation state in these terms see Miller, David (2000). *Citizenship and National Identity* (Cambridge: Polity).

7. Beck, Ulrich (1992). *Risk Society: Towards a New Modernity* (London: Sage).

8. For a powerful analysis of this aspect of globalization see Albrow, Martin (1996). *The Global Age: State and Society Beyond Modernity* (Cambridge: Polity).

9. See, for example, Soros, George (1987). *The Alchemy of Finance: Reading the Mind of the Market* (New York: Simon & Schuster), (1988). *The Crisis of Global Capitalism [Open Society Endangered]* (London: Little Brown); and idem (2000). *Soros on Globalization* (London: Public Affairs).

10. Soros, *The Crisis of Global Capitalism*, 101–2.

11. In the recent technology boom, the London-based fund managers, Schroders, under-invested in technology stocks relative to their competitors on the grounds that the prices were way out of line with the fundamental value of the shares. The result was that their funds, though they showed good growth, underperformed relative to the market, they lost their customers, and almost went out of business.

12. The importance of the project of modus vivendi, both in the global context and within national politics, has been argued persuasively by John Gray, whose analysis of globalization and contemporary society has much in common with those of Giddens, Beck, and Soros, on whom we have primarily depended here. See, for example, Gray, John (2002). *False Dawn: The Delusions of Global Capitalism*, 2nd edn. (London: Granta), and (2000). *Two Faces of Liberalism* (Cambridge: Polity).

13. For the history of human rights legislation see Klug, Francesca (2000). *Values for a Godless Age* (London: Penguin). Klug includes the text of the Universal Declaration of Human Rights as an appendix.

14. For a review of the impact of the Universal Declaration see van der Heijden, Barend (ed.) (1998). *Reflections on the Universal Declaration of Human Rights: A Fiftieth Anniversary Anthology* (Dordrecht: Kluwer).

15. Klug, *Values for a Godless Age*.

16. For analysis of these issues from different philosophical traditions see Taylor, Charles and others (1994). *Multiculturalism: Examining the Politics of Recognition*, (ed.) Amy Gutmann (Princeton: Princeton University Press); and Benhabib, Seyla (ed.) (1996). *Democracy and Difference* (Princeton: Princeton University Press). See also Patrick, Morag (2000). 'Identity, diversity and the politics of recognition', in Noel O'Sullivan (ed.), *Political Theory in Transition* (London: Routledge).

17. For a philosophical analysis see O'Neill, Onora (1996). *Towards Justice and Virtue: A Constructive Account of Practical Reasoning* (Cambridge: Cambridge University Press).

18. See Klug, *Values for a Godless Age*, for more detailed discussion of these objections.

19. Tony Blair, speech to the 1997 Labour Party Conference, quoted by Klug, *Values for a Godless Age*, 61.

20. Blair, Tony (1998). *The Third Way: New Politics for the New Century* (London: Fabian Society), 4.

21. See Bauman, Zygmunt (1993). *Postmodern Ethics* (Oxford: Blackwell).

22. For an elaboration of Confucian ethics and its post-conventional nature see Roetz, Heiner (1993). *Confucian Ethics of the Axial Age* (Albany: SUNY Press).

23. See O'Neill, Onora (2002). *A Question of Trust. The BBC Reith Lectures 2002* (Cambridge: Cambridge University Press).

24. For a study of the nature and role of law in a pluralistic society, see Habermas, Jürgen (1996). *Between Facts and Norms: Contributions to a Discourse Theory of Law and Democracy* (Cambridge: Polity).

25. For a useful discussion see Donaldson, Thomas J. (1989). *The Ethics of International Business* (New York: Oxford University Press).

26. See Moser, Titus (2001). 'Multinational corporations and sustainable business practice: the case of the Colombian and Peruvian petroleum industries', *World Development*, 29, 291–309; and for a more general review, Moser, Titus and Miller, Damian (2001). 'Multinational corporations' impacts in the developing world: a synthesis of contemporary debate', in Richard Starkey and Richard Welford (eds.), *The Earthscan Reader in Business and Sustainable Development* (London: Earthscan).

27. *Human Rights: Quarterly Review of the Office of the United Nations High Commission for Human Rights*, no. 1 (1999).

28. For discussions of various aspects of business and human rights see Addo, Michael K. (ed.) (1999). *Human Rights Standards and the Responsibility of Transnational Corporations* (The Hague: Kluwer Law International).

29. For an interesting attempt to build guidelines for multinational businesses based on human rights see Donaldson, *Ethics of International Business*. For discussions of the

limitations of such a rights based approach see de George, Richard (1993). *Competing with Integrity in International Business* (New York: Oxford University Press); and Velasquez, Manuel (1995). 'International Business Ethics: The Aluminum companies in Jamaica', *Business Ethics Quarterly*, 5, 865–82.

30. Roberts, John D. (2001) 'Trust and control in Anglo-American systems of corporate governance: the individualising and socialising effects of processes of accountability', *Human Relations*, 54, 1547–72, 1553.

31. Ibid., 1551.

32. Donaldson, Thomas J. and Dunfee, Thomas W. (1999). *Ties that Bind: A Social Contracts Approach to Business Ethics* (Boston: Harvard Business School Press). This also includes a good review of social contract theory in general.

33. Rawls, John (1972). *A Theory of Justice* (Oxford: Oxford University Press).

# INDEX

accidents, industrial 77
Adams, Frank T. 271
Addo, Michael K. 289
advertising 58, 80–1
agency theory 102–3, 186–7, 248
AIDS 89
air transport 138
Albrow, Martin 288
Alchian, Armen A. 286
Alexander, Richard D. 262
Alic, John A. 275
Alliance for Justice 272
American Civil War 73
American culture, dissemination of 141–2
American Declaration of Independence 239
American versus European
      perspectives 141–2
Amnesty International 248
anti-globalisation movement 33, 233
Argyris, Chris 227, 287
Arthur, Michael B. 199, 284
artists in hierarchical culture 49–51
Ashburner, Lynn 276
Ashcroft, Richard 274
Athenian society 53
Axelrod, Robert M. 262
Aymard, Maurice 265

Badaracco, Joseph L. Jr 215, 285
Bagdikian, Ben H. 279
Baier, Annette C. 286
Balazs, Etienne 47, 265
Bales, Kevin 273, 279
Balzac, Honoré de 60, 267
Banerjeee, Subhabrata Bobby 275
Bank of England 56
bankers 53, 55, 74, 76
banks and banking 61–2, 71–2, 93–5; see also
      bankers, financial institutions

Banque Royale 57
Barings 218
Barnard, Malcolm 282
Barney, Jay B. 286
Barry, Norman 155, 280
Barzelay, Michael 276
BAT 80
Bauman, Zygmunt 21, 161–2, 165–6, 198–9,
      243, 281, 284, 289
Baumgartner, M. P. 145, 279
Bechler, Jean 267
Beck, Ulrich 201–2, 232, 235–6, 282, 284–5
Becker, Gary S. 98, 274
Becker, Lawrence C. 286
Beiser, Frederick C. 278
Bellah, Robert N. 169, 263, 282
Bengton, Vern L. 282
Benhabib, Seyla 289
Bennis, Warren 207, 285
Berg, Maxine 265
Berle, Adolph A. Jr 77, 96, 270–1
Berman, Shawn L. 286
Bernstein, Basil 263
Bhopal 217
big man societies – see markets
Bill of Rights 238
bills of exchange 56
bimoral society 3, 168–76
Blair, Tony 232–3, 242, 289
Boatright, John R. 220, 286
Boesky, Ivan 106–7
Boisot, Max 263, 288
Bonney, Richard 264
Bork, R. 280
boundaries, social 53
Bourdieu, Pierre 114, 173, 265, 276, 282
Boxer, Charles R. 265
Bratton, Walter J. Jr 269
Braudel, Fernand 265

Brewer, John 265, 267
Bridges, William 284
Bryant, B. 284
Bryce, Robert 271
Bubble Act 57, 71–2
Buber, Martin 288
Buffet, Warren 283
bureaucracy 8, 111, 161–2, 167
Burke, James 218
Burns, James McGregor 285
Burroughs 79
business enterprise, growth of 54–8
business organization as moral
        community 27
Business Roundtable 215, 286
business schools 203, 229–30

Cadbury 79
Camerer, Colin 262
Cameron, Kim S. 272
capitalism, 'controlled' 66
capitalism, global 236
careers 180–2, 199–201
Carnall, Geoffrey 268
Carosso, Vincent 269
Cassis, Youssef 270
CEOs – see chief executive officers
Challenger space shuttle 217
Chandler, Alfred D. 268–70, 276
change, cultural 42–4
Channon, Derek 268
charity 243
Charkham, Jonathan 270
Charles, Nickie 284
Chaudhuri, K. N. 267
chief executive officers 23–4, 28, 184–91,
        209–12
    and self-interest 185
    as stewards 185–6
    remuneration of 185, 187–9
    succession of 219
child labour 77
China 47–50, 54, 137
Chiquita 81
Christianity 15, 42–3, 126–9, 233
Christie, Ian R. 265
churches 15, 160, 242
    attendance at 58, 126–7, 153
    decline of authority of 15, 126–9, 153
    in America 129
    in Europe 126–7
    Roman Catholic 38, 42, 53, 127
citizenship and consumption 114–16
City of London 56, 71
City of London 93–5, 245

civilization and cultural types 45–6
class structure 136
Clinton, Bill 118
Coase, Ronald 104, 275
Coates, A. A. Bob 275
Cobb, Jonathan 170, 282
codes of conduct 224–5
Coffee, John C. Jr 270
Cohen, David K. 279
Collier, Paul 272
commodification of morality 163–4
common good 17
common sense reasoning 116–19, 165–6, 168,
        222–3
    and economic reasoning 118–19
    definition of 116–17
communications technologies 17, 94, 138
Compagnie des Indes 57
companies
    and educational sponsorship 83–4
    bureaucratic 8, 62–6, 109
        failure of 180–1
        rise of 9
    chartered 61
    dispersed ownership of 74–5, 96
    hierarchical 62–6
    joint stock 61–2, 71
    legal personhood of 76, 78
    multinational 139
    political activity of 80–2
    transnational 85–6, 91
    with limited liability 62, 72–5
Confucianism 35, 222, 243
Confucius 286
consumer culture 80, 171
consumerization of political discourse 115
contraception 151
contract, social 250–1
contracts, economics of 102
corporate culture 110–11, 180–1
corporate governance 35–6, 186–9, 244–50
    failure of 96–7
corporations – see companies
Cottrell, P. L. 268
Cox, Harvey 107, 276
crime 122, 153–4, 157; see also fraud
crisis of morality 19–21, 122–4, 148–68
cultural boundaries, erosion of 136–44
cultural theory 5, 38–44
Cunningham, William 266
cyclical changes in morality 151–2

Daems, Herman 268
Daft, Richard L. 285
Dalton, Melville 63–5, 179, 216, 268, 283, 286

Darrah, Charles N. 193, 284
Davenport, Thomas H. 283, 287
Davies, Paul 272
Davis, Fred 282
De George, Richard T. 140, 279, 286, 290
Declaration of the Rights of Man and
    Citizen 238
Deetz, Stanley S. 30, 178, 180, 205, 277, 283
Delaney, C. F. 278
deliberative democracy 232, 240–1
Dellheim, Charles 271
demoralization 19–21, 119, 122–4, 157–68
Demsetz, Harold 286
dependency 156–8
deregulation 72–4, 83–5, 107, 139, 244–5
development, economic and industrial
    87–93
development, sustainable, 106
dialogic democracy 232, 241
divorce 122
Dodd, E. Merrick Jr 77, 271
Dodgson, Mark 287
Dollar, David 272
Donaldson, Thomas J. 251, 289–90
Donnellon, Anne 283
Douglas, Mary 5–6, 17, 38–45, 110,
    263–4, 276
Du Gay, Paul 111, 276, 281
Dubeck, Paula J. 284
Duncombe, Jean 282, 284
Dunfee, Thomas W. 251, 290
Dunnett, Dorothy 265
Dunphy, D. 284
Durkheim, Emile 8, 45, 51, 61, 167, 203, 261,
    263–4, 266, 285
Dutch East India Company 46, 48, 56
Dutch Federation 48–9

East India Company 46, 56
economic agency 12–13, 102–3
economic model of the firm 220
economic reasoning and ideas 11–13,
    98–105, 119
    dominance of 98, 106–119
Edel, A. 263
Edel, M. 263
Edgell, Stephen 282
education – see teachers
Edwards, Peter 283
Ell, Paul S. 278
Ellis, Richard R. 215, 285
Ellul, Jaques 161
Emerson, Ralph Waldo 156, 280
emotions 117, 165–6
Engels, Friedrich 60, 267

English society of the eighteenth century
    48–9, 57, 121
Enlightenment 15, 98, 121, 124–5
Enron 30, 81, 96–7
enterprise and self-interest, demarcation of
    52–4
enterprise culture 111
entrepreneurs 6–7, 69–70
    in hierarchical culture 50–1
environmental damage 88–91, 235–6
Escobar, Arturo 275
ethics and economic performance 190, 217
Etzioni, Amitai 274
European Community 137
European Convention on Human Rights 238
European versus American perspectives
    141–2
Evans, Eric J. 266, 278
evolutionary theory 37
Exxon Valdez 78

families
    and moral obligations 171, 194–7
    as moral authorities 16, 132–4
Farrar, Eleanor 279
Fehr, Scott A. 262
Ferguson, Niall 264, 269, 271, 278–9
Ferlie, Ewan 276
Feuerstein, Aaron 218
Fevre, Ralph W. 21, 116–19, 149, 165–6, 168,
    222, 277, 281
Field, Frank 280
financial crises 94–5
financial institutions 10, 93–7, 236–8
Finch, Janet 173–4, 282
Firth, Raymond William 263
Fitzgerald, Louise 276
Fitzgibbons, Athol 267
flexibility in organizations 111
flexible economy 12, 23–4, 109–14, 192, 228
flexible organizations, management in
    203–30; see also network
    organizations
Fohlen, Claude 269
Ford Pinto 217
foreign direct investment 139–40
foreign travel in hierarchical culture 50–1
Foucault, Michel 162, 261, 268
Fournier, Valerie 276
Fox, Loren 271
France 75, 94
Frank, Thomas 275–7
Frankfurt School 162
fraud in the workplace 215–16
Freedland, Mark 272

free market ideology 103–4, 106–7, 110, 158
  and critique of welfare 156–8
freedom 26, 155–6, 162, 197–202
French Revolution 125
French, Peter 271
French, Robert 288
Friedman, Andy 271
Friedman, Milton 98, 105, 155–7, 274–5, 280
Fromm, Erich 170–1, 272, 282
Fukuyama, Francis 20, 122–4, 127, 149–54,
    277, 280, 285, 287
fundamentalism 130

Gachter, Simon 262
Galbraith, John Kenneth 100, 274–5, 280
Galilei, Galileo 51
Gambetta, Diego 286
game theory 37
Garsten, Christine 283
Gay, Peter 278
Geertz, Clifford 263
Geisst, Charles R. 268–9
gender and morality 134
George, Jennifer M. 286
George, Peter 269
Gerbner, George 272, 279
Germany 75, 94
Gerson, Kathleen 196–7, 284
Ghoshal, Sumantra 263, 275
Gibbon, Edward 265
Giddens, Anthony 32, 173, 232–3, 235, 238,
    243, 264, 278, 282, 288
Gilligan, Carol 279
Gini, Al 284
Glass–Steagall Act 66, 93–4
global financial system 93–5, 236–8
  instability of 236–8
  and political system 237
global warming 90
globalization 17, 33, 85–95, 231–8
  and economic growth 86–7
  and American culture 141–2
  and environmental damage 87–91
  definitions of 235
  of business 140
GM foods 90
Goffee, Rob 284
Goldblatt, David 288
Gomez-Mejia, Luis R. 283
Graham, Laurie 193, 284
Grant, Robert M. 287
Gray, John 238, 289
greed 58, 90, 106–7
Greenleaf, Robert K. 208, 285

Greider, William 273
Grey, Christopher 276, 283, 288
grid-group theory – see cultural theory
Griffiths, Brian 280
Griswold, Charles L. 267
Grossman, Richard L. 271
growth, economic 86–7

Haas, Robert 218
Habermas, Jürgen 162, 289
Hall, John A. 265, 267
Hall, Peter A. 277
Hammer, Michael 283, 287
Handy, Charles B. 230, 288
Hannah, Leslie 270
Hansen, M. H. 286
Harris, Pauline 195–7, 284
Hatch, Elvin 263
having and being 170–1
Hawken, Paul 271
Hayek, Friedrich von 155–7
Hecksher, Charles 283
Heinz 79
Held, David 288
Henrich, Robert 262
Henry VIII 126
Herman, Edward 279
Hertz, Noreena 115, 271, 277
Herzenberg, Stephen A. 275
Hetherington, Kevin 282
hierarchies 6, 39, 41, 45–6
  problems of 6, 46–7, 63
high classification societies – see hierarchies
Himmelfarb, Gertrude 20, 149, 157, 267–8,
    277, 280
Hirst, Paul 288
Hodges, Anthony 288
Hodgson, Geoffrey 274
Hoenig, Jonathan 107, 275
Holocaust 161–2
homo economicus 99–100
Hope-Hailey, Veronica 276, 285
Howell, Signe 263
Huber, George P. 287
Hudson Bay Company 56
human concern 242–3, 249
human dignity 239–40, 243
human nature 37
  American and European perceptions of
    149–50
human resource managers 198
human rights 33–4, 238–43, 248
Human Rights Act 238, 242
humaneness – see human-heartedness

human-heartedness 243–4, 248–9
Hurst, James W. 269

Ignatieff, Michael 163, 281
illegitimacy 122, 157–8
immigration 175
incentive pay, pitfalls of 204–5
India 54
indifference 163–5, 222
individualising processes of accountability 248–9
Industrial Revolution 48, 121, 151–2
information and communications technologies 17, 94, 138
information revolution 151–2
Inkson, Kerr 199, 284
International Labor Organization 248
International Monetary Fund 85–8, 91–2, 95, 106, 139
international trade 48, 55, 139–40
Internet 138
Islam, 54, 130
Israel, Jonathan I. 265

Jackall, Robert 65–6, 180, 268, 283
Jackson, Kenneth T. 280
Japan, 75
Jaques, Elliot 276
Jensen, Michael C. 188, 283, 286
Johnson, Gerry 287
Johnson, Samuel 48
Jones, Eric L. 267
Jones, Gareth R. 286
Jones, Norman 266
Jones, Thomas M. 287
judges, perceptions of 132
Jung, Carl Gustav 128, 278
Jürgens, Ulrich 273

Kant, Immanuel 125, 278
Kanter, Rosabeth Moss 265
Karson, Marvin 268, 273
Katzenbach, Jon R. 191, 284–5
Kaufman, Allen 268, 273
Kaye, Joel 267
Kennedy, William P. 270
Kerr, Marion 284
Keynes, John Maynard 105
Kiern, Tim 267
Klug, Francesca 289
Knapp, A. Bernard 264
knowledge-based economy 31
Kocka, Jürgen 269
Koehn, Daryl 279, 286

Kohlberg, Lawrence 263
Körner, Martin 264
Kornhaber, Arthur 282
Korten, David C. 87, 93, 160, 269, 271, 281
Kotter, John P. 207, 209–10, 212, 285
Kramer, R. M. 287
Kristol, Irving 20, 158, 280
Kroszner, Randall S. 286
Kuhn, Thomas, S. 262
Kunda, Gideon 193, 284
Kynaston, David 269, 273

Lam, Alice 287
Landes, David 55, 261, 265
Lane, Jan-Erik 276
Langford, Carol M. 272
Lawrence, D. H. 51
Lazonick, William 270, 273–4
Le Jeune, Martin 287
leadership 27–30, 207–14
    and community 210
    and organizational change 207
    and stability 208
    and strategy 209–10
    and top management team 211
    authoritarian 208
    empowering 29, 208–9
    ethical – see moral
    heroic 190–1
    moral 30, 214–19
    participative 28, 208–9
    types or styles of 28–9, 208–9
servant or transforming 28–9, 208–9, 215
learning 31–2, 224–30
    process, management of 226–9
Leesom, Nick 218
Levin, Myron 272
Levinas, Emmanuel 165, 243
Levine, Dennis 106–7
Levitt, Barbara 287
Lewin, Kurt 287
Lewinsky, Monica 118
lifetime employment 183
limited liability 62, 72–5
Lincoln, Abraham 269
Lindner, Carl 81
Linklater, Andro 274
listening 210
Lloyd, Tom 265
London Stock Exchange 56, 71
Lopez-de-Silanes, Florencio 270
lovingkindness 243
Lull, James 279

Luttwak, Edward 66, 84, 107, 268, 272, 275, 277
Lyotard, Jean-Fraçois 108, 276

MacIntyre, Alasdair 165, 177, 261, 278, 281–2
Mackenney, Richard 267
Madsen, Richard 263, 282
male dominance 134
management
    and friendship 182
    and moral discretion 221
    as amoral 30, 177, 219
    as instrumental 30, 177–81, 219
    moral 30–1, 219–24
    unethical 218–9
management development 184
Mandeville, Bernard 58, 267
Mann, Michael 266–7
March, James G. 287
Marchand, Roland 271
Marconi 96–7
Marcuse, Herbert 162, 164, 199, 271, 281, 284
market for corporate control 187
markets; see also free market ideology
    and economic theory 103–4
    as cultural type 6, 39, 41, 51, 152, 220–1
    as God 107
    as institutions 160, 224–5, 236
Mars, Gerald 216, 286
Marsden, Dennis 282, 284
Marshall, Alfred 100, 274
Marx, Karl 60, 267
Mason, Jennifer 173–4, 282
massacres, 163
Masselman, George 267
materialism 101
Mathias, Peter 268–9
MBAs 203, 229–30
McCauley, Martin 266
McChesney, Robert 279
McCloskey, Deirdre 274–5
McGrew, Anthony 288
McKendrick, Neil 265
McNaghten, Phil 275
Means, Gardiner C. 96, 270
Meckling, William H. 283, 286
Megalli, Mark 271–2
Městrovič, Stjepan 117, 277
Meyrowitz, Joshua 279
Michie, Ranald C. 267, 269
Miles, Raymond E. 286
Miles, Robert H. 272
Miles, Steven 282
Milgram, Stanley 161

Milgrom, Paul 274
Miller, Damian 289
Miller, David 288
Milliken, Michael 106
Minow, Nell 273
Mintzberg, Henry 114, 265, 276
mistrust 248
modus vivendi 33
Monbiot, George 271
monetarization of society 163
money
    as dominant value 236
    as measure of good 100–1, 107–8
Monks, Robert A. G. 273
Monsanto 85
moral authority, decline of 14–17, 124–36
moral concern 242–3, 249
moral consensus, lack of 232–4
moral discretion 221
moral engagement 222, 243
moral leadership 30, 214–9
moral minimalism 145
moral pluralism 33, 44–5, 143–4
moral principles – see morality
moral reticence 157; See also moral minimalism
morality
    and gender 134
    and power 160
    and reason 165–6
    balance between rival principles of 149, 171–6
    changes of 42–4, 151–2
    coexistence of rival principles of 3–4
    commodification of 163–4
    conflict between rival principles of 22
    crisis of 19–21, 122–4, 148–68
    definitions and terminology 1–2, 261
    history of 5
    importance of 37–8
    in primitive societies 5, 38–9
    of power 160–3
    of self-interest 2–4
    market 2–4
    traditional 1–5, 11
        and markets 154–9
        and self-interest 155
Moran, Peter 263, 275
Morgan, J. P. 76
Morin, Fraçois 273
Morris, Tim 284
Moser, Titus 289
Mowlana, Hamid 272, 279

multinational corporations 139
Murphy, Kevin J. 188, 283

nation state, future of 33, 235, 237
Naumann, Katrin 273
Neal, Larry 267
Nelson, Benjamin 266
Nelson, Katherine A. 285
Nelson, William E. 269
network organizations 23–5, 27, 111, 180, 206:
    see also flexible organizations
    limitations of 154
New East India Company 56
New Labour 232
New York Stock Exchange 96; See also Wall
    Street
Noddings, Nell 279
Nonaka, Ikujiro 287
North, Douglass C. 287
Novak, Michael 20, 158, 280

O'Neill, Onora 289
O'Sullivan, Mary 273
O'Sullivan, Noel 289
Ohmae, Kenichi 288
opinion polls 117–18
organizations
    flexible, management in 203–30
    hierarchical 62–6, 109
        and moral practice 64–6
        problems of 63–6
    network 23–5, 27, 111, 180, 206
    post-bureaucratic 180, 203
Organization for Economic Cooperation and
    Development 248
Ouchi, William 263
ownership and control, separation of
    76–7, 96

Paine, Lynn Sharpe 283, 286
parental authority 133–4
Pascale, Richard T. 276
Patrick, Morag 289
pay – see remuneration
Payne, Peter L. 269
Peiperl, Maury 284
pension funds 96
Perraton, Jonathan 288
Peters, Tom 110, 265, 276
Pettigrew, Andrew 276
Peyrefitte, Alain 265
philanthropy 60
Piaget, Jean 263
Pliny the Younger 265

Plumb, J. H. 265
pluralism, moral and cultural 33, 44–5, 143–4
Plymouth Brethren 43
Polanyi, Michael 287
police, perceptions of 132
politicians, perceptions of 131
politics 114–16
    and economics 105–6
    market for 114
Pollard, Arthur 268
Pollard, Sidney 272
pollution – see environmental damage
Popper, Karl 262
Porta, Rafael L. 270
Porter, Roy 58, 265
Postan, M. M. 268–9
Postgate, J. Nicholas 264
post-industrial revolution 151–2
Postrel, Virginia 275
post-traditional society 232
Potter, Harry 173
poverty 87
Powell, Arthur G. 279
power imbalances in business organizations
    183–4, 205–6
Prendergast, Canice 285
price mechanism 103
Pringle, Judith K. 199, 284
private finance initiative 83
privatisation 83–5, 107, 139
property rights 34, 101–3, 240–1
    as superior good 155–6
    economics of 101–3
psychological technologies 161–2
public private partnerships 83
public relations 78–80
public sector, management of 13, 113–14
puffery – see advertising
Putnam, Robert D. 124, 276–8
Putternam, Louis 286

Radice, Betty 265
Rawls, John 251, 290
Redondi, Pietro 266
reflexive discourse 232
regulations:
    environmental 246–7
    financial 247
    of business and enterprise 52–3, 78,
        84–5, 244–50
    of markets 66, 78
    self-regulation 245–6
religion and free markets 158–9
religious marketplace 129

remuneration of CEOs 185, 187–9
reputations, business 79–80
responsibility, contrasted with duty
    232–3, 243
responsibility, unconditional 243
Rest, James R. 263
Ribaud, Jean 218
Ridley, Matt 262
Rifkin, Jeremy 200, 284
rights:
    and obligations 34, 241–2
    collective 34
        versus individual 240
    competing 241
    corporate 34, 241
    human 33–4, 238–43, 248
    property 34, 101–3, 240–1
        as superior good 155–6
        economics of 101–3
risk society 201–2, 235–6
Roberts, John 274
Roberts, John D. 248–9, 288, 290
Robertson, Joan F. 282
Robertson, Ross M. 270
Roe, Mark J. 74, 270
Roetz, Heiner 289
Roman empire 42–3, 48–9, 121
Rorty, Richard 149, 280
Rose, Hilary 262
Rose, Stephen 262
Ross, Stephen 283
Rostovtzeff, Mikhail I. 265
Rothschild, Emma 267
Rowling, J. K. 173
Royal African Company 56
rules 224–6
Rupp, Joachim 273
Ruse, Michael 278

Salomon Brothers 217–18
Schama, Simon 278
Schein, Edgar H. 286
Schiller, Herbert I. 272, 279
Schön, Donald A. 227, 287
Schumpeter, Joseph 104, 275
science and religion 128
Scott, John 270
Sears Auto Centers 217
sects 6, 38, 41, 43
security 182; see also careers
self, conceptions of 169–71, 248
self-improvement, ethic of 60
self-interest 11, 99, 106–7, 232
    and moral restraint 58–9

and selfishness 59
and survival 180–1
in economic theory 99–100
legitimacy of 10–14, 60–1, 107, 173–5
self-organization 206
self-regulation 245–6
self-reliance 20, 154–9
Sen, Amartya 274
Sennett, Richard D. 169–70, 193, 263, 276,
    282, 284
Shapin, Steve 277
shares, transferable 56
Shleifer, Andrei 270
short-termism 104–5
Singer, Peter 262
Sirico, Robert A. 158–9, 280
Sisson, Keith 283
slavery and slave trade 53, 56
    contemporary 89
small group societies—see sects
Smith, Adam 10–11, 58–9, 98–9, 103–4, 267
Smith, Douglas K. 284
Snell, K. D. M. 278
Snow, Charles C. 286
social contract 250–1
socialising processes of accountability 249
Sorell, Tom 287
Soros, George 94–5, 236–7, 273, 288
South Sea Bubble 57
South Sea Company 57
Soviet Union 48, 50, 53, 137
Spencer, Herbert 60–1, 99, 268
Spender, J. -C. 287
Starkey, Richard 289
state
    and business 71
    as in stitution 160
    as source of moral authority 16, 130–2
    nation, future of 33, 235, 237
Staves, Susan 267
Stiglitz, Joseph E. 87, 272
Stivers, Richard 21, 142, 149, 160–2, 279, 281
stock markets, collapse of, 93–5
Storey, John 184, 283
Strange, Susan 272
strategy 209–10
Strathern, Marilyn 264
structural adjustment 88
suburbanization 18, 144–7
suburbia, moral values of 144–5
Sullivan, Roger J. 278
Sullivan, William M. 263, 282
sustainable development 106
Swidler, Ann 263, 282

tacit know-how 228
Takeuchi, Hirotaka 287
Taylor, Charles 278, 289
Taylor, Frederick W. 283
teachers as moral authorities 17, 134–6
teams and teamwork 24–5, 29, 111, 191–5,
    211–14, 224
teamwork, ethics of 192–3
technology, domination of 161–3
television 18, 141–2, 146, 164, 167
termination of employment 181–4
Tesco 92
Tester, Keith 21, 163–4, 166–7, 222, 281
Thaler, Richard H. 262
Third Way 32, 232–3
Thompson, F. M. L. 266, 268, 272
Thompson, Graham 288
Thompson, John B. 279
Thurlow, Lord 78
Tipton, Steven M. 263, 282
tobacco industry 81–2
Torbert, William R. 208, 285
trades unions 43, 84
transnational corporations 85–6, 91
Treviño, Linda Klebe 285
Trollope, Anthony 60, 267
Truman, Harry 106
trust and trustworthiness 35, 218, 222–4,
    233, 247–50
turbo-capitalism 84
Tyler, T. R. 287

Union Carbide 217
Union Pacific 73
United Nations Commission on Trade and
    Development 86, 93
Universal Declaration of Human Rights 33,
    238–43, 247
Urry, John 275
Useem, Michael 271, 273, 283
usury 53

Van der Heijden, Barend 289
Van Helten, Jean-Jacques 270
Van Ness Myers, Philip 261
Vannoy, Dana 284

Veblen, Thorstein 163, 281
Velasquez, Manuel 290
virtues 243
vision, corporate 206–7
Von Crefeld, Martin 279
Von Krogh, Georg 287

Wall Street 71–2
Wall Street 71–4
Walton, Gary M. 270
Warde, Alan 282
Waterman, Robert 110, 265, 269, 276
Watson, Tony 195–7, 284
Watsuji, Tesura 286
wealth, measurement of 87
Weatherill, Lorna 265
Weber, Max 2
Webley, Simon 287
welfare state 20, 156–8, 201, 233
Welford, Richard 289
Wenger, Etienne 287–8
Werhane, Patricia H. 267, 286
Wheeler, S. 269
Whitehead, David 266
Wial, Howard 275
Wicks, Andrew C. 287
Wiener, Martin J. 270
Williamson, Oliver E. 39, 98, 263,
    274, 286
Wilson, Edward O. 262
Wilson, William J. 285
Wiseman, Robert M. 283
Wittgenstein, Ludwig 38, 263
Wolfe, Alan 19, 107, 145, 275, 278, 281
Wolff, Kurt H. 263
women in management 196–7
work, end of 200–2
work-life balance 194–7
World Bank 85–7, 91–2, 139, 247
World Trade Center 150, 164
World Trade Organization 86, 92–3
Worms, Jean-Pierre 278

Zacharias, Lawrence 268, 273
Zitkin, Richard 272
Zola, Emile 267